The Bedroom

The
Bedroom

An Intimate History

Michelle Perrot

TRANSLATED BY LAUREN ELKIN

Yale
UNIVERSITY PRESS
New Haven and London

Published with assistance from the foundation established in memory of
Amasa Stone Mather of the Class of 1907, Yale College.

Originally published as *Histoire de chambres,* © Éditions du Seuil, 2009; Collection
La Librairie du XXIe siècle under the direction of Maurice Olender.

Yale University Press books may be purchased in quantity for educational, business, or
promotional use. For information, please e-mail sales.press@yale.edu (U.S. office) or
sales@yaleup.co.uk (U.K. office).

Set in Bulmer type by IDS Infotech Ltd.
Printed in the United States of America.

ISBN 978-0-300-16709-2 (hardcover : alk. paper)
Library of Congress Control Number: 2017962733

A catalogue record for this book is available from the British Library.

This paper meets the requirements of ANSI/NISO Z39.48-1992 (Permanence of Paper).

10 9 8 7 6 5 4 3 2 1

For Anne,
Sarah, and Vincent

Contents

Translator's Note

THE TERM *CHAMBRE* in French is delightfully vast and ambiguous in its many meanings; we are far more specific in English and spell out whether we mean *room* or *bedroom* or *chamber, guild,* or *house.* Where there is a clear English referent, I have supplied it; where Perrot refers to a specifically French cameral practice, more than one kind of room at a time, or is employing wordplay, I have left the French term and given the closest English translation in parentheses. In some places I have preferred "bedchamber" where "bedroom" felt too contemporary. All citations are my translations unless otherwise indicated in the notes.

The Bedroom

Chamber Music

WHAT MAKES SOMEONE write a book?

Why write a book about bedrooms? It's a subject strange enough that it's surprised more than one person I've mentioned it to; my interlocutors have become vaguely worried to hear I'm wandering off into such questionable territory. The answer could be for personal reasons, unknown even to myself; this doubtless explains my more or less spontaneous response when Maurice Olender inquired what kind of book I might want to write. Or a taste for interiority, arising from the mystique of convents for young girls; I realized later the extent to which this was steeped in a world of fairy tales, with their magical canopy beds, and illnesses suffered through wartime in the anguished solitude of a grand Chekhovian house; the cool shade of an afternoon nap in a torrid summer in Poitou, so deep into the southwest that it's nearly Spanish; the anticipation you feel entering a bedroom with the one you love; the pleasure of closing the door to your hotel room in the provinces or abroad, after a noisy day cluttered with mumbling and idle chatter. These are the reasons, profound or pointless, why I decided to write about a place that is so saturated with intrigue and memory. My own experiences in rooms have also infiltrated this story. We all have our own rooms, and this book is an invitation to rediscover them.

Many roads lead to the bedroom: sleep, rest, birth, death, desire, love, meditation, reading, writing, search of self, God, reclusion (whether desired or endured), illness. From birth to death, it is the theater of existence, or at least its dressing room; the place where the mask is removed; the body undressed and relinquished to the emotions, to sorrow, to sensuality. It's where we spend half of our lives—the more carnal half, the drowsy, nocturnal half, the insomniac half, when our thoughts go vagabonding; the dreamy half, a window into the unconscious. The half-light of the bedroom only highlights its allure.

These are the axes that cut across my main interests: private life, which nestles there in different ways over time; the social history of the home, or of the worker, trying to find a "room in the city," or of women, trying to find a "room of one's own"; the history of incarceration and debates around the cell; the aesthetic history of taste and color, which can be observed from the accumulation of objects and images and the changes in decorative style; and the passage of time that goes along with it. It is not time that passes, Kant said; it is things. The bedroom crystallizes the relationship between space and time.

Another reason the microcosm of the bedroom attracted me was its explicitly political dimension, emphasized by Michel Foucault: "An entire history of space is still to be written. It would at the same time be a history of power, from global geopolitical strategies to local tactics of the home, of institutional architecture, of the classroom, or the organization of the hospital. . . . Spatial anchoring is a politico-economic form that must be studied in detail."[1] Incidentally, following Philippe Ariès, Foucault took the example of the thematization of rooms as a sign of the emergence of new problems. What role does the bedroom play in these "local tactics of the home," the dense networks of cities, the organization of the neighborhood, the house, the building, the apartment? What does it mean in the long history of the relationship between the public and the private, the domestic and the political, the family and the individual? What is the "political" economy of the bedroom? The bedroom is an atom, a cell; it relates to everything of which it is a part, of which it is the elementary particle, like the woodworm, minuscule in the minuscule, that so fascinated Pascal, the philosopher of the bedroom. For him, the bedroom was synonymous with the withdrawal necessary for tranquility (if not for happiness). "All man's unhappiness comes from one source: not knowing how to rest in a bedroom."[2] There is a philosophy, a mystique, an ethics of the bedroom and its legitimacy. What is the right to retreat? Can one be happy alone?

The bedroom is a box that is both real and imaginary. Its materiality is structured by four walls and a ceiling, floorboards, door, and window. Its size, shape, and decoration vary according to era and social milieu. Like a sacrament, closing the door protects the privacy of the group, the couple, or the person, and that is why the door and its key have become so important, so talismanic, and its curtains like the veils of a temple. The bedroom protects us, our thoughts, our letters, our furniture, our belongings. Like a rampart, it repels the invader. It welcomes us, like a refuge. As it narrows, it accumulates. Every bedroom is more or less a "cabinet of curiosities," equal to those assembled by seventeenth-century princes hungry for collections. What may be found in an ordinary bedroom is more modest: albums, photographs, posters, souvenirs brought back from travels—all these can sometimes make the bedroom a bit kitsch, a nineteenth-century museum saturated with images.[3] Anything can be included in these miniature models of the world. Xavier de Maistre, in his *Voyage Around My Room,* sets himself the task of mastering his immediate surroundings.[4] Edmond de Goncourt describes his bedroom as a box wrapped in its tapestries; among its objects could be found a coffer that had belonged to his grandmother, into which she stuffed her cashmeres and in which he would store belongings with sentimental associations.[5] "The interior is not just the universe but also the étui of the private individual. To dwell means to leave traces. . . . The traces of the inhabitant are imprinted on the interior."[6]

It is a metaphor for interiority, for the mind, for the memory (we record in a *recording room*), a triumphant image in the Romantic and even Symbolist imagination, a novelistic and poetic narrative structure. It is a representation that sometimes makes it difficult to understand the experiences it mediates. These figures are nevertheless at the heart of this book, and each chapter is organized around them. Fugitives, foreigners, travelers, and workers searching for lodgings; students lusting after a garret and someone's heart; curious, playful children; lovers of huts; committed (or uncommitted couples); women thirsting for independence or forced into solitude; the religious and the reclusive, hungry for the absolute; scholars who find in silence the answers they seek; voracious readers; and writers inspired by vesperal calm—these are the characters who populate this interior epic. The bedroom is a witness; a hideaway; a refuge; an envelope for the body, for sleepers, lovers, hermits, the lame, the sick, the dying. The seasons leave their mark, sometimes obvious, sometimes obscure; so do the hours of the day, casting their various lights and shades. But the night is no doubt the most important time of day. This book is a contribution to the history of the night; of interior (and even internal) nights; the stifled sighs of pleasure; the rustling of the pages of the book we keep on the nightstand; the scratching of pens; the tapping of computer keys; the murmur of dreamers; the meowing of cats; the cries of children, of abused women, of victims, real or imaginary, of midnight crimes; the whimpers and the coughing of the sick, the rattle of the dying.[7] The sounds of the bedroom compose a strange music.

A flip through some principal works of reference—from the *Grande Encyclopédie* to the *Trésor de la langue française*—suggests different evolutions of the word for a bedroom, some surprising indeed, especially when it comes to ancient origins. The Greek *kamara* refers to a space of shared rest among "friends," to which we might ascribe a martial posture. More of a barracks then. But there are even more complex examples. The Latin *camera,* an architectural term, is "the word by which the Ancients designated the vault, for those constructions that had them." The vault comes from Babylon. The Greeks didn't use it much, except in tombs: in Macedonia there were "funerary rooms with marble beds on which the dead were laid and left to decompose"; in short, they were holed up in bed.[8] The Romans borrowed the vaults from the Etruscans and used them to create pergolas *(cameraria)* under which to joyfully carouse, and with light materials—reeds even—they set about creating ceilings to the galleries of their villas, which, it so happens, featured nothing we would recognize as a "bedroom," not even of the conjugal variety. When they wanted to withdraw, to rest or to make love, the Romans had a space they called the *cubiculum,* a narrow area for the "bed," the root of the word a non-place, according to Florence Dupont. It was a small, tiled, set-back room used during the day or the night, equipped with a lock, sexual and therefore secret, because of the shame that was attached not to the act itself but to its advertisement.[9] Modesty is not only a Christian idea. The Romans used a stone *camera* for rooms that were closed at both ends, often used for funereal purposes. More cadavers.

According to Herodotus, by extension the term *camera* was used for covered chariots, "with a sort of tent or closed room, mysterious vehicles that the wealthy Babylonians took to visit the temple of the goddess Mylitta."

These must have been topped with hoops draped in fabric, "something we find . . . in many of our country carriages," as Léon Heuzey adds in his contribution to the *Dictionnaire des antiquités,* at the end of the rural nineteenth century; we might also think of the pioneers' covered wagons in the American West. Similar vehicles carried the young women of Sparta en route to the festival of the Hyakinthia in Amykles. Likewise, the Latin word *camera* applied "to cabins, rounded like cradles, that were located at the back of certain ancient ships, especially those transporting persons of distinction," the kind that can in fact be seen on Trajan's column.[10] There is thus an ancient link between the cabin of a boat and the bedroom that can be seen in the "captain's quarters," those of the second mate, and the chart room, where the machines are located. On a nineteenth-century cruise-liner, the very height of luxury, the cabin stood for certain ideals of comfort and privacy. Gustave Flaubert's Frédéric Moreau imagines himself with Madame Arnoux: "They traveled together, on the backs of dromedaries, under the awnings of elephants, in the calm of a yacht among blue archipelagoes."[11] A small, protective, soothing space, perfect for romantic intertwining.

A number of issues crop up around the bedroom, whether it be of canvas or of stone; vault, cradle, gallery, or cave; through its associations with rest, with sleep, nocturnal or eternal; with transport; with death. In each case it is linked to limits, to enclosure, to safety, even secrecy; it exists to protect young girls and women, the upper classes, and the deceased.

Things became more complicated during the Middle Ages, a period that deserves a more forceful semantic unpacking, and in the modern era, as the political began to intrude on the domestic realm. "There are few words in the language that have as many accepted meanings as the word *chamber*," Diderot and D'Alembert wrote in their *Encyclopedia,* which is particularly eloquent on this point. Diderot and the architect Jean-François Blondel divided the work, with D'Alembert writing on physical space and Diderot on its figurations. Blondel describes the different kinds of rooms—from the throne room to the king's bedroom, from the council chambers to the chamber of commerce, from which we derive the idea of the "bedchamber." "In general the word chamber refers to the place in an apartment designated for sleeping, and so it is called, according to the rank of the people who live there, and the decorations they have received." To the room, which he helped to shape during this period when the home was taking on new meanings, Blondel dedicates long digressions; he will serve as one of our guides.

Diderot is interested in the legal and political configurations of the room and is sensitive to overlapping meanings: "We took this word for places called chambers, in which people assembled to discuss various matters, then applied it to the people who assembled there, and then eventually to a space closed off by walls, pierced by a door and by windows, which became the simplest understanding of a *chamber,* and then applied it to any other space that had some analogy in the Arts with the usage of a small room or apartment, or with its character."[12] There follows an impressive list of definitions regarding justice, the police, finance *(chambre des aides, chambre des comptes),* communities, and politics (council chambers), which derive their names from their functions.[13] And let's not forget the arts and sciences and their various rooms (camera obscura, anterior chamber of the eye, artillery chamber). A number of rooms feature the names of the places they occupy or even their decoration: the extraordinarily large *grand-chambre* of Parliament in Paris is also called the "vaulted room" *(grand-voûte),* because it is vaulted above and below, or sometimes the "golden room" *(chambre dorée),* although the gildings from the time of Louis XII have not survived. The star-speckled ceiling of another room gave it its name. In the *chambre ardente,* or extraordinary court of justice under the Ancien Régime, hung with black curtains and lit by torches, those members of illustrious families who had committed crimes against the state were judged. There is also a moral or hierarchical meaning to the naming of rooms: the "upper House of Parliament" *(chambre haute)* for the House of Lords and the "lower" *(chambre basse)* for the House of Commons (as we once referred to the "high" and "low" court).

The vocabulary expresses the complex relations between the domestic and the political and their various (and often overlapping) spaces. Noblemen administered justice in their bedrooms, which is to say in bed; the bedroom became the *lit de justice,* a parliamentary session presided over by the king. We might then distinguish the retiring room for resting and the display room for public audiences and solemn occasions. In his final illness,

Charles V lay in a private room; as he lay dying, he was moved to the display room so that he might expire with befitting royal dignity.[14] However, the Bourbons had a tendency to show off their absolute power by receiving courtesans in their bedrooms, listening to their advice, and stretching out with them during meetings. Until the late eighteenth century, the king could attend the plenary sessions of the Paris parliament lying down; he spread out under a canopy. The bedroom therefore took on a public role as the seat of power—or at least as a symbol of it, as demonstrated by Versailles.

Democracy was cast in this mold: the Commons are lodged in the House of Parliament, and one "sits" in the Chamber of Deputies, today called the National Assembly. As Diderot pointed out, we have moved from the container (the *chambre*) to the contained (the assembly). Parliamentary representation is organized in a space where the architectural decisions have been made not only for practical reasons, but for ideological and psychological ones as well. The revolutionaries preferred the semicircle to the circle, which had long been chosen for its supposed egalitarianism, and adopted it in 1795; it is still in use today, though not without repeated debates, which often illuminate certain conceptions of political life.[15] The semicircle directs our attention to the podium, which suited the rhetorical eloquence of the revolutionary assemblies. They rejected the vocabulary of the *chamber*, which was too much associated with the Ancien Régime. The king gathered his advisers *(réunissait ses chambres)*. Citizens were not called together; they simply gathered. It is not surprising, then, that the Restoration brought back the concept of the chamber and wondered about the appropriate place for the podium. In his speech to the Chambers in 1828, and again in 1839 under the July Monarchy, the deputy Desmousseaux de Givré is particularly clear on this point: "The second inconvenience that I would note, I am touching with my hands: it is this podium in this chamber. And I ask of you, sirs, to unite these expressions: a podium and a chamber. Mirabeau told you that these are words that are crying out to be brought together."[16] The podium transformed the Assembly into a spectacle; in making room for the public in state deliberations, emotions were given precedence. For "one must not speak before a chamber as one would speak before the people."[17] Indeed, it is hard to imagine Mirabeau haranguing a chamber. The representative system is "precisely the substitution of public debate for popular debate, and the point of a parliamentary ruling is for the moderation of a debate to take place in chambers and not in a public place." Desmousseaux de Givré refused the theatricality of the podium. The delegates had to speak from their seats, as they did in England in the House of Commons; this meant employing a purely "private" eloquence, in imitation of the art of conversation. This is a question of exchange, of discussion rather than confrontation, to be in good company among legal specialists rather than political adversaries.[18] The debate was far from futile; it illustrates the different conceptions of parliamentary culture found in France and England. The chamber is the opposite of the forum; it is reminiscent at once of the Ancien Régime and of private space, so that is why it provokes republican ire. "Chamber" does not include "Assembly." The "Chambre des députés" is not identical to the National Assembly, even if, forgetting these conflicts, we use the two names interchangeably.

In this semantic slippage of the domestic, from the private to the political, the Provençal *chambrées* provide a now classic example. The *maison des hommes,* a typically Mediterranean space of masculine socialization, was located in a *chambro* (hall) or a *chambrette* and became a space of confabulation, of secret plotting and southern republican opposition.[19] It would publicly be called a "circle," while retaining this reference to—and reverence for—a round of conversation.

The *Trésor de la langue française* notes these different meanings and provides supporting citations. It distinguishes between the places where assemblies deliberate and the assemblies themselves or between the spaces specifically designed for people or to enclose objects, not to mention the *chambre du cerf* (hunting lodge) in the forest or the *cavité de cerveau* (brain cavity). A *chambre* can be high or low, beautiful (and often reserved for guests), good or bad, cold, strong, dark, light, black, furnished, unfurnished, or "stuffed" *(chambre étoffée),* as is the habit in the Netherlands, a reference to the furniture inherited by a widow after her husband's death. There are many different colored rooms in literature: blue, white, red, yellow.[20] The *chambrelan* (an artisan who works at home) labors there; the sick person "keeps" to it; the simpleton lets himself be *chambré* (duped); wines are said to reach the right temperature there *(vin chambré)*. We are wary of "bedroom" strategies; for example, young women are "bedded" *(mises en chambre)* by their suitors. Those who look after them tend to be female: chamber maids, parlor maids, ladies' maids—there is an entire hierarchy of them, crowned by the lady-in-waiting, who attends to a princess. Their male equivalents have a more elevated, necessarily aristocratic, rank in the court system: *valet de chambre* and "chamberlain" are as much titles as tasks, like the *chambrier du couvent* (officiate in the cloisters) or the pope's *camerlengo*, the administrator of the property and revenues of the Holy See.

The room that concerns us here is the private room, in all its meanings: the room in which we sleep, but not exclusively; the communal, conjugal, or individual bedroom, in all its forms and with all its associations—scriptural, mystical, hospitable, medical, cloistered, punitive, and repressive. The bedroom is an expanding space that becomes more and more specialized, one that is constructed through a sense of civility, intimacy, the evolution of family life or individual life; it has taken a considerable place in modern living, as in literature and our imaginations. We will be less interested in establishing an ethnography or a history of the bedroom, which has been amply sketched out elsewhere, and more in locating the multiple genealogies, the melodic lines where religion and power, health and illness, body and spirit, love and sex interweave.[21] With pleasure as our only aim, we will draw a few portraits, especially of the classical age of the chamber, the great cameral era that begins in the Renaissance and extends to our own days. It will principally center on the West, though it would be fascinating to extend the discussion beyond it. We will glimpse the legacy of the Orient, the attraction of its plush divans, its thousand and one nights soothed by the voice of Scheherazade. But what the bedroom or its equivalent might signify in Africa or the Far East, I cannot say much about.

Our subject will be the Western bedroom, then, especially in France; less in Germany; the Italian, through its associations with marriage and the Spanish through mysticism; and an approach to the English room with precaution. The word "room" has a double meaning, untranslatable in French.[22] The French bedroom has been scrutinized by sociologists of environment and has been the object of exhibitions and books that march through it without always stopping there; the small, transitory, hidden world of the bedroom has left few traces in the archives.[23] Ordinarily, it is a sanctuary of privacy from the government and the police, its nocturnal inviolability preserved even by the Revolution, which prohibited all home searches between sunset and sunrise. There are two exceptions, however: the notary, who makes his inventory after death, is the only one who makes a precise description of the furniture, drawn up by the aptly named *huissier* (bailiff).[24] The examining magistrate and his specialists, searching for clues to solve a crime, decode the "mystery of the bedroom," yellow or not.[25] Although potentially a crime site, the bedroom loses none of its interest for investigators, who proceed less on the basis of visual observation, the acuity of which has been greatly undermined by modern techniques, than by sampling bodily fluids (blood, sperm, saliva, sweat) to be analyzed in laboratories.[26]

The world of print has proved a rich source. The bedroom haunts books; from treatises on architecture or the decorative arts, decorating magazines, etiquette books, hygiene manuals, medical and social studies of habitat, and travel journals to personal and life writing (letters, diaries, autobiographies), to which it is intimately connected through their composition, we are told of its potential forms and uses. Libraries give us an abundance of bedrooms, dispersed like the pebbles scattered by Hop o' My Thumb to make trails in the forest. To discover them in a winding succession of texts was the central pleasure of this research. The bedroom was my thread of Ariadne and my cave of Ali Baba, enabling me to leap from one book or author to the next, led as well by the conversations I would have about it. Once my interlocutors got over their initial surprise ("Which *chambre*? The *Chambre des députés*?"), they would suggest ideas for me to track down ("Have you thought of XYZ?"), sharing their own experiences with me, sometimes permitting me to cite them. They were so helpful that this book bears their stamp and, in some way, belongs to them.

Poetry opens a window "lighted" by Baudelaire. And the novel is an inexhaustible source. In the nineteenth century, it accorded great importance to domestic spaces on which to stage worldly and familial intrigue. Balzac, Flaubert, Zola, Maupassant, and the Goncourt brothers devote many pages to them, not only through an interest in the picturesque, but also in a more sophisticated way, as an expression of character, of mores, of their characters' fates.[27] The *Comédie humaine,* the unhappy characters in *Les Misérables,* the torments of Madame Bovary, the dramas of the Rougon-Macquart family can all be given metaphorical, ideological, social, and psychological readings of their interiors. There is a physiognomy of the interior as well as the face, an archeology of "domestic relics" worthy of any object of national heritage treasure.[28]

Vice and virtue both leave their mark, as much as social success. In Balzac, to change your social situation necessarily implies changing or modifying your lodgings. *The Rise and Fall of César Birotteau* is swarming with observations like this. The perfumer and lucky inventor of *Pâte des sultanes* (The Paste of Sultans) turns his house upside down to give a ball, without forgetting to adapt the space for his women: "I will redesign your room," he tells his wife, and "I will create a boudoir for you, and give a pretty room to Césarine," his daughter. The grimy room belonging to Claparon, the false banker, with its hastily drawn-back curtains, two table-settings, "and napkins stained with the previous evening's dinner," indicates his depravity. Inversely, "the pure and simple life of Pillerault was revealed by the arrangements of his modest home, consisting of an antechamber, a sitting-room, and a bedroom. Judged by its dimensions, it was a cell of a monk or a soldier."[29] *Ursule Mirouët* depicts the symbolism of places where bedrooms act as pivotal points: M. du Portenduère's bedroom, left "as it was on the day of his death"; Ursula's childhood bedroom, where one can "breathe the scent of heaven."[30]

Zola built *Pot-Bouille* around stairways and the hierarchy of floors. In *L'Assommoir,* the rise and then the fall of Gervaise and Coupeau's relationship can be seen from the changes to their lodgings, the way they give up intimacy and return to promiscuity. Renée's room in *La Curée* indicates her sexual depravity, and Nana's failure is completed by her death in a hotel. Flaubert subtly uses the space of a room: Félicité's bedroom, or Emma Bovary's, represent their lives and their dreams. In his notebooks, he sketched out his plans for a metaphorical home: "On the ground floor (inferior state), the salon, simple and useful furniture. This, for visitors, is courtesy, easy access. And in the kitchen, giving onto the courtyard: the poor. The dining room? Hospitality, public life. The heart will be in the bedroom; beyond, the facilities, where you will dispose of your hatred, your rancor, your anger, all the filth."[31] The examples go on and on. They tell us not only what the bedroom is, but also what it represents as the realm of intrigue and as a signifying structure. This imaginary room, both producer of and saturated with images, interests us as a matrix for understanding other people.

The iconography of the bedroom belongs to this double register in an even more complex way by adding the supplementary horizon of the symbolic. An entirely separate book on the subject would be necessary—and not only on its decor. What does Van Gogh's deeply affecting room represent? What did the painter want to say about it? In medieval painting, which is especially coded, the Virgin is linked to the bedroom: births, the Annunciation, the Assumption, offering many scenes in rooms where a bed is always visible. Elizabeth's enormous childbirth bed is surrounded by matrons, while little Mary rests in her crib; the narrow bed in which the little girl lies as the Angel Gabriel visits her, or the dormition bed, where the Virgin lies with eyes closed, barely seems to be leaning back (she isn't ill), and is delighted in her sleep by angels; they carry her to heaven where she will join her son, as the Apostles watch on, delighted. Despite the materiality of this or that detail, taken from the banal objects of everyday life—a child's crib, a bolster, a pitcher, a pair of mules—there is no realism in these paintings, which are so eager to suggest Mary's virginity, her links with a cloistered femininity absorbed by the bedroom. The iconographic representation of the harem, a great theme of orientalist painting in the nineteenth century, follows a similar procedure. The tangle of bodies, the abundance of flesh spread out over cushions and draped in the folds of sumptuous fabrics, the odalisque languid in her humid, forbidden chamber: the seraglio invites the viewer to erotic reverie.

Dutch painting, seventeenth-century engravings (Abraham Bosse), the Intimist painters of the eighteenth and nineteenth centuries (Chardin, Greuze, Pater, Boilly, Laureince, etc.), the Impressionists and Post-Impressionists (Bonnard, for example) are much more attentive to interior scenes. Mario Praz drew greatly on this for his *Histoire de la décoration d'intérieur.*[32] He used the watercolors of interiors by certain artists—P. F. Peters, Wilhelm Dünckel, Fernand Pelez—and made himself a specialization; he foregrounded their power of suggestion. "This bedroom remains more alive in our memory than many of those upon whose floors our feet have trod," he writes of a work that captures in minute detail the decoration of an 1880s bedroom.[33] Mario Praz collected these watercolors, as well as dollhouses that reproduced these interiors in miniature with a fanatic attention to detail. He liked the way they stacked together.

Photography no longer constitutes reportage, in spite of its reality charge and the impression of contact argued for by Roland Barthes.[34] The photograph, in its pause, its pose, reveals above all the photographer's gaze. Eugène Atget numbered interiors among his favorite themes; in 1905 he had wanted to create a photographic and typological inventory of all the homes in Paris: the milliner's, the rentier's, the employee's; he was no doubt less interested in the lives of the worker or the writer, whose rooms were empty of their occupants, than in the stereotypes he hoped to capture and preserve.[35] And yet these photos are priceless. They brim with the sorts of things that escape the photographer's eye and in spite of him (because of him) inscribe the photograph in a specific temporality. They are the visual equivalents of the family studies carried out by Frédéric Le Play, with their richly detailed descriptions of workers' homes.

Certain writers have made the bedroom and the enclosure more broadly the site of their writing, the center of their reflection, and the point of recall. Great chamberlains like Marcel Proust, Franz Kafka, and Georges Perec belong to this group. The bedroom is a leitmotif in *À la recherche du temps perdu.*[36] It obsesses the mysterious animal of Kafka's "The Burrow," who seeks the protection of solitude as much as he dreads it.[37] It becomes the nightmarish stage for the "metamorphoses," where the sleeper becomes an insect to be killed. It is the "monad" of *Species of Spaces.*[38] "I remember," writes Perec, evoking the bedrooms in which he has slept, knowing he will never find the gas chamber where his mother perished.

These many rooms have been paced, surrounded, and dissolved by history. It is finally time to enter them.

The King's Bedroom

LET US ENTER our story majestically, through the king's chambers, as Louis XIV ruled they should be placed in 1701: in the middle of the marble courtyard, "facing the rising sun, in an Imperial centrality," pushing the neighboring chapel to the north, constructed entirely according to the king's needs—unlike at El Escorial, which places the chapel at its heart.[1] The space communicates the absolute power of the monarchy and its sacralization: the king replaces God in the four walls of his room.

In the cosmically vast estate of Versailles, a "summary of the universe," the symbol of the sun reigns over the organization of the whole, as well as in every detail. In the great apartments, built between 1671 and 1681 and decorated by Le Brun, each of the seven adjoining rooms becomes a planet, according to plans that we find as well in the princely dwellings of Italy, which the Tsarina Elizabeth borrowed for Saint Petersburg. The palace of the prince is bathed in a culture of allegory and performance that would have been recognizable to contemporaries, who would have read Versailles like an open book—for example, André Félibien in his *Description* (1674).[2]

The avenues radiate outward from the palace—which is to say, from the bed of the king. According to Julien Green, the king's bedchamber was placed so that "in order to go from one point to another, from his room to another room, the king had to make a number of steps that corresponded to the distance from the sun to another planet," according to the astrological principles that were found to underpin the pyramids of Giza.[3]

This cosmic will has no doubt been exaggerated in a frenzy of interpretation whose excess has been pointed out by Hélène Himelfarb.[4] Over time, it has given way to history, to the pictorial celebration of the exploits of the king, and, above all, to the everyday necessities that made the king's private quarters a center of power that operated slightly differently.

Nevertheless, in this constantly evolving château, where the work was ongoing and whose inhabitants were constantly moving around as members of the royal family and the court died, changed functions, and fell or rose in favor, creating a dizzying commotion, the king's chambers remained in place.[5] They were a fixed point, the beating heart of Versailles, and today they are the mythic anchor of memory.[6]

The King's Balustrade

The king's bedchamber served as both a space and a device, a material space molded from symbolism, in its design as well as its access.[7] Doors, antechambers, hallways, and stairways (including the king's private stairway) served as cannily hierarchizing filters, controlled by the bailiffs and the valets, scrupulous cogs in the "mechanism of the king" so majestically analyzed by Saint-Simon.

The material space of the bedchamber, however, escapes us. We don't know enough about it, given how greatly its decor was modified, endlessly replaced and dispersed, in an era that did not in any way value "antiques." If a member of the court died, his belongings were given to his household, including his servants; such was the case, for example, for Madame de Maintenon when she left Versailles for Saint-Cyr. What became of the king's furniture? What did the king see? What we see on our visits today is the result of historical reconstitution, partly based on our imaginings of what his room would have looked like. We just barely know that the room was covered in crimson velvet tapestries, enhanced with gold, a gold that weighed in at sixty kilos when it was removed in 1785.[8]

The bedchamber was a theater, with a briefly outlined stage. At its heart, a balustrade, referred to as the *balustre,* marked off the temple-like sanctuary. "To make sacred is to wall off. To create tension in a certain area. To surround with a barrier, a grille, a railing."[9] Only the highest-ranking valets and those to whom the king granted an audience were permitted beyond the balustrade—for example, foreign ambassadors. Even then, they were not allowed to go beyond the boundary of the edge of the carpet. When, in 1699, he received the ambassador Abdallah Bin Aycha, the king ordered the Baron de Breteuil to ask the Moroccan emissary to "stop at the edge of the carpet, just below the steps of the balustrade." Seated on a chair, the king "revealed himself one moment and concealed himself immediately afterward."[10] This was just one example of the many rules and regulations concerning the narrow access to the king and his chambers.

Rarely could one go beyond the balustrade. This privilege was granted to the Duke of Portland, the King of England's emissary to Versailles. The king, who had just taken some medicine, welcomed him, "which was a great distinction, and then compounded it by asking him beyond the railing to his bed, where no foreigner of any rank or character had set foot, except for the ceremonial audiences with ambassadors."[11]

To lean on the railing was almost a sacrilege, unthinkable during the time of Louis XIV, and the bailiffs kept watch to prevent this. Later, the discipline waned and postures relaxed, not without some complaint. In Louis XVI's day, when the Marquis de Créqui allowed himself this liberty, the bailiff reproached him: "Monsieur, you are profanizing the king's bedchamber," and the Marquis replied: "Sir, I am recognizing your exactitude."[12] The court laughed at an anecdote that would have been inconceivable under the Sun King. When the ritual becomes ridiculous, anything can happen.

The balustrade outlined a tabernacle, just as in church the choir separates the altar from the worshippers. In the king's bedchambers, it isolates the king's bed. Richly damasked and surrounded by heavy curtains, the bed was watched over by valets day and night. The first valet slept at the foot of the bed; he never left his post if the king was sleeping. He guarded him, just as he did the key to the wardrobe where the king's clothes and shirts were locked up.

"Where the king sleeps, power sleeps; his bed is the place where his physical body is reborn to life every day to carry out the mission of his mystical body," notes Édouard Pommier.[13] The king's bedchamber was "the frozen image of omnipotence," the privileged site of an etiquette that relied on a meticulous use of time and space, inspired by "the king's weakness for every little detail."[14]

The king's bed was the altar on which the transsubstantiation of the physical body to the mystical body took place, where two major rites of an unchangeable liturgy were celebrated and set the pace for daily life at court as in the rest of the country: the king's *levée* (rising) and his *coucher* (going to bed), an extremely codified ritual in the smallest of its moments, gestures, and players.[15] At the king's rising, the first valet would hold the right sleeve of his dressing gown while the first valet of the wardrobe held the left. In the evening, the privilege of the *bougeoir* (candelabra) allowed the king to bestow favor on this or that courtier. This was the case for the decidedly spoiled Duke of Portland: "One evening, the king gave him the *bougeoir* at his *coucher,* a favor that is accorded only on the most important of men, whom the king wished to single out. Ambassadors were rarely intimate enough to pay court at this hour, and if it did come to pass, they did not often receive this honor."[16] The *entrées* (admissions) indicated the various acts of the play.

Valets and bailiffs played a major role in carrying out this carefully choreographed process because they controlled the doors, limited access, and conveyed petitions to the king, permitting whomever they liked to clear a path to the king or even to speak to him. This was also the case outside the king's bedchamber or out of doors, during the short trips the king made to the chapel or in his carriage, in the gaps and free moments, briefly and secretly.

Once these rituals were accomplished, the king's day outside the bedchamber could begin. The *garçons bleus* made the king's bed, assisted by decorators. One of the chamber valets would guard the bed all day long, "keeping to the dais within the alcove railings." The bedchamber was at that time open to the public, except if the king was at his toilet. The visitor would bow down before the king's bed, like a worshipper genuflecting before the blessed sacrament laid out on the altar. The valet made sure of it.

The King's Chamber Valets

As a public space, the bedchamber—a term with many meanings—was also one of the most important mechanisms of the court and the kingdom. William R. Newton, who has scrutinized its functioning through archival research, describes the complexity of its workings, which would later inspire other palaces who wished to mimic the decorum of Versailles.[17] The Sun King's palace would prove an inaccessible and inextinguishable model.

The grand chamberlain would cede his prestigious role to the "highest ranking gentleman in the king's bedchamber." He was in charge of all admissions when the king was present. He was also in charge of the intimate service carried out by the *premiers,* or first *valets de chambres,* and the ordinary valets, the *ordinaires.* The *premier valet de chambre* enjoyed real power and distinct material advantages (appointments, favors, lodging, candles), as well as social advancements. It was always beneficial to serve in the king's quarters; it could be used as a springboard to greater success or as a means of gaining notoriety. And the role was hereditary, passed from father to son. The ordinary valets enjoyed more modest advantages. They lodged in smaller, contiguous rooms, where at least they had claim to the fireplaces. They were assisted by six *garçons ordinaires de la chambre du roi,* sometimes called *garçons bleus* because of their livery. Then there were the *huissiers ordinaires,* who manned the door at the outside entry to the apartment and decided who would enter or not; the sixteen *huissiers de la chambre du roi* watched over the balustrade and controlled access to the chamber itself, a task that required an astute knowledge of the court, its rights, and its privileges.

Among the other officers of the chamber, there was a parade of barbers; grooms of the portable wardrobe; the "groom of the stool," responsible for the portable commode, which Louis XV finally abolished, installing instead "English cabinets," a key step in the civilizing process; as well as a host of specialized valets: clockmakers, decorators, masters of the bucks and hounds, etc.[18] The "wardrobe" was a separate service. Its "grand master" looked after the king's clothing morning and night, each piece of which had to be laid out the previous evening, from the sleeves of his shirts to his nightclothes. All of these people had a very close physical proximity to the king.

Of this he was well aware, and he liked his bedroom personnel. "He treated his valets very well, especially the under-valets. He felt most at ease among them and spoke to them with great familiarity, especially those of the household. Their friendship and their aversions were often very effective," wrote Saint-Simon, who disapproved of the cult power of these subordinates, whose importance has been argued by Mathieu Da Vinha—especially that of the *premiers valets.*[19] Notable figures like Marie Dubois, present at the death of Louis XIII; Alexandre Bontemps, witness to the midnight marriage of Louis XIV to Madame de Maintenon; and Louis Blouin, who testified to his death throes, were equal parts confidants, chroniclers, inspectors, and spies for a sovereign who turned them into his "eyes and ears." Fittingly, their power lay in their position by the doorway to the chamber. Saint-Simon wrote of Bontemps: "Through him passed all orders and secret messages, private meetings and messages to and from the king, and all that was mysterious." The power of the valets was in their thorough knowledge of people's rank and their relationship to place—for example, their quarters—a rare commodity at Versailles. They alerted the king as a space became available, thereby allowing him to allocate it to this person or that one as it pleased him. To be housed at the palace was considered an uncommon privilege. Until 1700, the distribution of lodgings was not carefully administered. The politics of space had to do with favors and gratification. As masters of the chamber, the valets participated in a network of power that they created and incarnated.

The valets served both the public and the private body of the king. The "interior valets" had the keys to the chests. The "sleeping valets" slept at the foot of the bed. They witnessed his sleep, perhaps his dreams, his needs, and his nocturnal pains, and they were complicit in his loves, both legitimate and adulterous. The *valet de quartier* accompanied the king to the queen, to whom he devoted his nights until her death. The valet brought him there at night and took him back to his own room for the rising ceremony in the morning, a sequence that underscores the official, public character of the king's chamber. One did not make love there. The theater of the bed did not lend itself to such acts. A Christian curse continued to weigh on the flesh, a shame that led Saint Augustine to desire a different room for the conjugal act—one equipped with a lock.

The Panoptical Chamber

The king's chamber was at the center of a system of power that was panoptical, if not in reality, then via the king's will to know all, to see all. It was based on the double circuit of the gaze and the word. The king had a keen gaze: "He noticed everyone, no one escaped his notice, even those who hoped not to be seen," wrote Saint-Simon. And then there's that well-known phrase—"I don't know him at all. . . . That man I never see." The king required the presence of his courtiers at the time and place of their as-signation. The elaborate ballet of *entrées* set the rhythm for the *levée*, the dining, and the *coucher;* the *grandes*, the *premières* (also called *secondes* be-cause they came just after the *grandes*), and then the *simples* entered. His *familières* (intimates) saw the king in bed and looked after his physical needs; the *grandes* advanced once the king had risen. Once he had been dressed in his *robe de chambre*, the *premières* entered. When he was at his washstand, the *simples* were permitted to enter. When it came time for the *coucher*, the hierarchy was reversed, and the different *entrées* marked the stages in which the king was undressed and put into his bed. These grada-tions were indicated in terms of distance from the king's body. Proximity demanded or conferred honor. Thus the role of reader—not a particularly illustrious role; the king didn't like to read—was valued according to the adjacency it required. Racine once did the job.

The king's gaze had its limits, and yet the king wanted to know every-thing, including "what happens in private homes, in the business of the world, in the secret heart of families and liaisons." One must "slip in among our sub-jects and divine what they hide from us with the greatest care," he advised the Dauphin, his son.[20] To this end he devoted all his means: opening letters his underlings had intercepted and copied so that they might be cited if the need arose (private correspondence did not exist); encouraging the servility of his courtiers, "who on occasion spoke secretly to him in his cabinets, in the rear"—the famous "rear cabinet," which served as the back stage to the royalty; resort-ing to the help of the Swiss, predisposed to gallant public espionage; and, above all, enlisting the conniving of valets, who were the interceptors of peti-tions and requests for audiences and were always on the alert for mutterings, rumors, and gossip, to which the king indulgently paid attention.[21] Bontemps was particularly good at this: "It made him so accustomed to secrets that he made a great mystery of the smallest of things, and we laughed at this."[22]

The feeling of being watched, even spied on, created a desire to hide, to slip down the back stairs to avoid the king's omnipresent gaze. To avoid being heard, courtiers lowered their voices, whispered. Saint-Simon, wishing to send his *Mémoires* to M. de Rancé, abbé de la Trappe, to read and obtain his opinion, set a meeting at the castle but with great prudence: "I believe it would be useless to ask you to take certain precautions of secrecy, to lower the voice of whomever reads these papers to you so they cannot be heard outside of your chamber." It was necessary, he insisted, to "whisper in the ear," to meet in uninhabited apartments or in far-flung corners of the palace: "in the little salon at the end of the gallery, beside the Queen's apartments, where no one goes, because these quarters have been closed since the death of Madame la Dauphine," or "in a dark little passage between the tribune and the gallery of the new wing, where he lodges at the very end."[23] Despotism brings on strange games of hide-and-seek. The Duc de Saint-Simon was obsessed with thresholds that mustn't be crossed; forbidden passages; pulled curtains; open or closed doors, behind which he always suspected some hidden intent. Did he find the door closed when he went to visit Madame de Beauvilliers? He was surprised to see the Duchesse de Sully slip in, although the door was guarded, and suspected some plot. His *Mémoires* hum with murmurs and evasions. How could he build relationships, pursue his affairs, engage in his own intrigues in the simultaneously public and secretive court, woven of winks and whispers?

The "Little Favorites"

The king himself oversaw the distinctions that took shape in the space around him. He believed, or pretended to believe, that he was within everyone's reach, and in a way, this was true. The Palatine princess compared the inaccessibility of the emperor's chamber in Vienna, which was reserved only for the imperial family's intimates, to the public quality of the king's chamber in Versailles, where people could try to speak to him or visit the room in his absence. When he was dying, "a kind of crude Provençal peasant" who had heard the king was ill came to propose a remedy that would cure his gangrene. The king was in such a bad way that "the doctors let [the man] in without a word of protest."[24] But that is the nature of illness, to disregard boundaries and dissolve hierarchies.

On an ordinary day, the "Provençal peasant" would have encountered nothing but obstacles. He would have had to forge a path through the crowd, taking advantage of the king's movements; when the king went to mass or returned or when he went to his carriage, "the most distinguished, and even several others [would go as far as] the door of his study, without daring to follow him. That's where facility of access ends," wrote Saint-Simon, who was not taken in. "That way, you could barely say two words to him, in a very incommodious manner," or "if he knew who you were, in your wig, this was hardly an advantage."[25]

It was as complicated to obtain an audience in the king's study as it was to enter his chamber, which abutted it through a connecting antechamber. This was the king's true office, his place of work. There he received ministers and secretaries and gave all his audiences. It was more a question of function to enter the study, but *entrées* were just as filtered. Louvois's great privilege, says Saint-Simon, was to walk directly in, without warning or even without having made an appointment. But the valets stood guard, and if they were kicked out, they left the doors open so that they could hear and see in via the mirrors, which were the "great danger of the study"; it was an indication of the valets' power to control and obstruct.

"To go in back"—that is to say, into the rear cabinets—or His Majesty's private rooms was the supreme honor, reserved for the king's intimates, for secret or spontaneous audiences, for special meetings, often arranged by the valets. It was common practice, at least for princes, to have a place off-stage in this way, behind the scenes. Saint-Simon mentions it often, especially in his personal dealings with the Dauphin, "that admirable prince," with whom he had frequent *tête-à-têtes*. "I was the only one who had such free and frequent access to the rear cabinet, either at my request or at his. There, he revealed his soul." He remained nostalgic for these "impromptu" meetings when the Duc de Bourgogne held forth on his ideas about nobility, regretting its decline, deploring its "fatal, ruinous idleness."[26] "In back," one could speak more freely, more frankly; here could be found the tentative beginnings of public opinion.

The ordering of space was an essential aspect of the exercise of power. The distribution of apartments obeyed certain rules; the princes of the

House of France had priority. But the king upset the dynastic order by including alongside the "princes of the blood" his illegitimate children, born of his unions with his favorites—especially the children of Madame de Montespan, for whom he felt a particular devotion. The Duc de Maine, who was dear to Madame de Maintenon, and the Comte de Toulouse had the most beautiful of the apartments on the first floor. The Enfants de France, with their *remueuses* and governesses, occupied a large segment, a veritable nursery with a view of the gardens that had to be protected by iron bars from the public's desires.[27] Fate would prove to have a sense of irony: Marie-Antoinette was particularly preoccupied by the Dauphin's security.

Looking through archives and incredibly specific correspondence, William R. Newton discovered these changes alongside the complaints and the requests of those badly lodged courtiers, making a fascinating contribution to the history of the environment, as well as its sensibilities. They allow us to glimpse a strange world where luxury rubs shoulders with squalor. Those who benefitted, aware above all of their proximity to the king, showed a great faculty for compromise but also showed more and more a distinct need for rewards, whose criteria varied and were refined over time. The documentation, however, is inconsistent. The eighteenth century had much to say, but the seventeenth far less, to such an extent that there remain many uncertainties as to the princely, and even the royal, dwelling of this period. The king's chamber guards its mysteries. Is the center of the panopticon empty?

The favorites enjoyed spacious apartments, in the central part of the château, very close to the king, who displayed his bigamy (even polygamy) without self-consciousness—at least until his marriage to Madame de Maintenon, who put an end to his "royal harem."[28] For a long time, Madame de Montespan had unique access to the king, and she took advantage of it to send him notes or to speak with him—but not without equally unique precautions: "It was always at public times of day, but in the king's *petit cabinet* ... the two would sit at the back, but with the doors completely open, an affectation that she only employed when she was with the king and in view of the public chamber full of courtiers."[29] If it was just a quick word, "it was standing at the doorway, just outside the cabinet, in front of everyone." Did the king wish to reassure her of his love? Or did he, on the contrary, want to convince his critics there was no conflict of interest? What did this open door mean? The decline of Madame de Montespan was marked by her removal from the first to the ground floor, which did not adjoin the king's rooms, while she awaited her eventual retirement.

Conversely, the favor bestowed on Madame de Maintenon was fully revealed by the apartment she was given in Versailles, at the top of the grand staircase, facing that of the king and on the same level.[30] She occupied four fairly incommodious rooms, with a narrow bedroom at the end of a classic *suite*. After the queen's death (30 July 1683), the king moved across from his new wife, who little by little abandoned the services she had provided the Dauphine. The king took back the queen's apartment, though he did nothing with it, and that of Madame de Montespan, in which he installed his collections. Hélène Himelfarb has pointed out the "subconscious transference from a collection of women to one of paintings and statues."[31] Madame de Maintenon's apartment was remodeled to accommodate the king, and her chamber was enlarged. She stubbornly refused any more large-scale modifications and would not move to another apartment. At Versailles as well as elsewhere, she managed to achieve an almost royal stability.

The *Privance* of the King

As the site of spectacle, a theater, and the node and instrument of power, the king's bedroom did not really play a private role.[32] The king rose there and went to bed there but slept there very little. Not long after his *coucher*, his *premier valet* would conduct him to the queen, with his sword and his chamber pot, which he left in a hallway on a chair. The king was very respectful of his "conjugal duty," as Louis XV would be in the early years of his marriage to Marie Leszczynska, who would bear him nine children. In the early morning, the *premier valet* would go and get the king to bring him back to his own chamber for the *levée*.

This lack of intimacy was the case for all courtiers. The Palatine princess, suffering from culture shock, deplored this aspect of Versailles, which was even worse at Marly: "There is no private apartment, except to sleep and dress, but as soon as this is done, everything is a public performance."

She looked forward to welcoming her loved ones in the German fashion: "I will shut myself up with you and my uncle in a chamber, where I desire to be nothing but your Liselotte, as I once was," the princess wrote to her aunt, the Duchess of Osnabrück.[33]

"The king lacks nothing but the comforts of a private life," noted La Bruyère. Louis XIV longed for one. He had his grand apartments doubled with cabinets and rear cabinets, places of intimate passage, of secrets and confidential meetings, and where he placed his collections. He was accumulating houses: "I made Versailles for the court, Marly for my friends, and the Trianon for myself," he said. Above all, he visited his women, whose apartments were never too far from his own. At Versailles, Madame de Maintenon's transformed chamber allowed both spouses to work in a manner often described, particularly by Saint-Simon: he in an armchair, facing the minister, who sat on a stool, and she in another armchair, or in her famous "corner" on the west side of the chamber, an alcove beside a "duchess"-style bed. Madame de Maintenon's fan, which has been lost to us but of which we have a description by La Baumelle, depicted this room, where conjugality mixed with classic sociability, in its natural state. "The king works at his desk, Mme de Maintenon spins, Mme la Duchesse de Bourgogne plays, Mlle d'Aubigné dines." In love with a stability that perhaps reassured her, Madame de Maintenon sought neither luxury nor sumptuous decor. She preferred rooms that were not arranged in a row, a layout she detested. She liked soft fabrics, furniture that could be moved around, the accumulation of objects—all the padding and volume of the nineteenth-century bourgeoisie. Only the bed, surrounded by four bouquets of egret feathers, indicated her royal rank. Madame de Maintenon was always cold; she liked curtains, which kept out the drafts (which the king in his virility so enjoyed), curtains that could be pulled shut, thereby masking the alcove while the king worked. In the frequently chilly princely apartments, these curtains offered protection, enclosure, discretion. Saint-Simon writes of Madame de Montespan that she protected her status with gauze that may have seemed like curtains "but was nothing less than impenetrable."

Madame de Maintenon's room became the king's from 1683 to 1715, during those long years that this "incredible fairy" reigned. Saint-Simon minutely describes "the turning gears of the days and the times." He attributes a considerable influence to her, which she wielded discreetly. She listened without intervening, but she saw the ministers before their meetings with the king and was particularly attentive to the bestowing of jobs and favors. The only sphere that remained inscrutable to her was foreign policy, the least shared with women. Torcy, like Louvois, protected her from it by speaking of it only outside Madame de Maintenon's chamber.

The king never failed to pay her a daily visit, when he wasn't meeting with his council, for durations that varied according to the place where the visits took place: an hour and a half or more at Fontainebleau, much shorter at Marly and the Trianon. "The visits were always intimate, without prejudice to those that happened after meals," which were always more difficult to arrange. They usually ended around nine-thirty; Madame de Maintenon ate and went to sleep, all in the presence of the king and his ministers, until ten o'clock, when "the king would eat, and at the same time, they drew Mme de Maintenon's curtains." While traveling, she accompanied the king in his carriage, a mobile chamber. However, "she went to the king's chamber only when he was sick or on the mornings of the days when he had taken medicine."[34] She shared all the intimate miseries of the physical body, the seal of conjugality.

Her influence over the king was matched by her extreme dependence on him: she always had to be ready to respond to the king's desires. "No matter what state she was in, the king arrived in her chamber at his accustomed hour and did there whatever he had planned to do; at most she would be in her bed, sometimes sweating out a fever in great droplets." The king, "who feared the heat in her chambers," had the windows opened. "Thus did the king have his way, without ever asking her if she was inconvenienced." Madame de Maintenon reigned through her submission to his will. She couldn't always keep her curtains closed.

A homebody if not a hermit, Madame de Maintenon presided over her household and imposed her lifestyle upon it, preventing her subordinates from receiving anyone. These included the famous Nanon Balbein, who came from the parish of Saint-Eustache in the time of Scarron, "devoted, like her, and old . . . very possibly mad," who imitated her mistress in everything and served her devotedly. Her armchair was her throne, and the "sultaness" would not leave it even for the Queen of England. And yet this withdrawal was not sufficient. "While her chamber was a sanctuary, where only women entered in the closest familiarity, she still needed another retreat that would be entirely accessible."[35]

An aging Louis XIV shared a taste for these retreats, and they enabled him to flee the court that he had built and that was beginning to weaken him. The need for privacy wasn't born with Louis XV but with the *privance* of his great grandfather. "At the end of his life, the king—grown tired of beauty and the crowd—was persuaded that he wished, sometimes, for a smaller and more solitary life."[36]

Illness and the Death of the King

Secrecy shrouded the king's sex life, his sleep, his dreams, but also his suffering body, of which only his valets and doctors were aware. The bedroom is the place where care of all kinds is carried out, including both hygiene and medicine. Contrary to what has sometimes been insinuated, Louis XIV had a high standard of cleanliness and had a real predilection for washing. He would take *bains de chambre,* where he would observe several stages, according to certain prescriptions. He would rinse his mouth, which had been toothless since 1685. He would be shaved and his hair, which had been very beautiful in his youth, would be styled. He would choose his wig, which he would change several times throughout the day. The mirror, in frequent use at Versailles, showed him his own image. What did he see there?

Medical care was entrusted to the king's archiaters (physicians) and doctors. They were important, privileged people, well paid and well housed. Their influence only grew. Two in particular stood out: Daquin and Fagon. The former, connected with the school of Montpellier, was abruptly discharged, doubtless because this "Jew" asked for too much money; the discharge was an indication of a widespread anti-Semitism, which was shared by Madame de Maintenon, who did not care for him.[37] She took advantage of the discharge to promote Fagon, her favorite, who represented the school of Paris in its turn toward the English medicine of experimental observation.

The archiaters were tasked with protecting the king's health, thereby guaranteeing that of the realm. They moved freely through his apartments, entering his chamber day and night, sometimes remaining alone there with him—a supreme privilege. Fagon describes his first face-to-face meeting with His Majesty as a great event. Under the pretext of a persistent royal migraine, the king let Daquin go and was resting on an armchair in the antechamber when a valet came to summon Fagon. This was the beginning of his fortune. The archiaters spied on the body of the king and kept a chronicle of it. Stanis Perez, who brought back a biohistorical approach to the Sun King, published the *Journal de santé de Louis XIV* (Journal of Louis XIV's Health).[38] There he investigated the illnesses of the king in medical terms, which made an object of the physical body of a sovereign confronted with his daily humanity. He was a big eater and suffered from lightheadedness, headaches, vertigo, indigestion, vomiting, malodorous bowel movements, and recurring episodes of gout. By way of treatment he was bled, given enemas, or swaddled to make him sweat, to such an extent that in the morning his bedclothes had to be entirely changed. To fend off foul odors, which the king loathed, incense and orange-flower-scented sachets, the only scent the king could bear, were used. An image emerges of the king's chamber weighed down with pots, vases, utensils, and bedding, the air close from the windows being shut at night, the smells rank, the king surrounded by watchful valets. The king's sleep "was troubled by dreams, he cried out and was agitated. . . . He frequently talked in his sleep and sometimes even rose from his bed." When he was sick, "he cried out, spoke, tortured himself even more in his sleep than was usual." Watched over by his doctors and spied on by his valets, the sleeping king—a melancholy sleepwalker—fell prey to nightmares, anxieties, torments. The nocturnal bedroom, like a darkened theater, was submerged in the troubled waters of the king's psyche, its doors opened to an unconscious that eludes us.

The king's illness was a state secret, and something of that remains in the traditions of our monarchic republic. If the body of the king has become fragile, so does his power. The archiaters filtered news of the king and administered it in doses, strategic in their orchestration of public emotion.[39] The king was never seen recumbent, a posture that would undermine his virility and that was appropriate only to women, to queens giving birth.

There was one exception: images intended to celebrate the quasi-miracle that saved the king during his illness in Calais in 1658. The convalescent king—laid out on a canopy bed, Anne of Austria beside him—was an image of France brought back to life.[40] The security of the realm was embodied by the king's appetite, the correct functioning of his intestines, his robust health, his resistance to fatigue, his stoicism in the face of pain (notably when he had to have an operation to remove an anal fistula), his indifference to stormy weather, his insensitivity to cold. His frequent ailments, his incessant migraines, and his fluctuating moods all escaped the French public's notice, as well as that of his enemies, who might take advantage of them to conspire against him. He appeared well during the summer of 1715, his last summer.

The king's death throes pitched the chamber into disarray and disrupted the strict boundaries that had ordered it both inside and outside. Saint-Simon, who provides a daily chronicle that we will follow here, shows the functioning of the "mechanism of the king's apartments, since he no longer left them."[41] The king gradually withdrew, though he tried to keep up ordinary appearances for as long as possible. When he was ill, the king, mindful of state affairs, would gather his council in his chamber, which had become his cabinet, and would sometimes doze off. The rest of the time he retained "the greatest air of grandeur and majesty in his dressing gown." On 17 August, he held a meeting with his finance council from his bed. On the twentieth, he declined to visit Madame de Maintenon's chamber and sent for her instead. "He lunched in his dressing gown, seated in his armchair. He no longer dressed or left his apartments." He still rose for dinner (on the twenty-third as well) and continued to receive many visitors. The hierarchy of *entrées* was more or less kept intact. Madame de Maintenon and her ladies still entered, as usual, by the antechamber, while the courtiers were admitted for meals. The Duc de Maine retained his habit of "entering and leaving by the little staircase behind the cabinets, in such a way that no one ever saw him come or go." This was in contrast to the Duc d'Orléans, who, guessing himself unwanted, "made sure only to enter the chamber once or twice a day at most" and only came in and left by the door.

There were those the king called for and those he didn't, those who didn't venture to cross the threshold, and those who refrained from coming altogether. Madame and the Duchesse de Berry belonged to the latter group; "they almost never saw the king during his illness." On 24 August, the king sat up to dine, in his dressing gown, for the last time; he could not finish his meal and was put back to bed. He tried, nevertheless, to maintain his rituals, like that of having music every morning, drums and oboes, or of keeping to his meals. On the twenty-sixth, despite not having slept well, he dined in bed, "in the presence of those who had gained admission."

The chamber was invaded by doctors, who had a long habit of being there, especially Fagon, who slept there from the seventeenth onward, but also Maréchal and four others. The authority of Fagon, Madame de Maintenon's favorite, had reigned over the body of the king for so long but was curbed by the valets, Blouin in particular (who ranked highest among them), who managed to get hold (not without great difficulty) of the greatest doctors of the Paris School. The valets remained in the room except when the king was alone with his beloved Duc de Maine. Under pressure from Madame de Maintenon, the king had a codicil to his will drawn up, bestowing on the duke the running of the civil and military households, with the Maréchal de Ville-roy, "to such an extent that the regent [the Duc d'Orléans] no longer retained the shadow of even the lightest authority." This was the ultimate misdeed from a woman whom the Palatine princess called the "old *ripopée*."[42]

Father Tellier heard the king's confession and performed extreme unction. The king received the Duc d'Orléans, to whom he mentioned nothing of the codicil, and then the Duc de Maine, the Comte de Toulouse, and finally the princes of the blood, "whom he had spotted at the door to the cabinet." He had them enter his chamber and "said little to them, nothing in particular, or in a low voice." After his gangrenous leg had been re-wrapped, he called for the princesses, "said two words to them aloud, and, taking advantage of their tears, asked them to go because he wanted to rest." On the twenty-sixth, he delivered particular messages to various people. On the twenty-seventh, he burned his papers, with the help of Madame de Maintenon and his chancellor; what secrets did the flames devour? Madame de Maintenon remained by his side all day. On the morning of the twenty-eighth, "the king said something kind to her that displeased her and to which she replied not one word." He said he was sorry to leave her and hoped to see her again soon. This consolation did not please "the old fairy, who liked to think herself immortal." On the evening of the twenty-eighth, she left for Saint-Cyr with her ladies, with no intention of returning. The king was hurt by her absence and sent for her; she appeared the evening of the twenty-ninth. But on the thirtieth, after having distributed "the furniture she had left in her apartment . . .", she left for Saint-Cyr, never to leave again." Saint-Simon condemned her for what he saw as abandoning the king. He also points out the departure of the Duc de Maine, once the codicil was signed, and Father Tellier's indifference; as the king's confessor, he ought not to have left the king's side, but he fled the "vicinity of the bed," and, Saint-Simon writes, "all the interior of the king's bedroom, and the very cabinets, were scandalized by these absences."

The distance and coldness of the king's intimates contrasted greatly with the emotion of his subordinates, whom the king consoled. "He saw in the mirror over the fireplace that there were two of his valets weeping at the foot of the bed, and he said to them: 'Why are you crying? Did you think me immortal?'" The room was submerged in death, and it returned the king to the level of ordinary men.

In a way, by leaving, Madame de Maintenon and the Duc de Maine freed up access to the room, where even the great officers, who were habitually left out, could now enter. But not for long. The night and day of 31 August were "odious"; the gangrene had reached the knee and the thigh. At eleven o'clock, the prayer for the dying—a category in which the king now included himself—was pronounced. Then he fell into a coma, "which ended on Sunday the 1st of September, at eight fifteen in the morning, three days before his seventy-seventh birthday, in the seventy-second year of his reign."

Next came the "opening of the body," a visit to the king's interior. "They found all his parts to be healthy and intact, and so perfectly shaped that it was determined that he would have lived for over a century without the errors of which we have spoken and which put gangrene in his blood." Are we to believe that without overindulging in food and sex, the old king would have lived more than a hundred years? According to Saint-Simon, the king's interior—his most private chamber—revealed his destiny. This thesis has been challenged; the doctors had bit by bit imposed a diet to which the scrupulous, fragile sovereign had finally capitulated, hoping for a respectable longevity. The medicalization of the king's chamber humanizes him and desacralizes his power. It is the theater of modernity.

A few days before his death, Louis XIV asked for the Dauphin, his great-grandson. He had the child climb up onto his bed. He recommended that he be taken away, preferably to Vincennes. Everything should be cleaned before his return; the air of the château should be changed and that of his bedroom purified, instructions that say much good of his ways of life, physical and mental, hygienic and spiritual.

Louis XV never occupied this room the way his predecessor had. He didn't like the room, where he too had once been so cold. He would never cease running away from it, taking advantage of any illness to desert it. Early on, he went there to respect the ceremony of the *levée*. Then he ceased to do so, and the ritual fell into obsolescence. After having once been a site of spectacle, the king's chamber became an empty, abandoned theater. Certain ministers, like Fleury, thought they could keep the system intact by themselves carrying out a *levée* ceremony.

But everyone laughed.

Rooms for Sleeping

FOR THE GREEKS, the word *kamara* applied to any space intended for rest, and it was a long time before it came to refer to a place intended solely for sleeping and above all an individualized space. The things and the words we use for a sleeping space or an individualized space interweave in such a way that it is difficult to determine precedents. According to Beaumarchais, "When I say bed, I refer to the room." Is this true? *Chambre à coucher* appears in dictionaries only around the middle of the eighteenth century, although we may assume the idea is much older.[1] "A room of one's own," however, in which to write, dream, love, or simply sleep—Virginia Woolf's ardent wish for women—is a relatively recent invention whose Western origins I want to retrace, for this desire, or at least its practice, which today we employ as an inarguable mark of individualization, is less universal than it might appear. The Japanese had no notion of it. And even in Budapest, at the end of the nineteenth century, the sofas in the salon were transformed into beds, a practice that evidently preceded the bedroom.[2] In the eastern margins of Europe, the potential charms and the real nightmares of the communal habitat persisted for a very long time.

Communal Bedrooms

At the end of the eighteenth century, a doctor named Louis Lépecq de La Clôture visited the countryside of Lower Normandy to observe the "constitutions of epidemics."[3] He was astounded by the living conditions of the people there. Near stagnant ponds and dripping dunghills, some people slept in a kind of thatch-roofed hut, with no bedding, on hay that was stingily replaced, while others crammed themselves along with animals and poultry into a communal room where the doctor did note several box-beds.

The shearers of Louviers were hardly better off, though they did have a "room" without animals, in which there was sometimes a loom.

Before the bedroom, there was the room; before that, almost nothing. The rudimentary room improved as the countryside's fortunes grew in the nineteenth century. It was organized and furnished with wood made from fruit trees, according to regional styles—furnishings that, a century later, would become a gold mine for antiques dealers and the glory of museums of local crafts and popular traditions, relics of an idealized rural existence that had been tamed. Ethnologists have used these objects to try to understand daily life. Poring over judicial archives, historians have been interested in the family conflicts revealed in trials that were full of adulterers, child killers, parent killers, and arson; the mirage of family bonds and quaint cottages dissipates in those dossiers. They suggest, no doubt through exaggeration, the tensions of the rural house, accentuated by the changes in the law and the rise of an individualism that had little tolerance for the pressures of the group.

The communal bedroom was intergenerational and multifunctional and was a way of life for the majority of rural populations. In 1870, 70 percent of rural homes in Touraine featured only one "central room with a fireplace" where all its inhabitants lived together in 300–400 square feet. Everything in these one-level homes effectively centered around the fireplace when the cold came up from the ground and crept in through drafts. "In France, the doors close badly," noted Prosper Mérimée.[4] In 1875, the geographer Élisée Reclus described an Alpine house totally huddled up against the cold: "At night, all the windows and doors were closed to keep the cold from coming into the bedroom. Mother, Father, grandparents, children—everyone slept in a kind of shelved armoire, the curtains to which were closed during the day and in which polluted air accumulated throughout the night, worse than anything outside the curtains."[5] Elsewhere, the peasants slept wearing all their clothes, at least two to a bed, "sharing their fleas and bedbugs and vermin-ridden quilts."[6] The insalubrious quality of the air obsessed the hardened hygienist, who saw the box-bed, though widely used, as harmful and archaic. Jules Renard, whose *Journal* is a goldmine of observations on rural life in Burgundy, writes of "cold, damp bed linen. They slept wearing sweaters, underwear, socks, and dressing gowns, or they shivered all night." This in spite of wearing a cotton hat and sleeping under a heap of duvets. "I put everything I have in the house on my bed," said one woman. The beds were warmed, and folks slept under mountains of quilts and blankets. The beds resembled mounds for burrowing, and the sheets were rarely changed. "Peasants sleep for forty years under the same blanket without changing it, without even airing out the feathers. They change one sheet for every two. The most miserable sleep without sheets." The agricultural workers "slept on hay."[7]

Old age, illness, and death aggravated these situations. Around 1840, a young man called Tiennon (a sharecropper working for Du Bourbonnais, the spokesman for Émile Guillaumin) was pained to see his grandmother become progressively unwanted after an attack that left her unable to speak. "She needed someone beside her constantly to try to keep her spirits up, to feed her or help her drink when she was thirsty, etc." The women were weary and didn't want things to go on as they were. Tiennon himself could no longer eat in view of the bedridden woman and took his bread outside:

> I think wealthy people are lucky to have homes with more than one room, where the one you eat in is distinct from the one you sleep in. Each family should have its own bedroom, and consequently its own privacy. At least they can be ill without anyone bothering them. Whereas in the only room in the poorer households everything's a spectacle, and all the spectacles blend together; everyone's misery unfolds before everyone else's eyes, with nothing to be done about it. So it comes to pass that beside my dying grandmother, my little nephews are loudly shouting their joy at being alive, deafening her with their noise. Life carries on that way, indifferent to the agony of an old paralyzed woman.[8]

The grandmother finally died at the beginning of the winter, and the usual rites were carried out—the clocks were stopped, the troughs emptied—without any disruption to daily life. The curtains were simply pulled shut so that the meal could continue. Beside the bed, a candle was lit and a box tree branch watched over the body, whose rigidity surprised Tiennon's daughter, Clémentine. Under the Second Empire, having become a tenant and a farm director, Tiennon attempted to loosen the vise grip of communal living. In the central room, he placed only two beds, one for himself and his wife and, on the far side of the room, one to be shared by their servant and little Clémentine. Tiennon's putting space between the beds and using the corners of the room suggest he and his family were seeking a kind of privacy.

Françoise Zonabend sees developments in the use of the room in the Burgundian village of Minot, which she described around 1980 with an ethnographer's precision, attentive to the symbols woven into the order of things. Armchairs indicated the position of the master and mistress of the house; for the former, the chair was made of wicker, with a cushion, near the stove; for the latter, it was more modestly sized, in front of the window that faced the courtyard, beside a treadle sewing machine. "While sewing or knitting, she discreetly keeps watch over what happens outside, behind the thin cover of a few lively outdoor plants." The room also served as a bedroom. The bed was sometimes in an alcove or simply pushed against a wall; ample curtains, hung from a canopy, allowed for some privacy. The younger children slept in the same room, while the older boys joined the farmhand in the barn, where wooden box-beds had been installed. The girls stayed with their parents or slept upstairs if there was another bedroom, eventually used by newlyweds. The young servants slept on the landing on the stairway, as usual. Built by the village carpenter, the wooden beds were filled with materials collected from the farm. A pallet made from bales of hay formed the base, on top of which were one or two mattresses stuffed with hen or duck feathers dried in the bread oven, and these were then covered with an eiderdown quilt. "The higher the bed, the more beautiful it was."[9]

Communal life in a communal room: "Separated by a curtain, the generations slept side by side. In the big wooden bed tucked away in an alcove, the parents made love, the mother gave birth, the older people died. At the moment of the birth or death, the youngest children were kept away, while the other members of the family stayed." The thin line between the dead and the living, between the sick and the well, was offset by a strict discipline about the rules: "They gained in time what they lacked in space." This internal density was accompanied by a grave concern to defend the group against external threats. The room was rarely aired out so as to keep the heat in. Any traces of intimacy were erased. To leave the bed unmade was indecent. The women made sure bedclothes were kept neat by folding them with a large stick, the *baton du lit,* which was also used in Brittany, where the mistress of the house closed the box-beds at night to show them off to greater advantage.

Pierre Jakez Hélias provides a warm and thorough description of the Breton box-bed. With its illustrated panels, representing heaven, hell, and earth, it was the focal point of the bedroom, which might hold several others. He makes reference to one farm where three box-beds were in a line: one for the master and mistress, the second for the daughter and the servant, and the third for the three sons, until the eldest would join the two valets and his older brother in the stable. Each box-bed was like an apartment unto itself: "When its inhabitant entered, when he had closed the two sliding doors, he was at home." He himself remembers with nostalgia the one he had shared with his grandfather. In this "sleeping cabinet," the child felt protected. Of course, it wasn't easy to lay out your clothing after undressing on the inside, as you were meant to do. There wasn't much room, and it was impossible to totally stretch out; you slept half sitting up between hemp sheets and a quilt stuffed with hay. It is easy to imagine that childbirth, which took place here, was no easy matter. However, Hélias praises this "safe-box for sleeping . . . this fortress, this monk's cell . . . this private domain in a communal room," preferring it to all the subsequent beds in which he slept—hard beds at school, random beds in hotels, the mass-produced and standardized beds you find anywhere. He is mainly alone in his indulgence; beginning at the end of the nineteenth century, observers and pedagogues of the republic regarded the box-bed as the height of discomfort, an indication of a backward way of life that was happily on the wane. They were very glad that the box-bed had become an antique-shop curiosity. Pierre Jakez Hélias had to resign himself to its fate.

The communal room—the fate of the poor—was long in use among the poor, including those in urban areas. In the eighteenth century, 75 percent of Parisian households were concentrated in one room, says Daniel Roche, who made a study of postmortem inventories, where he could measure the progression of the individual bed.[10] "We had only one room," Jean Guéhenno writes, describing his family's home; his father was a worker, his mother worked at home, and they lived in a "hovel" in the suburbs before 1914.

> What a mess, what a hodgepodge. Why did the simplest life need so many *things?* . . . We worked there, we ate there, we slept there, we even on some nights had friends over there. Along the walls we had set up two beds, a table, two armoires, a buffet, and the trestle for the gas stove; we hung pots and pans and family photographs (as well as a few of the tsar and the president of the Republic). In front of the fireplace there was another cast iron stove, on which there always bubbled an earthenware coffeepot. . . . Laundry lines ran from one end of the room to the other, where the most recent wash was hung out to dry.

The "atelier" was next to the window, where the mother had her Singer sewing machine (which she called her "wheelbarrow") and where she pedaled away from five in the morning until eleven at night, fitting the uppers to the soles of shoes. In the middle of the room was a round table for meals. But "the wonder of the house was the mantelpiece." There all manner of objects accumulated: irons, alarm clocks, coffee filters, sugar boxes, Christ on a black cross, a statuette of the Virgin Mary, dust-gathering dried flowers, brought back from a cousin in the colonies, in colored vases. "Thus did we take our part . . . of pity, of joy, of the beauty of the world. All these things shone out from the mantel."[11] Jean Guéhenno was writing in 1934; in the activist writer's memory, the impoverished room is transformed into a cozy enclosure. This was not always the case; often violence broke out, defying the bindings of the body. Workers' lodgings put a somber face on the social question.

Communal Apartments

The same was true across Europe, including tsarist and Communist Russia. Katerina Azarova has written "the secret history of Soviet lodgings": "the communal apartment," describing its evolution in Moscow.[12] The "communal home" was intended to be a socialist utopia, but this never came to pass. It was based on a rational conception of space and services but could not hold out against social and demographic pressures, in particular the rural exodus, which was aggravated by the destruction of war. The legacy of the past weighed heavily. In the late nineteenth century, conditions were disastrous; 10 percent of apartments in Moscow were defined as "basement apartments" (a generous name for a cellar) and "bed-niche apartments," which, in 1898, housed 180,000 people. Many workers slept in their studios or factories. The Bolshevik revolution confiscated aristocratic mansions and bourgeois houses to transform them into communal homes. Each family was allocated one "individual room" and had access to the "common areas"—a shelf, a table, and the gas cooker in the kitchen and another shelf and a "corner" of the bathroom. In theory there was a schedule to organize the sharing of domestic chores, but there were always conflicts over whose turn it was to clean the toilets.

The "individual room" was the most problematic, especially when it didn't have direct access to the corridor. People and furniture were crammed inside; new couples lived cheek by jowl with older ones, and divorced couples could not part. Former maids could keep their rooms if they were small (less than a hundred square feet); otherwise they had to leave them to the family and sleep alongside their former employers. In the "niches," it was customary to section them off by a curtain, a screen, or an armoire placed perpendicular to the wall to shelter the beds. Often the beds were folded up during the day. "Couples were separated from their children or their parents by an armoire or a screen; this is a typical image of daily communal life." "Before I got married," says Nina (one of Azarova's interviewees), "I always slept with my mother, and my father slept on the table. We put in the extra leaf and covered it with blankets. I had no idea that usually parents sleep together."[13] What seemed normal in Paris at the end of the eighteenth century—to have a bed of one's own—was out of reach in Soviet Moscow in the 1930s.

Certain "middle-class" families attempted to maintain something of their former lifestyle by creating in different corners a sort of salon, dining room, or sleeping room with the bits and pieces of the furniture that remained to them. Furniture served the patrimonial, memorial function that is common among exiles. To not have any is a clue to their marginalization—and classes

them alongside drunks, ex-convicts, or other "deviants." The furniture
spilled into the corridor; every family was allowed to decorate its entryway.
(Later, a refrigerator would automatically be placed there.) The hallways,
then, were very cluttered and difficult to pass through. They also had a lot of
traffic because that's where the "communal" telephone was installed. They
were the site of rumors and conversations and of conflicts as well, for the lack
of privacy made it possible for everyone to overhear everyone else. Surveillance was constant, whether on purpose or accidental, and isolation was suspect. No one escaped the gaze or the gossip of the group. "Communal life is
when each inhabitant shares the individual room with the members of his
family and has no room of his own," said a respondent to one study.[14] All in
all, it was a disaster whose psychological consequences it is hard to measure.
In 1980, this was the way of life for 40 percent of households. Communal
housing was privatized by the Yeltsin laws in 1990 and 1991, and in April 1998
the figure was down to 3.5 percent. It persisted for longer in Saint Petersburg:
10 percent, according to Françoise Huguier, who carried out an astonishing
photographic reportage.[15]

Conjugal Bedrooms

The conjugal bedroom is linked to the couple and is central to the history of
the family, privacy, and sexuality—important themes in recent years.[16] This
is the space that concerns us here.[17] In the West, as far back as Ancient
Greece, the heterosexual couple has been the foundation of alliances, if not
necessarily of love, and accorded its own specific place, and a form of legitimacy, in contrast to the harems of the East. Could we think of the conjugal
bedroom as the frontier of civilization? At the very least, it indicates a way of
thinking about gender and sexual relations as historically constructed.[18]

"REMOVED FROM WITNESSES"

"Private life should be walled off; it is not permitted to seek out and try to
ascertain what happens in a private home."[19] Still less in a bedroom, the
heart of intimacy. Several factors contributed to its isolation. First of all,

prudishness and a desire to keep sexuality hidden away. The Romans—
who felt no guilt about sex—confined coupling to the *cubiculum*, "the room
before the room."[20] It was always impure, viewed from the perspective of
Christian morality. "What! The conjugal union, which, according to the
rules of the matrimonial code, is intended for the procreation of children—
does it not always seek out, with both illicit and honest motives, *a room removed from witnesses?*" wrote Saint Augustine, haunted by the flesh, like
most of the fathers of the early Church.[21] "The legitimate act of husband
and wife, while seeking to make itself known, does not blush at being seen.
. . . Why? Because that which is by nature fitting and decent is so done as to
be accompanied with a shame-begetting penalty of sin."[22] For the church
fathers, sin perverted nature, and the role of shame was to hide the sexual
act from witnesses and especially from children. Thirteen centuries later,
the prescriptions of Father Féline in his *Catechism for Married People* are
not much different:

> Spouses, as much as possible, must sleep in separate apart-
> ments, in beds closed off by curtains. If they must sleep in the
> same apartment, they must take the greatest precautions to
> avoid those who may also share that apartment, witnessing what
> happens between them. They must never allow anyone else into
> their bed, not even children of five or six years old; those who
> do so sin greatly, though they may give the usual excuse that
> they confine their relations to times when the children are
> asleep. This excuse is vain and frivolous.[23]

This Christian conception of sex, controlled by morality and hygiene, becomes more and more prescriptive and leads to separate bedrooms.

But the desire for intimacy also comes from within a couple itself
and an evolution of amorous feelings that tend to conflate bonding and
desire. To the extent that modern marriage is based on love, consent, the
free choice of individuals, and the shared goal of a mutually enjoyable
sex life, it requires the privacy of a shared bedroom.[24] When the honey-
moon is over, the newlyweds must prepare themselves for daily life under

the watchful eyes of the community. More and more it has come to be believed that the couple has a right to the time and space not only of a bed, but also a bedroom. In truth, the night is the only thing that properly belongs to them. That is when they come to each other. In the best of cases, there they share complicity of a "time that does not pass" in these "knotted places," as Louis Aragon puts it; in the worst, they share unfulfilling sex lives or the indifference of nights without lovemaking. The pleasures of such a space and the bother of contraception, so difficult to master—all of these things make the conjugal bedroom the locus of a secret history, the indissociable other side of communal existence, as well as an inexhaustible source for fiction. Aragon sings of Elsa: "These rooms here of which I speak are all the rooms, Elsa, that we have had together, as if there had been no other room but you, and it is true, for before you I was but the salesman of my own halted sleep, of ephemeral women," thereby ignoring "these knotted places called rooms or nests according to the animal species."[25]

Social categories have played varying roles in this isolating process, according to country and culture. In the rural communal room, the couple was luckier than the others, given their own private bed. The Italian patricians accumulated rooms and bedrooms. But when Mantegna painted the *camera matrimoniale* in the ducal palace of Mantua, he depicted the alliances of families in a solemn space of princely representation. The French aristocracy had little to do with rooms or conjugality; it divided the sexes and even assigned to women's rooms the function of receiving, which persisted for a long time.

The bourgeoisie, especially in England, was much more attentive to the notion of privacy. It became indecent to sit on a lady's bed. To enter her bedroom was the sign of an unusual audacity. "The English viewed the bedroom as a *sanctum sanctorum*," noted Balzac, nostalgic for the aristocratic way of life that was already being eroded. "No stranger was ever admitted to it; even members of the family only entered under urgent circumstances. In our country, this room is as accessible as any other. If the mistress of the house is feeling ever so slightly unwell, she will receive in her bedroom; there is something hospitable about this use."[26]

Architectural plans are very telling, and sociologists like Anne Debarre-Blanchard and Monique Eleb-Vidal have deciphered them for us.[27] They show the very late development of a specifically domestic architecture, the reconfiguration of the enfilade into a more functional arrangement of often numbered rooms, including the *chambre à coucher* (literally "room for sleeping"). An early example is in the work of Nicolas Le Camus de Mézières, who intended the bedroom to be mainly used for sleeping and recommended it be painted green, seen as a restful color. He designed alcoves and niches, where it was difficult to breathe, and placed an isolated bed, the "sanctuary of the temple," at the back of the room. For washing, he provided an adjoining "bathroom." For those voluptuous moments, he designed a mirror-lined boudoir, with a bed for "resting," intended to be placed in an alcove; he thought of everything to facilitate a "delightful retreat," and it is clear that he distinguished between conjugality and sexuality. The *chambre à coucher* was just one in a series of apartments (both large and small) in the vast mansion he designed, where he demarcated the master's and the mistress's sides of the house.[28] In these aristocratic homes, it continued to be the custom to separate Monsieur's room from Madame's, connecting them by adjoining cabinets. This proved a durable legacy; Viollet-le-Duc did the same in his bourgeois *Histoire d'une maison* (1873). Generally Madame was allocated the larger space—the *grande chambre*, where she could receive visitors as she always had and where Monsieur would eventually join her, following the tradition of the king and queen. In this way, her space was ultimately designated as the site of conjugality. Madame retained the power to close her door, but such was no longer the case in the smaller bourgeois apartment, where the two rooms became one. With this loss of her space, the married woman also lost part of her freedom.[29] In principle she reigned over the interior, but she no longer had a room of her own.

In time, the public/private distinction regulated the layout of the home, just as it organized the neighborhood. César Daly, an expert in this field, defined the system of allocating space that resulted from separating domestic and social life. The largest, most extravagant rooms were for public life. "Family life necessitated an interior apartment: intimate, comfortable." In 1902, Julien Guadet saw the bedroom as the center of the house,

"the most important mechanism for living, the private home." The bedrooms might adjoin one another, but it must also be possible to lock them:
"One turn of the key or throw of the bolt and the private life of the family
becomes inviolable in its fortress, which is the bedroom and its surround-
ing areas."[30] A few decades later, the binary of day and night would substi-
tute for that of public and private; it divided the apartment in two, "onstage"
and "backstage." In each case, bedrooms—moved up to the first floor and
facing north or relegated to the back of the apartment, looking out onto the
courtyard—were not given the best part of the house and dwindled over
time. In the twentieth century, we still complain about them. In 1923, Dr. P.
de Bourgogne deplored "the narrowness of bedrooms, sacrificed to the reception areas of the apartment, through a thirst for luxury and the need to
show off."[31] Today, these unregulated rooms seem ripe for redefinition.[32]

THE GOLDEN AGE OF THE CONJUGAL ROOM

In a way, the golden age of the conjugal room was established by royal couples: Victoria and Albert—masters of interior decoration whose collections
can be admired in London—accorded it a great deal of importance.[33] Louis-
Philippe and Marie-Amélie also decided to share a bedroom. At the Château d'Eu, the headboard of their bed was attached to the wall. The bed was
six feet tall, had four pillows and two nightstands, as well as a divan and one
single prie-dieu.

    For the middle classes, the conjugal bedroom became customary after
1840. These rooms were of modest proportions, placed not too far from the
children, frequently adjoining them, and were the natural center of a family
unit. Much attention was devoted to elements of comfort. Doctors were especially preoccupied by the precise volume in cubic feet of air in the room;
studies on hygiene focused at great length on the ventilation of the "tainted
air" produced by night breathing and calculated the amount depending on
how many people occupied the room and how many hours they slept.[34]
Until the late nineteenth century, the size of a room was measured in cubic
feet, rather than square feet. A fireplace was indispensable, but the temperature had to remain moderate, especially at night. The rooms were often ill

lit; what use is it to illuminate the temple of sleep? Lovers of nighttime reading—whose numbers grew during the nineteenth century—used a ton of candles, in spite of the risk of fire. Electricity, that enchantress, would change everything; the switch allowed for the room to become an individual space, an occurrence that hadn't been as possible due to petit-bourgeois parsimony, which held that reading in bed was too costly.

Much later, the arrival of running water would prove the decisive element.[35] Formerly, chamber pots had been hidden away under the nightstand. Basins and pitchers were inserted into dressing tables equipped with lids, and, more and more, in adjacent water closets, something that Dr. Bourgogne believed was crucial to the health of a marriage.[36]

COLORS AND DECORATIONS

The salon-bedrooms of the classical age were unequaled in their magnificence, especially when it came to textiles—tapestries, wall hangings, velvet bedding that matched the curtains, and so on. There was nothing like this in the modern conjugal bedroom, which was infinitely simpler; the walls personalized it. To repaint them, to reupholster them, was to take possession of the bedroom by modifying its physiognomy. Another way to do this was through wallpaper, whose use is relatively recent, dating back to the eighteenth century, and largely used in England among the working classes. According to Savary des Bruslons, it was first used by people in the countryside and the poor in Paris "to decorate and, so to speak, cover over certain places in their shacks and in their shops and bedrooms." In well-off houses, it entered through the wardrobe, hallways, and back rooms until it took over everywhere. First there was *papier d'Inde* and *papier de Chine,* in British blues, and then French manufacturers like Réveillon took over. Starting in the 1780s, we see more and more widespread advertisements for apartments to rent "decorated with wall paper."

In the nineteenth century, paint and wallpaper had a certain respectability and followed certain fashions generated by an active, prosperous industry, which standardized styles and colors. Never yellow; that was a "girls' color." Restful green was popular; blue was virginal, garnet reasonable, gray distinguished, and cream worked everywhere (and in the nineteenth and twentieth centuries was indeed everywhere). Muted tones were best for sleeping. The textures and the designs of the upholstering distinguished the bedroom from other rooms. There were never panoramas, which were displayed only in receiving rooms, but there were garlands, figures from myth or fairy tales, birds, griffins, flowers, or geometric patterns. Eventually they would be replaced by the cool uniformity and texture of Japanese papers. This reflected a certain neutrality of good taste, a calm "background" for love and sleep.

The bedroom was invaded by objects and keepsakes, as was the rest of the apartment, which became a gallery, a museum, a temple to the family. In his grandfather's living room on the rue d'Assas, the historian Michel Vernes once counted, as a child, more than six hundred knickknacks. The bedroom, however, was necessarily simpler and more intimate. Very few works of art or collector's pieces would be installed there; only the bits and bobs of everyday life. Around the clock, under a cover, could be found a pearl-studded wedding bouquet; the mantelpiece would heave with memories: boxes, little pebbles brought back from walks, shells gathered from the beach in summer, baubles acquired during travels near and far, and especially photographs, which brought the presence of loved ones into the heart of one's private sphere. The mantelpiece was an altar, accumulating the debris of an emotional landscape, both personal and collective.

The degree to which religion was present in the bedroom varied by era and custom. Above the bed could sometimes be found a crucifix or Millet's *Angélus*. In most Catholic countries, a few box tree leaves (blessed on Palm Sunday) would be slipped into the picture frame or under the cross. The most observant would place a statuette of the Virgin (picked up at Lourdes or elsewhere) on the dresser or on a stool and hang pious images on the wall. In the nineteenth century the Neapolitan bourgeoisie would add paintings of sacred art—sometimes up to eleven in the same room.[37] Women were especially attached to these practices, and their men left them to it, more concerned with their studies or their libraries. In this way, each bedroom—conjugal or not—became a palimpsest that required an attentive reading. The details personalized the decor.

For a long time, the bedroom was weighed down with furniture. Henry Havard's dictionary describes the bedrooms of great ladies, true havens of domesticity.[38] In Paris, the nineteenth-century postmortem inventories studied by Rivka Bercovici demonstrate an evolution: in a room from 1842, there were ten chairs, four gondola chairs, a fainting couch, a Voltaire chair, a padded armchair, and a cot; but in another room of 1871, there were merely a bed, a nightstand, and an armoire. As it became a more private space, the bedroom also became a more sparsely decorated and simple one—like the bedroom of a young couple from 1880, living in a five-room apartment in the rue Saint-Lazare; it was decorated in Louis XVI furnishings: a couchette in the middle, a canopy bed, three seats, a mirrored armoire, and a dresser—and that was a lot.[39]

Catalogues of furnishings published by department stores or specialty shops proposed model bedroom sets. After 1880, the mirrored armoire was inescapable (in one, two, or three parts), and it doubled as a looking glass and a storage unit. A couple decided jointly how to furnish the bedroom; the husband selected the furniture, a more serious job, and the wife the curtains and wall hangings. They had to choose wisely; their decisions would last a long time—in principle a whole lifetime. The Lévitan company promised "durable furniture"—in theory, it would last a lifetime. Fashion took inspiration from history, from the era of Henri II or Louis XIII, while the end of the nineteenth century saw the return of the eighteenth, especially the Louis XVI period, as can be seen from the Goncourts' house to a bourgeois home in Rouen.[40] The only glimmer of original bourgeois style was the Art Nouveau of the Belle Époque, which breathed new life into the furniture industry in the Faubourg Saint-Antoine. The height of monumentalism in the bedroom was marked by Majorelle, Serrurier, and Sauvage; they created the most beautiful bedroom that can be seen at the Musée des Arts décoratifs in Paris on the rue de Rivoli.

This kind of overstuffed decor provoked both aesthetic and ethical responses. At the end of the nineteenth century, William Morris and his disciple, Maple, "declared that a bedroom was only beautiful if it contained merely those things which are useful, and every useful thing, even a simple nail, should not be hidden, but visible. Above the bed: bare brass curtain rods. Only a few reproductions of masterpieces on the otherwise blank walls of these antiseptic rooms"—for example, Botticelli's *Primavera*.[41] Marcel Proust, however, preferred the layers of fabric found in provincial bedrooms.

APOTHEOSIS OF THE BED

At the center of the bedroom was the bed, the expression of a relationship to conjugality that has endured over the centuries.

Ulysses built his from the trunk of an olive tree. Upon returning to Ithaca, he joined Penelope there. "Now that we have returned to each other in this bed so dear to our hearts, you must watch over the belongings I have left in this house."[42] "The sign of the bed, with its erotic, conjugal connotations, is another of the secret scars and inscriptions of which only husband and wife are aware."[43] The conjugal bed is identity incarnate; women, to be sure it is their husbands who have returned, whose faces they have almost forgotten, ask for a description of the bed. To move the bed is to betray the husband.

For the Merovingians, "nudity was sacred, and the shared bed was a sanctuary for procreation and affection."[44] In Byzantium, the emperor and empress shared a room and a bed, which is represented in miniatures as being a very narrow space, but childbirth took place in another room.[45] In the master bedroom of the medieval château, a "matrix of lineage," the bed, throne of a conjugality controlled by the Church, was the place of conception and birth, the site of pleasure and no doubt of violence and deception, of the press of bodies that Georges Duby imagines to be cunning and shifty.[46] The garden, the orchard, or the forest were places where love could flourish more freely.

Sixteenth-century poetry celebrated the conjugal bed: "Fifty years one faithful to the other / Between them a bed without upset or quarrels," read one epitaph dedicated in 1559 by grandchildren to their lucky grandparents.[47] The poet Gilles Corrozet wrote in his *Blason du lit:* "O modest bed, O chaste bed / Where the woman and her dear husband / Are joined by God in one flesh / Place of a sanctified love, honorable bed / Somnolent bed, venerable bed / Keep your modesty / Avoid wantonness / So your honor may spread / And remain without besmirch."[48]

In the modern era, the marriage bed became widespread in the cities and the countryside. Marriage contracts make mention of it. Young couples strain to invest in it, scrimping on curtains and bedding to be able to afford a basic bed frame.[49] The bride's trousseau, which she and her mother have worked to assemble for years, provides sheets and embellishments, locked away in a chest or an armoire.[50] In the nineteenth century, urban working-class households would put themselves in debt in order to purchase a bed when they decided to transition from living together to marriage, a state to which all aspired because of the status it conferred. One woman threw acid in her partner's face because he wasted the money that was intended to buy wood to build a bed—that fundamental framework—and she could not tolerate such a betrayal—a rupture of their pact as partners.[51]

"The bed is marriage itself," according to Balzac, in his "Theory of the Bed." He describes "three ways of organizing [it]": two twin beds, two separate rooms, or one single bed. He rails against the "false chumminess" of the first, an option that is inconvenient for young couples and only really conceivable after twenty years of marriage, which have tempered the couple's ardors. Balzac condemned separate rooms, without explaining why, and argued for the shared bed, the scene of conversations and caresses, the site of the encounter and the exchange. However, this system presents nothing but inconvenience, and he himself avoids it! To share a bed is no easy thing. "It is unnatural for two to live under the canopy of a single bed," and to make love at appointed hours is an abomination. It is no surprise, then, that women avoid doing so, claiming migraines or modesty, feigning frigidity. "The married woman is a slave who must be placed on a throne," that great critic of bourgeois mores wrote elsewhere.[52] His panegyric to the marriage bed is the sort of ironic paradox to which he was accustomed.

Over time, the bed changed a great deal—in location, shape, material, structure, and size; ethnographers and art historians have studied the changes in detail, creating genealogies and inventories that may be seen in museums. The number and variety of beds grew. In the houses found in poorer Italian neighborhoods in the fifteenth century, there would be several per room. According to Havard, the seventeenth century was the "great century of the bed."[53] An inventory of the royal furniture at Versailles counted 413, of a wide variety of shades, according to the types of wood used, the hanging of the curtains, the moldings. The lists are interminable: Turkish style, Polish style, Italian style, canopy bed, boat bed, gondola bed, beds with curved feet and headboards, bassinets—all those of the kind that Perec wrote existed only in fairy tales.

In display bedrooms, the bed resembled a throne: sumptuous, ornate. Tucked away in an alcove or a corner, it appeared more modest. Or it could be lined up against the wall, between two nightstands. Or it could be placed between panels, often facing the window, and surrounded by curtains, intended to close it off if the room had to be unavoidably shared. In Polish-style beds, the majestic canopies would be covered in feathers. The fairly grandiose four-poster bed persists in the provinces until the present day and has had a bit of a renaissance thanks to certain decorators.[54] The need to surround the bed disappeared when a couple had four walls of their own. In that case, behind the closed doors, each had his or her own side of the bed, nightstand, candlestick, and chamber pot.

The bed became smaller in time and lower. Older beds were bigger because they were intended to include more people, and they were very high up, to the point that sometimes a stool would be needed to help one climb up into it. It was colder in low beds, and to be closer to the ground indicated a lower social situation. Spring mattresses, which were invented around 1840, a product of the industrial revolution, came to replace the older style of piled-up mattresses of the sort slept on by the Grimms' fairy princess, who slept atop a pile of mattresses yet was so sensitive she could feel a pea at the bottom. And little by little, the duvet took precedence over sheets. The expression *être dans de beaux draps* (literally, to be in nice sheets, but figuratively meaning "to be in a sticky situation") has more or less lost its meaning today.

THE MIDDLE OF THE BED

Nocturnal, sexual, sensual, potentially procreative, the conjugal room was both protected and constrained, shielded and controlled—above all by the Church, which made it the cradle of feudal lineage and the crucible of

Christianity. "Go forth and multiply"; nothing could violate the will of God the creator, and the sin of Onan was a crime, an attempt against life.[55] However, *coitus interruptus* was the most efficient way of keeping the birthrate down, and demographers have shown the French to be early adopters of this technique. "We cheat nature even in the countryside," said the demographer Jean-Baptiste Moheau, and wives were no doubt as much to blame as their husbands, pushing them off if they did not know how to "be careful" and pull out in time. The art of the fugue must be played in the conjugal bed. Priests knew this well and lent an understanding ear to the complaints of those who confessed to them. Could one refuse one's "conjugal duty"? The clergy did not think so and criticized the aristocracy for keeping separate bedrooms. "Their lives together become so much a matter of politics, of reserve, and of ceremony, that they can no longer give themselves freedom when it comes to natural things and cannot bear to sleep in the same bed, in the same room, or in the same apartment. They spend as much time apart as possible, through a natural aversion to nature and all that depends upon it."[56] The clergy blessed the marriage bed, "the place for healthy, sacred, divine love" (François de Sales), the only tolerated form of sexuality, and celebrated "pleasure under the sheets" rather than that "stolen in secret."[57]

What went on in the marriage bed remained relatively discreet in the nineteenth century, particularly thanks to the widely influential eighteenth-century writer and bishop Alphonsus Liguori, who was indulgent in the matter of sexual needs; in the twentieth century it became of great importance given the evident practice of "fraud," revealed by the declining birthrate, which also alarmed the French state. The pope got involved (in his *Casti Connbii* encyclical, 1930) and asked confessors to intervene and require the use of "natural methods." Young interwar couples saw themselves reduced to the hazards of the Ogino method, to charting the rise and fall of the woman's body temperature (responsible for many unwanted births), and confined to the "missionary" position, which reinforced the hierarchy between the sexes: man on top, woman beneath. For many observant Catholics, the conjugal bed became a hell of frustrated desire. Members of the Association for Christian Marriage addressed letters to the Abbé Viollet that testify to the suffering experienced by those whose desires were thwarted.[58] "I have often risen at eleven o'clock or midnight and fought until two or three in the morning against those desires that could not be satisfied," wrote a young woman whose husband refused to make love to her. "It only lasted a couple of years, two years at the most; I don't remember exactly. But I read, I worked, I prayed, and I did not return to my husband in bed until I was exhausted and often resorted to wrapping myself in a blanket and stretching out on the floor when I could not bear to feel the heat of his body so close to mine."[59] This was so much the case that the debate extended to the marriage bed itself: was it not wiser to resort, in the Protestant manner, to separate beds, which were more appropriate for chastity and spousal independence? So believed one letter writer, a dedicated proponent of twin beds, to whom another responded with a passionate defense of the "traditional marriage bed, the symbol of [the spouses'] union, and their haven." "Time is abolished on the pillow; the outside world is invisible. There, husband and wife are truly at home."[60] Is this really true? The conjugal bedroom is the final bastion of a Church that turned sexuality into its Maginot line—largely unsuccessfully.

In the eighteenth century, doctors (until then largely indifferent to sexuality) began to turn their attention to procreation and sexual health. They invaded the bedroom, declaring it "convenient" for observation and for a way of life that favored "harmonious pleasure," a condition for procreation. Alain Corbin has studied the quasi-erotic clinical discourse of those who followed Buffon and Virey—Cabanis, Roussel, Deslandes, Bourbon, Roubaud—those "officers of nature," experts on the "good coitus" upon which female pleasure was thought to depend. Nothing escaped them: no element of the "mechanism" of the "spasm" (orgasm) or the best positions and hours of the day (and it may well have been day and not night). The "peaceful husband and wife" were sexually active and satisfied; this was the ideal held by doctors and the state. It culminated during the French Revolution, which valued an honest household and preferred the People's Hercules to the scandalous sophistication of libertinage. Marie-Antoinette was painted as a modern Messalina; her supposedly deviant sexuality was thought to be one of her major "crimes." A good sexual regimen, considered indispensable to a healthy lifestyle, forbade masturbation (haunted by the specter of waste), as well as the homosexuality (seen as against nature) of the anti-physics. Medical morality made the marriage bed the center of normality. "The union of husband and wife cannot take place outside the bedroom, the sanctuary of their love and of maternity. A good bed is the only place where the work of the flesh may take place with any dignity," Dr. Montalban declared in a peremptory tone, prescribing the act taking place in darkness, without any mirrors or mutterings.[61] Was love meant to be deaf as well as blind?

It is not surprising, then, that soon after, Zola would exalt conjugality in *Fécondité* (1899), an epic of the procreating couple Mathieu and Marianne Froment, a foundational example of the family and the universal Republic. A number of scenes in this strange *roman à thèse* (one of the *Quatre Évangiles,* a blatant plea against Malthusianism and for a vigorous birthrate, the lifeblood of the nation) take place in bed or in the vicinity of the bed, presenting a number of different situations: pregnancy, childbirth, breast feeding, and the happy consequences of coupling, described in muted terms. When Marianne is pregnant for the fifth time, Mathieu installs himself a little iron bed next to the big walnut bed, which he leaves to his wife; he sleeps tenderly beside her, wishing to allow her to awaken each morning "like a queen." After each birth, his return to the conjugal bed is a new dawn. "Oh! this room of battle and victory, to which Mathieu returns, in his triumphant glory!" Zola contrasts this with the abortionist's "room of terror and horror," where poor Valérie Morange dies. Zola was personally very attached to the idea of the conjugal bedroom; in Médan, in the midst of his affair with Jeanne Rozerot, he still refused to keep a separate bedroom, even though Alexandrine, Madame Zola, asked him to.[62] His bedroom comprised classic conjugal furnishings, including a great copper bed facing the window, a desk, a large armoire with light woodworking, nightstands, seats, little round tables—and due to his extreme modesty, the threshold of his bedroom was forbidden to all. "Thus of this conjugal bed that husband and wife shared, in a bourgeois manner, all their lives, we cannot say much," writes Évelyne Bloch-Dano, imagining Émile's adulterous dreams.[63] From his balcony in Médan, he watched his beloved's window.

A couple's practices—their gestures and their murmurings, their desires and their satisfactions, their ardors and their lassitudes—are mostly lost to us. "There are things we must kept hidden, and I cannot think of anything more odious than conjugal love," wrote Prosper Mérimée, incensed by the publication of the letters of the Duchess de Choiseul-Praslin, who complained of having been sexually abandoned by her husband.[64]

The sweetness of the right to silence. Alexis de Tocqueville confided to Gustave de Beaumont that he rose later in winter, at seven o'clock instead of five (he worked until noon): "I am too gallant and attentive of a husband to leave my wife [Mary Motley] to shiver alone in her bed in this kind of cold."[65] The bed: a place of shared heat. "I long for our solitude, our tête-à-tête, everything that is the foundation of my happiness in this world," he wrote to Mary, to whom he was not necessarily faithful.[66] The most intimate couples are those who write the least, who make no mention of the essential, resorting to common epistolary conventions—"My dear wife, I dream of holding you against my heart"—except, perhaps, in times of war, which reawaken or ruin desires. In the archives of the Association pour l'autobiographie (APA), Anne-Claire Rebreyend found very revealing correspondence in this regard, like that exchanged by Serge and Diane between 1942 and 1944.[67] They dreamed of the bedroom to which they would one day return, sorry to see themselves reduced to meeting in a hotel.

How would they make love? They described what would happen with delightful precision. It is true that they were an adulterous couple aspiring to the legitimacy they hoped to find later on, even if it meant resorting to the sweetness of ordinary silence. A couple's silence is, after all, the best defense against indiscreet looks, familial allusions to sterile bellies or open legs, normalizing discourse, pressing injunctions. The encounter of their bodies belonged only to them, their unique story enveloped by the shadows of their bedroom, a novel of the world, buried in the hollow of the bed.

The death of a spouse marked the end of the conjugal bedroom. In well-off families, the widow (a more usual state than that of a widower) would eventually erect an altar to the departed and would continue to dwell among his furniture. She would save his place in their shared bed. The widows of Noirmoutier fishermen, as filmed by Agnès Varda, kept to their side of the bed, not even sleeping in the center, programmed until death to occupy the place they once occupied in their couple, in their love, in their lives.[68] Was this out of sadness for a lost happiness? Submission to marital destiny? Muscle memory? Who can say? The bed retains its mysteries.

Obliged to move into a smaller home, the widow would keep the furniture that was easiest to move and return to the single bed of her youth, to which she now, in a way, returned. She had to take refuge with her children, her ambitions reduced to an easy chair or a few objects. Mourning came with a purging.

In the countryside, the question of where older parents were to live was a thorny one for a long time, no doubt less because of a lack of space as for problems of authority, status, or domestic economy. In Alsace, widows or widowers had to abandon the alcove they occupied and restrict themselves to places designed in advance for such situations.[69] In Gévaudan, sometimes old women were installed in huts, like recluses. The lack of privacy of the communal room gave rise to unbearable tensions, which could provoke abuse or even patricide; judicial enquiries attest to deplorable situations.[70] A ninety-year-old mother was made to sleep on a bed of straw with a tarp for a blanket in an oven with a broken door; a sixty-eight-year-old father was confined to a bad room under the stairs. In an extreme case of sequestration, a widow was shut up on a bed of dried grass in the attic. There were cases of patricide.[71] The fate of the elderly was hardly better in urban working-class families; for men especially, who frequently had no belongings; a grandfather in Belleville, who had to move in with his children to survive, transported his bed from one home to another and had to bring suit against them to get back his bed, which they didn't want to return to him.[72] After a period of living with their children in narrow lodgings, the elderly—detritus of a broken home, of a time long ago—were sent to live in a hospice dormitory.

The conjugal bedroom held together only as long as the marriage—or at least as long as the couple took conjugal form, for there were others who did not share a room. It dissolved with the separation of the bodies that previously had necessitated the bed. Divorce. Death. Its lack of inheritors corresponds today to that of marriage—unmarriage—in contemporary society.[73] We have another, freer, less "conformist" conception of a union, one that is more interested in comfort and especially in sleep. To have separate bedrooms is becoming more and more widespread and does not indicate any lack of love.[74]

The conjugal bedroom corresponds to a crucial moment in the history of the family. The individual room preceded it and survives it.

A Room of One's Own

THE DESIRE FOR personal space is relatively universal; it is found across civilizations and historical eras. Sleep, sex, love, sickness, prayer, meditation, reading, writing—the needs of the body but also of the soul compel us to retreat to our own rooms, which may take many forms. Caves and huts, cells and corners, the boat cabin, the train compartment, the enclosed horse-drawn carriage—we have been unimaginably ingenious in devising ways to hide ourselves away. This has especially been true in places where collectivity comes to the fore; in a barracks, hospital, boarding school, or prison, a place to oneself becomes an obsession. When Jules Vallès became a monitor at the Collège de Caen, he was delighted to find himself in "a little room at the end of the dormitory, where proctors could spend their free moments working or daydreaming. The room looks out onto the countryside, full of trees, run through with rivers." There he could detect "the smell of the sea, which salted my lips, refreshed my eyes, and eased my heart."[1]

The crowd drives us to withdraw. It submerged Joachim Heinrich Kampe, who came to Paris, like so many young people, to see the Revolution: "I have torn myself away from the swells of this human river . . . and now am seated by the banks of it, that is to say, in my room. I'm trying to come to terms with this infinite mass of images, representations, and new sensations, to try to put some order to them, but in vain! The rushing of the human river crashes in through the windows, the doors, and the walls, invading my room, though it is some distance away."[2] His compatriot Georg Forster, like him attracted then disappointed in revolutionary Paris, came and went between the street and his garret, ruminating over a project that escaped him: "It has now been three or four hours since, half mad, I have been walking back and forth, taking refuge in my room, trying to remember. It's no use."[3] The ever-growing crowd, the increasing pressure of the masses brings with it an inextinguishable thirst, the frenzied quest for a room of one's own, a guarantor of personal freedom. This is what Walter Benjamin masterfully tracked in Paris in the early twentieth century; foot traffic moved through the honeycomb-like arcades, even when they closed at night.

The Right to Secrecy

Certain kinds of people show a more lively interest in private spaces: the young, workers without families, students in search of experience, single women, the exiled, foreigners, isolated elderly persons, or those who can no longer bear the rhythm of everyday life. There are many factors that lead people to a life alone in a room: those who are single, whether by choice or circumstance; those who have left or been left; those who are on the move or displaced; but also those who seek the sedentary life of study, of reflection and creation, or the aloofness from and the ebbing of emotions that public life demands. The servitude of the marital bed turns the stomach of those who are in love with love. Huysmans castigates "the misery of sleeping *à deux* . . ., the fatigue of the required caress."[4]

"I can sleep only when I am alone in my bedroom. I cannot bear communal life with anyone," Kafka admitted. "I hurl myself into solitude as I do into the ocean." This is modernity for Kafka, who felt so keenly the increasing, harassing, insidious penetration of surveillance and the gaze—those forms of panoptical control described by Michel Foucault—as well as their dissemination in the social body.[5] Hence the desire to hide away. "In our country," said Michel de Certeau, "opacity becomes necessary. It is founded on the rights of the collective, liable to balance the economy that, in the name of individual rights, exposes social reality in the naked light of the market and the administration."[6]

The bedroom is only one form of the right to secrecy. Even socialist utopias, so ready to hunt down egotism and to promote collective solutions, are careful to defend it. Victor Dézamy, author of the well-known *Code de la communauté* (1842), allocated to each of his "equals" a room of their own, equipped with all the comforts: "[all that is] commodious, useful, agreeable, salubrious"—two closets for storage; two alcoves, one for the bed, the other for the toilet; a bed with a box spring, the very latest in modern bed design; a sink; a nightstand; a table; seats and easy chairs, with everything on wheels.[7] His contemporary Eugène Sue was very attentive to the conditions of working-class housing and described a bachelor's bedroom with its iron bed stand, "pretty Persian paper," curtains, a dresser, a walnut table (the wood of the people), a few chairs, and a small bookcase. The right to the bedroom was practically written in the Rights of Man. It guaranteed independence and self-respect. Faunia, the protagonist of Philip Roth's novel *The Human Stain*, reproaches herself for sleeping beside her lover after sex. "I stayed. I stupidly stayed. Leaving at night—there is nothing more important for a girl like me. . . . I have a place to go, don't I? It isn't the nicest place, but it's a place. Go to it!"[8] She refuses to move in with someone who would ensnare her in the trap of "everlasting love." The bedroom guarantees freedom.

Sleeping Alone

"It's easier to sleep alone than as a couple," the poet Eustache Deschamps said.[9] His contemporary Montaigne replied, "I like to sleep hard and alone, that is to say, without my wife, in the royal way, a little too well covered; I will not have my bed warmed."[10] Georges Perec noted, "The bed is an instrument devised for the nocturnal rest of one or two people, but no more."[11]

The Roman retired to his *cubiculum*, the hermit to his cave or his hut. The grand medieval bed could accommodate five or six people, but as early as this period "[in] the bed, peninsula of privacy, grew the joys of solitude."[12] It could be the site of pain, welcoming the wounded, the ill, or those harassed by the fatigue of a long ride; you can throw yourself onto it to cry, especially in the modern period, when tears are fought back in public. "At ten o'clock at night, I returned to my bedroom to cry over our separation," one woman confided to her diary. "Distressed by sadness, I threw myself on the bed, where I sought to lose myself in sleep, but I could not."[13] Jane Austen's heroines took refuge in their bedrooms and gave way to the emotions they had been obliged to hide. In the bedroom, the

criminal hides himself. We nestle up in bed; it is a shelter, an island of protection, a piece of furniture that is celebrated, bequeathed, and represented
in medieval paintings, often in the exceptional circumstances of sickness
and death.

An increasingly refined physical awareness makes the very presence
of another person painful and reinforces the imperious demand for a bed of
one's own in all social milieux, especially urban ones. The number and variety of beds multiplies in a strange and poetic proliferation characteristic of
Western culture. The individual bed becomes widespread, initiated in Italy
during the Quattrocentro; in Paris by the end of the seventeenth century,
"even everyday people had real beds."[14] This aristocratic and especially
bourgeois practice became popular with the lower classes. In the nineteenth
century, workers revolted against the practice of communal bedrooms. "I
could no longer tolerate the contact of another man," said Norbert Truquin,
who worked on a construction site during the Second Empire. Having once
served as the seal of a conjugal union, the bed could be fought over when
those unions ended. "She didn't want me to sleep at home any more. So I
took back the bed that belonged to me because my former boss gave it to
me," said one defendant accused of a crime of passion.[15]

Hygienic and moral prescriptions contributed to the practice of quarantine, which acted as a barrier against all manner of contagions. The National Convention made this mandatory in hospitals (15 November 1793). In
the early nineteenth century, official regulations required that children
younger than fifteen sleep alone. The Church and the doctors agreed that
sleeping alone was the best policy, and the iron industry provided a solution: a bed that was light, mobile, affordable, easily transportable, spacious
with its clean angles, its metal base, its minimal fuss—it incarnated the democracy of sleep.

Perec celebrated the triumph of the bed. "The bed is . . . an individual
space par excellence, the elementary space of the body (the bed as monad),
which even the man crippled by debt has the right to keep. . . . We have only
one bed, and it is *our* bed." "I love my bed," Perec went on, remembering
the reading he did there, the imaginary voyages, the sweets consumed, the
terrors experienced there.[16] Each of us has our own memories of our bed.

We spend a third of our lives in bed. It is the overlap between day and night made material. It seals the shadowy alliance between ourselves and the night.

Sleeping

A man asleep holds in a circle around him the sequence of hours,
the order of years and of worlds.
—Marcel Proust, *Du côté de chez Swann*

First of all, we must go to bed. We undress; removing those clothes that weave together the way we appear to the world, we put off our old selves, as is written in Scripture. The public man is undone; the woman prepares for the night. At one time, this could be a ritual inspired by the ceremonies of the court. George Sand describes her grandmother's *coucher:* "The *coucher* lasted a very long time. My grandmother would eat a little bit, and then, while there were arranged upon her head and shoulders a number of little bonnets and fichus in cotton and silk, little quilted woolen things, she would listen to Julie's reports on intimate family goings-on and Rose's on the details of the household. That would last until two in the morning."[17] It was the hour of the daily assessment of domestic or personal matters; for the Christian it was the hour in which to examine one's conscience before plunging into the unknown night.

All bedtime rituals are not necessarily solemn, but it is always a moment of rupture. And then what do we do with our clothes? Between those who toss them anywhere and those who fold them carefully, there is a whole range of attitudes that speak volumes about our relationships to things and to ourselves; this is frequently a gendered division but not always. The bedroom of a single man does not have a good reputation but wrongly so; there are meticulous bachelors, like Kafka's Blumfeld, "between two ages," who cannot bear filth or disorder, who makes his bed as he likes it, starved, like his author, for peace.[18]

Next, we take possession of the bed. Some throw themselves "into the arms of Morpheus"; others slip furtively between the sheets or under the duvet, moves that suggest two different ways of living. There are also a variety of postures once one is in bed that are culturally determined on the whole; our ancestors slept half sitting up on shorter beds; we curl up in the fetal position or stretch out on our sides, on our stomachs, or on our backs, in the "missionary" position, like the one that the Church prescribed for lovemaking and also for death. There is nothing truly spontaneous in these attitudes. The "techniques of the body" asleep are no more natural than any others.[19] Dr. Lévy recommended the horizontal position rather than a lateral decubitus. However, "a dorsal posture on a hard bed has the inconvenient tendency to produce erections and nocturnal emissions."[20] And it is as difficult to move from standing to lying down in an apartment as it is on the battlefield.[21] A man who stretches out is viewed with suspicion and is always under threat. Those in power dread their powerlessness against the shadows, the risks of conspiracy, of nighttime assassination, practiced in Roman times. The easiest way to get rid of a tyrant was to lock him in his bedroom. This happened frequently in Rome; thus did Domitius perish. Women are a threat to an unarmed man: Delilah cut Samson's hair while he was asleep. Cleopatra debases Marc Antony. These defeated virilities sometimes inspire disgust: "I hate sleepers," said Violette Leduc. "They are dead people who haven't pronounced their last words."[22]

Falling asleep is an art and requires care. The bed must be neither too hard nor too soft; today this matters a great deal.[23] Some architects are very interested in the orientation of the bed and its position with regard to the window. Green, believed in the eighteenth century to be the most restful color for the body and the spirit—this was Goethe's opinion—is now used for delivery rooms.[24] Hygienists recommend a hard bed, a well-aired room, regular habits at appointed hours; one should avoid staying up late, stimulants, unsettling or arousing reading, and even intellectual work. They particularly warn against reversing day and night, a reversal that subverts the cosmic, divine, and civic order.

Being adrift in the night creates a profound feeling of anxiety and prevents us from falling asleep. It seems too close to death, which can creep up on those who are asleep. Even the religious—those who are specifically waiting for it—fear a too sudden arrival of death, which prevents the faithful from an organized, ritualized encounter with God. God warned, "I will come like a thief." Thus the recommendations to pray before bed, to examine one's conscience, to repeat contrition, to beg for forgiveness, to call on guardian angels for protection and to keep watch over the bedroom. To fall asleep is to leave on a voyage from which we do not know when we will return.

Children loathe breaking off the evening this way. They see bedtime coming a mile off and delay it as much as possible. This is why a motherly kiss at night is so important, as the opening scene of Proust's *Recherche* attests. "Once I was in my room," writes the narrator, "I had to close off every entryway, close the shutters, dig my own grave as I turned down the bedclothes, and wrap myself in the shroud of my nightshirt . . . before burying myself in the iron bed which had been placed in the room." Little Mona Sohier (now Mona Ozouf) was afraid in her Breton bedroom of the mid-1930s: "Monsters with claws crept along the floorboards, and I asked my grandmother if I could climb into bed with her."[25] Children like a light to be left on, the door open a crack, the shadow of a presence. But this anxiety isn't found only in children. Henri Michaux was particularly susceptible to it: "It is very difficult to sleep. . . . First of all, the covers are always very heavy, not to mention the sheets; it's like being in jail." Which position to lie in? asks the father in *Plume,* who cannot think of any that are not inconvenient. "For many people, going to sleep is an unparalleled torture."[26]

What about insomnia, these anxious moments when "night stirs"?[27] The shadows, the cracks in the ceiling, the creaks in the floorboards, the rustling that could be a mouse or even a rat, the beating of a butterfly's wing, the irritating whine of a mosquito, the sounds of muffled voices, of muffled steps, cautious and all the more terrifying, transform the bedroom into a hostile place full of traps, where each detail takes on outsized importance. In an unfamiliar bedroom, the risks are immeasurably greater. Insomnia invites in a depressing array of fantasies and phantoms. We dwell on our problems, our failed lives (at three o'clock in the morning we are always failures). The bed feels hard, uncomfortable. We turn and turn but cannot find sleep. We see, like Proust's narrator, the bedrooms we have known, in these vague recollections that distinguish and confuse them all at once.

The difficulty of falling asleep, the fear of losing the ability to do it, explains why we've turned to a whole pharmacopoeia of preventatives and curatives. We've abandoned the ones we inherited—lime blossom, orange flower, hot milk—in favor of more complex substances—laudanum, veronal, and opium, prepared by the apothecary, until our own day and the invention of sleeping pills, of which the French are among the most frequent consumers. Neurobiologists study sleep disorders, while psychiatry treats them with medicine.[28] A healthy diet ensures a good night's sleep, without which we cannot live a balanced life. To speak of a "good night's sleep" is to speak in terms of moral honesty, peace of mind, calmed nerves. It guarantees a productive day.

We must sleep but not too much. In Western culture, sleep does not have a good reputation. It is a sign of cowardice; the Apostles sleeping in the garden abandoned Christ to his last night on earth. "To sleep is to be disinterested," said Bergson. "Sleep is a vice," said André Gide, who only liked waking up and ensured that his bed always looked out on a window so that he could look out at the world. It was only in the second half of the twentieth century that sleep began to be considered an active function for the organism.[29] According to public health officials, eight hours is enough; a bit more is needed for children and adolescents, tempted by their endless evenings. Any more and the bed becomes a lascivious place, suitable for all manner of intimate explorations and unhealthful daydreams. Educators reviled the emollient laziness of the *grasses matinées* that Proust so adored.[30] To rise early is virtuous; to rise late is suspect. We cannot remain in bed any longer than is reasonable. On this point, here is Jeremy Bentham: "Sleep is not life, but the cessation of life; lying a-bed without sleep is a habit productive of relaxation, and thence pernicious to bodily health; and in as far as it is idleness, pernicious to moral health," wrote the author of the *Panopticon*.[31] The theorist of utilitarianism believed work to be the key to knowledge and poverty the result of a shameful indolence. Fortune favors the brave and the early to rise. Only reparative sleep is moral.

Then there are the "solitary pleasures" of the bed. In a journal addressed to her daughter, Madame de Krüdener encouraged her to resist "good food and voluptuous beds," where time is wasted. Even dreams worried this woman, haunted by impurity; she writes of the necessity of controlling them. "My soul stands on sentinel and keeps me from veering off course, so strong is my habit of self-surveillance."[32] Repression raised to morality also reigns over our dreams.

But how to control this surging, unfurling invasion of thoughts, images, and unknown sensations that we know well have long intrigued, frightened, and attracted us while we sleep? The history of the dream could be that of its contents but, above all, of its multiple interpretations.[33] Is it the voice of destiny, of God, of the beyond? Is it a manifestation of the body and of biological rhythms that can be scientifically explored or mysterious clues to the unconscious, the vestibule to our profound selves? (Our manner of reading was totally upended by Freud.) Dream narratives are an archipelago, a proliferating literature, explored in turn by saints (prolific recounters of their dreams) and by writers.[34] Drug taking altered the dimensions of a room; opium doubled the size of Baudelaire's bedroom: "The furniture seems to dream; it appears to be living in a state of trance, like vegetables, or minerals. The materials speak a silent language, like the flowers, like the sky, like the setting sun."[35] Other drugs—including alcohol—have more violent, more nightmarish effects. Under their spell, the bedroom fills with strange figures, insects, rodents, reptiles, monstrous creatures. The walls blister. The wall hangings crackle, sweat, fester. A repugnant fauna teems in the folds of the curtains.

Freud called dreams the "guardian[s] of sleep"; they dwell in the bedroom, which most of the time they ignore. The mind, freed of the weight of the body, floats free of everyday life, yet dreams are also very much composed of the space they inhabit; their sensations of expansion, oppression, crushing, and suffocation allow us to plunge into the abyss or climb stairs that wreath like smoke, scrolling upward in infinity, like something out of Piranesi. "I woke up with the sound of my room in my head," said Robert Antelme—the sound, not the shapes or the details, which the unreality of dreams disdains.[36]

The room opens up on the dreams that undermine and flee it. It dissolves as we awaken, when, like a swimmer reaching the shore, we find our feet. Finally!

This is sometimes called the dawn.

Loving

The bed—the intimate receptacle of the body—keeps its secrets. We confide our naked bodies to the folds of the sheets, those tattletales whose stains reveal so much, witnessing nocturnal emissions, the blood of a first period or its absence, signs over which mothers keep anxious watch, as do curious servants and gossiping washerwomen. A nightly palimpsest, sheets betray you like the unsettling "unmade bed" painted by Eugène Delacroix.[37]

In the bed, we smell our own bodies; we see them grow, change, tremble. We experience the disconcerting emotions that arise from sex. Masturbation provides new pleasures that girls hardly ever allow themselves.[38] Marie Chaix is no doubt one of the first to have dared to explore this in a text carried on the liberating wind of the mid-1970s: "Under the folds, a hollow beckons . . .; the young girl has just discovered the openness of her body. . . . She is frightened by the violence of a sensation that she never thought it was possible to create on her own."[39] Masturbation is the scourge of educators, the clergy, and doctors, who fear the planned or unplanned orgasm and the waste it includes. Outside of marriage, no question. One day, the single bed will become the marriage bed—a heterosexual bed, it goes without saying.[40] But until then?

To love is to discover the body of another, to undress it (*Déshabillez-moi* ["Undress me"], Juliette Greco sang tenderly), to caress it, and one day to make love to it. "Love: you will love, that is to say, you will want to sleep with a woman and you will for a time derive pleasure from sleeping with her," said a disillusioned Jules Renard.[41] How to make love? Where to make love? It is a question that obsesses the young, who are often reduced in the city to borrowed places, random shelters like public benches, abandoned corners of municipal gardens, the backseats of cars. Lovers must take the plunge, cross the threshold; "Come home with me" is the ultimate invitation, the "Open Sesame" of desire. To enter a bedroom with the one we love or desire is to take a decisive, uncertain step in a love story. This action is not the same for men as it is for women, at least according to older traditions; a conquering virility on one side is matched by a hesitant or ardent consent on the other.

Neither a young girl nor a well-behaved woman would enter a man's bedroom; she would be circumspect in opening the door, as this would signify that she is acquiescing. In Balzac's *Eugénie Grandet,* Eugénie violates a taboo in entering her cousin's bedroom, where she discovers his secret: money troubles. We know what it will cost her: she will be locked away by her father in her own bedroom. In Stendhal's *The Red and the Black,* Mathilde de la Mole tells Julien Sorel to meet her in her room one hour past midnight, but she does not open the door to him; he must borrow the gardener's ladder and enter by the window, just as he had once done for Madame de Rênal. The second time, he takes the initiative by using the same trick, knocking on the shutter and "hurling himself into [her] bedroom, more dead than alive." Was this proud young woman too disdainful to open her door to the son of a sawyer? Entry into her bedroom is a test, a barrier fraught with social and emotional power. Julien knows what is at stake, having so often "double-locked himself into his bedroom," his own safe territory.

Country homes and holiday resorts are particularly suited to sentimental intrigue and the exercise of seduction, being so useful for nocturnal circulation, secret messages, lights spotted, discreet knocks, and clandestine bedroom visits. Whether or not they jam in the lock, the keys do not always turn easily. Suitors must sometimes force delicate locks, holding the bolt behind them to be sure of their conquest, like the impetuous young man in Fragonard's *Le Verrou,* in which it is unclear if he has forced his way into the young woman's room or been invited in. The disturbing ambiguity of the painting is the source of its power for libertine suggestion. James Baldwin's hero David hesitates to enter Giovanni's room, though he is madly in love with him. To do so is not only to consent to this love, but also to finally accept his homosexuality.[42]

Lytton Strachey is more liberated. A dazzling memory: in the extravagant family home at Lancaster Gate, which he described so well, he had a bedroom on the top floor that was reached by a tortuous staircase. Coming home from a youthful summer evening, he writes:

> I opened the door and went in, and immediately saw that
> the second bed—there was invariably a second bed in every

bedroom—was occupied. I looked closer: it was Duncan; and I was not surprised: he had lingered on, no doubt, till it was too late to go home, and had been provided with the obvious accommodation. I undressed, oddly exultant, in the delicious warm morning. As I was getting into bed I saw all the clothes had rolled off Duncan—that he was lying, almost naked, in vague pyjamas—his body—the slim body of a youth of nineteen—exposed to the view. I was very happy. . . . I got into bed, and slept soundly, and dreamt no prophetic dreams.[43]

Lovers ask for silence, intimacy, discretion, anonymity, sufficiently thick walls to muffle their gasps and groans of pleasure (those of our hotel neighbors are intolerable), closed shutters, curtains that filter the unwelcome light from the outside. They are alone in the world. The real or artificial night, the unusual sight of day, protect their unique affair, of which the bedroom is but the indifferent frame.

Love escapes interior design. Do we remember the bedrooms where we've made love? The imprint in the bed marks the place where bodies have fused, "favors clung from each other in secret and silence."[44] "Our beds will be full of subtle perfumes / Divans deep as graves," wrote Baudelaire.[45] And the old French song about the middle of the bed: "Beauty, if you wanted to / We would sleep together / In a big white bed / rigged out in lace / For in the middle of the bed / the river is deep / all the king's horses / could drink there together / And we would stay there / Until the end of the world."

Praying

The retreat is an old practice that goes back to ancient Rome. There, they took refuge in the exedra, a niche set off from the main part of a space, often decorated with wall hangings, that was used to sleep, study, or write with a stylus. The silence of night was thought to favor inspiration and "elucubrations": *lucubrum,* a term that was initially positive before veering into the pejorative.

Christian hermits modeled themselves on ancient wisdom. They valued the absolute bareness of their cave or their hut, leaving the sinner in

absolute solitude with his God. The Spirit in the desert remained associated with nature, as in the case of the Solitaires of Port-Royal. These men
wanted to build several hermitages in the convent that took them in. "They
wanted nothing less than to build twelve hermitages around the abbey, to
which these men would retire, believed to have been called by God. At each
of their deaths, it would be given to a successor who had already been
tested. Each of them could go to church where a priest would say Mass,
without leaving. This is the earthly achievement of the ideal of Zion," wrote
Sainte-Beuve, with the slightest hint of irony.[46]

 "In classical rhetoric, as in monastic rhetoric, to retire to one's room is
the sign of a particular disposition of mind, the sign that the individual is
preparing to return to the 'place' of meditative silence said to be essential to
invention."[47] The prostration of the man in bed—open, offering, freed from
himself—encourages reflection. A number of prophets have had visions
when they were ill or confined to bed. Saint Bernard describes the *secretum
cubiculi*, the mystery of interior life; in his sermon on the Song of Songs, he
draws a line from the garden (time) to the storeroom (virtue) to the
bedroom: reward. "Enter the little room of your soul," said Saint Anselme.
To retire there is to look for God and to find oneself. Perhaps to find God
as well.

 The *cella* designates the lodgings of a solitaire, hermit, or recluse. According to Saint Jerome, a monk must live apart from the world. It is also an
instrument for mortification: its narrowness constrains and wounds the body.
In Syria, this sort of recluse would build himself a little room in which it would
be impossible either to stand up or to lie down to sleep. Hence the torpor
(acedia) that can come over the recluse, especially around the sixth hour of the
day. But reclusion was not necessarily the path to communal perfection. People were wary of excess, especially the feminine kind. The monarchy preferred
the convent to the cloister and the cell. The larger orders had certain rules for
collective life, balancing work and prayer, communal and individual exercise,
that replaced the cell with the group. The Grande Chartreuse planned, with
extreme precision, the alternating sequences and organized the cell as a
distinct space, with its garden, its furniture, and its objects. Weakness was
banished from the cell—or, if not, was to be instructive to its occupant. The

Chartreuse monks took this lifestyle to its greatest extreme. The Benedictines are less attached to it. Nevertheless, the Rule of Saint Benedict calls for monks to sleep dressed, in a single bed. In any case, between the sixth and the sixteenth centuries, dormitories rose to the fore, while cells declined. They returned from the Renaissance onward, during a period that thrived on walls and partitions as much (if not more so) through a demonstration of social distinction as through religious devotion. Priors and abbés were given more comfortable cells that locked with a key, the mark of their authority.

Retreat wasn't necessarily linked to the cell but above all to nature. Devotional thought of the seventeenth century exalted the forests more than the room. "I seek a desert place by morals unknown / There in the crevice of some ancient rock I want / To dig an obscure temple, and there make my home."[48] The "desert" was the "bare countryside," beside a river or a canal, an undergrowth, a "horrifying vale," as Madame de Sévigné said of Port-Royal. The seventeenth century sanctified the countryside, associating it with the soul and the garden. Walking provided contemplation and watching birds in their flight, or the progress of a slug, while the morning light played in the clouds. The soul became part of a solitary garden.[49] Gardening, botany, and mineralogy were recommended as occupations that lent themselves to meditation, more than shutting oneself up in one's room—a move that could be looked on with suspicion. Rousseau, the "solitary walker," is the secular inheritor of these contemplatives.

Solitude allows for meditation, contemplation, repentance. The sinner bares his body and soul before God. "If there is a happy moment for a sinner, it is now, when I am alone, in silence, when I am dressed only in my adoration."[50] Solitude befits prayer. "When you pray, go into your room, close the door, and pray to your Father, who is unseen," Christ counseled. Liturgical and private prayer have always coexisted in the Church. Although practiced individually, the latter is not without its rites and incantations. Mental prayer was seen as taxing and alarming, and some believers even said they were not able to do it. The clergy, in order to help them, divided it up into meditation, elevation, spiritual interviews, and even effusions, an abundant branch of literature that Abbé Bremond studied. Seventeenth-century mystics were more inclined to this interior prayer, which the Jesuits mistrusted, believing that a retreat into the self did not necessarily imply a retreat from the world. The Jansenists, more interested in good works, were equally suspicious of too much personal prayer and sought a more balanced division between work and prayer.

The bedroom therefore had a complex relationship to the cell. A cell was not a bedroom and must not become one, even for nuns. It must be austere to the greatest extent. For the most virtuous, a board sufficed as a bed or otherwise a straw mattress. "The beds shall be without mattresses, only bags filled with hay. . . . Experience has shown that even the weak and sickly can bear it," wrote Teresa of Avila in her constitutions.[51] Communal life was the ideal; "the sisters possessed nothing of their own; it would not be tolerated, not in the manner of food or dress; they had no coffer, no strongbox, no cupboard, no armoire but those that served the community; finally, they possessed nothing individually but only collectively. . . . The prioress must take great care when she sees one of her sisters form an attachment to something— be it a book, *or a cell,* or any other thing—she must take it from her."[52]

Not everyone went along with the reformers' crusade against personal property. The nuns revolted at this installation of the community at the heart of daily life, notably at having to eat at a common table and to renounce the "riches" they might hoard in their cells. "There was jealousy over who had the most beautiful rosary, the most jewelry, believing these things made them stand out as women who were worth something." Their Mother Superior exhorted them to turn in their jewelry, money, linen, all manner of "superfluous things." In a number of reformed convents strange processions formed of consenting or resigned nuns, who one by one turned in their little treasures.[53] But others balked and dissembled. The cell then became a bulwark of resistance to reform.

To fight the widespread tendency to lock the cell, Dom Claude Martin, the son of Marie de l'Incarnation and the prior of Marmoutier, left his door open so that the monks could speak freely to him. Moreover, this ideal prior greatly valued cleanliness; every Saturday he inspected and cleaned the cells, "scouring with his own hands even the utensils that were least seen," without letting the brothers trouble themselves. When he felt his death was imminent, he gave away all his gifts—notably a fur pelisse, no doubt a Quebecois present from his mother—and readied for his meeting with God by dressing all in white and having his cell (soon to become a mortuary) cleaned and bedecked with flowers.[54]

"Particular friendships," no matter how saintly, were also targeted. Teresa of Avila was particularly strict on this matter: "No sister may enter the cell of another without permission from the prioress, without risking serious misconduct." There should never be a workroom, which could be a zone for potentially dangerous encounters. In the intervals between services, "each sister would remain in her cell or in the hermitage designated for her by the Prioress," where she would work alone. Bodies must be kept apart: "No sister may embrace another nor touch her on the face or hands." So must their hearts: "We are capable of great blindness in the desire for those we have loved," wrote Teresa, starved for love.[55]

The cell lent itself to reading; the devoted devoured books—learned works for the clergy, for whom the cell became a *studiolo* worthy of the Church fathers, and more pious books for the women, whose confessors urged them to write. In 1669, Father Soyer recommended that nuns "relieve their memories through writing," counseling them to summarize every day in eight or ten lines, composed of "the reflections that had most touched them and the resolutions" they had made.[56] When she was overcome with violent ecstasies, Marie Martin-Guyard, the future Marie de l'Incarnation, "would retire alone to relieve her heart through her pen, writing the movements of her passion. And when the ardor had passed, she had her writings burned," much to the regret of her son, Dom Claude, who wrote her biography.[57] But writing, like retreat, should be turned to in moderation. During the Alumbrados crisis in Spain, certain contemplatives were reproached for "spending most of the day shut of up in their room reading books or giving themselves over to their devotions, calling themselves *'recoletos'* [contemplatives]."[58] And therein the very question of intellectual work comes to the fore.

Reading

The links between reading and the bedroom are ancient and varied. The bedroom is a refuge for the solitary reader. Eleanor of Aquitaine is depicted reading on her tombstone at Fontevraud. Alberto Manguel has written beautifully about reading in bed, a habit little known in the Greek and Roman periods, but no doubt practiced in the Middle Ages even in the convents.[59] An illuminated manuscript from the thirteenth century shows a monk seated on his cot, reading and writing with a stylus on a tablet. Nearby is a pile of books on a trestle table, and he is wrapped in a covering to protect against the cold in a little pious, intellectual nest. The cold generally plays an important role; Ralph W. Emerson describes the "icy room" where he read Plato's dialogues. "He forevermore associated Plato with the odor of wool."[60] "Reading in bed is an egocentric, immobile activity, during which one is freed from social conventions, hidden away from the world, and because it takes place between the sheets, in the domain of luxury and shameful idleness, [it] has a bit of the allure of forbidden things."[61]

Children and adolescents, who are often prone to napping for long periods or rising too early, have meaningful memories of reading. "Once our homework was finished, literature began, and up in the dormitory we read novels til our eyes hurt," wrote Flaubert, a boarder at the Collège de Rouen in 1832. Sartre made it a symbol of resistance: "Reading at night, in secret, authors who were banned or controversial, was a violation of the rules. . . . The daytime was our studies, sunlight; natural urges that we could not fulfill, that was classical learning . . . competition, gloomy bourgeois ennui. Night was literature, solitude, and hypnosis; it was the imaginary."[62] Against the daytime and submission to discipline, the night represents freedom. It is the best ally of those who love books and dreams, in the dormitory and even more so in the bedroom, where adolescents and women read long past any reasonable hour. In the nineteenth century, women read so voraciously that it worried the clergy and moralists who worried about the effects of novel reading on their productivity, their nerves, and their imaginations. The figure of the female reader stretched out on a sofa or a divan, or sitting up in bed, lips parted in pleasure, hungry for more, is a common trope in erotic painting. Women who read are dangerous.[63]

Lighting played a major role; the flickering flame of a candle in Delacroix's sketches represents "reading in bed," as does the more stable light of the oil or gas lamps made by Pigeon or Carcel, which allowed the reader

more control over her light.[64] The "yellow glow of a smoking oil lamp" of
Flaubert's dormitory was replaced by the regular brightness of electricity,
even if, early on, lightbulbs gave off a modest light that gave provincial fa-
çades a wan look. For a long time electricity was used only in the shared
parts of a house or apartment; it was too bright for bedrooms, in which a
quasi-curfew was installed. This explains Madame Cottard's suffocating
admiration when addressing Odette: "Speaking of eyesight, have you seen
that the *hôtel particulier* Madame Verdurin has just bought will be lit by
electricity? . . . Even the bedrooms will have their own electric lamps with a
shade that will filter the light. It is obviously a charming luxury."[65] The age
of the lamp on the nightstand had arrived, and it allowed for nocturnal reading to stretch long into the night without bothering anyone else; this was
one example among many of the influence of technology on modes of individual consumption. And with these, the invention of the *books on the nightstand,* those dear to our heart, which we like to dip into for a little taste, to
meditate upon them, or simply to be cradled by their soothing rhythms.
The Bible never leaves the nightstand of the devout, while libertines choose
"the sort of book you read with one hand."[66] As a child Colette devoured
Les Misérables; Manguel notes he preferred fantastic tales or detective novels. The book on the nightstand seals the alliance between the bed and the
reading that becomes part of the night and the room.

   "There are perhaps no days in our childhood that we have lived so
fully as those we believe we let slip by without having lived them: those we
spent with a favorite book," writes Marcel Proust, describing the happy
hours he spent in the room at Combray, "whose high white walls screened
the bed as if it had been placed at the back of a sanctuary" and was "strewn
with a heap of flowered quilts, embroidered counter-panes, and cambric
pillowcases," which gave it the feeling of an altar. He had to tear himself
away from the room for required promenades, which he abbreviated as
much as possible, but when he returned in the evening, what joy! "For a
long time, after dinner, the last hours of the evening housed my reading,"
with which he persevered if the end of the story was in sight. "Thus, at risk
of being punished if I was discovered, and the insomnia which would
threaten to last all night once the book was finished, once my parents went

to bed, did I re-light my candle."[67] And he was always disappointed and frustrated to reach the end of the book; they end so abruptly, destroying the worlds in which we have involved ourselves, the people to whom we have become attached. These endings send the reader away like an interloper, back to his own life, and dissipate the magic of vesperal reading.

Writing

The bedroom is the site par excellence of thought; mathematic vision, for instance, is best at night: "Mathematicians have the most difficult time explaining to their partners that the time they work most intensely is when they lay in the darkness of their bed," writes Alain Connes.[68] It is also well suited to personal writing, the sort that doesn't need recourse to a library, or to secondary materials: writing the self, for the self, for one's intimates. This sort of writing requires materials whose apparent simplicity belies their extreme technical refinement: table, chair, paper, pen, later the typewriter, and eventually the computer, and especially solitude and quiet, the sort only possible once the door has been closed and night has fallen. Night: the companion of writers lacking studies, who must try to work in corners they've carved out for themselves. A Russian diarist, Ekaterina Vadkovskaia, dreamed of having an office of her own in which to write her journal. She pictured it, she drew it, and she calculated how much money she would be given for her birthday, to try to buy it: "How I wish there could have fallen some money from the sky. I have such a beautiful office in mind for myself. . . . I have sketched it a number of times."[69]

All kinds of writing may be done in the bedroom, but some are, in a way, consubstantial with it. The travel journal, composed in stages, or the diary; meditations; autobiography; letter writing—all of this "personal" literature requires peace, a confrontation with the blank page. The origin of the diary is uncertain, not necessarily religious in use, although conventual retreats are apt occasions to make a written account, as was counseled in the seventeenth century. Nineteenth-century confessors encouraged the penitent to exercise this kind of examination and self-control, which was also cultivated by Protestant culture. Many adolescents—especially young women—first expressed themselves in its pages, taking advantage of the privacy it offered to write more freely, to make more personal claims; the journal of Henri-Frédéric Amiel is an unequaled prototype. The pious journal, which became the diary, was written at night, in the solitude of the bedroom, by the glow of lamplight. It could not be done in the presence of anyone else. It would be hidden in a drawer; for anyone else to read it would be a violation. The shared room of married couples was not favorable to its composition; most women stopped keeping their journals after they married.

Letters were another form of bedroom writing, a dialogue that required concentration, especially when it came to letters to family, friends, or lovers. What better place to read and write a love letter than the bedroom—or even the bed? These effusions had to be made before the candle burned down or the lamp ran out. George Sand wrote her letters at night, like Flaubert or Malwida von Meysenbug. "I seized the writing tablet, which is always kept before my bed, to write to you," wrote the latter.[70] Letters were a marginal form, somewhere between public and private writing, and therefore were a particularly appropriate form for women. This was the case for the *salonnière* Rahel Levin-Varnhagen, who did not want a traditional living room but a "garret," the opposite of the "open house" feel of urbane entertaining. She wanted a non-place, outside of society. From her garret she kept up correspondence with a vast European network of contacts, and she later kept it up from her Berlin salon.[71] "The letter creates a *correspondance* [passage] between two rooms and between two people," Diderot wrote to Sophie Volland on 28 July 1762.[72] Letters demonstrate the penetrative power of writing, the pleasure of which Proust captured in his first article for *Le Figaro:* "I thought of a female reader in her bedroom, which I so would have liked to penetrate; to her, the newspaper will carry this thought . . . or at the very least, my name."[73]

Most writers can write only in this state of retreat. For Kafka, it was an absolute and reiterated necessity. "To write is to open oneself to excess. . . . That is why we can never be alone enough when we write. . . . There is never enough silence around us, the night is never night enough," he wrote to Felice Bauer in January 1913.[74] And in February 1915 he wrote: "I want only peace, but a peace that those people do not possess. Which is understandable, for no one has as much need, in his ordinary being, for the kind of peace that I need; the kind of peace we need to read, to study, or to sleep is nothing compared to the kind of peace I need to write." Kafka dreamed of "setting myself up with a lamp and some writing materials in the heart of a vast, faraway cave" to be "the dweller within the cave."[75]

Of course, there are many ways to retire from the world: in a tunnel, in a garden shed, like Genet in his adoptive parents' yard, or in some abandoned barn. That is how Marguerite Audoux, a shepherdess in Sologne, accessed the pleasures of language, like her near neighbor Alain-Fournier. Ernst Jünger fled the routines of the bedroom: "Because my study was too close to the center of the house, I have set up a hermit's cell in the attic. . . . In rooms we have inhabited for a long time, this foreign energy is exhausted; they are like a plot of land that has been farmed for too long."[76]

Sartre was the antithesis of Kafka. He refused to write in his room, seeing it as a symbol of bourgeois comfort, and preferred to "live publicly" and write in a café. Simone de Beauvoir did not necessarily share his opinion, at least after the war. Did she get tired of writing in the busy, noisy Café de Flore? "I don't feel comfortable here. I'm feeling less and less capable of writing here the way I did all those years," she wrote in May 1945. She stayed at the Hôtel Louisiane. That spring of 1945 marked a new stage of her life, when the "force of circumstance" was warring with the "coming of age," and she experienced the pleasure of solitary creation on a physical level. "I have rarely felt so much pleasure in writing, especially in the afternoons, when I return to my room at four thirty and the air is still thick with the morning's smoke, where on the table there is some paper already covered in green ink, and the cigarette and the pen feel so right between my fingers. . . . And even inside, it is as if I feel myself unknotting."[77] The liberating energy flows freely between the bedroom, the writing, and the self, like the inhalation of the cigarette smoke, which was the writer's constant companion in those days.

In a 1980s book on writers' homes, most of those interviewed said they were relatively indifferent to their surroundings or were drawn to minimalism, as if still inspired by the religious model. They were much more vocal on the importance of the physical act of writing. "I would prefer a bare cell, four blank walls," said Dominique Fernandez. François Coupry disdained clutter: "When there are too many things in my space, I have to flee it." Pierre Bourgeade spoke of an ascetic existence tempered by tenderness: "My dream is the monk's cell, a prison, an asylum, four lime-washed walls, a long table on which to write. To look at the sky through a hole in a wall. To eat very little, in a bowl right on the table if possible. Few or no friends. . . . A woman who comes by from time to time. A child, too, to bury his head in my shoulder like a cat."[78]

"Soldier or monk?" Dominique Fernandez asks, his masculine terms betraying a desire for religious or military virility—something that did not appear in the same degree among women, who were much more specific about interiors.[79] There is an ascetic tradition of the writer's room, of the thinker, of the teacher. At 36 rue Mazarine Proudhon occupied "a student's room with a bed, a small number of books on a shelf, a few issues of the National and a review of political economics on a table."[80] According to the Journal of the Goncourts, whose misogyny is well known, there were two Sainte-Beuves: "the Sainte-Beuve of his upstairs room, of the study, of study, of thought, of mind; and another Sainte-Beuve, the downstairs Sainte-Beuve, the Sainte-Beuve of the dining room, of the family. . . . In the lower realm, he becomes a petit bourgeois, shut out from all the intelligence of his other life . . . stupefied by ladies' gossip."[81] The high and the low, the room or cabinet and the common room are as divided as male and female, creations from the trivialities of everyday life.

In his Schoolmaster's Manual (1889), Louis Chauvin describes the republican educator's room, fresh from the École Normale: an iron bed frame, white linens, and a few modest decorations "that prove that the occupant respects himself without trying too hard." Also a dresser or an armoire ("spotlessly clean"), caned chairs, a mat, a tasteful library, an easel with a blackboard for private lessons, a display case for an herbarium and his scientific collections, a mirror, an alarm clock, a birdcage. The only luxury was "an antique shawl taken from the maternal closet." Later, a piano or a harmonium. A few reproductions of works of art, plaster casts, or heliogravures. "In this sanctuary of order, work, and good taste," the schoolmaster could receive superiors, colleagues or the parents of his students "without blushing."

"What a difference between this and the neglected mess of the unruly bachelor!"[82] The bedroom as a model of civic and moral fiber.

The night is a release from daily obligations and disturbances that don't dare cross the threshold. It opens up a time to ostensibly be alone, a time for reflection, prayer, or creation; it allows favorable conditions for inspiration, whether it be from God, the muse, or Minerva's bird. "The foreign man shut himself up in his room, lit his lamp of inspiration and gave himself over to a terrible demon of work, demanding words from the silence, ideas from the night," wrote Balzac. "The paper was soon covered with ink, for the evening begins and ends in a flood of black water."[83]

Balzac's description is a romantic vision of writing that is certainly not universally shared. A number of writers, however, were familiar with the night. After a lively evening at Nohant, George Sand would climb to her blue bedroom, where she had built herself a "closet" in a kind of alcove. There, from ten at night to six in the morning, she would write thousands of letters, of which Georges Lubin has published twenty-five volumes, and several novels. Flaubert was less prolific but also wrote at night, feeling a violent need for isolation.

In May 1872 Arthur Rimbaud rented a "garret" on rue Monsieur-le-Prince; it has a view on one of the gardens of the Lycée Saint-Louis, with "enormous trees under my narrow window." "Nowadays I work all night. From midnight to five in the morning. . . . At three o'clock, the candle dies out; all the birds twittered at once in the trees: it's over. No more work. I had to watch the trees, the sky, caught by this incredible first hour of the morning." At five o'clock, he would go downstairs to buy some bread and drink himself silly at the wine merchants.' He went to sleep at seven in the morning, "when the sun brought the wood lice out from beneath the roof tiles." In June, he moved to the Hotel Cluny, on the rue Victor-Cousin, where he had "a lovely room, on a bottomless courtyard, about thirty-two square feet. . . . There, I drink water all night, I don't see the morning, I don't sleep, I suffocate." He hated the summer ("I hate the summer, which kills me when it starts to show a bit") and missed not provincial life but the waters of the Ardenne."[84]

Proust is the one who pushed the search for the "nocturnal muse" the furthest. Haunted by the fear of sound, he had the walls of his bedroom covered in cork. He bribed the workers so they wouldn't do the construction they were supposed to do in the apartment above. He lived in his bed. Yet Céleste, his housekeeper, used to say to him: "You never lie. Who ever saw anybody lie like that? You have just alighted there. With your white pyjamas, and the way you twist your neck, you look for all the world like a dove."[85] Marcel works in bed, with the help of Céleste, who glues the "quilling" *(paperolles)* or fragments of paper that he adds to his manuscript. She is the witness to his writerly torments. His joys as well. One morning, she sees him smiling—unusually—and asks him what has happened "last night in this room." "I wrote the words 'The End,'" he replies. This is the great event in the writer's bedroom: the end of the book, the prologue to the death of the artist, which occurs soon after. The period at the end of the work is the end of meaning, of the entire substance of his life. The nocturnal retreat was for Proust not only the necessary condition for writing, but it was also the indispensable prelude to a return to the self, a withdrawal into "this black internal chamber whose entry is condemned, so little do we see of the world."[86] The soul is a room without doors, as it is for Pascal, Flaubert, Kafka, or Emily Dickinson, for all those who made the interior life the center of their spiritual or existential quest.

In his Nobel Prize acceptance speech of 2006, Orhan Pamuk gave a lively tribute to the bedroom, sanctuary of creation: "Writing immediately suggests to me . . . a person who shuts himself up in a room, sits down at a table, and alone, turns inward; amidst its shadows, he builds a new world with words." First of all comes "the crucial task of sitting down at the table and patiently turning inwards. To write is to turn this inward gaze into words." He thought of his father, who left for Paris and spent his time in hotel rooms blackening the lines of a notebook. "When he was with us, like me he wanted only to find himself alone in a room to rub up against the crowd of his dreams." Orhan managed to do it. When he was twenty-three, he shut himself up to write his first novel. "I write because it pleases me to stay locked up in a room, all day long. I write to be alone. . . . I write because it pleases me to be read. . . . I write because I believe, like a child, in the immortality of libraries."[87] Many, many bedrooms line their walls with books. Most books are born of the secret room, emerging from the night or the interior day, which they resemble.

Writers' Rooms

Whence their attraction as early as the eighteenth century, when writers situated themselves in the "luminous" wake of great men. The "visit to the great writer" became a European rite for those who hoped to physically approach the mystery of a work.[88] Usually the visit was to the study, rarely the bedroom, unless they were one and the same, the sign of a respectable poverty, or in the case of illness, with the feeling of gaining access to the flesh and blood man. Paul Morand was stunned to find himself gaining access to Proust's lair.

How else to encounter the memory of a writer if not by visiting the places where he or she lived? "We love to visit their homes," writes Diderot; "we feel the softness of standing in the shadow of a tree under which they would have rested." The dispute at Ferney that set Wagnière, Voltaire's secretary, against the Marquis de Villette has rich implications for the uncertainties of the cult that began. What should be preserved and venerated? The marquis called for a "heart room": he sold the furniture and had an armoire built to conserve the heart, "which isn't there at all," sighs Wagnière; he would have liked to save the furniture and the authentic detritus of a writer's life—the torch and above all the writing desk—but he could not do so; Voltaire's niece had it all destroyed.[89] On one side, we see a corporeal, religious, reliquary approach; on the other, a patrimonial sense of objects, the witnesses and instruments of creation, those that the author used, the very things he touched: a material presence that could be quite moving.[90] In the educational tour of France she offered "young travelers," Madame de Flesselles included a visit to La Brède. "As all memories of a great man are interesting, we cannot visit Montesquieu's writing room without emotion, as it has been kept exactly as it was at the moment of his death. There is even a paving stone worn down by his very feet."[91] Authenticity, physical proximity, the stopping of time: what is it we're looking for in this desire to keep things "as they were"?

Aesthetes and Collectors

The fin-de-siècle dandyism exacerbated the need to remove oneself from the crowd yet to remain in the city, a necessary background that obsessed Baudelaire, a lover of the city as well as its cats.[92] The cult of the interior is typical of the "aesthetes and magicians" of the years around 1900, which were so rich for the decorative arts.[93] The "modern style" allied architectural invention and an extreme care for detail—even in the bedroom, renewing its allure. In their "artist's house," the Goncourt brothers housed an eclectic collection, a veritable compendium of different decorating styles.[94] Robert de Montesquiou, a friend of Mallarmé's and one of the models for Huysmans's Des Esseintes and Proust's Charles Swann, dedicated several volumes of his memoirs to the succession of houses he occupied—to the way they were arranged, the objects he had picked up, the rare editions that made his library one of the most refined of the nineteenth century. He dwells on the bedroom that he arranged in the attic of his father's mansion on the Quai d'Orsay: "I had imagined a satin wall hanging, all in mauve. . . . On the carpet (a dark violet), a low bed, which I had made with fragments of sculpted Chinese wood, in the form of a chimera; it seemed to me . . . that to go to sleep and to wake up in this chimera would give me engaging, reassuring ideas, which would enchant the entrance to the kingdom of sleep and embellish the return to the light."[95] A porcelain Japanese cat night light haloed his sleepless nights. However, the room lost its unique quality in the labyrinth of similarly ornate suites. An aristocrat with several bedrooms in his home can move among them without identifying with any of them. There is a kind of cosmopolitanism of the interior that Pierre Loti systematized in his house in Rochefort, whose bedrooms were stations in space and time.

Des Esseintes, Huysmans's hero in *A Rebours,* is fatally bored. He loathes the idiocy of fashion and the vulgarity of the masses. He hates his neighbors, suburban bourgeois, Sunday strollers. "He dreamt of some refined isolate place, a comfortable desert, a warm immobile arch where he could take refuge far from the incessant deluge of human stupidity." He hires an architect to design a rational, comfortable interior (like Barnabooth he took pride in his bathroom, which Montesquiou called his "bath chamber"), choosing the smallest details with great care. He chooses the colors, eliminating blue, gray, salmon, and pink, which were too effeminate, preferring red, yellow, and orange.[96] He picks out the material (wood, leather), the textiles. No oriental rugs, which have become too common, but "the skins of wild beasts" and the "blue fox-fur." Little of furniture is not antique; he has no knickknacks, only collector's items. Paintings by Odilon Redon and Gustave Moreau; rare plants; real flowers that looked fake; a sumptuously bound bibliophile's library. A "faint" light to preserve the black essence of the night; day filters "into the rooms through the windows and closed doors." Everything is arranged so as to muffle the servants' footsteps, invisibly, mutely waiting on a nocturnal house.

Every object is the result of a careful choice. In the bedroom he perceives two styles from which to choose: erotic or ascetic. Des Esseintes refuses a "sense-stimulating alcove," the "deceptive candor of a bed evocative of babes and chaste maidens," rejecting the inevitable enormous white lacquered Louis XV–style bed, the fruit of a feminine eroticism he doubts and disdains. Des Esseintes, the hardened bachelor, prefers a monastic cell, "a retreat for thought, a kind of oratory," with a small, narrow iron bed, a "fake cenobite bed," built with old tracks taken from a hotel ramp. For a nightstand, there is a prie-dieu.

We may discern a philosophy of existence in the choice of artifice over nature, "who eternally repeats herself"; it is a question of "substituting the dream of reality for reality itself." The house and the bedroom play a central role in this operation. There the collector may accumulate the fruit of his most secret quests and hide, for example, the painting stolen not to be sold or traded but merely to be hidden, forever. There the bibliophile can stroke the bindings; there the traveler can set out on the most fabulous pilgrimages, helped by naval instruments, spread-out maps, and detailed *Joanne* guides, stimulated by the rippling of the bath water, which seems, to him, to resemble the waters of the sea. Des Esseintes "procured himself thus, without even leaving his home, the rapid, almost instantaneous sensations of taking a very long trip. . . . Movement always seemed useless to him, and the imagination could easily supplement the vulgar reality of facts." This sophisticated man, who finds artifice to be the height of culture, creativity itself, meditates on ways to rebuild time and the suggestion of multiple spaces.

The bedroom thus becomes the "chamber of miracles," in the *Wunderkammern* tradition inaugurated at the end of the sixteenth century by the German princes, who made the apparently heteroclite accumulation of

objects the essence of knowledge and turned curtains into the secret machinery of their power. Louis XIV was doubtless inspired by them to create
the cabinets at Versailles.[97] However, these collections were designed to be
displayed at least somewhat publicly, if only locally. Their nineteenth-
century equivalents were much more private. They were less a collection of
scientific equipment and more an assortment of books, furniture, and paintings, but especially objects, the obsession of a century that made the knick-
knack into a passion and clutter an art of living. Montesquiou praises "the
rich frozen madness of objects that seem to be alive" and describes at great
length "the furious decorative arrangements, ornate apartments, magnificent installations" that possessed him.[98]

    In the following century, Mario Praz (1896–1982), the collector and
writer and the model for the *professore* in Luchino Visconti's *Violence and
Passion* (1974), attempted to analyze the psychology of interior decoration
and the philosophy of furnishing.[99] He argues for the testimonial and existential value of objects: "Man passes on and the object remains; it stays behind to testify, to evoke those who are no more, and to unveil, sometimes,
certain jealous secrets that a face, a regard, or a voice obstinately concealed."[100] Objects have the power to reveal. In *The House of Life,* a remarkable autobiography of a home and furniture, Praz describes his apartment
in the Palazzo Ricci in Rome on the Via Giulia. Room by room, object by
object, he makes an inventory of this overstuffed apartment (thirty paintings
on his daughter's walls alone), which is, nevertheless, organized; each object is placed as rationally as in an exhibition. He describes the history of his
acquisitions, as well as the events, places, and people associated with them.
For objects are bound up with material and sentimental life like knots in
fabric. They embody desire and memory. Each of them has a history and
tells a story. "I put so much of my soul into the cult of things, like the
furniture, which seem to most people to lack life. . . . I sinned in adoring
sculpted images."[101] There are two bedrooms in the apartment: the master
bedroom, which looks out on the Piazza Ricci, and his daughter Lucia's
room, whose metamorphoses reflect the way her life changes and the tensions between her and her father. Bedrooms are museum spaces as well as
memorials.[102]

Each of us has our chamber of miracles, our accumulations, favorite books, objects, photographs we like to look at, relics, layers of archives. Time passes and we don't quite know what's contained in these attics of our lives. The wisest thing is no doubt to dismantle them, as Pierre Bergé did after the death of Yves Saint Laurent.[103]

Seeing the World from the Bedroom

A "bedroom traveler," Des Esseintes is the inheritor of Diderot and Rousseau, those tired, disillusioned Enlightenment travelers, who saw travel as a waste of energy and reading an alternative to false mobility.[104] The book is the path to true adventure. "To travel is to read, to read is to travel. . . . Content yourself with reading. The objective voyage threatens to strip you of your identity," wrote Béat de Murat.[105] Kant, who never left Königsberg, was also of this opinion. Libraries, the collections in *cabinets de curiosité,* endless nights reading by the fire—these were the sources of wisdom and knowledge. Pascal, the philosopher of the bedroom, said the same thing.

The most famous of these arguments for a life lived through the bedroom is the *Voyage autour de ma chambre,* published by Xavier de Maistre in 1794. The text reads as a challenge to this troubled period. Its author, for that matter, appears trapped in immobility, for reasons that are unclear. He presents himself as a recluse, somewhat of his own volition, who wishes to protect himself from the tumult rocking Europe. He would reiterate his argument in another essay, *Expédition nocturne autour de ma chambre* (1825).[106] In actuality he did not at all live a sedentary lifestyle. Born in Savoie in 1763, hostile to the Revolution, de Maistre joined up with the tsar's armies, who were leading an expedition in Italy in 1799. He exiled himself to Moscow and then Saint Petersburg and took part in the Allies' final campaign against Napoleon in 1815. His argument for bedroom travel is no doubt both a tactic of distancing himself from politics and a philosophical posture inherited in the manner of Diderot and Pascal. Between the soul and the "Other"—the body, the material, the "beast"—to which we are all subject, he chooses the former and defends the right to the imagination. He undertook a voyage of forty-two days around his bedroom, "that delicious country that holds all that is good and all the riches of the world." He is writing to all those who were bound by that horizon: the penniless, the ill, those "bored with the universe." His valet, Joanetti, is his only link to the outside. But outside the curtained window the swallows sing in the elms. The fireplace and the area around it bring an essential comfort. The author details the furniture and objects: the armchair, the desk table and the letters saved for ten years (a sign of the sacred status of the epistolary), the library full with novels and poetry, the bust of his venerated father, and above all the bed, white and pink, "cradle, throne of love, sepulchre," scene of all the human dramas, which he declares in terms that are fairly conventional but unheard of in 1794. How can we understand this lauding of the bed in the midst of the European wars? He liked to spend the mornings there with Rosine, his dog and constant companion for six years. Wrapped in his dressing gown, his "traveling clothes," he moves on to review his paintings and engravings.[107] He dusts the portrait of Madame de Hautcastel, with whom he may have been in love, to rediscover the forgotten blond of her hair. He sleeps, dreams of Antiquity, stokes his fire, describes the poor who haunt the streets of Turin. In his second essay (1825), he describes sitting astride the window sill and contemplating heaven and the stars, while a female neighbor's slippers introduce a hint of eroticism in his Pascalian meditation. The window, like a balcony, transforms the world into a play. It keeps the outside in place, like a view. But what is the world seen from the bedroom?

Technologies like printing, engraving, and later photography and cinema (not to mention the computer) have allowed us to visualize the world, its countryside, its works of art, putting it all at our fingertips. Magazines, like the nineteenth-century *Le Tour du Monde*, illustrated collections, and projections transformed bedrooms into museums and performance halls. The magic lantern adds to the mystery of the bedroom in Proust's Combray, where Golo pursues poor Geneviève de Brabant.[108] There are no limits to the imagination when it invades the bedroom. This is the beginning of a revolution whose scale and effects neither Xavier de Maistre nor Proust's narrator could have anticipated.

From his sickbed, Proust felt as if he were floating on water. "I understood then that Noah could never have seen the world as well as from his ark, even from its enclosed cabin, and everything dark upon the earth."[109]

The possibilities of the internet have infinitely multiplied those permitted by travel. For François Bon, to write means no longer to turn one's back on the world but to welcome it through the screen. "Our imaginary spaces become accessible from the desktop." He has only one desire: "to stay in my garage, with my books and my screen."[110]

Oblomov or a Man Asleep

A tabernacle, a source of work and of life, the bedroom can also be a tomb, a synonym for drowsiness and unconsciousness, a retreat that condemns us to impotence. Bedroom theorists, strategists, and revolutionaries invite skepticism and even derision. They go around in circles, like horses on a merry-go-round, with no goal or ending, no effect on events, on the reality that Des Esseintes would have reduced to a dream. Hence the impatience of the young to throw themselves directly, greedily, into real life.[111]

Oblomov, the anti-hero of the eponymous novel by Ivan Goncharov (1859), incarnates the unrepentant retreat to the bedroom, the refusal of pointless agitation; he prefers the interior, and sleep, which confines us and leads us to death.[112] Oblomov, descended from minor Russian nobility in Saint Petersburg, is the heir to an estate called Oblomovka, the site of nostalgia for his lost childhood. A gentle dreamer, cultured and sensitive, intelligent and good, he is devoid of all prejudice but is skeptical, indolent, apathetic, in love with rest, and incapable of carrying out his plans, which are as vague as they are generous. He dreams of founding a Tolstoy-esque agrarian community and abolishing serfdom, a constant backdrop to the novel.

Oblomov is nevertheless constantly supported and encouraged by his friend Stolz, a German engineer, who is rational, hyperactive, a worker, an inventive entrepreneur—that is to say, Oblomov's exact opposite. Oblomov lives in a state of indecision, stripped of all ambition, allergic to conflict. He counters his friend's energy with total inertia. He is complicit in his own ruin, letting himself be cheated, but he prefers honest mediocrity to the effort necessary for gain. He seeks happiness in domestic peace and daily monotony, whose reassuring routine gives the illusion of time's having been abolished. He dreams of sharing this calm life with a woman to whom he could be faithful, "the light that illuminates the room." "Next to a proud, sweet, peaceful companion, a man can sleep without worry. He can fall asleep secure in the knowledge that upon awaking he will meet with the same humble and sympathetic look. And twenty or thirty years later, in the warmth of her regard, in the eyes of his wife, the same humble glow of sympathy will still sweetly shine. And so it will be until the tomb."[113] A life that flows gently, drop by drop: such is Oblomov's ideal.

Whence his predilection for the bedroom, which provides a kind of unity of place and time to this long, strange, poetic novel, a classic of Russian literature. The hero ignores the other rooms in his home, in which the seats are covered with sheets, a frequent practice in the provinces. He restricts himself to one room and one room alone, which served as bedroom, study, and salon. At first glance it is arranged nicely, in an almost Victorian style: "There was a walnut desk, two silk-covered divans, beautiful screens embroidered with flowers and exotic birds. There were silk wall hangings, rugs, a few paintings, bronze statues, some porcelain and a variety of little knickknacks. But the trained eye of a man of taste would have only found there a desire to respect the inevitable decorum of customs, in order to be free of them."[114] It was, in fact, full of the signs of neglect, with the dust, the spiders' webs, the things strewn across the floor, the leftover food on plates, the open books, the previous day's newspapers, the empty inkwells. Oblomov has only one servant, the lazy but faithful Zakhar, as resigned as his master to the eternal order of things. Oblomov spends the days in his slippers and dressing gown, "a true oriental dressing gown with no hint of Europe," stretched out on his bed—the very antithesis of the military posture or that of a man on the move. "The recumbent position was his natural state." In his rare periods of indecisive action, he would store away his dressing gown in an armoire; he would take it out again when he invariably gave it all up, and at the end he doesn't take it off at all. He sleeps, daydreams, meditates, and receives friends and family, who become more and more infrequent visitors, except for those who exploit him, taking advantage of his carelessness. "Like a lump of dough, you've rolled yourself up on yourself and you stay in bed," says Stolz to his friend, attempting to get him to get up, to come and go, to go to the countryside to visit his estate, to travel abroad with him, or even to marry Olga.[115] The girl has been given the mission of waking Oblomov up; she's fallen under his spell. Stoltz's suggestions frighten Oblomov, who retracts into his shell like a snail. "It's as if you're too lazy to live," Stolz remarks. "You sleep like a gopher in a hole."[116] Oblomov even swears off Olga, who, desperate to be close to him, ends up marrying Stolz. He "only felt calm in some forgotten corner, foreign to movement, to struggle, to life . . . a peaceable spectator of combat, like the desert sages who, having renounced the world, dig themselves a tomb."[117] He burrows into his bed, where he dies without a sound.

"Oblomovism," as described by Goncharov in a mildly critical manner, is a philosophy of existence that (according to Jacques Catteau, who wrote the preface) characterizes the impotence of the Russian man. This has to do with his eastern resignation, comforted by the fatalism of his Orthodox religion and his refusal of change, with an activism rooted in work, movement, and travel. Paul Lafargue, Karl Marx's son-in-law, caused a similar scandal for his praise of sloth, which actually has nothing to do with inertia but with leisure.[118] Oblomovism contains echoes of Pascal's thinking, his praise of wisdom, of renunciation, the nostalgia for a kind of happiness that is related to rest and frugality, which thrive in the bedroom. This novel of a man asleep is an epic of domestic life and illustrates the risks and attractions of being shut up in the room-trap, which, like Kafka's terrier, destroys its occupant in the end.

The bedroom with no exit terrified André Gide: "There are wondrous rooms to inhabit, but I have not desired to remain in any of them for long. Fear of doors that close, of traps. Cells that slam shut on the spirit. The nomadic life is that of the shepherd. . . . What would a room be for us, Nathanaël? A shelter in a landscape."[119]

A bedroom beyond the walls.

The Children's Room

THE CHILDREN'S ROOM is, today, a key part of furniture catalogues, which pay close attention to the little ones' needs. It also features in treatises on children's psychology, on early learning activity, and even on household ecologies.

Laurence Egill's beautifully illustrated book is telling in this regard.[1] The bedroom becomes a place *of* the child and *for* the child, preferably the child's alone, even if it means cramped quarters if there are several children. To each his own room. This is the central idea, adapted to the child who is considered to be entitled to his or her own personhood. Beyond questions of physical safety and psychological well-being, which lead to a preference for soft lighting and materials, rounded edges, and bright colors, there are no requirements at all—no imposed decoration scheme or prescribed ways of arranging the space. On the contrary, value is placed on fluidity, the possibility of adaptation to a multitude of uses. "Their tastes change as they get older. It's best to select furniture that can evolve over time with the child" and be adapted according to his or her size and preferences. "There is, indeed, nothing more sad than a child's bedroom where the child hasn't been able to have his say. He will feel so much better there if it is *his* room." Let him transform his bed into a tent or a playing field, and don't turn out the light. "If he wants to sleep with the light on, surrounded by stuffed animals, let him." Supply a range of smaller demarcated areas or "nooks." Develop a tolerance for junk, even for disorder. "The notion of putting things in their place is, for the child, understood in nomadic terms. . . . He needs the joyful mess to feel safe and very much *at home.*" Your child's room ought to resemble "a vast cabinet of curiosities open to the world." Respect the child's privacy and need for solitude. "Let him live independently in his room. No one can live without secrets." Still less so if we're dealing with a teenager, in which case it is best to "let him choose how to decorate his room on his own, even if you find his choices hideous." Freedom, privacy, individuality—these are the commandments that reign over the new order of childhood, far from the norms of traditional discipline, the rigidities of domestic decorum, so intolerant of an unmade bed, clothes and toys strewn across the floor, or the light left on.

The interior designer Vibel suggests several models: Robinson, Vitamin, Punk Rock, and Marie-Antoinette for a little girl, who "will fall asleep like a true princess."[2] And for their organic-crazed hippie parents, who want a "healthy, ecological" room for their baby, free of all chemicals, they propose a room with a floor that "they can lick and eat [off of]."[3]

The Crib and the Bed

Things were not always like this. The child first had to conquer his bed, that piece of furniture ignored by the post-death inventories carried out by Daniel Roche, even in Paris.[4]

Inventories more often mention the cradle. However, children's sleep is problematic. This brutal plunge into darkness and solitude is a difficult moment, one that engenders a rising fear of unknown creatures, of monsters turning up in their dreams, like those that Alice meets through the looking glass. Parents rock the child to sleep, singing lullabies in a gentle, monotonous, repetitive tone—one of the earliest folk literatures. The cradle is an ancient object. Medieval paintings provide us with many images of cradles, especially for the "birth of the Virgin." The Fécamp Museum has a wonderful collection. Often in wood and on wheels, they are sometimes equipped with a pedal that would allow the mother to rock it while she worked. Rousseau didn't like them: "I am persuaded that it is never necessary to rock children and that [cradle] use is frequently harmful."[5] On the contrary, "a woman should be seen beside the cradle of a child," said Jules Simon, who no doubt appreciated the paintings of Berthe Morisot, daydreaming beside her own cradle. The Larousse dictionary recommends placing it next to the mother or the wet nurse, both of whom are, in some way, devoted to it. The late nineteenth-century hygienists, however, were suspicious of the cradle for reasons of health and discipline. They sniffed at them, recommended frequently changing the bedding, decreed they should be made from wicker or covered iron, called them putrid, and, like Rousseau, warned that it was important not to accustom children to being rocked.[6] They preferred the rigor of the bed to the softness of the cradle, which has trailed behind it an enchanted wake of varying forms and names, like the *barcelonnette*.[7]

The cradle individualized the baby and protected it. Many infants were smothered in their parents' beds, in spite of the ecclesiastical regulations that forbade this practice for babies under a year old but accepted it thereafter. When a baby was bigger, it would join brothers and sisters, in a more or less undifferentiated mess of children, at least for the youngest. When they came of age, children were separated by sex. In the seventeenth century the Church made this an injunction that it assigned to the schoolmaster, the regent of a more fastidious sexual morality, judging from the attention paid to sexuality.[8] A manual titled *L'Escole paroissiale* was written with this in mind by a Parisian priest in the middle of the century, recommending that schoolmasters prevent children "from urinating in front of others, [a brother] never to sleep with his sister, not even with his father and mother, unless in the greatest necessity, in which case he will ask the parents to sleep at the bottom of his bed so that he may not observe or wonder about that which is permitted only to married couples; . . . if parents do not want to prevent their children from sleeping with their servants, sisters, or themselves, the Master in this case, after having explained the importance of this interdiction to them, will send [the children] away without delay."[9] At any price the confusion of bodies must be untangled. They were the source of forbidden pleasures, of violent experiences, of concealed incest, an anxiety of which we can read in Perrault's fairy tales.[10] This long ago blending of the sexes remains out of reach to us more than ever, in spite of Freud's best efforts to make the "primal scene" the foundation of psychoanalysis.

To leave the warmth of a bed, the heat of a body, the tenderness of a protective adult can be a painful experience. Little Aurore Dupin (the future George Sand) suffered under her grandmother's edict that she leave her mother's bed at Nohant: "It is neither healthy nor chaste for a nine-year-old girl to sleep with her mother," she recalled having been told, indignant at these outrageous insinuations. From the corridor, the little girl watched her mother's comings and goings. She would always be nostalgic for the "large yellow bed in which my father was born, which belonged to my mother at Nohant (the same one I currently use)," she wrote forty years later.[11] For many children, cocooning or seeking refuge in their parents' bed was to re-enter a lost paradise. Elias Canetti describes the joyous Sunday mornings when he and his brothers and sisters would harass their parents in bed, the one day it was permitted. Annie Leclerc describes the soft middle of the bed where, having left her own, she snuggled up between her parents, a fusional experience: "The body lightens to the point of melting completely, dissolving in the happiness of being 'between,' of being nothing more than be-tween."[12] I remember similar happiness, in an apartment in Clichy where we then lived and where, sometimes, to play a practical joke on me, my parents would switch sides. Why would anyone want to leave this peaceful warmth? Why leave childhood, the middle of the bed, as the old French song goes?[13]

Separating children from their parents at bedtime is a standard of moral decency for which the investigators kept an eye out when they visited the homes of the poor, smelling lust in the promiscuities of misery. "What are their sleeping arrangements?" asked everyone from the English philanthro-pists of the London Mission, the Baron of Gérando's visitor of the poor, and the followers of Le Play, drafting studies of the family under the aegis of the Société d'économie sociale.[14] The proletariat, moreover, didn't fight it; in its desire for comfort as much as respectability, it demanded a living space that would be large enough to accommodate this kind of separation. A room for the children and a separate kitchen became one of the minimum require-ments at the end of the nineteenth century. In her socially ascendant phase, the heroine of Zola's *L'Assommoir* believes it to be very important, creatively rigging up curtains or protective screens, which she then neglects in the pe-riod of her demise. Plans for employees' lodgings and cheap housing make allowances for a children's room more regularly than in bourgeois apart-ments, so much had it become a preoccupation of the morality police.

In rural or bourgeois homes, the children left their parents to sleep with the servants. They were given a more or less temporary corner: a straw or other kind of mattress, a bed frame, a pallet, a little makeshift bed that could be set up anywhere—in a nook, in a closet, on the landing, in a corridor, in a lean-to, or under a stairway. As they grew up, if they were lucky, they were given a *chambrette,* or little room, only for sleeping. In this sense, children were everywhere and nowhere. They moved throughout the house, the fields, and the town, territories whose resources they knew better than anyone, especially without their families. They didn't need their own space until very recently; no one thought to accord them any particular importance in laying out the home. In the 1979 special issue dedicated to "The Child and His Space," the journal *L'Architecture d'aujourd'hui* deals mainly with collective spaces—schools, game centers, pedagogical museums—and very little with the interior, except for one article, "The Child Discovers the House," on the spatial psychology of toddlers.

The Bedroom of the Enfants de France

At Versailles can be found the sketch of a children's bedroom that has been studied by William R. Newton. Louis XIV, a true family man, wanted the Enfants de France—both his legitimate and illegitimate offspring—to be raised close by him. Early on they were housed in the old wing, where, between 1680 and 1690, the Maréchal de La Motte-Houdancourt looked after the Grand Dauphin's three sons. By Louis XV's day, the princes' wing on the first floor was a kind of nursery. They were kept in a cradle until the age of three, looked after by their governesses, and subsequently slept in a bed surrounded by a balustrade, in the royal manner. Each room contained three beds, one for the wet nurse and another for the governess. Women ruled over this princely domain. At age seven, the boys "became men," and deciding who would be their tutor was an affair of state. In 1741, the children's apartments extended to eight rooms, of which six had fireplaces. In 1764, a wood-burning stove was installed so the Comte d'Artois would not catch a chill; a bit later, the walls were covered in padding so he could play without risk to his brothers, Provence and Berry: "The struts and the woodworking were cushioned up to a man's height so that in playing they would not injure themselves. These apartments, furnished with Savonnerie rugs and thick Gobelin tapestries, protected them from any danger. Their tutor hardly ever left them and left the tutoring, if necessary, to under-tutors." There was discussion of installing an iron grill "so that people could not see in."[15] A modern, attentive mother, Marie-Antoinette congratulated herself on the fact that her children were no longer behind bars and that they could enjoy the fresh air. "Mine will live below, with a little grill to separate him from the rest of the terrace, which may even teach him earlier to walk somewhere other than on the parquet," she wrote to her mother, the Empress Maria Theresa.[16] In 1787 the apartment of the Enfants de France had grown to fourteen rooms, of which thirteen had chimneys, and more than seventeen mezzanines, of which nine had chimneys for their entourage and servants. Warmth, security, and anticipation of hard play were integrated over time into these princely spaces, according to the spirit of the time.

Genealogies

The children's room, then, was not a pure invention of the Victorian era. We see it stutter to life in the châteaux of an aristocracy grown expert at separating children according to gender and age. However, until the end of the eighteenth century, architects more or less ignored childhood in the more and more reasoned plans they they drafted of the domestic habitat.[17] In 1768, Delarue specified the location of a room "for two children and a tutor" and one "young lady's room," along with a boudoir, on the same level as those of their parents, a specification that was a radical novelty. Le Camus de Mézières, in his remarkable treatise of 1780, devotes three pages (out of 280) to the "lodging of children in the home," which he situated on the mezzanine, not far from the servants, where the children would live along with a woman, a "governess or servant," until the age of five; after that they would be separated, and the boys would go to stay with their tutor.[18] He allocated them to an apartment of five rooms, including one "exercise room" and a bedroom. He gave precise instructions about wood-burning fires in order to minimize risks, recommended an eastern exposure, "essential for the health," and a colorful interior: "The children's apartments cannot be too gay: the colors used there should be agreeable; these things influence one's daily mood more than we know," he wrote, echoing the sensualist theories to which he adhered.[19]

It was no doubt through play that the need for a specific space arose. Inside, children will play anywhere, disturbing the grown-ups, overturning their father's office, and leaving their toys strewn around the house. The need to contain this "exercise" was first felt in England and Germany, where families were at that time bigger and the pedagogy more shrewd. The nursery appeared in the early nineteenth century in the country houses built by the English industrial bourgeoisie and, in parallel, the *Kinderstube* in the comfortable homes of the Biedermeier period; to "have a good *Kinderstube*" was to "be well brought up," according to the dictionary. This was what mattered. The nursery was normally composed of two rooms, one for playing and one for sleeping; the *Kinderstube* brought the two together but was more designed for separating the sexes.[20]

There was nothing of the sort in France. Out of ruralism? Rousseauism? "Can we imagine a more idiotic way of raising a child than to never let it out of its room?" wrote Jean-Jacques Rousseau, who railed against bells, rattles, and man-made toys.[21] "Instead of leaving it to sicken in the stuffy air of its room, it should be brought daily to the middle of a field."[22] He wanted to raise Émile in the countryside: "His room would in no way be distinguished from that of a peasant. What is the good of decorating it since he will spend so little time there?"[23] Was it a question of Malthusianism? "The question of the child is the question of the bedroom," remarked Colette, who had to wait for her sister to marry before she could have one. "Narrow dwelling makes miserly bellies."[24]

Viollet-le-Duc, in his *Histoire d'une maison* (1873), describes a children's bedroom, almost as an afterthought: "Everything must be anticipated," even accidents. There is little description of the receiving rooms and the nearby but separate bedrooms for Madame and Monsieur. It wasn't until the end of the nineteenth century, or even the early twentieth, that anything became systematic. And even then, the children's room is there but secondary, not far from the parents' room, which sometimes must be passed through to reach the children's room; the mother's surveying eye replaces that of the servants, who are relegated to the sixth floor of urban buildings. The children's room was often located at the end of a hallway, and no one gave any thought to what direction it faced.

Roger Perrinjaquet, the great expert on this subject, describes a generalized "contempt" for the children's room: "This tendency to overlook the child in the family apartment is not shared by all architects, but even when other suggestions are made, they often serve only to reinforce traditional arrangements." He mentions a stubborn blindness to it in modern architecture, including the Bauhaus architects or Le Corbusier, according to Marie Jaoul's autobiography.[25] Marie's parents hired "Corbu" to build them a house in Neuilly. Did she want her own room, separate from her brothers', the architect asked her. Yes, most definitely, she answered. But she was disappointed with the result: a hallway of a room, narrow, dark, and reached only through another room. The communal ideal to which Le Corbusier subscribed was hardly concerned with the spatial recognition of the child. Little Marie missed her old, dark, winding apartment. "I hated this communal life, and I had lost my territory even though I had my own room. . . . I locked myself in my room to read at night, without making a sound, so my parents wouldn't know. In the previous apartment, no one kept an eye on me. Here, in this house, you could see everything." Even the corners were "open." She hated the transparency of knowing "who was doing what, when." "The house made the rules," to the detriment of personal adventure.[26]

The second half or even the last third of the twentieth century saw the greatest amount of change in terms of urbanists' consideration of the domestic habitat and its division into "day space" and "night space"; it involved a revaluing of the bedroom. Where children were concerned, this always involves hesitating between the desire to isolate them and to include them, between sleep and play, individuality and collectivity. In the 1960s Paul Chemetov allowed for play spaces in buildings, like in the Scandinavian countries. Indifference gave way to concern or even anxiety. The master bedroom got smaller so that the children's space could expand, especially that of the adolescents, the guilty, misunderstood conscience of Western society.

Interpreting the Bedroom

The child, being vulnerable, sensitive, malleable, reads its new perceptions through space. It can be molded by its environment. Hygienists, who were truthfully more sensitive to the feet of furniture—of tables, of beds—were concerned abut airing rooms properly, the degree of moisture and heat. They feared excess, especially for babies. The Comtesse de Ségur recommended moderation: "Do not keep the child in a room that is too warm; the heat of the apartment will make him sensitive to drops in temperature. . . . Take care to change the air in the child's room at least twice a day," even if it is very cold out.[27] This opinion was shared by most doctors, haunted by the idea of all the carbon dioxide exhaled by children when they sleep. These great consumers of air had to be provided for.

The room became a means of shaping the child's character and habits. "As early as possible, each child should have his own room, where he can adopt orderly habits, putting aside and taking care of the things that belong to him—his toys, his books, his images," wrote Émile Cardon.[28] The doll's room was an object that could be rearranged endlessly; the toy chest helped promote a pedagogy of tidiness. However, in order to be respectful of the boundaries of private life, which it was sometimes accused of invading, the Republic restricted its efforts to school and left the bedroom to the family, which imbued it with the opposite of Christian morality. The Comtesse de Ségur was not a bedroom fanatic. In the storybook castles, children could roam freely and especially liked to play in the garden. They rarely slept alone—more often they were two to a bed, along with a maid. The bedrooms were on the second floor; one "went upstairs" to rest, to work, to pray, or even to be punished. To greet their cousins, Camille and Madeleine, the Comtesse de Ségur's granddaughters, put flowers around their rooms.[29]

Berthe Bernage, whose *Brigitte* books are about a woman at every stage of her life—as a young girl, a bride, a mother—and were bestsellers in the 1930s, taught young women how to set up a baby's room. Roseline is Brigitte's firstborn; the family lives in three rooms rented out by an elderly aunt, who decides to add another "for the little one," whose babbling and crying prevent her father from working.[30] It is to be "a beautiful room, full of light, big enough to dance in." Brigitte turns to "English fashion" to create a "pretty, pleasant, amusing nest." "The rooms were cream-colored, and I myself painted a pretty border of bouquets of roses." The curtains were a silky cream fabric with a large pink stripe—pink for girls. Every member of the family contributes to the room, which is inaugurated with a little party. A grandmother gives "a charming trundle bed with an ivory-colored lacquer." Another gives a matching armoire. The godmother gives a chest of toys. There is no rug; checkerboard linoleum "protects the precious parquet." There is a child-sized table and chairs, with cushions covered in cream and pink *toile de Jouy*, "printed with the animals from La Fontaine's fables." "The ceiling fixture sends out a very gentle, very cheerful pink light." On the walls, a few engravings depict childhood scenes. "Don't think for a moment I bought them at the shop. Not at all! They are little works of art, conceived and executed by good artists. My daughter must only have perfect things to look at." As a good Christian, Brigitte refuses to make the room a secular space; she places a "beautiful ivory crucifix" above the little bed, facing the "most maternal of Madonnas," escorted by an image of Thérèse de Lisieux, who will teach Roseline the "symbol of the rose." We are in the home of a young Christian couple of the 1930s, wary of "fraud," more familiar with the *Casti Connubii* than with the abbé Viollet.[31] Brigitte "already sees in her dreams two or three little beds—or even four! As many as we want! There is room in the room and in my heart." Once the room contains multiple children, will she call it a "nursery"? She is dying to do so, out of admiration for the ways the English have with their babies. But she wishes to remain "a little French mother" and congratulates herself on having found watercolors of childhood scenes at Versailles. "The Great Century will make my daughter more noble." This "in-the-know" young mother, who rejects her Aunt Marthe's suggestions, her Renaissance-style furniture, and her garnet-colored curtains, as well as the fashions proposed by her cousin Huguette, is set on reconciling tradition and modernity by choosing decorations that seem to her to awaken the senses and the spirit.

Roseline's room is a Christian translation of Ruskin and William Morris. Both believed in the power of environment. Between 1880 and 1914, artists turned to the child's bedroom, at least in the northern parts of Europe. We may begin with the walls, where the wallpaper—to be studied during interminable naps—became the first landscape of the child and would even one day be found in heaven, according to Henry James, and evoked so many childhood memories.

Wallpaper: The Language of the Walls

George Sand was particularly sensitive to wallpaper. She recalls "spending long hours in my little bed without sleeping, only contemplating the pleat of a curtain or some flower on the wallpaper."[32] At Nohant, a dark green tapestry excited her imagination. Sileni and bacchantes reveled in its borders; Flora and her dancing nymphs featured in its medallions. But a more serious reveler worried her, making her dread a certain place in the bed. "I pulled the covers over my head so I wouldn't have to see her as I fell asleep." She dreamed about her and in the evening dreaded the figures leaving their frame. "I didn't dare remain alone in the room. I was almost eight years old, and I couldn't look calmly at the bacchante before going to sleep."[33] She also remembered the floral tapestries in her grandmother's bedroom and as an adult found one that resembled them: "I was as delighted as a child to bedeck my bedroom with its foliage, whose every branch and every flower brought me back to a world of reveries and memories."[34]

These images feed the child's imagination. Anatole France writes, "I still see it, that room with its leafy green wallpaper and a beautiful color etching that depicted (I've since learned) Virginie crossing the ford of the black river in Paul's arms. I had some extraordinary adventures in that room."[35] Every year the young Marcel Proust returned to Prince Eugène in his dolman, a cheap engraving, no doubt given as a gift by the village grocer, that his grandfather had hung in his room, to the great consternation of his grandmother, who would have preferred a reproduction of Botticelli's Primavera, the only element of beauty that William Morris—apostle of the blank wall—in his hygienic austerity would tolerate. Mario Praz describes the tapestry in the bedroom of an old woman who was his parents' neighbor: a griffon in an endlessly repeating geometric pattern. "I had the curious feeling that I was sleeping in this room, from having seen this horrifying wallpaper in a pallid nocturnal light, like a nightmare, as if I had been sick in bed. It is one of the most mysterious of my childhood memories."[36]

In order to instill a sense of beauty in children, reproductions of great works of art would be displayed, preferably antiques; art photography made it possible to a widespread degree around 1900, as it invaded classrooms and, to a lesser extent, bedrooms. Fairy tales, legends, or instructive fables were integrated into wallpaper. "The more cheerful and warm your nurseries, the happier and more brilliant your children will be," according to the British architect Robert William Edis, for whom the "writing on the wall" was a major aesthetic initiation. A thriving British industry, dominated by Kate Greenaway and Walter Crane, and made commercially viable by Jeffries and Co., brought back the style and repertoire of *papiers peints.* The heroes of the classical and modern classical tradition—La Fontaine, Perrault, Grimm, Andersen—were joined by characters from literature and English and American illustrated books: Peter Rabbit, Winnie the Pooh, Felix the Cat, and soon Mickey Mouse invaded the walls and took over the toys, bringing about a considerable visual and affective revolution in the children's universe. We have yet to understand the impact this has had.[37]

In France, this movement had supporters in the form of Champfleury, Émile Cardon, and Marcel Braunschvig, who believed art was important for children. Unlike in Great Britain, it was the school rather than the house that seized this power; here it is more a question of the pupil than the daydreaming child. However, in the 1880s, Émile Cardon conceded almost timidly that "it is no small thing to decorate the child's bedroom with artistic images that are charming to the eye and provide the spectacle of joyful scenes."[38] There are also civic examples: the Third Republic preferred positive heroes like Hop O'My Thumb, who saved his brothers, rather than the disobedient Little Red Riding Hood, who got eaten by the wolf.

A whole series of events indicates a turning point. The key impulse was given by the World's Fair in 1900 and its continuation in 1901 at the Petit Palais on "childhood across the ages." In all the hubbub of the moment, two toy collectors, Léo Claretie and Henri d'Allemagne, appealed to the English tradition and created a society and a journal, *L'Art et l'Enfant,* supported by the pedagogue Marcel Braunschvig. "It would be better to decorate the house first," Braunschvig wrote. Energy was predominantly devoted to objects, like the animal toys of Benjamin Rabier, and then on the decor of the room, which was the subject of many exhibitions that were supported by public funds. One exhibition, "L'art pour l'enfance," organized in 1913 at the Musée Galliera by the Paris municipal council, encompassed all aspects:

furniture, panels and wall hangings, toys, fabrics, wallpaper. André Hélé (1870–1945) imagined a Noah's Ark with wood-sculpted figurines; he created a whole set for a child's bedroom, sold by the Primavera atelier in the Printemps department stores. A purified style, light colors, and rounded edges combined functionalism and aesthetics. The child's room began to feature in catalogues. This moment of grace, which was interrupted by the war, was a decisive one in terms of a growing spatial awareness of the child, and it would continue to develop in the dark during the period between the wars.

The Daughter's Room

No one seems to have taken much notice of adolescents until the 1860s.[39] That age was a threshold, a departure. In working-class circles, girls and boys were "placed" early. The bourgeoisie, both French and English, sent its boys to boarding school, middle school, or high school. Girls were educated less and tended to stay at home.[40] Adolescence is above all a gendered category rather than a social one.[41] Hence the distinction of the *chambre de demoiselle,* or young lady's bedroom, which appeared toward the end of the eighteenth century. This is the testimony of Rétif de La Bretonne, who was keeping watch: "I saw arrive a young girl who appeared to be very beautiful. . . . She was put to bed in her room, while I was put in a little room under a staircase."[42]

     The emergence of the young lady—her body scrutinized by doctors, her desires pored over by novelists—was accompanied by the invention of a space for her, a cloistered, protective space, located near her attentive mother. Somewhere between a cell and a boudoir, the young lady's room was modeled on that of the Virgin as represented by painters of the Annunciation: narrow bed, next to which the Virgin sits, reading or weaving, while the angel visits her. This is where the young lady was initiated into the domestic order. In the retreat of her bedroom she sewed, read, and wrote a familiar correspondence: her diary, which Catholic educators recommended as a way of examining one's conscience and the Protestants as a form of self-control. The room was saturated with morality, even religiosity, and was as closed-off as a tabernacle. It became consubstantial with the young lady herself. So every young lady dreamed of having her own room, which she could decorate, fill with flowers, and arrange her knickknacks. At boarding school, she would think about it. A young lady was judged by the state of her room. Before the rise of the magazine, etiquette books recommended that she take good care of it, this laboratory in which her character took shape. She too would choose flowered wallpaper, curtains (austere or filmy but opaque), bouquets (preferably flowers with subtle odors). She was to reject whatever was loud, luxurious, heady. Pious, she would fill the room with objects of piety. Musical, she was permitted a piano. Bookish, she was allowed a library, filled with "worthy" volumes.[43] Photographs would remind her of her loved ones, especially her ancestors, who set a respectable example. She would use her mirror sparingly. She would receive friends there but never a man. Her door must remain closed, like her legs. The rules of prudence necessarily have an erotic edge.

The young lady's room haunted the literary imagination to the point of fantasy. Victor Hugo lingers in Cosette's. Balzac inventories Césarine Birrotteau's, Eugénie Grandet's, and Ursule Mirouët's. As the perfumer César Birrotteau rises in society, his apartment undergoes a radical transformation. He gives his wife a beautiful bedroom, adjoining Césarine's, "coquettish, with a piano, a pretty mirrored armoire, a small chaste bed with unfussy curtains, and all the delicate little furnishings that young ladies adore."[44] For Balzac, a man who loved his metaphors, the arrangement of the domestic space says much about the soul. Ursule Mirouët's may be read in her bedroom: "In this room you might breathe in the perfume of heaven. The exact arrangement of her things attested to an orderly spirit, a sense of harmony that certainly would have struck anyone who saw it." The novelist's gaze stops at the doors of the armoire, "a great armoire containing, no doubt, her dresses and underthings," which should not be rifled through.[45] It is an ideal room for the ideal young lady that Ursule incarnates, luminously, always dressed in white and blue, the colors of matrimony.

Young German ladies were mad about Marguerite's room in *Faust*, "a small, well-ordered room," which Mephistopheles mocked: "Not all young ladies are so neat and proper." Faust notices it, and it piques his desire: "I feel, O young woman! your orderly spirit murmuring around me, this spirit that rules over your days like a tender mother, who teaches you to properly roll the mat on the table and to lightly powder the parquet with sand. . . . A hut would become, for you, a paradise."[46]

Young ladies had two approaches to this ideal room. Either they retired to it to escape from the world, to slow down their encroaching maturity, which they feared; they wanted enjoy this time in the chrysalis, dreaming like Emma Bovary or Jane Austen's heroines or even making art themselves. This was the painter Marie Bashkirtseff's desire, to find some authenticity on the canvas. Or, on the contrary, they sought to flee this prison, if not through love, then at least through marriage. "They have wandered around in circles, confined to the narrow room in which they've been given a deadly brainwashing," wrote Hélène Cixous.[47] How to escape, how to be elsewhere? Young ladies had a taste for travel writing, missionary adventures in faraway lands, love stories that unraveled over interminable *feuilletons.* They read in their rooms, by the changing light of their lamps, later than was allowed. Some dared to explore their bodies, but few would admit it. Marie Chaix describes "this unknown pleasure whose name [she] doesn't know." "Behind my closed door, I finally grasped the horror of the young lady's room. . . . In a room like this one, neither beautiful nor ugly, just a bit gauche, with its grays, its roses, its rosettes. I learned, patient and gloomy, to accommodate myself to adolescence."[48] Between boarding school and the conjugal bedroom is a transitional space of apprenticeship, a suspended time when everything is still possible.

This was a norm that continued to form the habits of young female teachers in their first provincial teaching posts, after studying at Sèvres or for the *agrégation.* Finding a room was their first worry, and they were the bread and butter of landladies who preferred these decent young boarders to young men with their dubious associates. Marguerite Aron recounts how she attempted to personalize her room, which was rented to her by a pair of spinsters in clogs. She describes "the little blue vases . . . , the dried branch, the cloth curtains around the alcove bed, the walnut chest of drawers, the worn carpet with faded flowers. I added my photographs to the mantelpiece and my engravings to the walls. . . . Then I was really at home."[49] How many sad little provincial rooms were filled with these young women, spending long, solitary hours preparing their classes, correcting essays, pausing for the daily tea ritual—their only luxury, left over from Sèvres. Women like Jeanne Galzy, Colette Audry, and Simone de Beauvoir have written about the challenges they faced, which one by one they escaped.

"Nothing is as solitary as a young lady," wrote Kafka.

Lucia's Room

In *The House of Life,* which the great collector and aesthete Mario Praz devotes to his apartment in the Palazzo Ricci in Rome, he spends one hundred pages describing his daughter Lucia's bedroom.[50] Of all the rooms, this one changes the most, in its furnishings as well as its decor. He had to make room for the child, whom his wife clearly wanted more than he did; she made him buy a crib, a *barcelonnette* in the style of the King of Rome (Praz is a great lover of the Empire style), in the hopes of exciting his paternal instincts—finally accomplished around 1936. Ten years later husband and wife were separated, but Lucia kept her room at the Palazzo Ricci, occupying it sporadically. It was updated in accordance with her age; for the child, everything was covered in pink, and the room was filled with custombuilt maple furniture, including a *lit galerie* inspired by a model from the Directory. All these "modern furnishings" disappeared, replaced by antique furnishings adapted for a young girl: a sober Empire bed in the shape of a boat, bought in 1925, with a mahogany nightstand, on which was placed a candle that was never lit but "could be used if the electricity went out." There was a round work table with multiple drawers, a "country bidet," like that which belonged to Pauline Borghèse, a desk, seats, etc. The author spends a long time discussing the bed, which once belonged to him and which he wanted to give to his daughter, in spite of what people might say: "Most people hesitate before buying an antique bed, some for reasons of hygiene, out of fear it will contain some vermin or microbe, but mostly for superstitious reasons, for it is certain that someone has died in it."[51] This single Empire bed, surrounded by a "crown" canopy with curtains to match the bedding, which he found after searching long and hard in secondhand shops, would stay with him all his life. The walls were covered in paintings, about thirty of them: portraits of women and children, genre paintings, and very feminine English conversation pieces from the eighteenth century. Lucia's room also contained many toys; a few stayed behind, like her miniature dollhouses, very Victorian, in the Chippendale style; Praz laments that they are too little appreciated in Italy.[52] But Lucia was a destructive child; she broke "an adorable doll with periwinkle eyes," which her father had saved from his own childhood and which he had given her "in a moment of unpardonable weakness." He felt its loss like a wound.

The story of this bedroom allows us to glimpse the disappointed love of an aesthete father, who didn't know how to express his love except by collecting or through the choice of an object, without understanding that neither his daughter nor his wife (an Englishwoman who left him because he devoted himself to *dead things*) really liked the things he gathered, even perceiving them to be a form of tyranny.[53] When, years later, she returns to her room, Lucia regrets that he took down the garlanded crystal chandelier, whose shimmers she used to track: "She reproached me for having replaced a cheerful object with a boring globe. Me, who had thought to stimulate her imagination with the stars scattered on the face of the globe, the color of lapis-lazuli."[54] This misunderstanding of things is a misunderstanding of hearts.

The Son's Room

The boy's room is discussed much less frequently. We think of boys outside, out of the house or far away, when they're at school; a boy looks suspicious, even effeminate or sickly, if he stays at home. However, many boys confessed that this was exactly what they wanted. Anatole France describes the decisive delight he experienced when he crossed the threshold to "my room." Neither large nor beautiful, with its cream wallpaper scattered with blue bouquets, Second Empire–style, it was, nevertheless, his: "As soon as I had my own room, I no longer recognized myself. From the child I had been the day before I suddenly became a young man. . . . As soon as I had my own room, I had an interior life. . . . It separated me from the universe, and I discovered the universe there. It's there that my mind took shape, where my mind was teased by—at first vague and far off, later frightening—

simulacrums of love and beauty."[55] François Mauriac hated the lack of privacy at boarding school: "Having a room where I could be alone, this was the frenetic, never-satisfied desire of my childhood and my youth. Four walls between which I would have been an individual, where I could finally have found myself."[56] Mauriac had an unquenched thirst to be alone, to read, and to be warm; his grandmother refused to light a fire. "Children need to build character," she said. "She had been raised without fires, and the head colds had never descended to her chest."[57]

We are of course talking about future writers, who were above all great readers, solitary boys—monks, some would have said. Today a teenager's room doesn't necessarily have this feeling of a cell. It's full of posters, concert posters, musical instruments, stereos, computers, gadgets of all kinds; out of their closets spill clothes and sneakers from their favorite brands, a key extension of consumerist practices that has made teenagers a marketing target since the 1960s. Access to the bedroom marks the teenager of the Trente Glorieuses.[58] The bedroom is the teenager's lair; the door is always closed. He has his "buddies" over for interminable conversations or jam sessions.

His parents demand a minimal amount of tidiness but respect his privacy. After his death, *The Son's Room* (the title of a film by Nanni Moretti) reveals to his stricken father an unknown side of the boy's personality: his tastes, his loves, his dreams. The dead child is entombed in his room. The experience of World War I no doubt had a great impact, as "Le journal d'un père pendant la Première Guerre mondiale," unearthed by Catherine Rollet, shows. The son is off at the front. The family organizes a kind of private religion in the middle of the house, "scrupulously maintaining the soldier's room so it will be ready for him one day," and creating, with photos and trinkets, a kind of "museum of war" display.[59] Should the worst come to pass, it will become a memorial, and the room will become an altar dedicated to mourning the dead, frozen in his eternal youth.

But when a son leaves home under more ordinary circumstances, this can also be experienced as a kind of mourning by those left at home.[60] Many parents dread the silence, hesitate to enter the empty room, missing the old mess, the slippers scattered everywhere. They keep it in that state for a long time, as if he were merely away on a trip and were going to return. It is difficult to resign themselves to using it for something else. Though necessary, though a kind of confrontation, the separation is difficult.[61] The son who leaves for good, even of his own free will, also suffers from this transformation, in which he feels the weight of time and fears being forgotten, the page irrevocably turned. "It was my room," he says (and she, the daughter, even more emphatically), slightly on edge, feeling a new affection for anything that belonged to him: the desk, the TV room, the bookshelves. He lived a part of his existence between these walls, and no trace remains. He hasn't even kept his stuffed animals, the dog or the bear that were his first friends, witnesses to his first doubts. "If the little dog moves, I will believe in miracles," someone close to me said to himself; the little dog did not move; he ceased to believe (and no doubt in God as well). Being alienated from his room, or from the memory of his room, is to be dispelled from paradise or his very life. One of my friends' wives confided to me that she decided to marry because her parents, without asking her, had given her bedroom to a grandmother. Chased from her territory, she hurdled toward a disastrous marriage. Giuseppe Tomasi di Lampedusa could not bear to leave the place of his childhood. He wandered his whole life in his imagination in the immense estate of Santa Margherita di Belìce and its three hundred rooms. Giuseppe "always mourned the room where he was born and where he was not permitted to continue to sleep."[62] In the child's room, and even more in the adolescent's, fundamental pacts and definitive alliances are made.

Childish Experiences

The urbanization of habitats changed our relationship to space and children's relationship to it as well. The Western child now has certain largely cultural needs and experiences of his room that he didn't necessarily have before. The child's room, to which he is often confined, is a space in which to play games, do crafts, read, work; it is a site of sociability and of the retreat that becomes necessary to him. "People bother me," says Vincent, age four. "What I want is to be alone in my room to play with my train." The child's room is well suited to this kind of infinite tinkering about, where dolls and dollhouses create a smaller version of the world, more so even than playing games, which usually requires several players and enough space. How much fun to lose oneself in these setups with their endless stories! Little girls try to imagine being mothers. Children's magazines give them instructions, such as *Francs Camarades,* which devoted several issues in 1945 to building a house, in a very postwar "Reconstruction" vein. Boys build the house; girls decorate it. "Girls use a paintbrush just as well as boys; they collaborate, then, on decorating the kitchen and the bathroom. But it is the arrangement of the children's room that gives them the most to do."[63]

Bedrooms lend themselves to the kind of endless reading whose delights Proust described. His passion (endlessly interrupted by the adults' schedule—interminable lunches, walks, dinners, turning out of the candles) was to take refuge in a garden or especially in his provincial bedroom, the blessed site of the siesta, with the windows closed and the drawn curtains letting a trickle of light in. If he didn't finish the book he was reading, "sometimes at the house, in my bed, for a long while after dinner, the last hours of the evening sheltered my reading as well."[64] Stolen hours had to be defended and were that much more delicious because of it. To read in bed—a childhood pleasure—was to be plunged into the sleep peopled with suddenly animate familiar objects, strange creatures, monsters surging from the shadows, ghosts springing from nowhere. Sometimes, in a half-sleep, the child may perceive a face leaning close to him, a murmur from the room next door, that of his parents perhaps, which still astonishes him. What happens there? If the door is cracked open, he may glimpse there strange words and gestures, maybe the primitive scene that Freud made the key of his future sexuality. The child's bedroom is the antechamber of sexuality— that of others and his own.

Many children are anguished in the evening and feel the arrival of night like a death. For Jean Santeuil, "going to sleep every night was . . . a truly tragic moment, whose vague horror made it that much more cruel." To say goodnight, "leave everyone, for the entire night," was an unbearable ordeal.[65] Children are afraid of the dark and cry when they have to go to bed. They're frightened of the shadows in their room suddenly turning hostile, the unknown threats lying in ambush, staring at them. Mauriac remembers the story of a thief that his maid told him: "He was climbing,

climbing, climbing. I heard the stairs creak and hid my head under the covers."[66] Children put off the moment when they have to go to sleep, kissing their mother longer than necessary, a kiss that Proust's narrator waits for at Combray like a necessary last rite. "For a long time, I went to bed early." The *Recherche* opens on this great scene of desire, of melancholy, of mourning, and of love, for which the bedroom is the theater. The early opera of childhood, of life itself, is played there, between the shadows. "Claire! Claire! The children sing at night when they're afraid."[67] Or they ask for someone to talk to them. Freud describes a three-year-old boy who helped him understand children's anguish: "Auntie, talk to me, I'm afraid because it's so dark." The aunt replies: "What good will that do you, if you cannot see me?" "I don't have to see you," responds the child. "As soon as someone speaks, it's light again."[68] The voice can dissipate nocturnal shadows.

But for children the room is a place to live out their shared adventure. In *Les Enfants terribles,* Jean Cocteau turns a no exit scenario into a fraternal drama of the impossible, exclusive, pure, and terrifying love between a brother and sister. Paul and Elisabeth are voluntarily imprisoned in the room where Elisabeth cares for Paul, who is wounded. "This room they shared was as it were a shell in which they lived, washed, dressed together as naturally as if they were twin halves of a single body." There, they collaborate on their "architecture of disorder," which they then destroy. They dream of leaving the room but cannot. They dream of having their own rooms and don't even consider using the empty room left behind by their dead mother. Even at the hotel, where their uncle invites them for strange vacations, they cannot sleep apart; they are endlessly brought back to a cohabitation that they loathe and desire. The friends who visit them in their room are drawn into their intrigue and become actors in a nocturnal theater, where they assume the roles that consume them. "Elisabeth and Paul, made for childhood, continued to live as if they occupied two neighboring cradles." They adore each other and tear each other apart. "Servants of an inexorable law, they brought [everything] to the room where the honey was made." To leave the room is to leave the other, to go to the outside, toward Michael, Elisabeth's American fiancé, whom she does not bring into their room, hoping, no doubt, to break the enchanted circle. "The future of these two rooms was taking shape. An astonishing speed pushed them toward the absurd, imagining they would occupy similar rooms in the future." We know that this future will never take place. Michael kills himself on the road, and the room is recreated, until everyone is dead. Death is the only force powerful enough to dissolve them.[69]

In the regained room, Paul "builds himself a hut like in Mme de Sé-gur's *Les vacances,*" with a screened-off bed. The hut in the room, under the table, with the sheets and covers, under a tent made out of a cape: this is, more than the room itself, an imposed space, which all children dream of; it is the only way they have of marking their territory, carving out a place where they can be among themselves, and build their world from nothing, like Robinson Crusoe on his island or the Swiss Family Robinson in their tree. It's perhaps a sexual fantasy, whose power Robert Musil detected: "The passionate intrusion in the body of another is but the prolonged taste children have for mysterious, criminal hiding spaces."[70]

Children appropriate the space of their bedrooms, which become their domains, the site of all their secrets. They are impatient to return to them after meals, where the heavy ritual and the adult conversations reduce them to silence. Mrs. Ramsay's children "disappear[ed] . . . as stealthily as stags from the dinner-table directly the meal was over . . . [and] sought their bedrooms, their fastness in a house where there was no other privacy to debate anything, everything."[71]

What might they talk about among themselves? asks Georges, Louis-René des Forêts's adult hero. "The childish voices unexpectedly seized him." A "mysterious curiosity" led him back to his room and nailed him "behind the half-open door of the children's room." Paul, the charismatic leader of the group, is leading the others in a strange role-playing game to force Georges to intervene and expose himself. They clam up before his muteness. And it is their exasperating silence that forces him to speak, as if in a panic. "Are you there, children?" he cries out, throwing himself through the door excitedly. "Are you still there?" But what can Georges hear but his own interior mono-logue, brought back to himself, to his radical alterity, by childish cruelty?[72]

The bedroom is a recent and—must we be reminded?—today nonex-istent territory for the majority of children in the world.

The Women's Room

MY GRANDMOTHER CLÉMENCE felt truly at home only in her kitchen, where she was the mistress of the house and all the things in it. She banished men from that space, believing they had no purpose there. In her room she spoke very little. A widow for nearly half a century, she spent a great deal of time in the kitchen, knitting, doing the accounting, reading novels from the Bibliothèque blanche or the journal *La Veillée des Chaumières* or distractedly saying the rosary. My memory of her room is of deep armchairs, cluttered tables, and especially a mixed odor of perfume, wool, linden, and camphor, as rendered by Raspail, her favorite remedy, which she liked to rub into her skin.

The bedroom is a woman's sacred space par excellence. Everything contrives to isolate them there: religion, domesticity, morality, decency, modesty, but also the erotic imagination, which pictures them dreaming at their windows or languidly reading, stretched out on a sofa, a divan, a bed, clothing slipping from their shoulders. They live in these bedrooms, working, reading love letters, devouring books, dreaming. For them to close the door behind themselves is a gesture of independence. They have looked out the window, traveled in their thoughts. "For women have sat indoors all these millions of years, so that by this time the very walls are permeated by their creative force," wrote Virginia Woolf.[1] This is why, more than men, women retain the silent memory of the rooms they have occupied and that have set the rhythm of their lives and their passage through time.

Femininity into Room

Many cultures assign women to the interior. "Any woman who shows herself dishonors herself." "A woman in public is always out of place"; both Pythagoras and Jean-Jacques Rousseau have said it in almost identical terms. Public space is the domain of men, that of business, politics, rhetoric, sport at the highest levels, power. A woman can only partially claim her place there. It is a question of function but also of sex, of the guarded and eventually veiled body.

The house is a woman's business, even among nomadic tribes. For the Tuaregs or the Berbers, the tent—a fragile anchor in the desert—is organized around the figure of the woman and always partitioned the same way: men and visitors to the right, women to the left.[2] The tent belonged to women as part of their dowry; they took responsibility for it. In a life lived through wandering, it stood for stability and hospitality.

Kant saw the house as "the only defense against the horror of the abyss, of the night, of unknown origins," the root of a human, domestic identity, and he assigned women a place there that was at once pivotal and subordinate. "She is the center around which children and servants are organized, and, to this extent, she is a person. But the moment she escaped, she became a rebel and a revolutionary." Whence the almost metaphysical necessity to domesticate her: "Women should be submissive, tamed, and kept at home, in the soft shadows of the furniture's glow."[3]

The bedroom represents a kind of enclosure identified with femininity itself, quite literally in Germanic cultures *(Frauenzimmer)* and more symbolically in Latin cultures, according to Freud.[4] Emmanuel Levinas compared the woman to the family crystal, "essentially violable and inviolable." "The feminine way of being is to hide herself, and the fact of hiding herself is the definition of modesty. . . . Woman is the condition of retirement, of the interior of the house and the habitat," independent of any singular presence.[5] An essence outside of existence.

This idea of enclosure derived from spiritual ideals. Saint Anthony recommended that women "close themselves up in their rooms, for it was in her bedroom that the sainted Virgin conceived the son of God."[6] The bedroom of the Annunciation is one of the great themes of medieval and Renaissance painting, with its bordered bed giving no hint of the sleeping woman's body, and it sets the model for the young lady's bedroom. This room is the setting for the greatest story ever told: the incarnation of God, the son of God made man in the body of a woman. The life of the Virgin

Mary, from birth to death, is frequently associated with the room, though she traveled a great deal in her son's wake along the roads of Galilee.

It is impossible to run through all the litany of precepts about the bedroom. Monseigneur Dupanloup, the bishop of Orleans and a specialist in girls' Christian education under the Second Empire, advised pious women to retire from the world and domestic worries: "Study makes women love their homes, which remind them of the joys of working for others. How little need have we then for visits and company! What a joy to retire to the room, to rediscover one's books and drawings! How quickly do we run, and with what a light step, to return to our homes!" The worthy bishop recommended that women develop "the art of lost moments" and that young ladies know how to close their doors.[7]

Secular institutions shared this desire for preservation. When toward the end of the nineteenth century, at the instigation of Dr. Bourneville, Parisian hospitals replaced nuns with nurses, they built them a convent-like dormitory, which seemed preferable to the risks of the bedsit.[8]

Nineteenth-century Anglo-American writers like Edith Wharton, Alice James, and especially Charlotte Perkins Gilman described and sometimes denounced the claustrophobic atmosphere of their velvet-lined homes and their cozy bedrooms.[9] But this did nothing to quell the ardent desire for a "room of one's own," a space that Virginia Woolf famously claimed was a necessary condition for creativity, along with a minimal income on which to live. The bedroom has been claimed by many women of all ages and diverse conditions, from the woman who works at home to the writer, no matter how she chose to live. Emily Dickinson, the American poet, shut herself up in her room in her parents' house in Amherst and would never leave it for the rest of her life. But even those women who went traveling, perhaps more than others, appreciated the friendly calm of the bedroom—even the liberated women of 1968, mostly lesbians, whose autobiographical testimonies were gathered by Françoise Flammant.[10] Always on the move, they invested a great deal of energy in their houses and in their vagabonding lives.

Thinking about the women's bedroom is therefore as complex as its many functions and practices. It swings from a place of constraint to one of freedom, between duty and desire, real and imaginary—distinctions that are difficult to distinguish in the semi-darkness, where boundaries are blurred.

Assigned Rooms

The *gynaeceum*, the seraglio, the harem, the medieval women's room—these are just some of the major models of enclosure whose way of operating largely, if not totally, escapes us. This way of bringing women together excites men's fantasies even more than their company (what do they do when they're together?); it is to men that we owe the material or literary images that historians have attempted to decipher.

According to Paul Veyne, who analyzed the "mysteries of the *gynaeceum*" according to the frescoes of Pompeii, "the *gynaeceum* was no doubt less mysterious for Greek women than for their husbands, who shut them up and then worried afterward, or for the historians who dreamt of it as a harem."[11] This was an oft-repeated idea in the nineteenth century, when the term *gynaikeion* was used to refer to an "apartment of women" and whose exact outline is unclear. Archaeology has uncovered no trace of this kind of segregation, unless the women were held upstairs. Their objects have been found everywhere in the house, so it would suggest that they circulated freely. The Athenians were more confined than the Romans. The differences between the sexes, which were strongly marked in Greece and even more so in Rome, were not established through a partitioning of space or a rigorous arrangement of rooms. On Greek vases, and especially on *pyxides* (perfume boxes), women are shown with other women, at their toilette or other domestic activities, in a space bordered by columns, with objects like mirrors that, associated with beauty, "are a metaphorical expression of a certain attitude toward women."[12] There is no question of this being a realistic depiction of daily life but a representation of femininity. The *gynaeceum*, to which Penelope lends her image of the faithful wife, has a reputation for austerity, its virtues discovered in the eighteenth century at the same time as those of Greece itself. It served as a model for Rétif de la Bretonne's *Les Gynographes*. In order to reform social mores and "put women in their place," he advocated for these *gynaeceums* to be rebuilt; there women would be free and only husbands and fathers could enter.[13] In his view, the *gynae-ceum* incarnated an ideal harmony between the sexes that contrasted with the violence of the lustful Orient.

In the harem (literally, "sacred thing, reserved") and the seraglio (palace of the Sultan of Constantinople), the space was complicated by religious (the weight of Islam) and political references. "Having been raised on the seraglio, I know its every nook and cranny," said Bajazet in Jean Racine's play. Those of us who weren't can only study the ways in which the Occident attempts to penetrate an unknown world created by its own obsessions.[14] Beginning in the sixteenth and especially during the seventeenth century, there was a great expansion in travel narratives (by Baudier, Tavernier, Chardin). They fed the political thought of the philosophers (Montesquieu, Voltaire) who saw "the Grand Turk" as the quintessential despot. This monstrous tyranny was based on the ways he ruled his home, which was organized around the seraglio. It was a "mysterious center, closed on itself, without windows, almost without doors, a microcosm where the entire despotic state is reflected," according to Alain Grosrichard, who deciphered the "structure of the seraglio" in the gradation of its obstacles and its sexual functioning. In the succession and interlocking of courtyards, gardens, and closed-off rooms, each wall stands for a taboo, and each space is devoted to one function and one alone. "Every time a threshold is crossed, a new and uncertain destiny is encountered but one that always leads from one prison to another." It was a question of doors, from the most modest to the most "sublime."[15] It was a system of keys and gatekeepers.

In the heart of the seraglio, the harem, gathered women whom only the prince was allowed to see and to pleasure and of whom he expected heirs—a key objective. Even the doctor was not allowed to see them; to listen to their heartbeats, he passed his hands through a tear in a curtain. The young virgins lived two to a room that resembled a nun's cell, in such close quarters that one bed was separated from the other by a black eunuch. Reading, writing, and embroidery took up most of their days, while they waited for the moment when the sultan would toss a white handkerchief at the one he'd selected for that night. His power was to have unblocked access, free rein, over female bodies, unreserved and unlimited access to their variety, their availability, their use. This made the seraglio "a place of fantasy, whose power to fascinate we cannot quite appreciate . . . unless we understand its profoundly metaphysical roots."[16] This was an almost godlike power of man over woman, a door to push open, a virgin to penetrate, as she waited for him, available, reserved, under guard. The European erotic imagination ran away with the seraglio, giving this name to debauched places in eighteenth-century Paris, gorging itself on the *Thousand and One Nights,* taking it as a synonym for endless love, never satisfied, and the beautiful odalisques that Ingres, Delacroix, and their imitators so enviously painted. Sometimes bodies accumulated to the point of nausea.

Two aspects of this are particularly intriguing: eunuchs and the relationship of women to them. Depending on whether their castration (carried out between the ages of seven and sixteen) was partial or complete, they were either white (officers of the seraglio, tutoring children) or black and guardians of the women whom they were not to let out of their sight. The ugliest black castrati were specifically sought for their impotence and their tendency to highlight the prince's beauty. They were assisted by old women and ordered by an *odabashi* (head of chamber) with a knife at his waist, whose job it was to spy on the young and to punish them—to obtain pleasure from them as well, in some cases.

A perpetual suspicion weighed on the sexuality of these seraglio women, who were presumed to be burning with an almost hysterical orgasmic excitation. By way of precaution they were forbidden to keep pets, monkeys or male dogs, which might try to have sex with them, and entire cucumbers, which resembled dildos. Their "vicious appetites" led them to lesbianism, a given within the walls of the seraglio and even more at the hammam. Women deployed a thousand tricks to communicate among themselves—for example, the exchange of letters and salaams, little objects in the form of a rebus—to express their love. Or they would dress as boys, assisted by the presence of the eunuchs, who added to the general confusion of the sexes, and by the plotting of the old women, fueled by their own desires. Far from being passive, they seem to have experienced an intense sexual activity that gave the seraglio an erotic density on which Western Orientalism thrived.[17]

According to Fatima Mernissi, numerous sources—stories, minia-tures (but who created them?)—show hyperactive women, armed, armored, on the march, astride fast chargers, voracious.[18] Fatima's grandmother Yas-mina's favorite story was called *La Dame à la robe de plumes* (The Woman in the Feathered Dress)—such a lightweight dress was perfect for escapes. "A woman should lead her life like a nomad. She should always be on the alert, ready to flee, even if she is loved. For according to Scheherazade, even love can pin you down, become a prison." Fatima describes her childhood in a contemporary Moroccan harem, which no doubt bore little resem-blance to the Ottoman seraglio. It was a conflicted hotbed of sociability and feminine apprenticeship but nevertheless a form of enclosure that strictly regulated women's access to the outside world. The doors and the win-dows faced the courtyard, never the street. "As a little girl," her grandmother told her, "you had to learn to be wary of words if you didn't want to live like an idiot. A window that does not face the outside—I hesitated to call it one. A door that opens to an interior courtyard, or a walled garden with guarded doors, is certainly no door. You have to be aware that it is something else."[19] It was an experience of the limits, her granddaughter attests.

In medieval castles separation was of another kind, more binary in a sense. The women's room was the opposite of the men's hall, the place of chivalric, homosocial culture, the cement of the feudal agreement.[20] It has been interpreted in contradictory ways. Jeanne Bourin, author of the novel on the subject *(La Chambre des dames),* made this warm feminist place the center of the drama of the Brunel family, of which Mathilde and her daugh-ter, Florie, are the main heroines. Hearts, bodies, and hearths aflame, lofty and good sentiments, intimate conversations—everything contributes to paint an image of an amorous, sensual, and happy thirteenth century. This delighted readers, to judge from the sales (more than one million copies sold). The novel devotes entire pages to the sweetness and harmony of the home:

> In the warmth of the room, where the scent of the fire joined
> that of the perfumed candles, an atmosphere of intimacy was
> created that hung over the memory of each of those who could

recall a happy childhood there, the memories unleashed by a shared past that was still so close at hand, as the two women went to their knees in order to abolish anguish and time by praying in harmony. Then, more calmly, they began to embroider, one very close to the other, fondly planning the future for the child yet to be born. [21]

Régine Pernoud wrote the preface to a recent reprinting, bringing the eye of an acclaimed historian to this reassuring vision of a Christian, female Middle Ages.

Georges Duby does not share this perspective. The women's room was in his view a "disturbing space," "a closed-off little world, insidious, the field of an obvious internal terrorism" and at the mercy of masculine domination, in particular that of the lord, whose power was not so distant from that of the sultan but was carried out by the knights, whose power theoretically stopped at the door and who were obsessed with its closure. During the day, the ladies sewed, talked to each other, took care of the children and the sick, who were allowed at that time to enter their space. They sang "weaving songs" they composed. But at night, what did they do among themselves in their shared beds? Literature describes an intense nocturnal circulation among these "insatiable females," consenting and provoking the desire of men who would slide into the room, "a field wide open to unrestrained virility." Adultery, incest, rape, and illegitimate children were the result of a sexual ardor for which courtly love was only a strategic cover, a mask, an illusion. The "medieval male" was in fact dark and brutal, hot and sweaty. Even if Duby later provided a more nuanced account, he has always railed against sentimentalized representations of the period.[22]

In this way, the women's room was distinct from the *gynaeceum* or the seraglio. More air was allowed in, and more men, too. The women who lived there seem to have had more freedom to read or even to write. Certainly the orchard is a more appropriate setting for courtly love. The enclosure of the garden provides more freedom than the shelter of a shared room. Nevertheless, the women's room was a step toward a more egalitarian conjugality.

The Convent and the Cell

We have often conflated the convent and the seraglio, which share many of the same formal traits: virgins sworn to a supreme master; strict enclosures, guarded by the clergy, a form of eunuch; women alone among themselves, suspected of hysteria; the use of scourging and flagellation to tame their urges and the amorous desires that they might feel for their confessor or their companions. Another avid site of erotic literature, the cell figures as an island of masturbation and lesbianism; the youngest are initiated into pleasure by their elders, like Diderot's mother superior, who guides Sister Suzanne.[23] The young and the old alike give themselves over to the pleasure of the dildo. The convent could even be said to exist to marginalize lesbianism and, by separating it off, to protect society from it. But how much reality is there in this imaginary oasis?

We know the rules of the convent better than the practices that took place there. We know more of the excesses (mystical or sensual) than of daily life, lost in the murmurings of prayers. Haunted by sin, the Tridentine reforms of the seventeenth-century Council of Trent reinforced the rigor of the cloister, which became a major question symbolized by the famous "Guichet Day" at Port Royal; thenceforth parents were no longer allowed to enter the convent.[24] Even when traveling, nuns had to maintain a certain retreat, avoiding hotels and preferring the solitude of a carriage, and always keep the modesty of the veil.[25]

The rules were strict about furnishings, as well as the size of the cell. A minuscule space of about one hundred square feet, it should contain only what was absolutely necessary: a bed, a prie-dieu, a place for books, a chair, a table. No personal belongings were allowed; just a few images of saints or reliquaries on the wall, with the mother superior's permission. The slatted bed was made of a straw mat covered with two muslin sheets and blankets (one in summer, two in winter). It was sheer luxury compared with most people's standards of living; in a way it was an echo of an artist's studio, and a number of young girls described their rooms at the convent with great pleasure (like George Sand at the English women's convent). However, some of the sisters were unable to bear the pressures of this communal lifestyle and would shut themselves up in their rooms and be driven mad there.

According to the rules of Saint Benedict, nuns were not permitted to "nestle . . . like secular people." Cushions and pillows were allowed, but many had to content themselves with a straw-filled mattress. They would not undress much; modesty forbade uncovering the body and looking at it. Nuns could remove their shoes and their dress but had to keep on their underclothes, veil, and scapular. To sleep they would stretch out on their backs, hands folded on their chests, like recumbent figures on a tomb. They were to have edifying thoughts. Sleep is a voyage similar to death, which may surprise them at any moment, making it a difficult time; the impurity of their dreams must be surveyed. Evil may prowl in the darkness of the cell; temptation may invade it, as it does (according to the clergy) tend to assail women's bodies, homes for lust.[26] For the sisters of the convent, night was a battle.

Of course a cell is not a bedroom. But in its purified austerity, it shares certain aspects: solitude, separation, discipline, and also a minimal amount of furnishings, protection, autonomy, retreat, and the nocturnal portion of life and the self. It illustrates the ambiguities of cloistering women, lodged between constriction and salvation.

Everyday Life in the Bedroom

From birth to death, the bedroom is the stage on which women's everyday lives are played out. When they share a room, they work more for others than for themselves, continually busy with chores, especially oriented around the bed, which they make in order to maintain the respectability of the home, or the sick and helpless for whom they care, or the dying, whom they watch over and bury. They were born to this task; it is transmitted from mother to daughter in rural areas, interrupted by urban disorder, which offers them the deliverance of escape. In these shared rooms, do women manage to carve out a space for themselves? Do they even think of this? How is the need for privacy born? Where can it take refuge? In objects perhaps; in a box, a pile of laundry, a handkerchief, a headscarf, a prayer book, an image, a mirror? Perhaps in a stool or a seat by the chimney or a place by the wall, a corner, or some kind of nook in which they can rest and dream? We know so little of their desires, their suffering, and the strategies they adopted to escape from the group, of their potential indifference, and their capacities for interior exile.

In the home, these women did not have a space of their own, unless it was in certain circumstances having to do with the body or sexual difference, which markedly affirmed itself in two main ways: marriage and childbirth.

The nuptial chamber was to be devoted to the union of two bodies, the fusion of two sexes. But it was the woman—the virgin—whom we tend to associate with the bed, the bloodied site of the penetration that marks the entry into womanhood. The nuptial bedroom differs from the conjugal bedroom in that it is an altar on which to accomplish a rite of passage, frequently a public or semi-public act that at one time required heralds or spectators. Any sign of impotence was shameful; this was the only factor the Church would allow as grounds for annulment. The privatization of marriage—a major event in the history of Western love—gradually eliminated the need for witnesses; banished the gaze; closed the door, the bed, the curtains. Horrified by the acts of the flesh, Saint Augustine called for its total invisibility. Shame drove him more than modesty or desire, which was deemed impure. Centuries later, this bedroom terrified the young Colette, who, at the age of thirteen, attended a country wedding:

> The newlyweds' bedroom. Under the Turkey red curtains, the high, narrow bed, stuffed with feathers, bursting with goose-down pillows, the bed where ends this journey steaming with sweat, incense, the panting of livestock, the steam, the fluids. Later on the newlyweds will come here. I couldn't imagine it. They will sink into these deep feathers. There will be between them that dark struggle of which my mother's hardened candor and the lives of animals have taught me too much and too little. And then? I fear this bedroom and this bed, which I couldn't imagine.[27]

Soon the newlyweds will flee to the country, or a hotel, on more and more distant honeymoons designed to protect their privacy. There will be no more nuptial bedroom but a nuptial moment, the "wedding night," detached from a specific place or associated with mythic places—Italy, or Venice above all—that are shrouded with secrecy. The act will be experienced unequally: the man who takes the lead will do so relatively indifferently, while for the woman it will be fraught with meaning, the completion of her entry into "women's state," a domain in which she will dwell until menopause. The evolution of social mores and the fact that marriage is less frequently the first stage of a couple's relationship have happily dissipated the uneasiness of this bedroom, which persists in narratives of "intimacy" in the 1920s and 1930s.[28] Recent news items have brutally reminded us that for some, virginity remains the seal and the threshold of a woman's integrity, over which men mean to maintain control.[29]

Of all life events, giving birth is the most feminine. Until doctors came on the scene through the practice of the Caesarian section in the seventeenth and eighteenth centuries, succeeded by obstetrics, childbirth belonged to women and told us much about their sociability. Matrons and midwives surrounded the laboring woman from her first pains. They helped deliver the child, cut the umbilical cord, washed and swaddled the newborn, and fussed over the mother's bed, bringing bedpans and pitchers of water. Men were not permitted entry; they kept their distance. It was well looked upon to project a certain virile indifference. The banality of childbirth could not interrupt work in the fields.

Medieval paintings show an ethereal, joyful, and friendly version of childbirth. In a room bathed with light, elegant women buzz around a peaceful-looking bed where a serene mother reigns supreme (often Saint Anne, holding little Mary in her arms). Blood and pain are absent. The reality was something else altogether, as the high rate of infant and maternal mortality even until very recently shows. Childbirth is far and away the most dangerous moment of a woman's life. Many die in childbirth, a factor that significantly lowered women's life expectancy. Everything worked against them: a badly positioned baby, the lack of hygiene, polluted water, a lack of time to rest before and after the birth. Puerperal fever was a great danger and caused eighteenth-century doctors great concern. The birthing took place just about anywhere: in a stable, in the communal room (even in the twentieth century the kitchen table and utensils were still used), in Breton box-beds, in spite of their narrowness. Until World War II very few elements had changed. However, the security offered by the medicalization of childbirth led more and more women in cities to prefer to give birth at a clinic or a maternity ward than in their home. A major scene of feminine life would disappear forever, its practices and central players permanently outstripped by scientific progress. Childbirth was no longer a "private affair, a women's affair" but a public issue under the remit of doctors. The history of this serious transformation has been studied.[30] Only its spatial effects interest us here.

We will note that maternity wards were the first site of the hospital to offer private rooms (Paris, 1863–1870), thanks to the efforts of Dr. Stéphane Tarnier (1828–1897), less for reasons of privacy than contagion. Puerperal fever was, he argued, linked to promiscuity. Tarnier first recommended that the number of beds per room be reduced to no more than ten; then he suggested small rooms devoted to one bed only, honeycombed around the nurse's station and limiting to the greatest possible extent contact and internal circulation. Yet the patients protested. They believed that by imposing "a form of sequestration to healthy laboring women," they were being treated like delinquents or as if they carried the plague. They were not completely wrong: German hygienists blamed the badly washed hands of those delivering the babies. Eventually, Tarnier was forced to revise his plans.

The genealogy of the women's room can be tracked through architectural plans. In France in the eighteenth century, Jean-François Blondel was the first to allocate a *chambre de demoiselle* for a daughter, located not too far from her mother's room. In the nineteenth century, young ladies' bedrooms were common and reflected the degree to which adolescence was being taken seriously. An erotic suspicion hung around the virginal bed; this explains why certain educators defiantly recommended that young ladies not return to their beds between rising and going to bed but avoid them carefully. A symbolic fact about the events of 1968: they began at Nanterre on 22 March because students there were claiming the right to enter the girls' dorm rooms. Female students would enter male dormitories, but male students were not allowed entry to the females' because to cross the threshold

of a young lady's room was to penetrate the intimate sphere, and it constituted a prelude to lovemaking. It was up to the girls to take the initiative.

Marriage did away with this provisional solitude. But before becoming narrowly conjugal, the feminine bedroom was a space for receiving and
socializing. Let us turn to the story of the *ruelle*.

The Blue Bedroom and the *Ruelle des Précieuses*

The *ruelle* (literally, little street) was a space between the bed and the wall
that became a receiving place thanks to Catherine de Vivonne and her followers, the *précieuses*. Abraham Bosse's famous engraving shows how it
was laid out: a woman presided on a bed, dressed like a statue on a day of
procession, fan in hand, while on the three sides of the bed would gather
several ladies and a few men. They would talk. Catherine de Vivonne, the
Marquise de Rambouillet, detested the scramble for favor at court and had
retired from it. On the rue Saint-Thomas-du-Louvre, she had a beautiful
mansion built that would contain "all the commodities of a great house,"
including two bathrooms, sumptuously decorated with sculptures and al-
legorical paintings. Her health was not good, and she was often pregnant
(she had seven children, including the future Julie d'Angenne, Madame de
Montausier, who would become her associate in sociability); she therefore
received guests lying down on her four-poster bed, submerged in pillows
and ribbons. "I can see her in a recess where the sun does not enter," Mademoiselle de Montpensier remembered, in an alcove like a grotto, but filled
with books and paintings. Only two or three could enter at a time. This was
the famous "blue bedroom," which was no longer one, according to an inventory of its contents in 1652: a divan, ten chairs, two stools, some shelves,
some tables, some paintings, an adjoining cabinet.[31]

The marquise subsequently enlarged her "circle," eager to build a
"selective court," a "court within the Court," a little "gang" whose participants would adhere to the same code of politeness and refinement. Conversation was their mode of exchange and literary and linguistic critique their
common activity. A passion for books and writing united these women,
many of whom were unmarried; they were mad for novels, which cultivated

an elegant melancholy. In their literary utopia, "no one who did not have her own library would be included." The marquise had disciples who had joined the initial group and received in their own apartments; she always preferred the sanctuary of her blue bedroom and a companion chosen for her personal values. She must behave in a queenly manner, be chaste as Artemis, practice self-restraint, lead the conversation, prefer the elegance of the smile to the vulgarity of the laugh. Ethics and aesthetics inspired the *précieuses* to proselytize; they wanted to make love a principle of civilization. "Their government was peaceful, their politics were to study ways of turning all conflicts and wars from their empires" and to attract all persons of quality "in order to put the empire above every alcove," said the historian Antoine Baudeau de Sommaize in his seventeeth-century *Grand dictionnaire des précieuses.* In summary: we have the empires we can manage. But the political and cultural influence of the *précieuses* is not to my point. What is fascinating is the kind of power—female, it so happens—that can be exercised by a bedroom turned into a salon that has no intention of taking the king's place but whose object rather is to police society through conversation and literature. The city was experimenting with a civil sociability, which would soon be suffocated by Versailles, though destined to return to the fore. The *précieuses* prefigured the *salonnières* of the Age of Enlightenment and the first women of letters.

The concept of the bedroom-salon that the *précieuses* created endured for a long time. In hers, George Sand's grandmother would receive "old countesses" who would instruct little Aurore in the "graces" she lacked in her mother's more modest Parisian apartment, which she preferred. Madame Récamier would recline on a divan to receive her visitors. Their counterparts in 1848, petites bourgeoises with little money, gathered "at the home of whomever had the most chairs." And until the 1860s postmortem inventories listed a great many chairs in bedrooms that served as rooms in which to sleep and to entertain. The Comtesse de Bassanville recommended having a love seat and chairs and that the nightstand be put away during the daytime—an intimate furnishing that should be taken out only at bedtime. This was the end of a traditional usage, of which the countess did not approve but that lingered on.[32] Nostalgically, in 1930 Paul Reboux recommended taking out the mirrored armoire and disguising the bed in order to create "a little salon that would give directly onto the proper one and form a more intimate sitting room, to which ladies may retire to talk or smoke."[33]

Nevertheless, in the nineteenth century in France the conjugal bedroom soon became only a bedroom with one bed, used only for sleep and lovemaking. It was not particularly feminine, even if women spent more time there, having their hair done or writing letters. If they were widowed, the room became the "maternal bedroom" described by François Mauriac as the point around which his childhood and adolescence revolved.

Servants' Quarters

Modern and contemporary cities contain many single women, lodged in dark, ground-floor apartments or on the upper floors, in maid's rooms, garrets, hovels, or concierge's loges. The loneliness of women is a widespread social and demographic phenomenon. It has several sources: labor migrations that have affected women as much as men, though in different ways, especially domestic ones; girls who have been seduced and abandoned and often left to raise children alone; women who have outlived their husbands and been left dependent and without resources. Women's poverty lurks in all the niches of big cities.

It's not only men who migrate; migration has been reevaluated from a female perspective, in the present as well as the past. Since the eighteenth century especially, young women have come to the city to try their luck there. Take, for example, Marivaux's Marianne and her trials and tribulations. Most of the time, such women find placements as servants and are consequently summarily "fed and lodged." At one time they would have contented themselves with a pallet in a corner, under a stairway, or in a hallway. Then came the rise of the *chambre pour domestiques* (servants' quarters). In the eighteenth century, the sexes were kept separate, out of concern for the lust that might arise from their contact. Rétif de La Bretonne was especially aroused by the bedroom of a young maid in his father's house. Having a maid's room is therefore relatively recent, but it spread as far as Russia in the nineteenth century—in the city anyway, for in the countryside

sexual promiscuity was rampant and responsible for many unwanted preg-
nancies and infanticides. For a servant girl on a Breton farm, to have a bedroom meant only to have a bed.[34] In the châteaux everyone was more
comfortable. Their eaves today retain the trace of female servants having
lived there and having been better looked after than valets or grooms.

Few female servants stayed for very long in one post. Domesticity was
volatile and turnover high. Good houses, however, hoped to attract a more
stable personnel; we learn of this via memoirs (George Sand's *Histoire de
ma vie*) or through literature (Flaubert, Proust), where we can detect a certain nostalgia. Female servants had rooms in which they were confined by
age and the rooms' distance from their families. Françoise in Proust's *Recherche* has a daughter whom she sees regularly; the narrator, who tells us so
much of what she says, maintains a respectful distance from her room,
whose threshold he does not cross, respecting its alterity. Flaubert describes
Félicité's room on the last floor of Madame Aubain's house in Pont-
l'Évêque, where she has lived for half a century. The room is lit by a skylight; the furniture—a large armoire, a camp bed, a vanity table—is less
important than the objects accumulated like so many memories. "This
place, to which she admitted few people, resembled both a chapel and a
bazaar, so many religious and miscellaneous things did it contain. . . . One
saw on the walls: rosaries, medals, several pretty Virgins, a holy water stoup
made of coconut shell; on the chest of drawers, covered with a sheet like an
altar, the shell box Victor [her deceased nephew] had given her; then a wa-
tering can and a ball, penmanship notebooks, the illustrated geography
book, a pair of girl's boots; and on the mirror stud, hooked on by its ribbons, the little plush hat!"[35] Each of these relics is associated with an event
or an episode in Félicité's life; she practices a religion of remainders. They
testify as well to her fervor and her curiosity. She keeps any old thing her
mistress throws away: Monsieur's old redingote, artificial flowers, a portrait
of the Comte d'Artois, and especially Loulou, the parrot left to Madame
Aubain by a relative, which Félicité stuffs after he dies of the cold in the terrible winter of 1837. This jumble, this bedroom museum, is her entire life,
whence the drama when she is asked to leave. Her room turns out to be an
illusory home, a way station en route to nowhere. Many old servants have in

their twilight years been rudely confronted with their dependence and their deprivation.[36]

In the nineteenth century, the urban bourgeoisie (eager to be served as cheaply as possible) called on young women, often from the country, placed by relatives or special agencies, as "maids-of-all-work." Anne Martin-Fugier has described the conditions in which these servants lived: the interminable workdays; the exploitation by their mistresses, sometimes cantankerous, who measured out their food; and the frequent sexual harassment by men tempted by this fresh young flesh within arm's reach.[37] Émile Zola's magisterial epic of a Parisian apartment building, *Pot-Bouille,* tells the *roman noir* of the sixth floor, where the *chambres de bonnes* (maids' rooms) were systematically built by Haussmannian architects. Real estate speculation and a desire for social segregation converged in this use of the eaves of the buildings. They were reached by a service staircase and a narrow hallway, where the rooms were numbered. In the hallway were one or two sinks and a toilet (notoriously insufficient and badly maintained). These were minuscule lodgings, garrets lit by a tiny window looking out onto a small courtyard, a sordid well where the smells of cooking and washing wafted up from below. Badly insulated by thin walls and ill-closing doors, to which everyone had the key, they were noisy, stuffy in summer, and freezing in winter. There was no heating (no chimney), and the young women made up for the thinness of the covers by stacking their clothing on their wobbly iron beds. A chair and a chamber pot composed the perfunctory furnishings. They were full of cockroaches and water bugs; they were smelly, noisy, dirty, and provided no privacy. Servants who lived there were alone and exposed, vulnerable to contagious diseases, especially tuberculosis, which thrived in these unhygienic surroundings, and which medical inquiries described as rampant. Abortions and infanticides—the "crime[s] of the servant" as Victor Hugo called them—concerned them above all. Parisian maternity wards were full of maids. They were susceptible to the boredom and depression that results from being uprooted and lonely. In *La Figurante,* Léon Frappié describes the character of Armandine, who came from the outskirts of Orléans and who serves her masters so thoroughly that she doesn't know what to do with her free time. On Sundays, for fourteen years, she packs and unpacks her trunk.

Of course there were more tranquil rooms and servants who felt protected there, even lucky. Some described their years in service as a relatively happy time of apprenticeship and savings. Little tokens could be more remunerative than a salary. Parisian workers, it is said, sought out "serious" servants for their housekeeping skills and their ways of economizing; with their help, they were able to pay off their debts and build a family. These were the lucky ones. Not everything was so dark on the sixth floor; some managed to escape their miserable rural fates. There were risks but also the chance of freedom.

These *chambres de bonnes* nevertheless constituted a "social question" that was repeatedly posed by researchers and feminists. Marguerite Durand's newspaper, *La Fronde,* in 1899 asked its female readers—often employers themselves—to become aware of such mistreatment: "We do not care strongly enough for other women's social situations." The feminist activist Jeanne Schmahl advised creating housing for maids like there was in Great Britain, founding societies to help combat their loneliness and raise morale, or even providing lodging for them in their employers' homes. But employers feared a lack of privacy—and the smell maids would bring with them! Madame Vincent, a renowned feminist, took up their cause before the National Congress on Civil Rights and the Suffrage of Women in 1908. Drawing on various reports, she put forth a few demands. Maids' independence should be respected—they should be able to stay in their sixth-floor rooms, which guaranteed them a certain amount of freedom—but the space must be completely overhauled, equipped with running water, bathrooms and a common room in which to brush clothes and empty waste; men and women should be separated by two separate stairways; the rooms should be tiled and centrally heated; the iron beds should be fitted with metal box springs, etc. Worthy wishes indeed.

A number of laws and decrees specified an employer's responsibilities, at least in the region around Paris. A decree of 22 June 1904 set the requirements for a room: a minimum of 86 square feet (700 cubic feet), a pipe to ventilate smoke, one or several bay windows. One water closet was required per six rooms. These were more or less the same prescriptions in tsarist Russia.[38] All of this indicates a growing consciousness of an

intolerable situation. But in practice, nothing changed. "Our rooms are un-
inhabitable," said the maids polled by the Social League of Buyers (1908).
In 1927, Augusta Moll-Weiss, the founder of the École des mères (School
for Mothers), deplored French homeowners' inertia; in Great Britain and
especially Switzerland they were much more enlightened.

Maids' rooms did not change much more than the maids' conditions.
But they stopped attracting young female migrant workers. Brittany, which
had supplied so many young servants to the point of caricature, became reluctant to send its young women to the capital.[39] The secular posts for nurses
and nurse's aides available in the Parisian hospitals were a more attractive
and more respectable occupation. Soon, with the onset of World War I,
there was a genuine crisis of domesticity. "We can no longer be served," the
ladies of the houses complained, having to consent to certain modifications
on behalf of these "girls." The crime committed by the Papin sisters in their
mistress's bedroom in 1933 caused society to look with horror on the condition of servants. This type of interpersonal relationship, which cast the lin-
gering odor of feudalism over a democratic society, had become unacceptable.
World War II put a definitive end to it, under this form at least.

The maids' rooms became very sought after by students, who no
doubt were unaware of their original history.

Working at Home

Working at home became a widespread practice in the cities at the end of
the nineteenth century within the context of a rationalizing manufacturing
industry, which relied on a rigorous division of work and on the widespread
adoption of the sewing machine. To have a Singer was the ambition of many
working women, who would purchase it on credit, to be paid off in install-
ments.[40] Many married women hoped to use it to earn a little money while
staying at home to look after things there. As a secondary income, it worked.
But if they found themselves alone, through abandonment or widowhood,
the women's situations worsened. This was all the more true as salaries
ceaselessly fell in this sector. Their days became longer; they no longer left
their homes, except to deliver their work and look for work—but at least

they had the appropriate clothes. Tuberculosis was rampant, and hygienists worried as much for the seamstresses as for the clients they threatened to contaminate.

In the early twentieth century, the Office du travail carried out inquiries into linen seamstresses in all of France and those who sewed artificial flowers predominantly in Paris.[41] These were exhaustive, precise, quantified inquiries, including tables, analyses, and hundreds of extremely interesting monographs, inspired by the methods of Le Play and carried out directly in the field, in areas that were not usually the subjects of investigation. Those who carried out the research sprained their necks in dark corridors; jumped at barking dogs (the seamstresses' frequent companions); and dealt with the mistrust of some of the women, who evaded and resisted their questions or sometimes outright refused to respond, especially when they were asked about their budgets. Most of them, however, were cooperative, even pleased to be asked questions; it was so rare that someone showed interest in their lives. The investigators sometimes quoted them directly, giving us the chance to hear voices that are usually inaudible.

The investigators were not interested in lodgings first and foremost but in standards of living, although they judged the "domicile" where the work was carried out to be of the utmost importance. Though today it has become more rare, at that time it was common practice for a *chambrelan* to work "in the bedroom"—and the *chambrelans* were usually female. They were of interest for reasons of hygiene and economics —for example, how much of their budget was taken up by rent? In Paris and in other big cities, it was a large percentage—sometimes half their annual spending. Since the time spent at work couldn't be reduced and rent was continually on the rise until World War I, these women had to delve into their clothing and even their food budgets to pay it.[42]

Such seamstresses lived in one single room, were more usually found in Paris than in the provinces, and represented 31 percent (135) of the linen seamstresses polled and 25 percent (42) of flower makers—an especially miserable minority whose circumstances were worsened when they weren't alone but had to look after children or elderly parents. Cohabitation was more widespread than is commonly believed. The investigators described the homes in minute detail. They calculated the air cubage, a key concept in those air-obsessed days, and the size of the rooms, less often the surface area. They mentioned the windows, the chimneys, heat and light sources (mostly gas), and the furnishings, always summarily, where there sometimes survived a vestige of a former social status. They were concerned about hygiene and cleanliness more than comfort (which was nonexistent) or decoration (totally absent), noting shredded wallpaper and filthy tiles.

Many factors were at work: family relationships, previous social situations that left splintered bits of furniture and certain habits of cleanliness. Madame A., age sixty, the widow of an employee at Crédit Lyonnais, occupied a mansard room of 600 cubic feet on the sixth floor near Notre-Dame-de-Lorette. "You could not find a better kept home. The red tiles are so clean they shine; the little black stove as well. 'It's my only luxury,'" she said.[43] The neighborhood mattered greatly; better to be a linen seamstress in a good building in Saint-Germain or Notre-Dame-de-Lorette than a flower maker in Belleville, Charonne, or Ménilmontant. The level of skill mattered as well; the seamstresses who made "little flowers"—forget-me-nots, Parma violets, and mimosas for hats and other ornaments—were less qualified than those who specialized in roses (and who suffered from chronic illnesses caused by the aniline dye) and earned less than one franc per day in the season of high demand, which lasted six months at the most. These months of frenzied activity alternated with the "dead seasons," which lasted interminably and are typical of professions that are so dependent on fashion and the market. Each lodging is the end of a particular road, the expression of a social situation, where family and work are indistinguishable.

For a few examples of this sad report on the Belle Époque, take the case of two sisters, ages forty-five and fifty-six, linen seamstresses making aprons for women and chamber valets. For thirty years they lived in one room—stuffed with boxes, with blistering wallpaper—that served as both atelier and bedroom. One iron bed for the two of them, a round table, a sideboard, a sewing machine, a few chairs. Clothing was a problem; when they bought shoes, the sisters had to restrict what they ate.[44]

By comparison, the life of a sample garment maker, a forty-six-year-old widow, seems enviable. During the "rush" period, she worked ceaselessly, looking after neither herself nor the house, seriously limited by the regulations, which stipulated when she could use her noisy machine. She made five francs a day. From time to time, she would go all out and celebrate. For her daughter's engagement and marriage, she paid no attention to how much she spent and went into debt.[45]

The worst off were those who were alone (whether widowed or single) with children. Madame F., a forty-year-old widow, a bodice seamstress, lived with her eleven-year-old daughter in a room of 150 square feet, for which she paid 120 francs a year out of the 500 she earned. The room was dark and low-ceilinged and overlooked a small courtyard; it was located in a tenement with deplorable standards of cleanliness. It could be reached only by ladder. The room was furnished with an iron bed stand, a child's cot, a few chairs, a stove, a table, and a sewing machine.

Worse still was the home of Mademoiselle P., a forty-year-old single mother of an eleven-year-old girl who was anemic and "pre-tubercular." They lived in the rue de Charonne, in a mansarded slum of seventy square feet on the fourth floor, and it had to be accessed by a stairway and then a ladder. Inside: a single bed, a table, two chairs, a stove, a gas lamp. Water and the toilet were in the courtyard. Raised in a convent, where she had learned to sew linen, Mademoiselle P. did the finishing work on men's shirts. She was worn out, denied herself on her daughter's behalf, and sustained herself on slabs of Brie, "the seamstress's pork chop."

Older women, who were slower workers, had a difficult time making ends meet. A seventy-three-year-old linen seamstress, the widow of a postman, lived reclusively with her dog Lili in a big, light, clean room near the Bon Marché. It cost 230 francs a year, which was an exorbitant amount for her to spend, but she insisted. Obsessed by her rent, she would go to get her pay only the day before rent was due. Two incidents disturbed her budget's fragile equilibrium: buying a few sous' worth of poppies and marshmallows and a broken lens in her glasses.

Madame S., sixty-two, paid sixty francs per year for a tiny mansarded room, clean but full of bugs. The bed took up a section under the window; she could not sit up in it. She made a fire where she cooked a soup every three days. A linen seamstress with painful joints, she dreamed of moving to a hospice for the old, just like Madame L., sixty-nine, who had to take care of her sick mother and therefore never learned to sew anything more complicated than little flowers, a job that brought in little money. "She made rose hearts with tendrils." She ate once a day, a meal of eggs and lard. For one hundred francs a year, she rented a room with two windows in Belleville. "To get there, you have to hunch over as you climb a staircase, a real neck-twister." She dreamed of being hospitalized in the old people's home in Brévannes, but she didn't know anyone who could help her apply.[46]

The seamstresses sometimes united in their solitude and would live several to a room. These women's homes long attracted the interest of observers like Villermé (1840), who stressed above all the economic reasons for such female cohabitations. The Office du travail examined a few of these. Madame P., forty-eight, a specialist in little flowers who had been abandoned by her husband, lived in a 280-square-foot room in the Grandes Carrières in the northern part of Paris. It was "very clean and well-kept," but she preferred to work at an atelier: "It's more lively here than in my room. But when you get old no one cares about you." She hoped at least to share the room with a friend to reduce costs. Mademoiselle C., forty-eight and single, lived in a bedsit in the same neighborhood for 3.50 francs a week, on the ground floor above the mouth of a sewer. "This room looks revolting: the floorboards are nauseatingly dirty; the disorder is such that kitchen utensils are next to her garments. Everything has gone quite wrong for this sickly, demoralized, miserable seamstress. When she doesn't have enough money for gas, which is measured in half-litres, she buys candles. 'My rent is killing me,'" she said. Moving in with Madame P. was a big relief.[47]

These rooms housed the deepest miseries. And yet the women who lived in them were not homeless; they were disgusted by vagabonds and the life of the street, which was so dangerous for women. They held on to their rooms, which served as both refuges and places of work. They clung to them like lifelines.

A porcelain painter from Limoges was in a better situation, and in 1903 the Société d'économie sociale devoted a celebratory monograph to this model worker, who was saved by the paternalistic union and by working at home. A widow of fifty-seven, she shared a large room of 480 square

feet with her three daughters (ages thirty-four, thirty, and twenty-two). It
served them in all possible ways—they worked there; they ate there around
a folding table (more usually they would lunch quickly, without sitting
down); and they slept there, in two large wooden beds. It contained a walnut table, a porcelain mantelpiece, photos, little cups, a sewing machine, a
stove, a large armchair for the mother, and a red cushion for the cat. (Seamstresses loved having pets.) Under the portrait of a friend stood a chest of
drawers that held the family's few luxuries: a pendulum clock, knickknacks,
a statuette of the Virgin, a rosary from Lourdes, and mementoes of first
communions.[48] From an investigator's moral perspective, this room was a
model of all the virtues.

Chambre Close

Did prostitutes have their own bedrooms? No. They were lucky to have a
bed! In 1811 an ordinance that passed in Paris specified that "under no circumstance can the same bed be used by two women at the same time." The
state wanted to be sure "that each woman would have her own bedroom
entirely separated from the others; [these] did not formerly exist and gave
rise to innumerable disturbances."[49] Separate beds, separate bedrooms, furnished with as much linen and water as needed for minimal hygiene: this, at
least, was Dr. Alexandre Parent-Duchatelet's wish.

In 1836 Paris, the site of his famous investigation, Parent-Duchatelet
observed three kinds of prostitutes. One was a "free" category, "who owned
her own furniture, paid taxes, and, judging from appearances, differs not at
all from other members of society." These were sex workers, more or less
independent, free from all constraints and networks, as the call girls of today
see themselves. This residue of a more widespread form of prostitution,
more integrated into the city, was at that time in decline. Next came another
set of unregistered girls—part-time workers, servants, seamstresses, even
housecleaners—who wanted to make a little extra money on the side. They
had recourse to boutiques and mezzanines, where they displayed themselves in windows in spite of the curtains required by the police. In the *maisons de tolérance* (licensed brothels) they rented rooms that were sometimes

very expensive, costing between three and ten francs per day. For this price, they received a clean bed, a mirror, and a sofa. An advantage of this arrangement was that they didn't have to declare their earnings, could choose the clients they liked, and could change lodgings when they wanted to.

Parent-Duchatelet had no patience for these clandestine sex workers, these *habituées* of the *maisons de passe* (low-class hotels renting rooms by the hour), who escaped the control of the sanitation police and spread syphilis as well as other sexually transmittable diseases. In the eyes of Parent-Duchatelet, the great regulator who advocated a limited, well-defined network of *maisons de tolérance* (*maisons closes* is a twentieth-century term), these freelancers were a plague.[50] He wanted a system of *dames de maisons,* who would be licensed by the police and would keep an eye on the girls, who would be assigned special cards allowing them to be "visited." These girls would even enjoy a certain luxury in their situation, which would be very attractive to some, dazzled by the gilding and the services they enjoyed—they wouldn't even have to make their beds. This appearance of luxury quickly dissipated, judging from the instability of the workforce, which quickly became aware of the ways in which it was being exploited.

Colonial prostitution, the third kind mentioned by Parent-Duchatelet, was the worst example. Social and ethnic hierarchies combined to construct a system that culminated in constraint and imprisonment. We are not speaking here of *maisons tolérées* but truly *maisons closes,* closed off, found in red-light districts like the famous Bousbir in Casablanca, which was built to serve the "needs" of a military clientele.[51] Christelle Taraud has traced the origins of this kind of prostitution, while Germaine Aziz has examined the mechanisms in an exceptional autobiographical narrative titled *Les Chambres closes.*[52] An impoverished Jewish orphan who was sold at a bordello in Bône in 1943, where she was raped, Aziz was subsequently caught in a prostitution ring that brought her from one establishment to another in colonial North Africa. Here she is at the Chat Noir in Bône: "The room has no windows. It is lit by an electric lightbulb filthy with fly dirt. A sink, an enamel bidet—the first I'd ever seen—an armoire, a chair." She found minimal decor everywhere, at the Lune Rousse in Philippeville and even at the more upscale Sofa in Algiers. The room was not only the site where exhausting work was carried out, but also a prison described from within. "In the evening, the room smelled of sperm, sweat, dirty feet. The scent of it stuck to my skin." Getting out was very difficult, even dangerous. "Sometimes when I had had enough, I would barricade myself in the bedroom, push the bed and the armoire against the door, and stay there, crouched in a corner, like a trapped animal, imprisoned in this stuffy room, without light, without air, where sometimes the smell of stale sperm was so strong it made me nauseous. It was an odor that would haunt me for years."[53] She would finally manage to escape, though the attempt visited violence and bullying of all kinds.

The bedroom matters somewhat less in this field of hastened sexual encounters, where it was important to "show off." However, over the course of the century, a desire for refinement and comfort was born. Middle-class men abandoned bordellos, which were too down-at-heel, leaving them to soldiers and workers and preferring the more attractive "assignation houses," which gave them the illusion of carnal intimacy.[54] The setting, the sexual accessories, the satisfaction of the most varied fantasies became even more important in a more personalized atmosphere.

Courtesans and Kept Women

It became fashionable to keep a dancer or an actress, to purchase her furniture and install her in a flat somewhere in order to at least partially enjoy her charms. One had to be very wealthy to buy oneself a monopoly on such a woman, as did Zola's Count Muffat for Nana or, on a different scale, Proust's Charles Swann for Odette de Crécy, who winds up marrying him. The homes of actresses and demimondaines fascinated novelists and the general public. In *Nana,* Zola looks askance at the bedroom and the bed. Nana's first apartment, when she is a star at the Variétés, has "a garish luxury, golden chairs and console tables . . . the odds and ends of a secondhand dealer." But Nana cultivates her bedroom. "The bedroom and the toilet cabinet were the only two rooms that the neighborhood decorator had seen to"; the cabinet especially was "the most elegant room"; she received visitors there in its patchouli-scented comfort. When she becomes Muffat's official mistress, she transforms into a "chic woman" who sets the fashion for all of Paris. She moves to an *hôtel particulier* on the Avenue de Villiers, and she transforms it top to bottom "without spoiling it too much," having domesticated her penchants, which still, however, shape her taste. Most of the time, she neglects the ceremonial apartments on the ground floor to live on the second, where she keeps three little rooms: a bedroom, cabinet, and salon.

> She had redone the bedroom twice already, the first time in mauve satin, the second in lace over blue silk, and she still wasn't satisfied; she found it bland and continued to seek out new patterns and colors. On the elaborately upholstered bed, which was as low as a sofa, there were twenty thousand francs' worth of *point de Venise* lace. The furniture was lacquered blue and white under designs in silver filigree, and everywhere lay such numbers of white bearskins that they hid the carpet. This was a luxurious caprice on Nana's part, as she had never yet been able to break herself of the habit of sitting on the ground to remove her stockings.[55]

The little salon in pale pink silk recalls the voluptuous sofas of the seraglio. The door to the toilet cabinet, where the scent of violet had replaced patchouli, was almost always open and allowed a glimpse of the white marble bathtub. But when she falls in love, Nana returns to simplicity: "She dreamt of a light, pretty room, returning to the ideals of her former life as a florist, when her highest ambition was to have a rosewood cupboard with a plate-glass door and a bed hung with blue reps."[56] It's a nice dream for a *grisette* who has become unreachable: to have a room of her own, like Mimi Pinson.[57] Nana dies of smallpox, alone, in a room at the Grand Hotel, which Henry Céard, the famous gallant, had described for the author in some detail.[58]

    The more refined snobbery of Odette de Crécy reflects the changing fashion. The Louis XVI style succeeds the fad for Orientalism, itself to be succeeded by the lacquered white Art Deco movement. Toward 1890, Odette, now Madame Swann, has downgraded to "hideous" what she called "chic" only a few years earlier. "In the room where she was most often found . . . she was surrounded by Saxe porcelain. . . . She was afraid for it, more than for her little Chinamen or vases of long ago, that it wouldn't survive the clumsy touch of her servants."[59] She would henceforth prefer over her Japanese dressing gowns the light, frothy silk of her Watteau peignoirs, which symbolized a physical hygiene that (as she put it) was more important to her than contemplating the Mona Lisa.

The world of gallantry has a strict hierarchy, and "kept women" have nothing to do with the prostitutes in the bordellos—especially when they are stars, free to choose their male companions like their interior decor. Sarah Bernhardt's bedrooms were the subject of fantasies—the animal skin tapestries, the black satin padding, the human skeleton, the fake coffin, the enormous four-poster bed buried under blankets bordered with swans. The actress Cécile Sorel's baroque featherbed was also much admired.[60]

Living off sex seemed, in short, to make more sense than living for it. The heroine of Zola's *La Curée*, Renée, is a crazed lover, a hysteric, according to the psychiatry of the day, greedy for pleasure, a desire that reinforced a perverse view of her quasi-incestuous relationship with her stepson. In Zola's eyes—that virtuous, sensual Republican—she incarnates the depravity and degeneration of the business class, reveling in the orgiastic luxury of the winter garden, a "hellish passion, out of Dante." Renée's apartment is "a nest of silk and lace, a marvel of coquettish luxury." Zola describes the bedroom and cabinet at length—the debauchery of fabrics, soft colors and heady odors, the theater of love whose altar is the bed. "A large pink-and-gray bed, whose woodwork was hidden beneath padding and upholstery and whose head stood against the wall, filled at least half the room with its flow of drapery, its lace, and its silk figures with bouquets falling from the ceiling to the carpet. It was like a woman's dress, rounded and slashed and decked with puffs and bows and flounces; and the large curtain, swelling out like a skirt, brought to mind some tall, amorous girl, leaning over, swooning, almost falling back on the pillows." The bed, "this monument whose devout ampleness recalled a chapel decorated for some festival," a sanctuary for sex, cast the whole room in semi-darkness. "The bed seemed to stretch out till the whole room became one immense bed," saturated with the imprint—the shape, the warmth, the smell—of Renée's body.[61] It is assuredly one of the most beautiful beds in literature, to which we might add the work of Courbet or Manet's *Olympia* to round out the exquisite pleasures imagined by men.

Her Own Room

The female desire for a room of one's own resounds across the stages of life. Teenagers don't want to share rooms with their sisters, who keep different hours.[62] A maturing young woman wants to leave the family nest. Simone de Beauvoir writes of the joy she felt when she could rent a room at her grandmother's, near Denfert-Rochereau, after passing the *agrégation* in September 1929: "Finally I was at home when I was home!" She transformed the living room into a bedroom, inspired by something she saw in a magazine, *Mon Journal,* which described exactly what she needed: a divan, a table, shelving along the walls; she would long remain faithful to a minimalist interior. She didn't care much for decoration, and above all she valued her freedom. "All I needed to feel fulfilled was to be able to close my door."[63]

Migrant workers, in the country or abroad, needed a room in the city to be able to enter the workforce, the fashion industry in the nineteenth century, administrative services in the twentieth. They were all candidates for the urban sixth-floor maids' rooms. Jeanne Bouvier moved to Paris in 1879 to escape the provincial fate of a mill worker, having worked as such in Isère since she was eleven years old. She knew the maids' rooms well, how there was no way of making a fire or cooking. "Rooms with a chimney were not within my purse's reach." When she earned more in a sewing studio, she decided to buy some furniture. She bought a bed on layaway and could finally build a fire in her hearth, while dreaming of a country home for her twilight years.[64] Marguerite Audoux left her native Sologne, where she was a shepherdess, went up to Paris, and worked in various studios before settling in the one she described in her second novel. Single young female workers who were susceptible to being seduced, abandoned, and left to look after the children also had an intimate knowledge of the attics. Audoux's Sandrine, a young seamstress with tuberculosis, had a room that "was so

small that the bed took up the entire length of it on one side. The other side
was taken up by a table and two chairs; it would have been difficult to sit
down in the space between them. The floorboards were coming up everywhere, but what really stood out in the room were the photographs of children."[65] This was a way of making this space in the city a woman's own.

"Where we live, it's not just a room," say contemporary female migrants from Central Europe and North Africa, whose testimonies were collected by Perla Serfaty-Garzon at the beginning of this century. "It's a shell,"
a "refuge," a beacon with a view of the rooftops of Paris. In time of upheaval,
the room becomes a dwelling for these women in exile. Furniture (nonexistent) counts for less than the objects that reconstitute a familiar universe—
photographs of their loved ones. "I had a room of my own and I started
decorating it. . . . I could leave things there. It was really my home."[66] To
open up her trunk or her cardboard box, unpack her things, decorate the
walls, learn the view of the city—this is to take the time to mark her territory,
to catch her breath during this "in between" moment before moving on
with her life and her goals.

How can one write without a minimum of money and a room of one's
own? Virginia Woolf asked in her magnificent text of that name. Under the
pretext of giving a talk on women and fiction at Oxbridge (a frequent con-
traction of "Oxford" and "Cambridge"), she asks about the role that wom-
en's silence has played in history and what kept them from making art.
What happened to Shakespeare's sister? Why did she not write? Could she
have if she wanted to? Did sixteenth-century women have their own bedrooms? What did they do there? Woolf thinks of "the doors that have been
shut upon women" and their diverse stories, which they alone can tell, as
she herself tried to do in a number of her novels.[67] To write these stories,
they need at least a small income and a room of their own. Virginia Woolf
and her husband, Leonard Woolf, each had their own bedroom, according
to common British practice in well-off families. One day, receiving the
Webbs at Hogarth House, she was horrified by Beatrice's brazenness: "To
my horror, in came Mrs. W[ebb] early next morning to say Goodbye, &
perched in all her long impersonality on the edge of my bed, looking past
my stockings drawers & pot."[68]

Here is Christine de Pisan (1364–1430) in the early fifteenth century, in her *studiolo,* which resembles the bedroom of the Annunciation; but she is alone, writing. After her husband's death, she retired from the world. "Willingly I am alone / For the mourning that I must silence / before people, gives me sorrow / and to complain to myself / and to restore a day of joy / I put myself willingly / inside a little study."[69] This is how she has herself depicted in the miniatures that decorate her writings. With one stroke she appropriates the clerk's masculine pose.

Then there is reading, which for so long was stingily meted out to women, judged to be contrary to their purpose and dangerous for their imaginations. The female reader is a favorite theme with painters, who associate it with eroticism because it is carried out on a divan or a bed.[70] For many women, as late as the beginning of the twentieth century, reading was a stolen pleasure, practiced semi-secretly in bed, in the evening, by the light of a rationed candle or gaslight.[71] Girls received less of an education than boys, so they had to claim knowledge for themselves, gleaning it from a personal store of books and newspapers, in a concerted autodidactic effort that became possible after the invention of the printing press made books readily available; women's thirst for knowledge increased during the Renaissance. Gabrielle Suchon (1632–1703), a former nun from Burgundy (once she left the convent she continued to cover her head with a veil), spoke of the "school of the bedchamber." That is where she taught herself Latin, the language of the clergy, which was off limits to women, and composed the treatises that made her the ancestor of female philosophers.[72]

Writing was an even more delicate task. Female authors had difficulty conquering their public and private spaces and carving out for themselves the privacy they needed to write in the midst of the family and the home.[73] Edith Wharton wrote in bed, the only place where she felt comfortable, corset off, body free; she filled up pages while a secretary gathered them to type them up.[74] Emily Dickinson never left her father's home. One day, she took her niece Martha to her bedroom and closed the door. "Marty, here's freedom," she told her. This is a familiar gesture to Jane Austen's heroines, always ready to withdraw, in search of an interior life. George Sand was passionate about nocturnal writing. When her lovers went to sleep, in the silent house she was free to give rein to her desires. The time belonged to her; she stole it from no one. The night was her study.

Simone de Beauvoir's Bedrooms

In the rooms she rented, Simone de Beauvoir made sure that there was a writing table present. In Marseille: "This isn't the bedroom of my dreams—a massive bed, chairs, and an armoire—but I thought the large table would be convenient to work at."[75] Like Antoine Roquentin in Sartre's *Nausea* (whom she used as a model), she didn't care for cozy interiors. In Rouen, she left a "delicately furnished room, where the windows opened up onto the silence of a large garden." She preferred the Hôtel La Rochefoucauld, "where I could hear the reassuring whistle of the trains."[76] In Paris, she developed the habit of working in cafés, like Sartre. "I never worked in my bedroom, but in a booth at the back of a café." Nevertheless, her idea of home was different from his and was partly dictated by the restrictions of wartime. In the various hotels where she stayed—the Mistral, the Louisiane on the rue de Seine, the Chaplain—she sought a room with a kitchenette where she could feed the "family" (Olga, Bost, Wanda, a few others) that had grown up around Sartre and herself. She was proud when she could make the most of the meager rations they were allocated or could rustle up here and there. "I did not share the condition of the housewife, but I had an inkling of their joys."[77] Sometimes she envied the housewives. She had long dreamed of a "small apartment that I would arrange to my taste. I was not particularly interested in playing the bohemian."[78] Near Lyons-la-Fôret she rented a cottage that fulfilled all her girlhood dreams. "I offered her what she had often dreamed of, in many forms: a little house of her own." But she had neither time nor money, and living in a hotel released her from all obligations. "I had Paris, its streets, its squares, its cafés." In 1945–1946, Sartre and de Beauvoir went to live in two separate rooms at the Hôtel de la Louisiane. Sartre's room was a shambles. "In his room there was a slow daily accumulation of dirty dishes, old papers, and books; you could barely walk in there."[79] Moving in with his mother in 1946 saved Jean-Paul from his domestic concerns. The days of writing in cafés were over for this couple who had become too famous to sit there in peace.

Simone left the hubbub of the Café du Flore and from then on chose to write in her room. "For three weeks I have not left my room. . . . It's both restful and productive."[80] However, she was growing tired of it. "I grew tired of living in hotels; I was too exposed there to journalists and their indiscretions." She was too well known; public spaces no longer offered the anonymity she sought. In the autumn of 1948 she moved into a furnished room in the rue de la Bûcherie, and she did it up a bit: "I hung red curtains on the windows, bought bronze floor lamps created from designs by Giacometti by his brother; I hung things I've brought back from my travels all around the walls and from the enormous central ceiling beam.[81] From her window, she could see the Seine and Notre-Dame. "My way of life had changed. I stayed at home quite often. This word was invested with new meaning. For a long time, I had owned nothing, no furniture, no wardrobe." Now her room was filling with exotic clothing and "worthless objects that were precious to me" brought back from her wanderings. She bought herself a phonograph, began collecting records, and would spend evenings with Sartre listening to music. "I liked to work at the window; the blue sky framed by the red curtains looked like something out of Bérard."[82] She was ready for a "room of one's own." In 1952, she fell in love with Claude Lanzmann. He described the "one room flat, entirely upholstered in red, which she occupied on the last floor of 11, rue de la Bûcherie."[83] It was the beginning of a long relationship: "We lived together as lovers from 1952 to 1959. We even managed to live for two years in one room of 270 square feet and were . . . legitimately proud of the way we got on."[84] In 1955, the success of *The Mandarins* (which was a best seller and won the Prix Goncourt) allowed de Beauvoir to buy a little apartment in the Rue Schœlcher, where she would live until her death in 1986. In this "studio" (as she called it), weighed down with memories, she was happy to receive the "family," which had grown and changed, on the "yellow divan," which the novelist Claire Etcherelli has described, as well as Sartre, who was often ill. The *Force of Circumstance* had quietly imposed itself.

Do women writers today have offices less often than men? They are more willing to write in their bedrooms. According to a 1982 study, which is already out of date and not very rigorous, it appears that women do prefer to write in bed, like Françoise Sagan, Anna de Noailles, and Colette, who at the end of her life no longer left her *radeau lit* (raft bed); propped up on her pillows, in her "lofty solitude," she wrote on a table designed for use in bed that had been given to her by the Princesse de Polignac.[85] Marie Cardinal could work only "lying down . . . just about anywhere: in hotel rooms, in a sleeping bag." She never wanted to settle in. Danièle Sallenave has sung the praises of the bed most eloquently, turning to the example of illustrious predecessors: Joubert, Pushkin, Proust. "It would seem one can only write well in bed. . . . For the bed is a place like no other. While at one time it was a place of birth, of suffering, and of death, today it is still the site of our dreams and our pleasures. This is not insignificant. The walls of the bedroom can absorb our dreams, its ceiling like that of the pyramids, bricked up from the outside and turned entirely toward its dazzling interior."[86] The body of the writer, whether male or female, is a suffering body that is soothed by the sheets.

Leaving the Room

To the soft folds of the bed, Simone de Beauvoir preferred the solidity of the table. She refused to be weighed down by domesticity and the alienation of the housewife. This is one of the central themes of *The Second Sex*. During a trip to Tunisia, in a troglodyte village, she saw an "underground cave where four women squatted," four wives of varying age, who were joined by a superior "young man dressed in white [. . .] smiling, solar." The four women only went out at night, "silent and veiled." In "this dark lair, the kingdom of immanence, matrix and tomb," de Beauvoir saw a symbol for the female condition.[87] She was disturbed to see her young female colleagues play the provincial housewife with an ardor that approached alienation.

Above all, this indefatigable walker loved the fresh air and hikes in the Alps or in Provence, which she walked from top to bottom, backpack and all. These peregrinations gave her a feeling of happiness that infuses a certain lightness into *The Coming of Age*. A number of women, especially during the nineteenth century, were emancipated by traveling, eager to explore a world that had been closed to them for so long. George Sand, an urban *flâneuse,* rustic rider, nature walker, and European explorer celebrated the virtues of a "path without a master" and saw birds as a kind of spirit animal. "As long as there is space before us, there will be hope," and "Life is a road whose destination is life."[88] Such thoughts didn't prevent Sand from enjoying the contentments of life at Nohant, her refuge and "paradise" or from conferring great importance on her real and imagined bedrooms.

Contemporary feminists vigorously contested the idea of enclosure as being intrinsic to women's "nature." They claimed the practice of traveling and nomadism as a philosophy and a way of life.[89] Otherwise, there was always the option of escape through daydreaming, of perching by the window like Emma Bovary. "Emma was leaning on her elbows at her window (she would often sit there: a window, in the country, takes the place of the theater or a public walk)."[90] She would travel through the mind, like all recluses. Flaubert wrote to Mademoiselle Leroyer de Chantepie: "Widen your horizons and you will breathe more easily. If you were a man and were twenty years old, I would tell you to set off on a tour of the world. Well! take a tour of the world from your bedchamber."[91] There are no limits to the imagination.

A woman's bedroom is a balcony on the world.

Hotel Rooms

FOR THE CONTEMPORARY traveler, the hotel room is the basic requirement for a good trip. In it one expects to find a place to retreat from the world, quiet and a comfortable bed, functional heat or air conditioning, a table for writing, gentle lighting, closets and drawers for clothes, and, above all, a private bathroom and toilet. The tourist escaping to the country will appreciate a nice view rather than a window on the courtyard; the aesthete, the old wood of provincial furniture; the loner, sweet privacy and security; the lovers, the haven of a deep bed, the protective intimacy of the walls and the curtains; the businessman, the convenience of services and a minimal guarantee of comfort. Hotel chains compete vigorously to offer levels of comfort in accord with their rating and cost.

From one side of the planet to the other, the traveler knows what he may expect; for those who travel for work this uniformity is both reassuring and tiresome. They run the risk of feeling disoriented or nauseatingly satiated. The modern hotel room negates originality.[1] It strives to create the opposite of adventure. Travelers turn up with their bags, and the hotel provides the wifi, bolstering this feeling of an identical anywhere.

This was not always the case. The hotel is one example of a long history of modes of hospitality open to travelers, from caravanserais to furnished rooms to palaces, as well as inns, the history of which Daniel Roche has traced from the Middle Ages to the nineteenth century, while Catherine Bertho-Lavenir has looked at their contemporary incarnations.[2] The hotel depends on the vagaries of travel and modes of transportation yet has always provided a break from them. The inn was linked to the horse and the hotel to the railroad, just as the motel depends on the road and the automobile. Technical progress creates its comfort and individual requests shape its form. Most of a hotel's occupants are merely passing through. In the past, they might stay for longer periods of time, the poor by necessity and the rich by choice. The proliferation of facilities reflects the diversification of needs.

Compared with earlier forms of hospitality, the hotel room offers an unheard of level of luxury. Merchants or pilgrims hoped only for a place to keep their horses and a bed—or even a place in someone else's bed. The inn was a site for encounter, seduction, and intrigue; it represents all the dangers—if not mortal, then financial. It has long attracted a bad reputation, in frequent evidence throughout literature. For example, in the mid-nineteenth century, the *Livre d'or des métiers*—mass-produced, with illustrations— demonstrated the staying power of the threat of the *classes dangereuses.* Through page after page of picturesque images, vagabonds, bohemians, derelicts, and rogues of all sorts haunt the "everyday refuge of those contemptible races, the foul gathering place of outcasts," "some of the most notorious places of all time, ever-disgusting hovels."[3] Tragic news events like the story of the Auberge des Adrets, which were endlessly retold in the *feuilletons,* contributed to this dark period for inns. They needed time to become respectable, comfortable, even "charming." It took a steady growth in the inflow of guests and the refinement of their sensibilities, the distillation of which can be found in the hotel room. Starting in the seventeenth century but especially during the economic growth of the eighteenth century, when the market and exchanges flourished, an ever increasing number of travelers began to demonstrate new demands and aversions. The description of the inn becomes a common literary genre. In novels from Marivaux to Fielding to Diderot it was the crossroads of possibility. Among the recurrent themes, we find a contrast between the frequent quality of the food at French inns and the appalling mediocrity of the rooms, to which English travelers (whose industrial progress made them more demanding) were especially sensitive.

"Miserable Holes"

Arthur Young described the hotel industry on the eve of the French Revolution in his series of reports, *Voyages en France.* In reality, Young would stay in a hotel only if there were no better option available, preferring to

enjoy the hospitality of his many correspondents. He distinguished between hotels—urban and well equipped, though unequally so—and country inns, which could be disappointing, even revolting, most often "awful,
dangerous holes," essentially pigsties. The Barque in Cherbourg is "little
better than a hog sty." In Aubenas, its equivalent was "purgatory for one of
my pigs." In Aubagne, the inn (which nevertheless had a good reputation)
was just a "miserable hole" in which "I have one of the best rooms, without
glass to the windows." He declared the Croix Blanche in Saint-Girons, in
the Ariège, to be "the most execrable receptacle of filth, vermin, impudence,
and imposition that ever exercised the patience or wounded the feelings of
a traveler. . . . I laid, not rested, in a chamber over a stable, whose effluviæ
through the broken floor were the least offensive of the perfumes afforded
by this hideous place." The inns of the Languedoc were no better. A disciple of Adam Smith, Young attributes this to the lack of traffic in the region.
He has a litany of complaints about the rooms: dirt, vermin, bad smells,
noise, a lack of water for washing or bells to ring for a servant, so one would
have to "bray for the girl to come"; he also notes the squalor: "the necessary
houses [are] temples of abomination." The rooms are badly arranged and
have beds crammed into them, sometimes up to four to a room. The walls
are covered with several layers of paper or old tapestries, which become
nests for mites and spiders; at best, they are lime-washed. The doors and
windows close badly; it is cold in the drafts. People make a habit of spitting
in the stairwell, which disgusts Young, especially as the premises are rarely
cleaned: "Mops, brooms, and scrubbing-brushes are not in the catalogue of
the necessaries of a French inn."[4] Young does, however, praise the widespread use of the bidet, one in every room, "as universally in every apartment, as a basin to wash your hands, which is a trait of personal cleanliness"
(and no doubt a contraceptive practice?), a habit that he wished were practiced more often in England.[5] The bedding is generally of good quality, and
he appreciates that the sheets have not been dried before the fire, as they are
in England.

Of course, urban hotels (only they merited this name) were more luxurious, especially in the north and the east, where they were much more advanced than in the backward Midi. There were excellent hotels, often with

aristocratic names, in the cities—for example, in Nice (the Hotel des Quatre Nations), in Nîmes (the Hotel du Louvre), in Rouen (the Hotel Royal), or in Nantes (the Hotel Henri IV). At this last hotel, rooms or apartments could be rented that included a "reading room." This just had one drawback: a lack of funds or insolvency meant people would shut themselves away in their rooms, and it bothered the chatty Englishman. "We are so unaccustomed in England to live in our bedchambers that it is at first awkward in France to find that people live nowhere else. At all the inns I have been in, it has been always in bedrooms." But the same is true in private homes—for example, at the home of the Duc de La Rochefoucauld, whom Young visited: "Here I found that everybody, let his rank be what it may, lives in his bedchamber."[6] He attributes this restrained sociability to French parsimoniousness. In the late eighteenth century and for a long time thereafter, the French bedroom was a *ruelle*, a place for receiving visitors, while the English bedroom was becoming more specifically meant for retiring and sleeping. The eye of the traveler picked up these differences in social mores from the contrasting uses of the hotel room.

Stendhal: A Room with a View

Forty years later, in spite of the political upheaval, the hotel industry hadn't changed much. Stendhal hiked through France as a "tourist," in search of national treasures; he was industrious by profession and artistic by taste but also a keen observer of the transformations that were taking place. "This is why I'm keeping this journal. . . . It is because France is changing so quickly that I dare write it."[7] The journal bears witness to the state of the country, whose hotel rooms nevertheless indicate a certain backwardness.

In his journal, he is vehemently angered by hotels' refusal to modernize. As a city dweller, thoroughly Parisian, Stendhal talks more about hotels than inns. He detests the provinces, especially in the middle of the country (he never visited George Sand at Nohant). Bourges, a petty little burg, is redeemed only by its sublime cathedral. At the Boeuf Couronné in the rue Bourbonnoux, he occupies "a room that is terrible to see . . . where a fat servant handed me a stinking candle in a dirty candelabra; I am writing this on a chest of drawers." In this setting, he is served "such a disgusting dinner that in order not to be sick I was obliged to ask for some Champagne," a not disagreeable medicine. Luckily, it is summer, without which "the vile little chimney by the window" would barely have warmed the room. In Tours, a few days later, at the Grand Hotel de la Caille, he is dying of hunger and freezing. He has a difficult time obtaining hot water. "I nearly broke all the bells, I banged like an Englishman, I asked for a fire, I was prepared one—which is to say my room was filled with smoke—and an hour and a half after I'd asked for the hot water, I was able to make some tea." This is what Young (who had no bell) could obtain only "by braying after the girl."

Stendhal deplored the fake luxury of damasked fabrics and the absence of a *cousinière* (mosquito net); at the otherwise well-reputed Hotel de Jouvence in Lyon, he is told by a valet that there aren't any. No one ever asks for them. The lack of tables, the noise, and especially the bad quality of "provincial candles," which requires him to travel with his own, impedes his reading and writing; he is repelled by the communal meals and small-minded conversation. "For a traveler to read instead of to look is no doubt a failure; but what else is one to do with those moments when the pettiness of provincial life makes one sick?" Unlike Young, Stendhal voluntarily takes refuge in his bedchamber and wishes it were even more welcoming, even more *snug*, to use his word; Stendhal was a devoted collector of books in English.

When we spend more time in a room, we begin to attach more importance to the exterior, the location, the "view." Stendhal is very attentive to these. In Grenoble, at the Hotel des Trois Dauphins, where Napoleon stayed on his return from Elba, his window gave onto a "sublime drive of chestnut trees," lit by the emperor's crepuscular recollections—the landscape of memory. In Nantes, it opened on the Place Graslin, "a pretty little square that would be remarkable even in Paris." In Saint-Malo, unhappy with his room on "an impossible street," he moves to another one on the third floor, "from which there is an impressive view over the rampart. I grew drunk on this view, and then I read half the book I'd just bought." In Honfleur, he chooses "the only room in the inn that faces directly onto the sea," a perfect witness for the "desire for the coast," which Alain Corbin has described.[8] In Le

Havre, at the Hotel de l'Amirauté, "from a beautiful room on the second floor
. . . that is happily empty," Stendhal follows the movement of the tugboats,
the sailboats, the steamboats, peering through his lorgnette. He describes in
great detail—like his contemporary, J. M. W. Turner—the "yellow-brown
smoke" that invades the air: "The enormous clouds of smoke mingle with
the bursts of white steam that stream and whistle from the machine valves.
The profound darkness created by the coal smoke reminded me of London,
and to be honest this pleased me, at a moment when I was saturated with the
petty meanness of bourgeois France. All this activity pleased me, and in this
sense Le Havre is the truest image of England that France can offer."[9] Sometimes the copy is far inferior to the model: Liverpool was completing 150
buildings a day, and Le Havre 12–15! The "view" of the countryside framed
by the hotel window, or, more fleetingly, by the window of a train compartment, became a form of appropriation or even representation of the world.
The "beautiful view," here is of commercial industry and its heady smoke, a
synonym for the progress and circulation of goods that was so typical of England in the view of Stendhal, simultaneously Saint-Simonian and interested
observer. Would he remember this moment, so difficult to capture in all its
movement and activity? "We only remember in detail the landscapes that
have bored us a little."[10] The photographer's lens would soon make this
possible.

The "Hygienic Room"

It became more important to have a "good" room than a "beautiful" one.
The former combined both interior and exterior qualities. It had to be a
pleasant place to spend time and offer a satisfactory layout, with a convenient
location downtown (and after 1850, it had to be near the train station). It must
provide privacy and protection but not be too cut off from the world. By the
middle of the nineteenth century, the development of commerce and tourism
had raised standards of comfort and hygiene in the hotel industry, which was
becoming more organized and industrialized. Certain tourist guidebooks
(for example, *Joanne* and then the *Michelin Guide*), organizations like the
Touring Club (founded in 1900), and the Automobile Club contributed to

the higher standards by asking tourists to fill in questionnaires and through the assignment of rankings and distinctions (stars).[11]

There was a great deal to do. The *Joanne* guide of 1861 complained that certain regions, "for lack of decent hotels," remained totally inaccessible "to women who would like to visit them." The railway companies and their "travelers' hotels," necessary auxiliaries to train stations, laid out the first rules. Beginning in 1905–1906, the Touring Club had a systematic policy that was applied by the grand Parisian hotels. Inaccessible to most tourists, the palaces created an attractive ideal. The Touring Club established a model of the "hygienic room" and showed a prototype of it at the 1905 World's Fair. Its watchwords were order, simplicity, and cleanliness, and it obeyed Pasteur's standards: glazed wallpapered or gloss-painted walls that made it easy to clean (once a year), beds on raised legs to make it easier to sweep beneath, quilts, bedspreads, and thick curtains without pompoms or frills. Water must be available and plentiful. A sufficient number of English "commodities" (at least one per floor) should have porcelain fixtures.[12] Dust and microbes were to be hunted down and chased out by regular cleaning and disinfecting.

These efforts were at first concentrated in the big cities. But the Touring Club went after deepest provincial France, an impoverished region. Even before 1915, the small elite who drove motorcars had begun exploring it; in 1907, the club targeted this group with a promotion of "pretty" country inns, boasting "available clean beds, white sheets, light walls, clear window panes, doors that close properly, abundant water, plenty of light. Order, simplicity, cleanliness—that's all it takes for [a] happy room, a room in which [one] can breathe, to become a palace." It was "a ferociously bucolic model," notes Catherine Bertho-Lavenir, who emphasizes the normative and discriminating power of this hygienic ideology; travelers became its agents by responding to the questionnaires inserted into their guidebooks, which asked them to update prices in effect and reflect on the quality of services offered.[13] This was one of the first forms of organized consumer power.

A bit later, around 1920, the Automobile Club of France started a bedroom and bathroom competition that was significant for the way it brought together these new expectations. There were three main categories on the program: (A) first-class hotels in large cities or resorts, (B) second-class hotels for secondary cities, and (C) inns. Rooms were grouped according to size (400 square feet for category A and 150 for category C), the presence of private water closets, and the organization of "hydrotherapeutic installations." Hot running water was necessary for category A and optional for category B, while the inns (category C) were required to have "a fixed or mobile toilet, whether or not connected to the water system."[14] Only the first-class hotels had electric lighting and "steam" heating. The others were lit with alcohol, and the heating sources were not specified. The illustrations show fairly dismal rooms but vast, well-equipped toilets, these having become a central criterion of comfort.

   In this way, hotels diversified according to place and function: travelers' hotels near the stations, run by railway companies; resort hotels, like the Grand Hôtel de Balbec or, as late as the 1950s, Monsieur Hulot's Hôtel de la Plage, were legendary figures; spa hotels or pilgrimage city hotels (see the Hôtel des Apparitions in Zola's *Lourdes*); hotels for people just passing through or that rented by the hour.[15] They obeyed different criteria and did not offer the same standard of room or service. There was an infinite distance between the grand hotels and the bedsits, which housed often miserable migrants of all origins. The lodging is a social marker that reached its apogee in the hotel. An entire world separates the palace from the furnished room.

Palaces

The English word "palace" began to stand in for the *palais* around 1905 and soon embodied a traveler's heaven on earth, like the luxury ocean liner, a symbol of luxury in the twentieth-century European imaginary. Jean d'Ormesson has sung its praises: "Palaces! Houses of dreams for those from elsewhere, halfway houses for millionaires, layovers on the road of *luxe, calme, et volupté*." They incarnate "the place where poetry meets money . . . where beauty can be found in the tumult of the universe." The palace is a dream machine, always unique, famous for its founders and its clientele, its pomp and its drama (deaths, crimes, suicides, scandals), a "world of extravagance and dark passion." It could never belong to a "chain," as that would erase its singularity, the connotation of these famous names: the Carlton, the Ritz, the Grand Hôtel. Its desire for distinction indicates a nostalgia for an aristocratic age that began to decline in the 1880s (in Balbec, Proust's Madame de Villeparisis and the Baron de Charlus maintain the illusion) and was totally dead a century later, making it all the more alluring to d'Ormesson. There you can catch the scent of "a sort of sweetness in living, already chilled by death; a maximalism that was still elegant; an age that did not want to die but was already struck by the illness that would carry it off" and that was beginning to gnaw at it.[16]

Born of history and the market, the palace is a hybrid. It takes up residence in the noble homes of the eighteenth century, their former owners having been forced out by the Revolution; under the censitary monarchy they were "embellished" with luxury. This rehabilitated the term "hotel," which had previously been banned.[17] After 1850, this conversion was amplified by the necessity of attracting a greater number of travelers, drawn to Paris or London or Vienna by the world's fairs and the railway system. The Grand Hôtel du Louvre was created for the 1855 fair by the Grand Hôtel des chemins de fer company. The Grand Hôtel Saint-Lazare faces the railroad station and collects passengers accordingly.

The century from 1860 to 1960 was the age of the palaces, which formed a universe in which moneyed travelers circulated—with Valéry Larbaud's Barnabooth as their spokesman. They combined two models: modern Anglo-Saxon know-how and a French taste for courtly ceremony. The former was more concerned with comfort, especially in the bathroom, and the latter was attentive to decoration and reception. The former triumphed at the Carlton and the Hôtel du Louvre; the latter, at the Hôtel Meurice. The successful palace hotel reconciled the two; this accounted for the success of César Ritz, in the hotel he named after himself.

What makes a hotel a palace, to begin with, is the sumptuous quality of the lobby, the entrance hall, the ornate curving staircase, the bright lights, the heavy draperies, the abundance of seats. Then there is the quality of service, the availability of numerous alert and discreet personnel: the porters, receptionists, valets, and chambermaids, who can be reached at the press of a button, an electric signal, and later a telephone, each deploying his or her charms as necessary. Finally, there is the reputation of the clientele, those who pass through as well as those who stay—of which there were many at this time, especially in the south, where there was a revolving door of regulars returning year after year. The court model was always present, in the vocabulary and the mores, the subtle alliance of deference and familiarity, obsequiousness and respect, according to the codes of politeness and the everyday rituals that created the "civilization of customs" at the palace, subtly analyzed by Proust's narrator of *Within a Budding Grove.* It was a closed world of intrigue, rumors, and nods; of gazes, love, and desire, all of which Thomas Mann dramatizes in *Death in Venice.* An intensely narrative space, the palace has given rise to an immense literature of its own. When the palaces closed, their relics have been fought over, as was recently the case at the Royal-Monceau (June 2008), which was cut up, sold at auction, and systematically torn apart by those who loved it, leaving room for something new.

In the universe of the palace, the room is not the most important component. In the photo albums that are devoted to palaces, it is underrepresented, appearing much less often than the salons, the kitchens, or the cellars. As a place of intimacy the room is less spectacular, less visible, more frozen in its use and its furnishings, repetitive and anonymous. A regime of housekeepers reigns over the hierarchy of floors and over the army of valets and chambermaids, who each have their own distinct roles and who live under the eaves, sharing—until World War I—the home reserved for clients. In time, the in-house staff was reduced to include only the drivers.

The most extravagant rooms combined to form "suites"; the smallest of them was large enough to include a sitting area. The bed (king-sized in France, a double in England) was for a long time housed in an alcove; it had a canopy and curtains, with a Louis XIV allure. But the eighteenth century was having a renaissance, with the Goncourt brothers as its principal zealots, and it became the last word in "stylish" furnishing. The local artisans became adept at reproducing it. Nostalgia for the Ancien Régime, along with a taste for the good life, hovered over the palaces, inspired by an aristocratic model that continued to dictate social codes, down to the vocabulary and the curve of the seats.

The Anglo-American clientele appreciated this but required more comfort, especially in the bathroom. This area lagged behind, however. The Grand Hôtel du Louvre (1854), the largest hotel in Europe, in the center of Paris, boasted six hundred rooms and seventy salons. Baths were on offer at any hour of the day but in collective installations. Half a century later, of the four hundred bedrooms of the Elysée-Palace (1899–1919), only a third featured private bathrooms. At the Carlton in London, every room had one. Hygiene remained mediocre behind the façade of grandeur; valets continued for a long while to empty chamber pots.

The Carlton provided a model for César Ritz, who worked there at one point. The Ritz, in the Place Vendôme, was inaugurated with great ceremony on June 1, 1898, and aimed to feature the best in comfort, hygiene, dining, and privacy.[18] Private bathrooms and toilets were now standard for each room; César and his wife Marie-Louise provided the greatest refinements, with enamel porcelain bathtubs, white marble toilets, and toilets covered with ribbed seats, which curiously resembled commodes. In the bedroom, the walls were painted white; the fabric was dust-resistant; the curtains were triple layers of tulle, light canvas, and sateen, which filtered the sun; there were ample closets and drawers deep enough to store wigs, braids, and chignons; the light-colored carpet matched the drapery and the bedding; the bed was made of copper, which was preferable to wood, with a mattress cover, light quilt, and densely woven sheets that were changed every day and ironed by hand. The mantelpiece was bare—no clock or candelabras—while the desk had writing accessories, blotting paper, and paper embossed with the hotel's arms. The indirect lighting scheme provided diffuse light. There was no aggressive telephone but electric buttons to summon the staff. Soundproofing could not yet block out all noises; Proust could hear his neighbor's water running in the shower. He found some delight in the relative proximity of other people's bodies, which contributed such an erotic charge to the hotel room, a place for sleep and for love, personal, shared, and intuited, an act resented by neighbors, imagined by servants, and testified to by unmade beds and sheets where their occupants had left their imprints.

According to one journalist, the Ritz was like a hotel that had been started under Louis XIV and finished under Félix Faure. Memoirs of

Versailles slowly disappeared in favor of hygienic preferences, which called for a new aesthetics, theorized by William Morris and certified by Proust. "A room is only beautiful if it contains things that are useful to us."[19] It should be bare, functional, unpretentious, showing its joints, he wrote, not without regret for the warmly overstuffed rooms of yesteryear. However, the Ritz pleased him so much that he moved there and entertained there and sold off his silverware, no longer having a use for it.

In the great capitals of Europe (like Berlin, which had the Hotel Adlon) or on the Riviera, the palaces also live off the glitz and glory of their guests (or even their scandals); the guests are linked to these places through habit and appropriation and transform them from hotels into homes—though it is unclear if this changes their meaning or completes it. They return, year after year, to "their" room and are angry if they find it occupied by someone else (a good manager knows how to avoid this). Others live there year round, becoming part of its fabric or overstaying their welcome.[20]

The palace is exceptional, an island paradise in the sea of mean or mediocre hotels that made up most of the offerings during this period. The furnished room was its exact opposite, and many recent studies have attempted to reevaluate its functions. For more than a century, furnished hotel rooms, sometimes called bedsits, housed migrants, people from the provinces, and foreigners—those who wished to work in the city, especially in Paris. Most were only "birds of passage," returning home during the low season, at least in the building industry, which exploited temporary labor. But especially after 1880 a greater number settled definitively, bringing their families or starting one. Hence the need for a larger, more permanent place to live. Furnished rooms and bedsits were a means for the lower classes to integrate themselves and build a more settled life, the very opposite of the luxurious or mediocre hotel stay but more volatile. We will return to this below.

Love and Death

The variety of uses and experiences of the hotel runs the widest of gamuts. What do we know of the humblest of them, beyond the most banal, ordinary experience? Henri Michaux, the "man of a thousand hotels," attempts to give voice to this as he describes one character: "He lived in the most modest of rooms. It was really too narrow. He felt that it would drive him mad." He changes rooms, and this doesn't help; "rooms for the broke always have some defect."[21] This is a truism that applies just as well to the hotel as to the bedsit.

We know little of the everyday life lived in these rooms, just a few bits gleaned from rare inquiries, autobiographies, memoirs, or fragments jotted down on the back of a postcard of happy memories or tragic events. This is all the more true given that hotel guests tend to want to maintain all the anonymity their hotel rooms allow them—slightly more now than in the past, when guests had to fill out police forms and state their identity, which they had to invent if they were on the run. The privacy of the hotel room was a guarantor of liberty, and it explains the role the hotel room has played for those who are persecuted, in exile, delinquent, fugitive, or in love—all those who for one reason or another are in flight.

The hotel room welcomes all sorts of love, from legitimate to clandestine. At one time it sheltered the wedding night of moneyed young newlyweds. Lovers meet there, some returning to the same room, which becomes a part of their lovemaking; others constantly change rooms, the better to hide their furtive assignations. Jean Paulhan and Dominique Aury skipped among all the little hotels in the Seine-et-Marne region, where they knew all the train stations.[22] An employee offering a key with a vaguely suspicious and knowing look; a room number; curtains pulled in the middle of the day; if possible thick walls to muffle the sighs, the whispers, and the panting of lovemaking—all these contribute to an ease of passage, a relative security, an instant of eternity. Happy are those lovers who may enjoy an entire night to make love, sleeping together like an ordinary couple. Most often they must content themselves with furtive moments, lasting no longer than necessary. But do lovers remember these rooms? How important is the bed, assuming it doesn't squeak too much? Are the premises important? If so, is it because the ardor of love eventually cools or that mad passion makes lovers forget everything but each other? For Marguerite Duras, passion lives in the hotel room, "in the shadow of a hallway facing a door open to the outside." "I would have wanted you for myself alone, with / the world in the shape of a hotel room," wrote the poet (Louis Aragon to Elsa Triolet).[23]

Sexuality lives in the hotel room, and sometimes overwhelms it. So does death—and not just metaphorically. The hotel managers of the Riviera were always afraid their tubercular guests would die; some of them came to the hotel expressly for that purpose. The managers created systems for the rapid removal of the bodies. At the Ritz, a special exit was created to avoid any contact between the living and the dead, whose corpses would certainly tarnish the festive appeal of the palace—a sign of the erasure of death that is scandalous in contemporary society. Alice James was dying in London of an incurable cancer in a South Kensington hotel; the room was pleasant and calm, but to die she would be transported, she imagined, to her brother Henry's home, "it not being aesthetic to die in a hotel." Her friend Katherine reassured her, however; she had nothing to fear; everything would be carried out "with perfect decency": the body would be carried out via the service stairway so as not to disturb anyone. "They have strange ways here, of shutting all the windows and doors as soon as a person dies." Perhaps to avoid the bodies turning black? That was her nurse's theory.[24]

Whether foreseen or sudden, death is an accident contained in every journey. The deaths of the poor don't receive much attention; a mention in the police log book at the nearest commissariat or a short item in the local newspaper is all the fanfare such an incident attracts, while the death of a writer or an artist haloes a hotel with glory. Plaques remind us of the death of Strindberg at the Pension Orfila in the rue d'Assas, of Joseph Roth in the rue de Tournon, of Oscar Wilde at 13, rue des Beaux-Arts, to mention only the sixth arrondissement of Paris. Diane de Furstenberg underscores the sumptuous decor of Wilde's last refuge—"a few touches worthy of a dandy"—and the affinity that future guests may enjoy: "All those who have stayed in this room . . . have thus been able to enter the world of the writer."[25]

The hotel can be a depressing place. Finding yourself alone between its four walls after a play or a concert can be, for an artist, a relief or a test. The searing contrast between the grand finale at the theater and the sometimes sordid decor of the hotel can be a real comedown. The pianist Martha Argerich has described the boredom she felt in her youth coming home to her hotel room after a triumphant recital. No one is waiting for you there. This is why she later launched a project to house young musicians. "We have everything—glory, money, applause—and we brood alone in a hotel room," said Rachmaninoff.[26] Melancholy lurks in empty, anonymous hotel rooms.

People commit suicide in hotels, through the window or in the room. The double lock guarantees such desperate people the necessary solitude to hang, shoot, knife, or poison themselves. The writer Jacques Vaché put an end to his life on 6 January 1919 at the Hôtel de France in Nantes, room 34, on the second floor. Joseph Roth killed himself at a hotel. In Nazi Germany, a number of suicides were linked to anti-Semitic persecution. "Veronal in a hotel," notes Victor Klemperer of Arthur Sussman in his journal.[27] Such was also the fate of Walter Benjamin and so many other political exiles, whose hotel rooms were their last address. This is the tragedy of the hotel room in times of war, of exile, of persecution. But also in times of ordinary depression. Cesare Pavese swallowed twenty sleeping pills on 27 August 1950, in a room at the Albergo Roma in Turin, his favorite city. "Silence is our only power," he wrote.[28]

Singular Experiences

Some wealthy writers chose the hotel as a way of life or used it as a literary device. Their experiences are not necessarily representative, but each one, in its singularity, within the confines of the biography or the novel, at least gestures at a shared history.

BARNABOOTH: THE DANDY'S ROOM

Valéry Larbaud, who loved hotels, made Barnabooth his hero and his spokesman. Barnabooth is one of the richest men in the world (unlike his author). He manages his American father's fortune, which was built on speculation and gaming, especially casinos. A traveler without luggage, he buys objects as he needs them, later destroying them or distributing them to his staff upon his departure, like the dying at one time gave their clothes to

their servants. He travels throughout Europe, appreciating art and museums, an unfettered cosmopolitan. His travels, which he chronicles, are for
him an aesthetic as well as an ethic; he wants to liberate himself from "the
demon of real estate," that "stain [of] the caste that destiny hopes to imprison."[29] He wants to rid himself of the image of the idle young billionaire
that follows him around, instead hoping to be seen as an ascetic dandy and
voluptuary. Through travel, he hopes to discover the world, Europe especially, as well as himself. By keeping a diary, he hopes to "see things in themselves." He writes of the "duel to the death between me and him [his
self-love] in the prison-house of my soul. . . . I follow him from room to
room, into the furthest reaches of the storerooms." He dreams of escaping
the room, a metaphor for the soul. "Leave myself, but to go where, and to
give myself to whom?"[30]

Travel allows him to have neither roots nor attachments, to escape
homes and women. "Woman is a limit." She embodies the boredom of virtue: "Affairs begin with champagne and end with chamomile."[31] The train
and the hotel make this liberation possible; Barnabooth wanders from palace to palace. At the Carlton in Florence he rents an entire floor, "a suite of
windows on the Arno, a dining room, a smoking room, a bathroom as big as
a bedroom." The bath is his supreme pleasure: "A bath was prepared for
me. The noise of the hot water churning into the bathtub, the rising steam,
always bring voluptuous thoughts to mind," unlike the repulsive figures of
the "bachelors without bathtubs, who smell like shut-ins." In the futuristic,
scientific house he plans to build in Kensington or Passy, the bathtub is
his first priority. He plans all the details, in contrast to the sparseness of
the bedroom. "The bathroom especially should be twice as big as the bedroom, which ought to resemble a simple hospital room, white, tiled, and
rounded."[32]

"Two hundred rooms, two hundred bathrooms"; according to Valéry
Larbaud, such should be the "proud motto of the modern hotelier." In a
1926 article dedicated to Jean Paulhan, he offers a condensed description of
his personal experience of the grand European hotels, beginning with the
palace-hotel in Bussaco and ending with the Villa Bianca in Rapallo.[33] As
a sickly youth, he spent a great deal of time in the hotel rooms where his

parents left him; none of them could have helped him reflect more on the sheltered life that was his.

Larbaud appreciated the fact that a hotel could serve as a retreat: "A hotel room has an almost unlimited power to isolate." How and why was this power found in a shared space, "a banal space, offered equally to all, somewhat like the passage of time, which can never go quickly enough?" In this suspended space-time, we feel ourselves in transit, awaiting some meeting or some vague happiness that will no doubt never arrive. The hotel keeps its distance from the town that moves around it and in which we know ourselves to be foreign. "It's like staying in a train station, always expecting the final departure." This impression of suspense, of nowhereness, is amplified by the act of putting the key on the board and not in one's pocket, confirming a feeling of exteriority. Larbaud recalls a grand Parisian hotel (the Hôtel du Louvre, no doubt) where he spent long passages of his childhood. In his room, where he had his dinner brought to him by a meticulous and silent maître d'hôtel, he could hear the movements of the crowds that passed by without anyone sparing a glance at the window from which he observed them. To see without being seen: the panoptical position of power, which can produce an extreme feeling of isolation.

MARCEL PROUST: THE ANXIETY OF THE NEW ROOM

Proust's experience is different and contradictory. He fears change and therefore all new rooms, to which one must acclimate; this is is a recurrent theme of the *Recherche*. From the first pages, the narrator describes his nocturnal anxiety: "The hour when an invalid, who has been obliged to start on a journey and to sleep in a strange hotel, awakens in a moment of illness and sees with glad relief a streak of daylight shewing under his bedroom door . . . I became uneasy, as though I were in a room in some hotel or furnished lodging, in a place where I had just arrived, by train, for the first time."[34] At Balbec, the first night, it was impossible to sleep. In his room at the Grand Hotel, everything seemed threatening: the height of the ceiling, the curtains, the glass doors on the bookshelves; "a strange and pitiless

mirror with square feet, which stood across one corner of the room," un-
nerves him. "It is our noticing them that puts things in a room, our growing
used to them that takes them away again and clears a space for us. Space
there was none for me in my bedroom (mine in name only) at Balbec; it was
full of things which did not know me."[35] Only custom can vanquish the
darkness of things and help us forget them. At the end of his stay, the narrator has tamed his bedroom to such an extent that he wishes to return to it
the following year and trembles at the manager's suggestion that he might
find him a better one. Moreover, he experiences the return to his room in
Paris as a new exile.

Visiting Doncières, the narrator regretfully leaves the officer's room,
where Robert de Saint-Loup was putting him up, to return to the hotel.
"And I knew beforehand that I was doomed to find sorrow there. It was like
an unbreathable aroma which all my life had been exhaled for me by every
new bedroom, that is to say by every bedroom." Happily, the eighteenth
century hotel retains "a superfluous refinement of structure and decoration,
out of place in a modern hotel." His room, at the end of a torturous hallway
and an unexpected stairway, looks out onto a discreet courtyard and is filled
with antique furniture, a good fire, an alcove bed, and charming nooks.
"The walls held the room in a close embrace, separating it from the rest of
the world." His solitude, "while still inviolable, was no longer shut in." The
room has a certain charm that calms him and gives him "the sense of liberty." He feels at once isolated and protected. It allows him to find a poetic,
"velvety" sleep and to awaken serenely.[36]

The room at Doncières resembles Jean Santeuil's room, which Proust
describes, in an almost ethnographic manner, as his ideal room: large, with
a not-too-high ceiling; lined with soft, thick carpeting; electric lighting
operated by a series of buttons; "a large bed, not too long, not at all sad,
separated from the room, but plunged into silent happiness." The window
looks out on a courtyard carpeted with Virginia creeper vines, which Jean
spies through a curtain, "quickly pulled to return more completely to the
bedroom . . . full of poetic promise."[37]

In the end, Proust likes provincial hotels, where there are traces of
other lives; this inspires him.

As for me, I only feel happy when setting foot in one of those provincial hotels—on avenue de la Gare, on the port, near the church—with the long cold corridors where the outside wind successfully fights the effects of the base heater . . ., where every noise disturbs the silence by displacing it, where the rooms retain a shut-up perfume which the wind comes to wash, but can't erase . . .; where, in the evening, when you open the door to your room, you feel as if you're violating all the life that has remained scattered there . . .; of sometimes touching the nudity of this life in the aim of troubling myself by its familiarity . . .; and so we feel like we're shutting this secret life in with us, when, trembling, we lock the door."[38]

A poet of hotel rooms, Proust is nourished by their materiality. At the end of his life, he lived part-time in a hotel. At night, he wrote in his bed.

JEAN-PAUL SARTRE, "THE CAFÉ MAN"

Sartre is the antithesis of the bedroom. He refused the idea of home, marriage, monogamy, or conjugality. He felt happy only in a café: "At a café, I can work. . . . What is it that attracts me to a café? It is a place of indifference, where others exist without noticing me and where I take no notice of them. The weight of a family would be insupportable to me," he wrote to Roger Troisfontaines in 1945.[39] Almost thirty years later, Sartre wrote to John Gerassi: "Until then [1972], I had always lived in a hotel, worked in a café, and ate at a restaurant. It was very important to me not to possess anything. It's a form of personal well-being; I would feel lost if I had my own apartment, with furniture, and things that belonged to me."[40]

The private realm was, in Sartre's view, synonymous with bourgeois life. He hated secrecy and advised transparency. The rue de Naples, with its wall-less, mystery-less interiors attracted him as a model. "The whole street went by my room and slipped on me," says his alter ego Roquentin in *Nausea*. The historian, who is writing a thesis on the Marquis de Rollebon, spends his life between the library, cafés—the Rendez-vous des cheminots

on weekdays, the café Mably on Sundays—and his room in the Hôtel Printania, above the rue des Mutilés and the building site of the new train station. The worksite, the fence, the old station, the noise of the trains and the
business travelers resonate in the brick building, where "the slightest noise
could be heard between floors," and form a world at once gray and colorful
(there is a certain Expressionism in Sartre), ordered and monotonous.
Roquentin catalogues the repeated sounds: the steel grinding of the tram-
way; the footsteps from room 2 ("the one with the bidet"); the snoring and
the washing up of the girls in the kitchen, his neighbors in room 16, who
take turns, always in the same order. "What is there to fear in such an un-
changing world?"[41]

Roquentin could have lived elsewhere. He has been to see other poetic, tranquil neighborhoods, with furnished rooms in bourgeois houses
with views of the sea. He describes one with great precision, perhaps the
room of a married, established son. The mistress of the house brags about
it: "And you know, it's a real little home, very cozy. You would surely be
happy there. At night you can't hear a sound, you'd think you were in the
country. It's very agreeable for working; in summer you can open the windows, and the linden trees nearly come into the room."[42]

But Roquentin refuses "the pretty little room, the dear little room,"
which "exists by itself" and "very slowly cracks open." This is precisely
what he flees: this insipid peace, this pastoral tranquility. His hotel room
has no shutters; colors and noises rush into it. "All that men do at night, I
hear." The room is a void, a hole in a sieve, an impersonal niche.

> This room does not smell of man; it does not retain the imprint;
> I could live here for ten years in the midst of furniture that is
> merely functional; I would leave no mark on it; I would always
> only be passing through. . . . And others could come after me,
> and they would find nothing left of me in this room without
> memory." "I write. . . . I feel free. . . . I *am* this light house with
> red bricks, turned toward the northeast. . . . What do I have to
> lose? No wife, no children, no particular purpose in this world.
> I am not a leader, not a manager, or any other sort of idiot.[43]

The hotel room, an ethical, existential choice, is the condition of liberty that writing requires; this is Sartre's philosophy of the bedroom, influenced by Christian asceticism but also by a phobia of domesticity and separatist elitism.[44] In any case, no one else thought so carefully about the way of life in a hotel room.

This was Sartre's way of life initially. He lived his beloved hotel life from 1931 to 1946 in Le Havre and then in Paris, in a variety of hotels on the Left Bank (in the sixth and fourteenth arrondissements).[45] In October 1946, he went to live in the apartment his mother had bought at 42, rue Bonaparte, and lived there until it was bombed in 1962 as a reprisal for his engagement in the Algerian War. He moved to a studio apartment on the boulevard Raspail, where he stayed until 1973, when, losing his sight, he went to live on the boulevard Edgar-Quinet, not far from Simone de Beauvoir.

Simone shared, to a certain extent, his preferences. She also spent time in cafés, restaurants, and hotels. When she looked back, she gave a chronicle of their itinerant life, notably the time at the Hôtel Louisiane, where a writers' and artists' colony of sorts grew up around them and where the famous Egyptian writer Albert Cossery recently died at age ninety-four, last witness to a vanished time.[46] However, as we have seen, Simone eventually tired of this lifestyle. In time, she developed a more pragmatic relationship to the hotel, one that was less concerned with ethics, one that was more temporary, and one that made it a more nuanced space.

JEAN GENET: LIFE AND DEATH IN A HOTEL

Jean Genet was more radical and for a long time more broke; he saw himself as a "martyr" who proudly owned his marginality and refused even the basic luxury of owning furniture. In any case, all attempts he made to settle failed, as Edmund White has shown in his sensitive biography.[47] Poverty ran in the family; his mother, who worked as a servant and had him when she was very young, lived a hand-to-mouth existence and died at age twenty-eight in the Hôpital Cochin. He passed his life like a monk in a series of cells, but in a way, this formed him and became a necessity. As a child in Alligny-en-Morvan, the village where he was placed, he spent hours reading and dreaming in the toilets at the back of the garden. When he was a teenager, he was sent to Mettray, a juvenile detention facility where he was shut up in a completely dark room, where even the ceiling was painted black. For three months, he squatted in complete solitude, and in the various institutions where he was imprisoned, he eventually came to prefer life in the slammer. He acquired an extraordinary capacity for communicating and an ability to write anywhere, which he described in his final book, *Prisoner of Love.*

Hotels were appropriate spaces for Genet, who chose wandering and sexual freedom as a way of life and who associated them with his travels and lovers and with his desire for anonymity, for escape. He was perpetually in flight, always feeling himself to be hunted down, always having to feign another identity. Sometimes he would take a random train, get off in a little town, often without interest. He would bed down in the closest hotel, which was generally wretched. Sometimes he would take up with the waiter at the local café, whom he would return to visit. On the walls he would tack up photographs of Eugen Weidmann, the last man to be publicly guillotined in France (1939). He often changed "bunks," even in Paris, where he drifted from Montmartre to the Butte-aux-Cailles, with a marked preference for the proletarian quarters of the Left Bank, in the thirteenth and fourteenth arrondissements. He was a disorderly guest, burning holes in the mattresses with his Gitanes, strewing leftover food behind him; hotel managers didn't care for him. When he became famous, Gallimard had to pay the tabs he'd run up; when he had a bit more money, he wasn't above stopping in at the palace hotels, and he resided for a time at the Lutétia. His bohemian tastes were not at odds with luxury, and he demanded a certain bodily hygiene. He had his own soigné style, a "little hoodlum's" elegance, as Jean Cau put it, who saw him often in the 1950s. His vague desires to set up house never really came to much. In 1950 he rented a one-bedroom apartment in the rue du Chevalier-de-La-Barre, and he had it repainted and furnished at the Samaritaine's expense; he left a few months later. In the spring of 1957, he did it again, buying a one-bedroom apartment in the rue Joanès, near the Porte de Vanves in the south of the city. He eliminated the kitchen, for which he had no need, and decorated the place with his lover, Java. There he entertained his new passion, the young Moroccan Abdallah, an army deserter

whose uniform he kept hidden in the cellar. But he wasted no time in resell-
ing the place to some Americans who would inherit the uniform and the
(vain) police searches. He fled across Europe with Abdallah, who, abandoned, would kill himself a few years later, in the maid's room into which
Genet had moved him.

"I was born a vagabond. . . . My true country is any train station. I
have a suitcase, some linen, and four photos: Lucien, Jean Decarnin, Abdallah, and you. . . . I go to Paris as infrequently as possible," Genet wrote to
Java in 1962. More of a nomad than ever, he would sometimes abruptly leave
a hotel, abandoning even his pajamas.

However, one day—or rather one night—in Turkey, the nomad felt the
fleeting desire for a place of his own. He recounts this paradoxical and
almost mystical experience in *Prisoner of Love:*

> The desire to get rid of all external objects was this traveller's
> principle, so it must have been the work of the devil, God's
> devil, that after a very long time, when he thought he'd really
> divested himself of all possessions, he was suddenly invaded,
> one can only wonder via what orifice, by a desire for a house, a
> solid, fixed place, an enclosed orchard. Almost in one night he
> found himself carrying inside him a place of his own. . . . It was
> a situation both flimsy and funny. I went on rejecting real prop-
> erty, but I had to deconstruct the property inside of me, with its
> corridors, its bedrooms, its mirrors, and its furniture. And that
> wasn't all: around the house was the orchard, with plums on the
> plum-trees which I could not put in my mouth because every-
> thing had been for so long inside me. . . . To carry his house and
> furniture inside him was humiliating for a man who had shone
> one night with his own inner aurora. . . . For my humiliation
> made me aware that it was *my* house, *my* furniture, *my* light, and
> *my* interior. Did that last expression mean the inside of my
> home, or the vague, uncertain place put there to conceal a total
> void: my inner life, which is sometimes called, with equal lack of
> precision, my secret garden?

Genet was very moved, though not without irony, by the iconography of Orthodox churches, which represented the passing of the Virgin Mary, carried to heaven by angels along with her "little stone house."[48]

When he was stricken with throat cancer, for which he refused chemotherapy, Genet returned to Paris. He liked to stay at the Hôtel Rubens, near Gobelins, but it was full, so he went to Jack's, a mediocre little place. On the night of 14 April 1986, he tripped on the bathroom step. He was found unconscious the next morning. He died at the hotel, just as he had lived there.

Traveling Women

What about women? We don't hear as much from them, although they were much more *voyageuse* (travel-hardy) in the nineteenth century than they had been previously. A woman alone in a hotel is always suspect. Flora Tristan describes this when she was traveling around France; in the Midi, especially in Montpellier, numerous hotels refused to take in single women for fear of prostitution. In *On the Necessity of Welcoming Female Travelers* (1835), Tristan advocates opening, just for women, hotels equipped with libraries and maintaining a rigorous level of privacy—an early example of a women's hostel. George Sand was also a great traveler, but she never went anywhere alone and was often dressed like a man, the source of many misunderstandings. When she made a cheerful trip to the Alps with Liszt and Marie d'Agoult, the innkeeper pretended to confuse her gender.[49] A lover of gardens and countrysides who liked the open road and the "masterless path," Sand found the hotel room to be of little interest, and she would summarily note if it was clean or full of cockroaches.

A woman alone is a cause for concern. She is perceived as a floozy, a tease, a lady adventurer, the heroine of a serial novel—a woman of the demimonde, or worse, who will probably come to a bad end. Zola kills off Nana in room 401 at the Grand Hôtel, on the less expensive fourth floor— "death requires no luxury"—in the same posture of abandonment that brought on the syphilis that was now rotting her body. "The room was empty. A great desperate sigh rose up from the boulevard and swelled the curtain. 'To Berlin! To Berlin! To Berlin!' " The Second Empire was dying at the same time, in the palace where there roamed the courtesans who embodied its luxury.[50]

The single woman traveler would not dare to go out at night; she would remain in her room to preserve her reputation and avoid unseemly encounters. That is why women traveling for work—for conferences, symposiums, all kinds of salons—in predominantly masculine industries were (and are) often lonely; they had to remain in their rooms to avoid being hit on. As we've seen, actors, artists, and writers experienced this melancholy returning to their rooms after a performance or a book signing.[51] Colette intimately knew the provincial tours of café concerts, as she knew the moment of retreat, when the "vagabond" kept her distance from men who might come a-wooing. "I don't like anyone to enter my messy, smelly room. I have become physically intransigent, which is entirely agreeable to me." The heroine of her novel *L'Entrave* chooses "hotel life" to flee the conventions of family life, of the enslaving life of a couple, and writes, in summary: "The little that a woman may perceive of herself is not the calm, round light of a lamp lit every evening on the same table, which shows it to her." She sleeps with her lover in the afternoons but sleeps alone at the hotel. "The double-locked door" protects her privacy; luxuriating in hot, perfumed baths, she enjoys the pleasures of her own body.[52] The hotel room safeguards her freedom.

Freud's Rooms

The unmarried couple is also suspect. The mistress passes as the wife in order to avoid arousing suspicion. Freud's wife Martha was exhausted by his travels and asked her sister Minna to fill in for her; the travels they made in Italy have raised a number of questions, obviously concerning Sigmund's sexuality. Did they have one or two rooms? Separate or adjoining? Did they sleep together? Freudians and anti-Freudians alike have torn each other to shreds over the question. They have scrutinized Freud's apartment in Vienna, where Minna lived, and the hotels where he vacationed. One researcher thought he had found proof of an affair by looking at a hotel register in the

Engadin, where Freud had written "Dr. Freud und Frau"; he believed it was evidence of Freud's passing Minna off as his wife and of an affair that skirted incest. The *New York Times* even published a picture of this hotel, with twin beds and television, as if it had remained exactly the same. Then it became clear that the researcher had made a mistake; the numbers of the rooms had changed. A Swiss psychoanalyst stayed in the notorious room (number 11, which had become 23) and described its configuration: a two-room suite, separate but adjoining. How reassuring. Élisabeth Roudinesco has published a summary of this extraordinary affair in the *Nouvel Observateur* and dedicated a well-argued seminar to the Freudian "scenes of private life."[53] Elsewhere she has published travel correspondence among Freud, Minna, and Martha, with a title taken from Freud: "Our heart tends toward the South."[54] It is a detailed chronicle of travel and hotel stays, especially when it comes to prices—to which Freud was keenly attentive—and local gastronomy, which he also appreciated. This cheerful, friendly correspondence is totally lacking in amorous charge. They are the postcards of an average bourgeois looking after his comfort and his budget, in love with Italy, antiquity, and antiques; they tell us much about Freud, a voracious traveler who wanted to see everything; who passed through places without staying; about his tastes, his education, and his imagination; they contain nothing concerning his sexual behavior. Clearly his heart "tend[ed] toward the South" more than toward Minna.

Hotel Novels

A site of possibility, a theater for the imagination, the hotel room is an ideal setting for police novels or sentimental intrigue. It has received varied, refined treatment: Agatha Christie satirizing the English beaches, Simenon in the gray provincial hotels where Inspector Maigret stayed, Raymond Chandler suffering under the shadows of alcoholism and a breakdown, Paul Auster in his New York ramblings. It is a place of encounter, of rupture, of flight; the scene of the crime, of love, or death. In Julien Gracq's novel *A Dark Stranger,* Allan's room stirs the curiosity of a group of friends at the Hôtel des Vagues. They watch it at every hour of the day, looking to see if the shutters are open or closed, if the door is banging in the hallway—especially Christel, who loves Allan and is desperate to be loved; she spies on the room, a sanctuary of indecipherable intimacy, where he moves "like a bee in a closed room, bumping against the window." One evening, the window is as shadowy as Allan, a sign of his imminent death; he has poisoned himself. "Again he heard the door open, and, calm, he saw his final hour approach him."[55] Allan's room is a figure for his unfathomable mystery.

The literary hotel room defies anthology, like all the others, but more so because of its infinite cinematic and textual possibilities. It is easy to get lost in its labyrinth. Two novels (among others) that have adapted it for the stage, turning it into a central set-piece are *Grand Hotel*, by Vicki Baum (1928), a best seller reprinted many times, and *Suite à l'Hôtel Crystal*, by Olivier Rolin (2004).

The Grand Hotel in Berlin (no doubt inspired by the famous Adlon Hotel) serves as a backdrop to a number of plots that weave the protagonists together: Kringelein, an accountant who knows he is going to die and has come to the hotel to realize his dream of luxury before he does; his contemptuous boss, Preysing, a businessman, who has come to negotiate a deal that will ruin his reputation; the (fake) Baron Gaigern, a penniless dandy and seductive con man, a bit like Arsène Lupin; a Russian ballerina in decline, Grousinskaia, who is still beautiful and is embarked on an affair with Gaigern that will kill him; and Dr. Otternschlag, mutilated in World War I, who lives in the hotel, a "frozen picture of solitude and detachment," addicted to morphine, a lucid observer, a pessimistic student of destiny who has established his general headquarters in the lobby. These varied characters weave together to form the life of the Grand Hotel, which is the true hero of the novel. Through its complex machinery, the author, without excessive realism, sketches the decor, the atmosphere, the noises, the smells, the facilities, the traffic, the illusions. "Every hotel is but an enormous joke," says the doctor to the accountant, who thinks the Grand Hotel is the antechamber to paradise because it is the most expensive. People sleep badly there: "Many insomniacs dwell behind the closed doors of a hotel asleep." The apparent equality masks a hierarchy that can be seen from the quality of the rooms. Room 216 is wretched, and Kringelein, who wants a room as luxurious as his boss's, has to plot to get another one, number 70, "with a bathroom," which he has no idea how to use at the outset of the novel. "Room 70 was a nice room. It contained walnut furniture, hand mirrors, silk-upholstered chairs, a sculpted table, and lace curtains; on the wall, still life paintings depicting fallen pheasants; on the bed, a silk quilt. . . . On the desk, an impressive bronze *écritoire,* in the form of an eagle, its wings outstretched, as if to protect two empty inkwells." But the hotel transforms its guests: "Strange, what happens to those who stay at the Grand Hotel; no one comes out exactly the way he has gone in through the revolving door." The door turns and turns and turns, like the ever-changing stream of visitors; such is life.

Olivier Rolin—the Perec of the hotel room—has a very different perspective. Like the author of *Species of Spaces,* who undertook to "make an inventory, as precise and exhaustive as possible, of all the places where [he] slept," Rolin makes a list of forty-two hotel rooms around the world, as far afield as Buenos Aires, New York, Helsinki, Port Said, and Vancouver or as close to home as Nancy, Montélimar, and Brive-la-Gaillarde. The narrator takes refuge there as he tracks the faceless heroine, Mélanie Melbourne, who slowly disappears without a trace. He follows the same format as he describes each room: size, layout, walls, floor, ceiling, paintings, furniture, objects, fabric, curtains, radiators, engravings and their subjects, windows, window panes, views, closets, adjoining rooms, bathrooms; everything is described meticulously, in stark contrast to the vagueness of the plot and the fluidity of the characters: women seduced, spies on the run, sleazy dealers, morally dubious operators for a shady deal that turns on the narrator. But the vagueness doesn't matter very much. It is not a narrative but a poem, an oratorio, a dizzying succession of hotel rooms that would be impossible to memorize. The "suite in the Hôtel Crystal" in Nancy, which lends its name to the novel's title, is the forgotten, unreachable room. "The Hôtel Crystal is an empty space, a warehouse for imaginary merchandise, the hotel of the novel, if you like."[56] It is empty like the rooms described, indiscernible from each other, becoming confused in their uniformity, like a veil covering the story and the world. The fictional structure hides a metaphysics of travel—a travel with no exterior, no countryside—and of the hotel room as a way of relating to time and space that its opacity causes them to intermingle. The hotel room becomes utilitarian, generic, serial, a place to pass through; it loses the singularity, the poetry, the sense of possibility beloved by Kafka.

Kafka at the Hotel

"I love hotel rooms," Kafka said. "In a hotel room I am immediately *at home,* truly." He suffered from the lack of privacy in the family apartment: "My room is a hallway, or better, a track that links the living room and my parents' bedroom," he wrote to Felice Bauer, his perennial fiancée.[57] The room was cold, dark, noisy, and totally exposed. His mother went through his things. He couldn't write there. It reinforced his phobia of people. "I've always been afraid of people, not people themselves that is, but that they would intrude on my ridiculous being. . . . That includes those to whom I am intimately linked—the thought that they might enter my room has always terrified me. It's more than a symbol of this fear."[58]

This is why the hotel room was, for Kafka, a haven; it offered him isolation and quiet, allowing him to enjoy the silence and to write all night long: "a place where I feel especially at ease."[59] To hold the key to such a place, even temporarily, gave him a profound feeling of freedom. Michael Walzer sees the hotel room as a basic form of democratic inscription, the symbol of a modernity that Franz Kafka embodied and that dissipated at the same time as it became globalized.

Workers' Rooms

WORKERS' ROOMS ARE enigmatic, more than others, in spite (or because) of the novels that have explored them, the investigations that have described them, and the alienating screen they deploy. Behind the window panes of compassion, astonishment, or condemnation, what do we see? What can we glimpse of these lives in these tiny spaces, among the heaps of belongings, anonymous objects, bizarre piles created by "people who have nothing"? What do we know of these workers beyond sociology—an instrument of comprehension perhaps but one that can become an insidious mask of individual hardships?

But a social approach imposes itself. To be fair, it is doubtless somewhat artificial to refer to "workers' rooms" as a branch of the family tree of rooms, like "the king's bedroom" or "the children's room." They are a key part of a social problem: that of housing, which has been a pressing issue for over two centuries in the wake of urban and industrial migrations, which disintegrate the traditional habitat. Moreover, the world of the proletariat is not uniform, and there was a great variety of habitats and situations. In some cases the room was an entire home or sometimes just a room, in the English sense of the word, a stopping place in a migrant's long struggle. Migrants would arrive in the city to try to earn a living; where should they live? Servants were "fed and lodged," but employees, who were subject to the market, were not; it fell to them to find a bed or a "room in town." Of course such migrations were rarely made blindly; they generally followed patterns established by family or neighbors. The most recently arrived had to muddle through with the help of those who had preceded them and who would house them, at least for a time. But migrants accumulated in the centers of cities that were not at all equipped to absorb them or on the outskirts of factories that were indifferent to their fates, creating densely populated zones with a degraded quality of life for a potentially "barbaric" population—at least in the contemporary imagination.

In all the European countries, the "housing question" gave rise to all kinds of investigations that produced a rich source of information and knowledge but that were also overflowing with images, fantasies, and the construction of norms. While revealing in some ways, they also make it difficult to understand what the inhabitants themselves knew; such inhabitants are as opaque to us as people in far-away nations. Doctors, philanthropists, specialists in social economics, architects, novelists, and later photographers (whose lenses were never neutral) haunted these exotic territories, and we are dependent on what they saw.[1] These data have been pored over by historians and urban sociologists, beginning with Louis Chevalier's notorious book, in which he may be suspected of having succumbed to the romance of the *classes dangereuses,* through recent studies that have been careful to precisely analyze the functioning of this system and its realities.[2]

Life Every Which Way

Investigators who visited proletarian neighborhoods were initially struck by their deprivation, the lack of privacy, the smell, and the way people lived on top of one another. In 1770, Dr. Lépecq de La Clôture was horrified by the place where the wool combers and shearers lived in Louviers; to it he attributed the epidemic of pestilential fever. After they left the workplace, the combers and shearers retired to "low, narrow rooms, partly dug into the ground, where fresh air rarely enter[s] and [then] only by opening the door; water gathers when the rain is heavy. This hovel houses an entire family: father, children, the elderly, sleeping every which way, like animals, on a plank bed that was never covered with enough hay. . . . The healthy were all mixed up with the sick, and the living with the dead."[3] The Norman doctor looked with a medical gaze, not a moral one, barely a social one, unlike his nineteenth-century counterparts, who tried to address the problem of poverty, the subject of an ever-increasing number of studies and perspectives.

In 1835, Dr. Guépin invited the reader to enter the dark, damp rooms in the rue des Fumiers in Nantes: "Look at these three or four badly supported beds, which lean to the side because the string that attaches them to worm-eaten supports has itself given way. A straw mattress, a quilt made of scraps, rarely washed because it is the only one, sometimes sheets or a pillow. No need for an armoire in a house like this. Often a weaver's loom and a spinning wheel comprise the rest of the furnishings."[4] Guépin condemns misery rather than intemperance, which Dr. Louis-René Villermé finds more troubling. In 1840 Villermé was commissioned by the Académie des sciences morales to tour regions where the textile industry was thriving in order to create "a portrait of the physical and moral state of the workers" there. He visited more homes than factories, convinced (like many of his colleagues) that these were the key to the workers' misery. In Mulhouse, the workers "are crammed into bedrooms, or small, unhealthy rooms, located near their place of work. I've seen . . . some of these miserable lodgings, shared by two families, each in a corner, on a heap of hay thrown on the floor supported by two boards. . . . A single, miserable pallet for the whole family, a small stove for a kitchen and a heater, a crate or a box for an armoire, a table, two or three chairs, a bench, a few pieces of earthenware comprise the extent of the furnishings" in these homes, rumored to be rented by Jewish speculators (revealing an ever-present anti-Semitism).[5] In Sainte-Marie-aux-Mines, "the whole family sleeps in one room, where the equipment is set up." In the rue des Étaques in Lille, it's even worse. The poorest live in the caves where they eat, sleep, and even work. "In several of the beds that I have just mentioned, I have seen people of both sexes, of very different ages, most without shirts, and repulsively dirty"; their feet are so caked with scum that they seem to be African, the worst mark of degradation.[6] "Fathers, mothers, children, adults, the elderly, all crammed in, on top of one another. I can't go on. . . . The reader will try to fill in the picture, but I warn him that if he wants it to be a faithful one, his imagination must not retreat before any of the disgusting mysteries that accumulate on these filthy sheets, at the heart of darkness and intoxication."[7] "Disgusting mysteries," according to police conversations, seemed to refer to dangerous copulating and incidents of incest. The question of sleeping arrangements especially preoccupies Villermé, who notes in detail the use of sheets (many homes do not have any), the number of beds and how many people sleep in them, the separation of parents and children and of sexes and ages. In Amiens, he sees one room per family but several beds. "The parents share the biggest one with the youngest children, the girls have the next biggest, and the boys the smallest. Furthermore, it is quite usual to find the two sexes sharing a bed until the age of 11, 12, or 13—that is, until they make their first communion or when the priest recommends separating them," as was the case in rural families during the seventeenth century.[8]

Common decency condemned this way of life, associating it with abject misery. In *Les Mystères de Paris,* Eugène Sue describes the Morel family, whose five children sleep on the same straw mattress. A disgusted female correspondent sought his help to put an end to a similar situation in a household she knew about: "The daughter, who is getting very big, is obliged to share a bed with her brother in the same room as their parents." They must find "a healthful lodging composed of two rooms, so the children can be apart from their parents, and a divider must be found to separate the son from his sister, which would require a third bed."[9] Subletting, which was rare in Paris but common in the provinces, saw a worker's household let a bed to lodgers passing through; this also raised suspicions.

The proletariat was thought to have an unrestrained sexuality: exuberant, irrepressible, torrential, almost savage, similar to those of Africans, another "primitive" group of people to whom its members were often compared, if only for the color of their skin, tan through exposure and the lack of washing. The color black was seen as unsettling, satanic, nocturnal.[10] The workers' bodies sustained fantasies of fertility, power, and force, which fed on images of their way of living all jumbled together. Fantasies also attached to the deviant sexuality of incest, which the utopian Socialist thinker Charles Fourier said was widespread. It was an unrestricted reproductive sexuality, unbridled, pullulating: "Only workers multiply like rabbits. . . . They are a real herd of beasts, which nauseate me in the streets," one of the characters remarks in Zola's *Pot-Bouille.*[11] And the growth of this demographic, which is out of proportion to the earth's resources, is the basis for Malthus's concern. The Protestant pastor worried about the population rising too quickly and wisely recommended a curb in the birthrate, submitting the conjugal bed to the austerity of moral restraint. We know that Marx resented this bourgeois solution to proletarian misery. He felt they should be able to have all the children they wanted. "Go forth and multiply": socialism took a biblical view of humanity. Émile Zola made himself its lyrical prophet in *Fécondité,* an epic devoted to reproduction. As against the exhaustion of a degenerate bourgeoisie, he saw the fertility of the people as the source of a national and humanist power. He praised the beauties of the workers' conjugal beds in this strange, baroque poem to germination and generation, written in the solitude of his hotel room during the foggy exile in London that followed his condemnation for having written *J'accuse* in response to the Dreyfus Affair.

These fruitful unions assumed that the workers had all the comforts they needed. But the poor hygiene that resulted from the lack of necessary equipment (no water, sanitary facilities, or sewers) and the filth connected with the density of habitation transformed the places they lived into hotbeds of pestilence, toxic miasmas. High infant mortality, rickets, tuberculosis, alcoholism, the spread of epidemics (cholera, smallpox, measles, typhus), and the consequential low life expectancy derived from such sordid habitats, the smell of which assaulted visitors.[12] The Second Republic was very concerned about these conditions. In 1848, hygiene commissions were created. Though ineffective, they were at least a sign that the authorities were becoming aware of the noxious effects of insalubrity on public health. The Third Republic made hygiene an important issue and declared a war on slums, blamed for all manner of evils, to the point of stamping out the harmful effects of "worker exhaustion," which was no doubt more serious still.[13] Investigators drew up a "sanitary record" of the big cities (especially Paris), creating inventories of buildings to knock down and neighborhoods to clean up. Their questionnaires became ever more precise, according to the cubage of air: "What is the capacity of bedrooms relative to the number of beds that are found there, taking into account size, height, length, and width?" "Are the rooms equipped with ventilation outside the windows and doors (like chimneys, pipes, etc.)?" They also wanted to know about lighting and the state of the floors and walls. In 1878, these were the guidelines for an investigation into the "insalubrious bedsits of Paris." Dr. du Mesnil, who led it, mentions particularly bad cases. At 9, rue

Sainte-Marguerite (near the Faubourg Saint-Antoine), in a crooked house where the running water left a lot to be desired, he counted twelve beds in four parts of the building and only two bathrooms. "The courtyards, as well as the windows on the landings, are covered, in many places, with fecal material. Plumbing is as rare as bathrooms," and in what a state the bathrooms were kept! Three or four beds were jammed into bedrooms that were often devoid of a fireplace, damp, dirty, with worm-ridden paneling. Worse still was 103, Quai de Valmy: "The courtyard, the bathroom, the hallway leading to them, the stairway, the two galleries, the plumbing, the lodgings—that is to say everything—is in a state of indescribable uncleanliness. Papers, rags, urine, excrement, you can find it all. . . . The lodgings are full of vermin." The pages that follow are a litany of filth and foul odors. Dr. du Mesnil advises that the state intervene, as was the case in other countries, where bedsits were subject to draconian regulations. They were feared because their effects were felt "not only by those who live in them, but by the entire race, whose vitality is impacted; they are an assault on the nation, on its very structure."[14] These habitats were a public health issue and were at the heart of a more rigorous politics of hygiene that was, nevertheless, more discursive than effective.[15]

These habitats represented a moral issue as well. "Without a home, there is no family; without a family, there is no morality; without morality, there are no men; without men, there is no country," wrote Jules Simon, the father of the Republic, whose opinion was shared by his follower Louis Rivière, a member of Frédéric Le Play's Société d'économie sociale; he advocated an aesthetic vision of the worker's household, especially urging that workers have a garden.[16] The Société began carrying out research on the family under the Second Empire, according great importance to the role of the good housewife and domestic harmony—a catalyst for social peace. It provided incomparable sources of information; it was the only one to cross these thresholds and make such precise, legalistic inventories of the contents of a home. Its studies emphasized the "honest ease" of the homes that were well organized enough to serve as models. At the cabinetmaker's home in the Faubourg Saint-Antoine, the carpenter's in Paris, or the glovemaker's in Grenoble (all skilled artisans), we notice the frugality of everyday life, not its extreme poverty. And the investigators provide us with an exemplary portrait, though we cannot assess the degree of its likeness to reality.

Finally, the home is a symbol of success or social integration. For Agricol Perdiguier, who was known as Avignonnais la Vertu (known for his writings on the *compagnons,* or members of workers' brotherhoods), his room was a haven of dreamy, virtuous privacy, and it was much admired. Zola treats Gervaise Macquart's bedroom in *L'Assommoir* like a parabola reflecting her rise and fall. Her relationship and future plans with Coupeau take shape around their dream of a bedroom. "As soon as they had a bed, they would rent there," she imagines, visiting the "barracks" of the Goutte-d'Or, where she had picked out a sunny corner. After their marriage, they "get furnished"; they have a little room for the children, a small kitchen, and a big bedroom that they use for both sleeping and receiving visitors. "It [is] really a beautiful room," and they take care to close the curtains of the bed and to decorate the room with engravings and photographs. But as their relationship unravels, the room is slowly emptied until it is totally bare. Gervaise is thrown out because she can't pay the rent and is reduced to sheltering behind a stairway, in a little nook like a dog, where she dies. Her downfall is linked to the dissolution of her bedroom.[17]

An improvement in workers' moral standards had to be processed through an improvement in their homes. Philanthropists of all stripes believed this, as did management, the Socialists (or at least the Fourierists, like Godin and his Familistère, or Social Palace, in Guise; the others were more or less indifferent).[18] The need to house an imported workforce led the big industrialists (such as Kœchlin, Dollfuss, and Schneider) to build housing estates for workers, which were powerful instruments of disciplinary paternalism. Built by architects to be rational, hygienic, and standardized, these estates embodied the idea of minimalist housing. The distinction between cooking and sleeping and the need to separate parents and children led to a more strict definition of the bedroom, which was often situated upstairs and retired to only at night, at a distance from the everyday life of the street and the garden. It was, nevertheless, a key part of the house where workers rested and regenerated their energy. It was a worker's dream.

Workers' Everyday Lives

Leaving aside talk of their habitats, how can we understand workers' everyday lives? What did they want? The first thing a young worker needs, having recently quit his family in the countryside or abroad, is a place to live. If not a room, a bed somewhere. In this way, the need arose for bedsits and furnished rooms, whose function from nineteenth-century Paris to our own day has been studied by Alain Faure and Claire Lévy-Vroelant.[19] It was a vast, volatile industry that affected a wide range of people and depended on thousands of independent landlords or hotel managers. Around 1880, there were around 10,000 landlords for 200,000 tenants. In 1930, more than 350,000 Parisians (11 percent of the population) lived in furnished rooms. At the end of the day it was also a very integrated system that played a necessary mediating role until the 1920s. It was a flexible system that adapted to an ever changing demand and the turnover of the workforce, the needs of which fluctuated in keeping with the proximity of work, the desire to settle down, and familial situations. No one stayed in a bedsit for very long, at least not if it could be helped. After World War I, however, accommodations became more rare, and the system entered an irreversible decline—evidence of a general crisis in workers' lodgings. Often foreign-born migrant workers (Portuguese, Algerian, African) were limited to hostels or the *banlieues,* or they piled dangerously into sordid hotels. This is still the case and worse; homelessness is still rife.

The most striking aspect of this history is the role of the consumers, not at all passive agents, "users" who are "producers," as Michel de Certeau puts it in his analysis of the "thousand ways of poaching" that weave together to "invent" the everyday.[20] People move between jobs or between rentals; they make use of market potential, at first in the center of the web and then on the peripheries, and then they return to the center, in an incessant Brownian motion that has been identified in most of the big cities.[21] Asked to take what they can get, in mediocre conditions, they look for something better, moving frequently, sometimes skipping out on the bill, eager to improve their lots and to "get furnished." Let's see where they take us.

Chambrées

At first workers converged in "communal rooms," as Villermé termed them in his description. In Sedan, "as in all industrial towns, single men live in pensions. For 25 or 30 francs a month, they *sleep two to a bed,* are fed, cleaned, given candles, and a small amount of beer at each meal."[22] Young men were not admitted below the age of twenty and needed parental consent. Two to a bed was standard practice in most of the textile cities that Villermé visited—Reims, Rouen, Tarare—and it included the foreign female workers employed in silk milling.[23] How many beds were there per room? Villermé doesn't say, nor does he use the word *chambrées* (hostels), which became widespread after 1840. The 1878 *Annuaire statistique* describes a *chambrée* as "a room containing several beds intended to house tenants who have *no familial links to one another*" (emphasis added). The answer to "How many beds per room?" is at least four, or five on average by 1880, often many more, especially at the beginning of the period.

The term *chambrée* has several meanings. In the south of France, it refers to working-class men's societies, which emerged in the eighteenth century (though they had no doubt been around for much longer), set up in fairly rudimentary private rooms with a fireplace, a table, some chairs, some glasses; the men met to drink, to play games, to talk. Nevertheless, the meetings were pretty much clandestine, held upstairs, in rooms with balconies so as to be able to identify visitors and keep a lookout. The term *chambrettes* has nothing to do with size but with the modest origins of the participants. It means not "little room" but "little people" and was a virile Mediterranean form of socializing, according to Lucienne Roubin, a *maison des hommes* that could be compared to a Turkish *oda*. Men did not feel at all at ease in the house, which was dominated by the women's kitchen. Maurice Agulhon has showed how the *chambrées* were politicized and became "circles" in the nineteenth century.[24] But these southern *chambrées* were used to pass the time, not to spend the night; this was not the case in the north. With the military barracks as its origin, the word *chambrée* applied first and foremost to soldiers, with a virile, matey connotation. "Soldiers live gaily . . . and socialize in the *chambrées*," wrote Voltaire. Camus has written, superbly, "Men who share the same rooms, whether as soldiers or prisoners, create a strange bond; as if having left their armor behind with their personal clothing, they unite each evening, beyond their differences, in the ancient community of the dream or fatigue."[25]

The impressions we have of workers' *chambrées* are less glorified; they raise the suspicions that usually greet groups of poor men, ragged and smelly, with the usual waves of xenophobia against gaunt Italians or anti-Semitism aimed at shoemakers or down-and-out Jewish tailors. However, beyond their miserable appearance, they represented forms of collective solidarity comparable to what is found in housing for African workers today. Workers stuck together not only by provincial origin (Bretons, Auvergnats), but also by national, ethnic, local, or professional origin (in the rue de Lappe, there were blocks where people from the Auvergne lived and shared a collective kitchen, overseen by a woman from the village). Largely seasonal construction workers, whose everyday frugality has been described by Martin Nadaud, preferred this kind of organization, often outsourced by the site foreman; from year to year they would leave their tools in a shed and return to the same beds. The rooms were regularly cleaned, but that didn't do anything to prevent the bodily odors from steaming off of their sweaty, hastily washed bodies. The workers tried to do up their own little areas of the rooms. On the walls they wrote the names of their villages, their wives, or their vows—"sometimes a random word of love; everything jumbled together, like their lives," wrote Vinçard.[26] The future Communard Eugène Varlin believed in this communal lifestyle and lived in a community of young bookbinders in which six men shared the housework—and the charms—of a woman who looked after their linen and their sexual needs, sleeping now with one, now with another, in a way that would be Fourierist if it had been egalitarian.[27]

The freedoms of the masculine *chambrée* contrast starkly with the discipline of the Lyonnais "silk convents," which cropped up beginning in the 1840s, following the American model in Lowell.[28] The silk convents received a massive number of country girls (up to one hundred thousand at the height of the system) who were placed from the age of twelve until their marriages in silk and spinning mills. They worked fourteen hours a day under the watchful eye of secular forewomen and lived in *internats* (dormitories) kept by nuns of an order specifically created for this purpose. At night, they slept in these overpopulated dormitories, but each had her own bed, as was not always the case in the village or in smaller factories. The harshness of rural life in this era made life in the *internats* tolerable. They were a safeguard of morality for parents, who were said to be lucky to have daughters; with the girls' salaries, they could pay off their debts and lay manure; they signed three-year contracts and paid a fine of 50 centimes a day if they broke them; hence their hostility to strikes. Daily life consisted of prayer, mass, monotonous work (usually carried out in silence), and a few rare distractions (the girls were allowed to return home only once a month); it was of a convent-like austerity, which was very unlike the often joyful untidiness of the masculine *chambrées*. At the beginning of the twentieth century, the young female workers could no longer bear it. They began to strike against the long days, the now intolerable discipline. Ringleaders emerged, like Lucie Baud, who left behind a rare autobiography and, later, killed herself out of loneliness and solitude. It is not easy to be a rebel. The silk *internats* finally disappeared in the 1920s and 1930s.

All in all, the *chambrées* were better for the workers; they were "an asylum open to the very poorest in the very heart of the city." However, they were never the predominant mode of housing that we sometimes imagine. In Paris in 1895, they made up only 3 or 4 percent of furnished rooms. The number of beds per room was temporarily raised—five on average in 1880 (as noted), seven in 1895—to respond to a growing demand for individual beds. But the *chambrées* declined irrevocably due to their lack of hygiene and a growing desire for autonomy.[29] Young people especially wanted to rebel against the authority of the older generations that was built into the system; they wanted to make love more freely, build a home, have a little corner or space of their own. Nadaud was reprimanded by his father for his behavior; he left his room near the Hôtel de Ville to live in a room on rue Saint-Louis-en-l'Île. Émile Souvestre, another defector, celebrated his freedom: "A chair, a chest, a cot—this was all the furniture I had; but at least I was on my own. The space between these four walls belonged only to me. No one came—as in the *chambrée*—to eat up my air, to disturb my silence, to interrupt my singing or my sleep."[30]

The *chambrées* no longer met the needs of a more varied population, which had become younger, more feminine, and especially more family-oriented.

Furnished Rooms and Bedsits

The changing population explains the success of the furnished room and the bedsit, whether those were kept by landlords who may or may not have had permits (or were even clandestine) or by official hoteliers. Furnished hotel rooms—of which many photographs have survived—were generally quite small; they advertised their offerings ("furnished hotel"; "furnished rooms") and their facilities ("water and gas," "every comfort," "modern comforts").[31] They often featured a restaurant or a billiard hall (with "wine, coffee, liquor") on the ground floor. They had a variety of names, from those of their owners (Maison Margain, Hôtel Deoyez), meant to inspire confidence, to the names of provinces or cities (Hôtel de l'Aveyron, Hôtel du Nord, Hôtel du Midi, Hôtel de Périgueux), or they proclaimed themselves the Grand Hôtel, the Hôtel Éden, the Hôtel de l'Avenir. They saw pass through them tens or even hundreds of thousands of migrants. In 1856, 6.3 percent of the population of Paris (about seventy-five thousand people) lived in "furnished rooms," more than a third of them in certain neighborhoods (Belleville, Saint-Merri). They were mostly workers, sometimes students, and, more and more often, foreigners (there were two hundred thousand foreigners in Paris in 1914). This called for the proliferation of all kinds of bedsits, offered by unscrupulous landlords: a room, a closet, a nook, an area under a stairway, or even a simple bed in a corner. Opportunistic, clandestine, and either temporary or permanent, such rooms defied nomenclature and evaded the census.[32] This is why they exasperated the local administration and police.

There were numerous advantages to living in a bedsit. First of all, the fact of having a key on the board or, better, in one's pocket inspired a feeling of independence; the holders of such a key could go upstairs or come downstairs whenever they pleased. They had a place where they could leave their things. They were able to prepare food, to sleep alone or with the company of their choice, and to escape the hold of the family, which sometimes weighed as heavily as the rules of the *chambrée*, especially for the young, male or female. Joseph Voisin, a carriage painter, initially stayed with his uncle André but found the atmosphere deadening and was delighted to find "a room of my own" in the rue Galvani. "[I could be] free to come and go, free to do what I liked with whomever I liked, without having to be accountable to anyone." Jeanne Bouvier, an orphan, went up to Paris from the Savoie, first as a servant (where she was housed) and then as a seamstress; she lived with her cousins, who demanded fifteen francs a week to feed and house her. This was very expensive, and she left to stay in a small furnished room in a hotel. "Family is nice; a bedsit is better." For generations of people from the provinces, the Parisian hotel permitted them to acquire residential autonomy. "The furnished room may be sordid, but at least it's yours—your own home."[33] This meant a lot, even if, on a practical level, the material conditions were more restrictive. The hygiene was worse than mediocre, the rooms were noisy, there was very little privacy, and there were too many people, as a room was rarely rented to one individual and sometimes seven or eight people would be crammed inside it. And then the hotels or buildings in which these rooms were found were often dilapidated, dirty, insalubrious, noisy, and without privacy. It was far from ideal.

Proper bedsits were more scattered than the hotels, so they tended to group together. "A bedsit is rarely alone," wrote Alain Faure, describing the morphology of the system. Moreover, rooming houses—even housing estates—were built for this purpose—for example, at Pointe d'Ivry. Bedsits arranged themselves into hives whose every compartment was full; they were especially present in the center of Paris, composing the *îlots insalubres* that hygienists like Paul Juillerat (who coined the expression) said should be torn down, without worrying about the populations that clung desperately to this center of salvation. For being downtown was of the utmost importance; it was where work was available, where one could built a network, find some security. Why come to the city from so far away only to be exiled once again to the peripheries, cut off from it all? "The bedsit was an impoverished form of urbanization for the impoverished."[34] The city, against all odds, was there to be loved, not merely withstood. Further afield, the *banlieues* at first served as foils to the city before becoming industrial and residential centers in their own right. They tell a totally different story of lodgings in housing estates; they house another kind of bedroom.

In the nineteenth century, those who were newly arrived in Paris from the country, the provinces, or abroad sought housing in Les Halles, the Marais, and the Montagne Sainte-Geneviève, or they would walk up the Faubourg Saint-Antoine toward Charonne, Belleville, and Ménilmontant. They were more reticent to try their luck in the thirteenth arrondissement, which had only recently been built up, though it hadn't attracted many settlers.[35] In the rue Nationale and the rue Baudricourt and as far as Pointe d'Ivry, the outer limits of the city, the very poorest and most recently arrived tried to set up home—women (working as servants or seamstresses) or exiles (Lenin, for example, in the rue Marie-Rose). As a last resort, the famously sinister neighborhood of Jeanne-d'Arc could be tried, where housewives tried to mask their misery by hanging curtains on the windows.

A room or a closet designated the cramped space of the bedsit—sometimes both, but not often; that was the greatest luxury. Single men and women, workers, and broke students crammed themselves into closets without fireplaces or windows.[36] In the Latin Quarter, Jules Vallès found a lean-to under a skylight at a *frites* seller's. He had to enter it hunched over; he could only lie down in it and then only in the fetal position. "I forced my fingers to curl when I want to stretch out. It's a habit you acquire. . . . I could come home at any hour I liked; I had my own key." And, he noted with irony, "I could have ended up in one of those sad old rooms with all the space you need to pace in! I could go for a walk, but what then? I would be always wandering instead of reflecting! Prancing about, moving my legs from side to side in an oversized bed, like a courtesan or an acrobat!"[37] He even managed to take in a friend who in order to sleep had to hang his legs off the staircase. All students aren't from well-to-do families. The luckiest stayed in modest pensions, like the pension Vauquier, and the poorest looked at the closets with envy.

But the basic component of the bedsit is the "room"—that is, "any room large enough to contain a bed (at least five by seven feet)." This was the smallest possible room, hardly better than a closet. In 1896, 91 percent of lodgings had only one room; the figure had risen to 97 percent by 1911. One room thus became the norm in a bedsit. People from the provinces— Corrèze, Brittany—and especially foreigners banded together and rented in the same buildings. They tried to organize themselves, to find a way to cook together (an obsession of the poor). They rented by the night or the week, rarely by the month, with no lease or security, constantly surveyed by suspicious landlords, aware they were occupying less desirable rooms. "Slumming in a bedsit" was looked down upon and made them look down on themselves; the bosses didn't want to give work to people who lived "in a room"; girls were reluctant to come over. So everyone who lived there was always trying to leave; the bedsit population was volatile, to such an extent that the Second Republic asked itself: How can we give suffrage to such nomads? A law of 1850 required three years' residence for one to obtain suffrage. It indicates the perpetual suspicion that weighed on those who lived in the bedsits, hotbeds of ruffians and tuberculosis. Attention to sanitation control began under the Second Republic, and its standards would become more specific in time. The Conseil de Salubrité at the police prefecture recommended outlawing the practice of sleeping two to a bed and reducing the number of beds. An 1878 ruling required 130 square feet per person, raised to 150 square feet in 1878; it focused on air cubage as well: 380 cubic feet per person in 1890. The ruling also required "sufficient" access to water and one toilet for every twenty-five people. Even if they were rarely respected, these rulings introduced potential control over landlords and hotel keepers who were always at fault.

Supply diminished, but there still remained a considerable number of bedsits on the market. In 1954, 12,000 hotels and furnished lodgings were counted in the census, with a capacity of 204,240 rooms in Paris and 61,000 in the *banlieues;* the occupancy rate was 1.4 in Paris and 1.6 in the *banlieues.* Bedsits numbered around 400,000 renters—some 7.5 percent of the population. Most of the hotels were "lacking in comfort" when they weren't outright squalid. They housed the broke, the young, the newly arrived (many Algerians), the abused (women). In the 1950s, the sociologist Andrée Michel studied 276 Parisian households located in noisy, dirty, dilapidated furnished hotels.[38] These rooms were rarely redone by hotel keepers, who were concerned only with their profits. Renters would do the repainting themselves, replace the lightbulbs, solder leaky pipes. Some secretly bought their own furniture. There was no hygiene, no bathrooms or showers, not even shared ones; only 45 percent had running water in toilets or sinks; some hotels turned off the water during the daytime. Central heating was also available in only 45 percent of bedsits. The rooms were tiny: bedrooms measured ten by thirteen feet, not more than 130 square feet per household. The furniture, although basic—a sofa bed, camping material—took up the whole surface. The walls were thin; there was no privacy. Children crossed paths with prostitutes, who had the nicest rooms. There was no security; rents were agreed on only for a few days. One young family was batted from one hotel to another. A woman who had been deported in 1941 and lost everything lived precariously from day to day upon returning home. Renters also moved around with the hotel, depending on the needs of the clientele. The management—fearing above all that the bedsitters would *stay*—refused to allow folding beds or baby carriages. There were frequent conflicts; renters who united against illegal rent rises were taken to court and accused of a "Soviet plot" by the management's lawyer. Algerians, North Africans, Africans in general were especially badly treated. Anything could be used against them—and the Algerian war hadn't even begun yet.

Half a century later, the number of available bedsits again declined. According to Claire Lévy-Vroelant, who has described the system's decline (but also its persistence), today there are no more than a thousand furnished hotel rooms in Paris, and these were long ago outpaced by a general improvement in hotel facilities that began to be more specifically aimed at tourists.[39] The bedsits were relics of another age, eyesores in a renovated market; they were finished off by the construction equipment that dug up and transformed working-class neighborhoods. They were destroyed without being replaced. Those that remained resembled "cement shantytowns"; the fire at Paris-Opéra in the summer of 2005, which claimed several victims, revealed how hazardous they were. For an all-too-fleeting, emotionally charged moment, the cameras entered rooms where numerous families, often African, were crammed together; their work, often in the cleaning services, kept them in the center of Paris. They were there awaiting or hoping for something better, like their predecessors of the past: Limousins, Bretons, Italians, Poles, Jews of Central and Eastern Europe.

"Getting Furnished"

The bedsits had their limitations. It was easy to grow weary of them, of the rudimentary furnishings, and the landlords' whims and abuses. The desire would arise to be *dans ses bois,* or *dans ses meubles*—to "get furnished," to buy furniture and live among it. Charles-Louis Philippe, a lowly employee at the Paris police prefecture, lived in a bedsit in the rue Saint-Dominique and wrote to his mother (25 October 1896) to complain of the noise, the vulgar lack of privacy, the filth: "Life in the hotel is pathetic. We live next door to lowlives, who argue and fight every hour of the day and night. The rooms are disgusting and badly kept. To give you an idea, they haven't changed my bedding in three months. My basin and chamber pot have layers of filth that have been there for so long they can no longer be cleaned off. . . . If you want a decent room, in a decent hotel, it costs an insane amount of money, so I will always have to live in a notorious bedsit, with hoodlums for neighbors." He asks for some money "to buy some furniture," a move that would be cheaper than the bedsit in the end, an argument that his mother did not understand. Jules Vallès said the same to his father: "Give me a little money for a few pieces of furniture, enough to do up a monk-like corner where I can take shelter." He found an empty room near Contrescarpe for eighty francs, payable in advance. "I beg of you, make this sacrifice that will spare me so much danger and pain."[40] He had no more success; it was difficult to persuade one's impoverished, tightfisted parents.

It was best to look out for oneself, or even to buy on credit, on subscription. This is what a number of young workers did when they "went up" to Paris, eager for work. Jean Grave, a shoemaker, easily found work in the capital in the mid-1870s, but he was badly housed. "I didn't want to stay in a bedsit, so I took out a subscription at Crépin's. When I had paid half the price of a bed, a dresser, a table, and a few chairs, I moved into a room I rented in the Cour des Rames. I was home." This was a good phrase to describe one's owning a minimal amount of furniture. When Jeanne Bouvier left her family, she suffered in the filth of the bedsit: "The hotel repulsed me even more, as it was disgusting and patronized by a bad element. I couldn't clean it the way I would have cleaned my own home. . . . Going without little treats or pleasures caused me no pain, but to go without cleanliness was intolerable. I made all kinds of sacrifices to buy what I needed to live on my own." To the indispensable "furnishings" she added linen and kitchen utensils; she whitewashed the walls. "It wasn't luxurious, but it was home."[41] Georges Navel, a factory worker in Ménilmontant between the wars, put it forcefully: "Pushing open the door to the bedroom, love and real life began, which would help me bear life at the factory. I had left behind my solitude. Anne was still sleeping."[42]

To live one's "real life" meant to love freely. Young workers had precocious sexual lives. They made love in factories, in pits, in bistros. In England, "there are cabarets where boys and girls go upstairs two by two; in general sexual relations began around 14 or 15."[43] They left their families at a young age to set up more or less stable homes of their own. Cohabitation was an ordinary way of life that irritated the self-righteous, and that charitable organizations like the Saint-François-Régis in France or the London Mission in England tried to control. Constraints, economic necessity, and the social gaze shaped people's behavior, and marriage began to be seen as an ideal, or at least a socially desirable objective, to which the bedroom was the conduit.[44] Young people sought space and minimal furnishings that could be added to over time, with increases in their pay and the arrival of children. First one room, then a closet. First a wooden bed, then a table, chairs, dresser, curtains. Some would manage to create a domestic space. Others would only accumulate things and misery.

This, at least, is what several studies carried out by Frédéric Le Play's Société d'économie sociale would have us understand; its investigators did not shy away from passing moral judgment.[45] There are good households, which manage to get on. They have morality, a bit of religion (signaled by a crucifix, a statuette of the Virgin, a few pious images), a good work ethic, a knack for enjoying the social advantages conferred by the factory, a solid connection to the earth, and payment in kind, which limited the inconveniences of having a cash salary. They avoided living together without being married and, above all, emphasized the woman's role as housewife, the key to a balanced diet and budget. For in French homes, more than in English ones, she was the "minister of finance" of the family, as well as its doctor. Ingenious and versatile, she knew how to take advantage of a good deal, boil leathery meat, cook leftovers, prepare a lunchbox, mend old clothes. It was important to her to add to her husband's salary, complementing it with whatever extra money she could bring in by cleaning houses, babysitting, doing laundry, running errands, making deliveries, or working at home. The at-home sewing industry—using the famous Singer sewing machine bought on credit, described above—created new opportunities, which market competition transformed into a fatal trap. At the beginning of the twentieth century, investigators from the workers' bureau looked into the "sweating system" in the bedrooms of female workers.[46]

Though they did apply a normative gaze, Le Play's investigators were not without their merits. Their practice in the field and their rigorous methodology were subject to a precise, standardized questionnaire; they looked carefully at a household's expenses and profits, believing that the budget summarized a family's way of life; they had an attention to detail unequaled in the social literature of the time, making their descriptions of interiors almost legalistic inventories—no doubt they were inspired by those made by notaries; finally, they had a desire to explore the connections built up between the history of the family and the place where it lived, information that lends a personal, sensitive tone to their observations.

Workers' Interiors

It always worked the same way. Studies would describe the various aspects of the family—the ages of the father and mother and the ages and genders of each of the children; the location of the lodging within the building, its layout and size, the number of rooms, lighting (number of windows or skylights), and heating (chimneys, fires). Then there was the listing of furniture. First, the beds (number, material) and bedding (mattress, box springs, sheets); they were always discussed on their own, an indication of their importance. Then the various other kinds of furniture, with a note as to their age and state; the utilitarian or personal objects that gestured at decoration; the state of the walls, paint or wallpaper, and the curtains. Clothes—like furniture and objects—were also inventoried and evaluated in great detail, an indication of their value as property. The studies concluded with a terse, general statement of the investigator's impressions, his judgment as to the moral and material situation of the family, legible to him as the degree of "order and cleanliness."

Let's push open a few of these doors. For an annual rent of 180 francs, the Parisian carpenter lived with his wife and two children (a boy of twelve and a daughter of seven) in a fifth-floor apartment in a mediocre building in the ninth arrondissement; sixty-two renters were subject to the tyranny of a concierge, who played, then as now, an essential role in the life of the building and yet was almost always confined to a poky *loge* on the first floor. The lodging—220 square feet in total—included two rooms: a tiny entryway; a bedroom with a fireplace, lit only by a window and a skylight; plus a small attic in the eaves for putting dirty laundry. The parents slept in the main room, and the children slept "each separately in the entryway," which was also fitted out as a kitchen with a table, a wood-burning stove, and a few shelves. The furnishings, which were estimated at 868 francs, had "none of the signs of luxury that indicate[d] a tendency to live a bourgeois life." There were three beds; the parents' included a walnut fold-up bed frame, three woolen mattresses, two "ordinary" feather mattresses, a feather bolster, two pillows, a "common" bedspread, a fleece wool blanket, a white calico quilt, and a pair of curtains; there was a cot for each child, a little cherrywood bed with a straw mattress and two little calico curtains. The use of the curtains indicates a desire for privacy. In the bedroom, all the furniture was made of walnut: an armoire with double doors, a nightstand, a dresser, a table covered in waxed canvas, and six straw-bottomed chairs. There was also a sculpted wooden pendulum under a glass cylinder, a frame with a colored image, a little statue of the Virgin Mary, a birdcage with accessories, and a few books (devotional, history, cookery). "The lodging is as clean as the restrictions of space will allow, given the necessity of cooking food in the bedroom fireplace or in the stove in the entryway." In the bedroom, the investigators noticed the cage: "The worker voluntarily looks after a bird that was given to him; his wife takes care to feed and clean the elegant cage." Workers—especially female workers—liked to have pets around—birds, cats, and even dogs.[47]

In Gentilly, a weaver specializing in shawls at a Parisian factory collective brought together an old way of life, like the chamberlain of yore, combining home and atelier. For six people (including four children, ages ten, eight, six, and four), he had a large room divided into four sections: a nook for the kitchen, a dining room where the boys slept (the youngest in a cradle), and a closet for the girls' beds. The parents' room doubled as a living room. It included a fireplace with a marble casing and a screen decorated with painted figures. The housewife took great care to protect this room from the children. It was newly decorated with fresh wallpaper and red-painted tiles. In addition to the walnut bed surrounded by white calico curtains, there were a few pieces of furniture brought by the wife's dowry, including a screen and a dresser. Though somewhat damp, the whole place "breathed order and a taste for work."[48]

Others had it worse. The quarryman's family on the outskirts of Paris crammed six people (the parents plus four young children) into a room of 160 square feet, with tiled floors, three beds, and a cradle; the sole luxury was a walnut sideboard.[49] The water porter had enough for five people in one room (130 square feet), for the parents and a cabinet (65 square feet) for the children.[50] The furniture was ramshackle and badly taken care of, partly inherited; it was dirty because of the lack of a kitchen. The Parisian tailor paid a rent of 140 francs a year for a 180-square-foot room in a hallway on the fifth floor; the room was one of twelve in a row; the couple slept with their two-year-old son and at the foot of the bed placed a trundle bed for their elder son.[51] The investigator's comments emphasize the indecency of the situation, aggravated by the fact that the parents were unmarried. The room was stuffed with cheap furniture, bought secondhand and haphazardly maintained: a dresser, a trunk, a walnut table, four tattered chairs, a wood-burning stove, a mirror, four vases, and two birdcages. The investigator found this hodgepodge to be an indicator of the erosion of morals in a profession that had lost any ability to anticipate the future. "The old workers are dying on the pavement," it was said in the industry. Tailors—who were often to be found at the *goguettes,* cabarets that the investigator looked down upon—were not the correct sort of people in his opinion.

Interiors tell stories about the families who live there. In this sense, there is a strong contrast between a linen seamstress and a toy maker in Lille.[52] Seduced and abandoned by a locksmith, the former lived with her seven-year-old daughter in a 108-foot-square room, with no fireplace, that she rented for six francs a month. The walls were bare, the furniture dilapidated: a wobbly table, sagging chairs, and a bed made of four planks (called a "cholera bed," manufactured in haste during the 1849 epidemic); this was the background for a far too frequent female misery, shared by the toy maker. Forty years old, separated from an alcoholic factory worker, working at home, she lived with her two sons (seventeen and thirteen) in a few tiny rooms fixed up in an attic, which she tried to imbue with an air of "genteel poverty," according to the investigator. In the bedroom (130 square feet) there were two iron beds: one large one, which she shared with the younger son, and a smaller one for the elder; there was old walnut furniture and a combination dresser and basin; old-fashioned knickknacks decorated the mantelpiece—a bell jar over a bridal veil, a crucifix, some old engravings and photographs, a coffee set. This motley array of objects, the remnants of a long-ago prosperity, attest to the worker's degradation; the investigator suggests that she was ruined by a *sublime* (alcoholic worker) and driven into the sweat system.[53]

A Parisian locksmith and blacksmith, a certified artisan, was better off.[54] For 250 francs a year, he rented a two-bedroom apartment on boulevard de la Chapelle, in a relatively recent building with eight hundred other renters. The three rooms of the apartment had oak parquet floors and a fireplace, covering 300 square feet. For this couple and their five children, it was a tight fit. But the investigator is pleased to note the care lavished on the couple's bedroom, at a far end of the apartment. The walnut bed and box spring were made up with white calico sheets; there was a night table, a washstand, an armoire with double doors, two straw-bottomed chairs, and an iron cradle for the eighteen-month-old baby. On the mantelpiece stood a pendulum under a dome, with bronze figurines. On the walls, there were a gilded wooden mirror and six frames with images and photographs. The wallpaper was worn from humidity and northern exposure, but the window was hung with colored Indian curtains.

The Parisian maker of luxury cabinets was living the high life, with two rooms for five people (parents and children of eighteen, thirteen, and eight). The fact of having a living room and the quality of the furniture in the parents' room—a mahogany bed, a mirrored armoire, a sofa, a number of decorations on the mantelpiece, an orange-flower crown, a birdcage—indicate the family's middle-class aspirations. All this in 215 square feet—a space that was very annoying to the family, who was very concerned about hygiene, having "replaced the priest with the doctor," as Pierre du Maroussem, that subtle observer of the Faubourg Saint-Antoine, put it.[55]

By comparison, the fitting supervisor's lodging at the Familistère de Guise was palatial: two mid-sized rooms and three small rooms for five people—a real apartment with an eat-in kitchen.[56] The parents had a large bed with a box spring (an indication that the furnishings were very modern), no curtains on the bed, a nightstand, some paintings and vases, an old carpet, a mirror and some photographs, and an engraving showing "the great *familistère*"—and that was just the beginning. This qualified worker, selected for the study for his competence and morality, had a relatively comfortable quality of life; it "pleased him to decorate his home," the investigator notes, adhering on this point to the "social solutions" of an industrialist and innovator like Godin, who believed the worker's home was crucially important. It was the "equivalent of riches" and the foundation on which to build a work ethic.[57]

Life a User's Manual (for Workers)

As far as lodgings went, workers were subject to certain imperatives that shaped their desires. What did they want? Above all, they wanted to live close to work; this led them to look first in the center of a city where jobs were to be found. This was also true for women, who were always in search of a few hours of work with which to supplement their husbands' salaries. In the Haussmannian period, workers dug their heels in and refused to leave the center of the city to be "deported to Cayenne" (that is, to the *banlieues*), even if two families had to be crammed into one apartment. They attempted to pay a rent that would not exceed a fifth of their budget, which was already devoured by the cost of food (50–70 percent).[58] To maintain appearances, they were prepared to spend more on their clothing than on a quality of lodging that would still remain out of their reach. But we should not conclude from this that workers didn't care about where they lived.[59] All recent studies (for example, by Magri or Faure) refute this overhasty image of workers' resignation to insupportable conditions. This is not the case.

Workers continually sought to improve their lots in life; this is one of the reasons they moved around so much. The end of every rental term in Paris resulted in more or less furtive moves from one apartment to another, not only in order for a worker to avoid paying the rent, but also in an effort to better lodge a rapidly growing family. Carts called *diables* (which Atget captured in his photographs, shafts striating the sky) were used to transport a summary amount of furniture—a bed, a mattress, rags, pots and pans. The anarchists of the Belle Époque, who declared war on "M. Vautour" (an imaginary proprietor), supported the badly housed with militant activism.

What were the workers looking for exactly? A small separate room in which to prepare, cook, and store food was a priority not only because of the smoke and the smells—proletarian noses were as easily offended as any others—but also for reasons of order and hygiene and a reluctance to mix food and sleep. Even in a narrow room one could hang shelves to put away food and utensils; a wood-burning stove or camping stove could be used to cook instead of the fireplace in the bedroom, which was in use during the winter. The need for a kitchen was most pressing but not necessarily as a space to eat in; because there wasn't enough room, most inhabitants ate *sur le pouce,* or on the go.[60] But the family meal in the evenings and on Sundays, around the table (preferably a round one), was increasingly valued. CGT union posters calling for the eight-hour work day in 1906 illustrate this ideal, contrasting the ramshackle family of an alcoholic worker with the family seated at a table, a steaming soup tureen brought in by a comely housewife, whose husband carries a copy of *La Bataille syndicaliste* in his pocket. Below these two scenes the following is written: "Long days make unhappy families/Shorter days make happy families" who come together to eat dinner. A reduction in the work day and an improvement in one's living arrangements went hand in hand.

Then there was a desire for a second room that would allow the bedroom to be less crowded and to separate the parents from the children, boys on one side, girls on another. This double bodily segregation was an entrenched part of the worker's lifestyle. Workers interviewed as part of a parliamentary enquiry in 1884 emphasized the degree to which this modest requirement was important to them, along with the presence of more shared toilets. Of course, they said timidly, "people aren't asking to have their own toilets"; this was a still inaccessible luxury, unthinkable at that time, when the sewer systems and water distribution networks were still unfinished.[61] At the least they wanted to sleep comfortably.

Two rooms: this is all it would take to be able to have a bedroom—a real one, with a "marital bed," the foundation of the couple—that would allow for a relative amount of sexual privacy. We can imagine the ordinary frustrations that would reduce the act of love—so dependent on the look and the sigh of pleasure—to a hasty, brief coupling. According to a 1909 Board of Trade report, although French workers were the worst-lodged in Western Europe, by the beginning of the century they had achieved at least this modest quality of life. By this date, 80 percent of workers had two rooms, and 20 percent still had only one. According to Charles Garnier and Auguste Amman, "one single room without a fireplace houses the most profound misery; one room with a fireplace, which serves as both bedroom and kitchen, is the poor worker's lot; if the kitchen is distinct from the bedroom, we've reached a relative degree of comfort. The existence of a dining room suggests a more elevated situation: this is normally the maximum level of comfort that the working classes can achieve."[62]

For lack of a better arrangement, the smaller children slept at the foot of their parents' bed; the older ones slept in the kitchen. There were a number of foldaway cots and light iron beds. People hung curtains and sheets and used screens or movable walls. Unable to enlarge their homes, people resorted to carving them up. Just as in the Russian communal apartment, corners become rooms or imitate their uses; the same is true for meals, which were served on side tables, as in the eighteenth century. This required constantly putting things away, transforming them, making modifications—this is what Zola's Gervaise (in *L'Assommoir*) does in the apartment she and Coupeau live in after their marriage. The apartment is very adaptable, optimal even: a large room, a smaller room, and a kitchen. "Étienne's bed took up the smaller room, where there was just enough space for another child's cot. They were very proud of the larger room. Come morning, they closed the curtains to the alcove, white calico curtains, and the room was transformed into a dining room, with the table in the middle."[63] It took a certain energy to keep up appearances, one that in time began to lag.

In the constricted setting of these narrow lodgings, an infinite number of details indicate a desire for appropriation: the choice of wood, of wallpaper, of an object or an image, the presence of books. The massive furniture—usually walnut—was almost always bought secondhand. The usual trio of "bed, table, chairs" was joined by a nightstand (only one; there was rarely enough room for the bed to be placed in the middle of the room), a washbasin with accessories, and a dresser, which was the worker's favorite piece of furniture, rivaled only by the armoire, first with a door then with a mirror, as in the bosses' own homes. Sometimes there would be an easy chair, a chest, or a sideboard, suggesting a rural heritage. To "get furnished" was to break with the bedsit, to render an amorous relationship concrete—a couple's union, their entrance into a shared life, their plans to have children, to set up house. Gervaise "was religious about furniture, wiping it down with maternal care, her heart broken by the slightest scratch."

The mantelpiece and the dresser served as display cases; on them were lined up pendulums, orange blossom wedding bouquets under bell jars, porcelain figurines, knickknacks, cheap rubbish sold at a reduced price by some retailer in order to create loyal customers, religious figurines (found not only in the homes of Leplaysian workers). At the home of Lise and Agricol Perdiguier, on either side of the mirror "were hung little black festooned velvet cushions, on which rested a family medallion and a silver watch, the only jewelry in poor households." On the cornice of the armoire, Gervaise placed the busts of two random "great men": one of Pascal, and one of Béranger, no doubt turned up at some secondhand shop, an

indication of the cultural aspirations that characterized her relationship
with Coupeau at that time.

The only free space in these lodgings were the walls, which became
the object of a greedy desire to occupy the space—one that was at the same
time decorative and utilitarian (everything that couldn't be put away was
hung from the walls on nails or hooks). When one moves into a new home,
the first thing to do was whitewash the walls, repaint them, hang some new
paper over the old, layering fashions and periods. Since the eighteenth century, hanging wallpaper (popularized by the working class before the bourgeoisie started using it) has been synonymous with renovation. Charles
Blanc, the brother of the socialist Louis Blanc, emphasizes its democratic
character: "The wallpaper industry addresses a double need for the less
well-off: the need to close oneself off and the desire to hide the bareness of
the walls that separate the man from the world."[64] A light wallpaper gave the
Perdiguiers' bedroom an "air of liveliness." The interiors photographed by
Eugène Atget feature papers with flowers or stripes. A worker in Romain-
ville nailed a mirror, frames, and hooks on a wallpaper dotted with bouquets of flowers.[65] The walls were cluttered with an army of decorations:
reflective glass, rather than mirrors (a still rare luxury), pious or historical
pictures, genre scenes that Le Play's investigators deemed "bawdy," family
photographs, which became much more frequent after 1880.[66] Walls were
like a second skin. The workers couldn't get enough of pictures, which they
took from the press. They liked the colorful covers of the newspapers, including the lavishly illustrated supplements of the *Petit Parisien* or the *Petit
Journal.* A glove maker in Grenoble pinned up a portrait of Louis XVIII.
Gervaise chose a *maréchal de France;* she admired the decoration of her
neighbor, Goujet the blacksmith: "images from ceiling to floor, cut-out
pictures of men, colored engravings affixed with four nails, portraits of all
sorts of people, torn out of the illustrated papers"; it was a joyous, baroque
explosion of images, an indication of an avid curiosity.

Goujet was a model worker who lived with his widowed mother in a
young girl's room and also had "a narrow bookcase hung from the wall."[67]
To read was a sign of distinction, an expression of the worker's dream.
Gauny, a parquet layer, was sorry he "could not live until death with our

books."[68] Which books? We know relatively little of the workers' book-shelves. According to Gilland, "good books" filled the oak shelves in Agri-col Perdiguier's home, and these doubtless included many titles on *compagnonage*. The studies by Le Play's investigators sometimes provided lists. There were professional manuals (the famous *Roret Guides*), cookbooks, history books, religious books, political books. An independent carpenter in Paris, an activist, lined up the books for his profession next to socialist books, like Marx's *Capital*, Louis Blanc's *L'Organisation du travail*, and the works of Eugène Sue and Victor Hugo.[69] The elite workers were great readers of these books, as indicated by the library at the Amis de l'instruction, created under the Second Empire and conserved "as it was" in the rue de Turenne.[70]

There were curtains everywhere—around the beds, in the bathroom, on the windows—even in the miserable lodgings in the Cité Dorée that Atget photographed.[71] This suggests a search for contentment represented by the interior, a victory over adversity, the recreation of a universe. "Almost everything that surrounded Agricol Perdiguier was odious and repulsive, but once inside his home, it was like finding oneself in another world."[72] Perdiguier's wife Lise, a linen seamstress and dressmaker (she was George Sand's), hung muslin curtains on the windows. Virginia Woolf notices the same gesture, not without condescension, in the suburbs of London in 1915: "The vilest little red villas are always let and that not one of them has an open window or an uncurtained window. I expect that people take a pride in their curtains and that there is great rivalry among neighbours. One house had curtains of yellow silk, striped with lace insertion. The rooms inside must be in semi-darkness; & I suppose rank with the smell of meat & human beings. I believe that being curtained is a mark of respectability."[73]

Lodging Workers

For a large business, a place to lodge workers was imperative.[74] It was a way of attracting manpower and keeping it in place, of disciplining it, of creating "the indefatigable little worker" necessary for its expansion.[75] Early "barracks" were replaced by housing estates on a large scale, conceived by architects who developed rationalist ideas about workers' homes—more basic for the miners and more refined for the metalworkers.

Miners were originally country folk. In Carmaux and elsewhere, care was taken to provide them with a bit of garden more than a living room or bedroom.[76] In the countryside where *Germinal* was set, inspired by Anzin (in the north), the population was dense both indoors and out. "In the middle of the fields of wheat and beetroot, the miners' cottages of the Deux-Cent Quarante settlement slept under the black night. One could vaguely distinguish four immense blocks of little houses sitting back to back, barracks or hospital blocks, geometric, parallel, separating the three large avenues that were divided into equally apportioned gardens." At number 16 of the second block, in the Maheu house, "thick shadows drowned the only bedroom on the first floor" in the odors of a sleeping bedroom. It was a square room with two windows, light yellow walls, and rudimentary furniture: an armoire, a table, two old walnut chairs, a pitcher on the ground next to an earthenware pot that served as a toilet, rags of clothing hung from nails. Three beds were shared among six children, boys and girls ranging in age from nine to twenty-one. The parents slept on the floor near the baby's crib—Estelle was barely three months old.[77] It is a somber painting, largely reconstructed from Zola's own fieldwork.

The Société industrielle de Mulhouse was founded by the Protestant textile industry, with strong Germanic influences, and was much more innovative. To comply with his orders, the engineer Émile Muller drew on the notion of the English cottage. In groups of four, back to back or side by side, the *carré de Mulhouse* (Mulhouse square) houses featured gardens, a common room on the ground floor (referred to as the *chambre d'habitation* [living room]), and one or more bedrooms upstairs, plus a basement and an attic. The rooms were approximately 100–130 square feet. This relatively luxurious model was rarely improved on, and it inspired many similar living arrangements, at least in the larger factories.[78]

The Schneider family, who ran Le Creusot, implemented well thought-out spatial and residential policies.[79] They preferred the stability of workers who owned their homes to the unreliable flux of renters. There were places for children and young women to learn how to keep house—as noted, having a good housewife was an essential part of a harmonious way of life. Indeed, the performance of housekeeping was rated by inspectors. Order, hygiene, and morality; these households were designed to promote such commandments. What was surprising about these workers' *cités*, or neighborhoods, was the amount of land given over to gardens, the way the space was privatized, the way the bedroom was moved to the upper floor, and the stricter definition that was applied to the room used for sleeping. This at least is what we see on the sketches for the plans, which indicate a certain way of thinking about society and the family. French workers disliked the control exerted within the *cités*, but though they resisted in some ways, they usually got used to it. In this sense the *cités* were a relatively useful introduction to the modern workers' homes, which emerged slowly and from multiple directions.

There were many contributing factors that are not our concern here.[80] The housing estates of the first half of the twentieth century had little to do with the workers, who were much more strongly impacted by the *habitations à loyer modéré*, or council housing (*HLMs*) after World War II and by the development of the *banlieues* and the new towns. A decisive change came in the late twentieth century, when workers became homeowners. From then on, they were more invested in their homes than the cities where they were found, according to Michel Verret, who has studied this shift.[81] The city was too far away; workers only went there for meetings. Their major claim-staking had to do with the privatization of space. "By turning the manager's surveying gaze away from his private home, the worker carved out a freedom that was so precious that he was willing to pay the price of distance and fatigue." The factory was only too present. "For the worker, owning his own home meant above all that he did not have to be in someone else's space but in his own, where he could be himself." Workers invested (on credit) in home furnishings; they could decorate as they liked, with a surprising taste for home improvement, though more often in the living and dining rooms than in the bedroom.[82] The bedroom was specifically used for sleeping and took on associations with privacy that were both acquired and imposed. In a way, the workers' bedrooms were dissolved, becoming ordinary rooms according to their functions, their placement, and their arrangements. Hidden away from the public gaze, attention was no longer lavished on them; instead, the most personal objects were given refuge there: wedding photos, crude images, religious objects—perhaps a crucifix over the bed—linen in the dresser, clothes in the closet. Workers had a sharp need for privacy since it had been denied them for so long. Modesty was an acquired honor.

After two hundred years of claim-staking, individual and collective protests, everyday efforts, and incremental gains, workers were finally at home. How well or badly they lived is another question. They had distanced themselves from the poor man, who lacked bedrooms and dividing walls.[83] The poor live precariously, looking for a corner of the city to sleep in, preferring that to the dormitories of homeless shelters, where there is no privacy and the fear of being shuffled along. They set up tents, put down their mattresses, unfurl their sleeping bags or their blankets in some corner on the outskirts of town or, less frequently, under the entryways of buildings (which were eventually closed off and protected with digicodes), at the limits or in the hearts of our cities. Against all odds, they maintain the right to a space of their own. The bedrooms of the homeless have no walls; their living spaces haunt the city.

Makeshift Homes

There are, today, almost one hundred thousand people in France living on the street (*sans domicile fixe,* or *SDF*), eight thousand of whom are in Paris, though it is difficult to ascertain the exact number.[84] Slightly more than 6 percent are there by choice; the rest, through the oppressive necessity of crisis. They are not antisocial; three out of ten have jobs, and four out of ten are registered with the unemployment office and are looking for work. They are not itinerant by choice but are underpaid workers with nowhere to live or with homes that have been closed to them because they could not pay the rent or the bills. We tend to call them simply *sans domicile,* fixity being a secondary characteristic, however difficult to ignore. A third of them are young people, many are foreigners, and more and more are women (in the 18–24 age group, there are as many women as men). Some have provided testimony or even written about the difficulties of living rough for women, who often have to look after children.[85] The life of the *SDF* calls for resourcefulness, energy, and a refined knowledge of the geography and offerings of a city. A metro station, a park, a square, a bench, or a table become important locations in a space that can become more and more closed off and controlled. Some shelters are more acceptable than others. When the temperature falls, some go to a shelter every night. But where to put their belongings during the day? To address this problem, some nonprofit groups have opened "lockers," like left luggage areas in train stations. Living rough isn't really a choice, except for the several thousand hardliners or "drop outs," who more or less correspond to the vagabonds and bums of yesteryear.[86]

Throughout history, many have chosen to lead an itinerant life. In the nineteenth century, the forests and the cities were the unmanageable territories where vagabonds (more rural figures) and bums (more urban) took refuge—in barns, in huts, on porches, in courtyards. They have been hassled by the police and progressively marginalized by the norms of a stabilizing society that makes citizenship dependent on the home (the right to vote, for example). In the twentieth century, geographic shifts in population accentuated the need for housing; precarious forms of housing proliferated. Slums, shantytowns, all manner of improvised housing grew up around the edges of major towns and cities.

Around Paris, the ragpickers' shacks built up in the "Zone" on the northern edges of the city, pushed out toward the outer boulevards, and then to the *périphérique* (ring road). After World War II came the *bidonvilles* (shantytowns), so called in 1953 after the container towns that grew up in the suburbs of Casablanca. These were notable for their permanent structures, as well as a certain density of inhabitation (around three hundred people in sixty homes). The *bidonville* in Nanterre, where Algerians and Portuguese converged, was mostly made up of families, a structured, mutually supportive society whose ingenious functioning and processes of acculturation have been analyzed by the ethnographer Colette Pétonnet. "The *bidonville* takes on an essential role, that of a successful transition."[87] It was also a means of resisting the obligation to live in improvised housing or in an *HLM*. The latter was greatly in demand, though initially out of reach for many, and served as a normalizing space where only "suitable" people were allowed to live. The layout of the apartments in the *bidonvilles* did not always please new occupants, who suffered from the lack of privacy and the configuration of the bedrooms. There were always too few or too many, and they were badly laid out; there were never enough for everyone. Denounced by Abbé Pierre in the winter of 1954 and targeted by the policies of Jacques Chaban-Delmas, who found them intolerable, most of the *bidonvilles* were destroyed. Some inhabitants experienced the obligatory rehousing as a painful tearing away, a loss of identity. *Bidonvilles* cropped up here and there, in the suburbs of Marseille, for example, and even in the Bois de Vincennes; in the autumn of 2007, two hundred people (alone or in groups) took refuge there in permanent structures.

Destitution, but also a savage desire for autonomy, drove these inhabitants to defend their spatial independence. Caravans are not only the preserve of travelers, but also a form of resistance to proletarianization. A Portuguese family (a couple and two children) rented a cramped yet tidy and colorful caravan, which they furnished like a boat cabin. There was a galley kitchen with a camping stove. "During the day, they put away all the sleeping equipment to make more space and unfolded a table and chairs. Everything was impeccably organized, compensating for how narrow the space was with a mania for rational organization," which took up most of the mother's time (she was twenty-nine years old), while the father (who suffered from depression) labored as a construction worker.[88] Such was the lot of many poor households. Zola's Gervaise did the same in her room in the Goutte-d'Or. But furnishings today are more lightweight than they were when *L'Assommoir* was written.

Camping material was most convenient, and mobile homes were a good solution. Camper vans replaced the caravans of the 1950s, which were specifically intended for tourism, and these were incredibly successful; introduced in 1967, by 1994 they numbered over a million. They still served as open-air hotels and became more and more comfortable. "In some of the vehicles, you can even find real bedrooms *[sic]*, with a bed that you can move around and a partition separating it off from the living room," proclaimed one advertisement.[89] Thirty-five thousand models were sold in 2005. The older ones were reclaimed or rented by less-well-off customers, who made them their homes. According to a 2006 report, one hundred thousand people were living year-round in camper vans or mobile homes. In Marseille, out of six campsites open all year, there were 250 permanent rentals, or 570 inhabitants, out of which 197 households received benefits. Several nonprofit groups sent by representatives led a campaign to acknowledge them as permanent homes, with post codes allowing them to be declared official residences.[90]

An official residence remains the key to social integration and is coveted for this reason. This is what an investigation by Xavier Godinot for ATD-Quart Monde revealed; he researched four different life narratives in the Philippines, Burkina Faso, Peru, and France.[91] In the Philippines, Mercedita lived under a bridge and returned there repeatedly. In Noisy-le-Grand, a suburb of Paris, Farid and Céline fought long and hard to obtain a flat in a small estate run by ATD. They were lucky. "Without a home, you are nothing. You don't even exist on this planet," Farid said, describing the years when he had no fixed residence. "Not having a home means you're outside twenty-four/seven with a bag on your shoulder. You're pounding the pavement all day and even all night." It's impossible to find a job or vote; it's especially difficult to raise a child. Farid describes their happiness when they were granted a home:

> The last night at the hotel, and especially the first one we spent in the flat, we couldn't sleep at all! I couldn't stop looking at the walls, measuring them, looking at the kitchen. It was as if someone had said to me: 'Come on, we're going to take a little walk in Paradise.' We cooked, we made coffee, we woke up whenever we liked. It was a change, a really big change. We found our rhythm: coming home, having a sink, our own toilet. I had never had a home or a rent receipt.

To have a bedroom, a key—this was a decisive change. "The key was something incredible," said Farid. "The day I had a key and a rent receipt, I saw how many doors opened up to me. I was always shaved, bright-eyed, well-rested, wearing clean clothes. Everything was in place. I could show up for work in view of the bosses. I could live with my wife." The home plays a major role in a difficult integration process. Eventually the couple found a flat in an *HLM:* "We had one bedroom. Karim [their child, whom they'd had to give up] also had a bedroom." They could take back their child, now that they had a place to raise him, and find work. Farid found a job as a building concierge.[92] This narrative shows the extent to which one's lodging is crucial, even more today, perhaps, because of strict requirements about stability and social control. The right to housing, which forms the basis of citizenship, ought to be a human right.

At the same time, migrations are increasing. On the doorstep of Calais, where the Sangatte camp has been closed, clandestine immigrants (Afghans, Kurds, Sudanese) in transit to England (350–600 per week) have built makeshift shelters out of bits of construction debris, sheet metal, blankets, rags, clothing, cardboard, and branches; the police regularly teargas and burn the camp, reducing it to a misshapen, reeking mess. For two years, Jacques Revillard photographed these ephemeral shelters, preserving their memory in color. He made them visible and saved them from oblivion.[93]

As soon as the makeshift home is stamped out in one place, it crops up somewhere else, reflecting the mobility of its inhabitants, who search for a better life. Currently 6 percent of the urban population in developed countries and 43 percent in developing countries live in shantytowns. The townships of South Africa, the *favelas* of Brazil, and the slums of Bombay rival the scale of the vast urban conglomerates of Kenya, where Kibera is one of the largest shantytowns in the world. The American sociologist Mike Davis has argued that the increase (which began in the 1980s) in an informal economy and an unhinged urbanization is the key to the "global shantytowns" toward which all our societies are heading. "If nothing changes, the future of humanity will be life in a cardboard box."[94]

Nevertheless, the dream of a room of one's own lives on, as tenacious as it is fragile.

Sickbeds and Deathbeds

The Death of George Sand

GEORGE SAND DIED on 8 June 1876, at ten o'clock in the morning, in her bedroom. Since that spring, she had been ill. On 8 May, she wrote to her editor, Buloz, who asked when she would work again; she replied: "Without being ill, I have been uncomfortable and unable to work for two months. I think I will be able to return to work, but I cannot promise when." Nevertheless, she was planning to return to Paris, as she did every spring, in two weeks. On 22 May, she wrote to Maurice Albert: "I have been ill for a few months, but I hope to recover soon and return to my scribbling." She even proposed writing a review of Ernst Renan's *Dialogues et fragments philosophiques* (having greatly appreciated his *La Vie de Jésus*), which would be published after her death. On 28 May she wrote to Marguerite Thuillier: "Your old friend suffers greatly from a chronic illness of the intestines but is in no danger. It is just a question of patience, and I have a great deal of it." She wrote regularly to Dr. Henri Favre, who usually treated her in Paris. On 18 May, she wrote to him: "I am fighting my own demons with patience. The crises are more frequent but less severe." She replied to his questions on 28 May: "I do not feel any onset of senility." But she suffered from unrelenting constipation: "I have had almost no natural evacuations for more than two weeks; I wonder where this is leading, and if I shouldn't expect a sudden departure one of these mornings."[1] She did not fight for her life but did everything she could to take care of herself. "Delicious weather. I'm not suffering very much," she noted on 29 May, in the last entry in her *Agendas*. On 30 May, in her last letter (to her cousin Oscar Cazamajou), she wrote, "I am still under the weather." She had nine days left to live.[2]

212

We are exceptionally well informed about Sand's death.[3] Dr. Favre, aware he was witnessing a historic event, left a detailed account, written during the night of 8–9 June, as he watched over her. "Alone, in the contemplative silence of dawn, I am writing to you from the desk of the strange woman who was George Sand. . . . In this eighteenth-century castle, she is there, on her deathbed, surrounded by flowers and foliage from her park. While the storm of a family drama rumbles, the birds sing in the verdant trees." The drama concerned the conflict between Sand's son Maurice and his wife Lina as to what should be written on the death notice; Maurice wanted to use his title ("Baron"), while Lina was against it: "I don't want to be brought closer to an aristocracy that detests us. . . . I am, and wish to remain, the daughter-in-law of Mme Sand"—that is, of a George Sand who never compromised with the aristocracy.[4]

According to Favre, the death throes lasted a long time but were gentle at the end. He prayed for his patient and friend, kissed her forehead, and asked for a lock of her white hair. He made sure the priest did not enter, for she didn't wish him to. "The priest prowled around the victim, whom he wanted to mark with his insignia. He could walk in the paths under the trees, he could sit in the chairs in the salon, but he had no hope of entering the sickroom." Anticlerical and deistic, Favre saw himself as "God's only representative" and funeral director, to help "this diaphanous little soul" rise to the spirit world.

The journalist Henry Harrisse, Sand's intimate friend and a great admirer of the "marvelous writer," took up a serious investigation of the doctors and witnesses, whose "responses were compared and submitted to careful inspection," in an effort to untangle the various roles played. He describes Sand's last days with clinical precision: the ballet of the six doctors (local and Parisian) and their rivalries at the deathbed of the famous writer.

Sand's state worsened on 31 May after she was prescribed a laxative (of ricin oil and orgeat syrup) by the young local doctor, Marc Chabenat. It had no effect beyond pain and vomiting. She was suffering greatly from what we call "intestinal occlusion." Her cries could be heard as far as the other side of the garden. "She is lost," said Dr. Papet, joined by Dr. Pastel of

Saint-Chartier. The latter contacted Favre, though he did not care for him. Favre arrived in Paris on 1 June and left with the goal of bringing back a surgeon. On the second, a surgeon called Péan arrived at Nohant with Dr. Darchy (who came from the Creuse region), called for by Lina, who trusted him. The doctors decided on an enterostomy with stomach tube and an injection of twelve siphons of seltzer water, a very painful operation. "Mme Sand suffered horribly during the operation but had significant relief afterward," noted Chabenat. On 5 June, Favre returned with Plauchut, Sand's right-hand man, with no illusions.

Sand was humiliated by the nature of her illness. "A nasty malady," she called it. She had such modesty and spoke of her body so little; she hated inflicting the sight of her soiled sheets on the people around her. "She kept her children and friends away from her sickbed so they wouldn't see the traces of her illness." Letting them see it horrified her, especially her two granddaughters, who were never far away. Lina brought them in briefly for a quick goodbye; Sand said to them: "Be good. I love you." Maurice came to the threshold, and she asked him vehemently to leave.

Sand slept on an iron bed, specially installed in the middle of the room, facing the fireplace. Solange, her daughter, reoriented it so she could look out the window. To see the garden? The weather was terrible, cool and rainy—autumnal weather. She was surrounded by women: her daughter Solange, who had run to her side from Paris, in spite of her brother's reticence, Maurice believing he was in control of everything; her daughter-in-law Lina; the "devoted" Solange Marier, a nurse. On the evening of the seventh, she said her goodbyes to Maurice, Lina, and Lolo (little Aurore). She insisted on being bathed. Harrisse called her an "ermine": she was obsessed with cleanliness, wanted to be completely white. She asked to be fed. "I'm hungry," she said but didn't eat. She murmured, "Leave greenery," enigmatic words that have given rise to infinite interpretations.

In the night of 7–8 June, Sand suffered greatly. Her position had to be changed constantly. "Have pity," she said, as if she were imploring death. The doctors left, prescribing morphine to ease her pain. She entered a stupor and said almost nothing else. Then her gaze became fixed and vacant. The men came in to witness her last breath; her cousins Oscar Cazamajou and René Simonnet and Dr. Favre were present. Maurice, exhausted, was asleep; the girls woke him up. They kneeled down. She died around nine thirty (ten o'clock according to the declaration). When she died, Dr. Favre, ever theatrical, stood up, raised his hands over the body, and swore "As long as I live, your memory shall never be sullied." Why on earth was he so afraid of any staining? The following night, he recorded his account, as the doctors once had for Louis XIV.

Solange closed her mother's eyes. Along with Solange Marier and Mlle. Thomas (a maid), she prepared the body, dressing her (we don't know how) and transporting her to her own walnut bed, where the body was laid out, the face covered with flowers. According to the younger Alexandre Dumas, her right hand, "adorable and polished like ivory," remained uncovered. Solange sat up with the body during the night of the eighth, with a few close friends who succeeded her. The following night, only the servants remained, obliged by the smell of the rapidly decaying body to remain in the adjoining workroom. The morning of the tenth, the coffin was displayed in the vestibule of the chateau so the faithful could pay homage and throw laurel leaves in place of boxwood.

Sand wanted to be buried in her garden, near her loved ones, with no monument, only "flowers, trees, greenery." She wanted, in short, to become Aurore once more. She left no instructions for her funeral. This gave rise to some debate.[5] Solange wanted it to be religious, while Lina thought it should be civil. Maurice thought so as well, but he let himself be convinced by his sister, who invoked the "religious beliefs of the population," suggesting that local friends—Dr. Papet and his associates—would not attend a purely civil funeral. Dr. Favre, who was supposed to be a free thinker, rallied behind this position. He justified himself as follows: "It's only here that I feel myself to be at the heart of the Celtic race. [Pan-Celticism was one of the doctor's favorite subjects.] There is no pompous ceremoniousness here. . . . The Church is here to be of service, not to triumph." The Abbé Villemont, the vicar of the parish, whom Favre had thrown out so unceremoniously while Sand was dying, sulked and refused to preside. But the archbishop of Bourges, Msgr. de La Tour d'Auvergne, who was aware of the issue, agreed to do so. Gustave Flaubert attended the funeral of his dear "troubadour" and was devastated at the religious rites accorded his agnostic friend, "who died perfectly impenitent"; the services were notable for the fervor they inspired in the local population, country folk in their wide-brimmed hats; the number of Parisians who attended (Prince Napoléon-Jérôme, Ernst Renan, and the younger Dumas all made the trip); the quality of the speeches; the message sent by Victor Hugo (which Maurice read out), celebrating a woman who was remarkable for her life, her work, and her political engagement. She was, in sum, a "great woman."

Everything combined to make this death an exemplary scenario of the new ways of dealing with death, where tradition hesitated, jostled by modernity. In this bedroom laboratory, we witness the meeting and the confrontation of the public and the private, the body and the soul, the priest and the doctor, men and women, brother and sister, Paris and the provinces. We hear the footsteps of children and the echoes of the century; the conflict between the Ancien Régime and the Revolution plays out around the deathbed. We hear the voice of the ill, who wants to live, but not at any price. Sand refused degradation and suffering and left us a mystery: what were Aurore's final wishes? What did she mean by her last words, "Leave greenery"?

The Deathbed

George Sand had a short illness and a quick death. She died at home. The doctors especially looked after her, easing her pain and banishing the priest. Only her family surrounded her in her final moments; her daughter took charge, perhaps more than Sand would have wished (she distrusted Solange). But to care for the body and the soul was the role left to women. Her friends came later, hesitating at first to enter the room. The neighbors came as far as the vestibule and gathered outside, between the courtyard, the square, and the church. Her death was related in the same manner as those of kings, a sign of the "consecration of the writer" that crowned the literary nineteenth century. This was unusual for a woman.

This "beautiful death" is an entry in the genealogy of the Western "arts of dying," long recorded and developed, whose origins have been described by Philippe Ariès and Michel Vovelle, along with its codification in the seventeenth century.[6] The terrestrial ending to human life, the solemn entrance into the world to come, whose existence was not in question, is as much the concern of the group, of the community, as the individual. This explains the public nature of death.

The "deathbed" is its central (and only) scene. For a long time it took up the entire stage and was abundantly represented in medieval iconography. The "long illness," the result of medical progress, makes the sickroom possible. Socially and spiritually certain death is preceded by random illness. It is death that occupies and preoccupies the living—above all, its "hour." We fear sudden death, as if God were threatening humans with abduction. "I will come like a thief," said Jesus.

Even today death disconcerts us. A heart attack or a stroke can brutally change our lives, as Joan Didion describes, seeing her husband collapse and die. "Life changes fast. Life changes in the instant. You sit down to dinner and life as you know it ends."[7] This shock reverberates through the book, in which Didion relates what she went through. Sudden death is stupefying; it plunges us into a kind of distress that we feel even more profoundly in our era of deferred death. At one time, this was known as a "bad death."

Anticipating one's death, being able to prepare for it, organize it, and attend it would be the best death. We want to die in our homes, surrounded by the ones we love. "I would like to die in my bed, with the whole household in tears around me," said the novelist Louise de Vilmorin. "To die in bed" is the proletarian's dream, knowing full well that death comes early to those who live on the streets.[8] "Yes, at the end we can want to die at home. . . . After slaving away all my life, I'd gladly die in my bed, in my own home," Gervaise says to Coupeau.[9] We know this won't be her fate; she'll die outside, like a dog. For it isn't so easy to achieve this ideal or has become more so only recently. In the communal room of yesteryear, it wasn't easy to make room for the dying person. All were going about their lives around him or her. The old and bedridden were a burden. The sick moaned and bellowed; those who were in the death throes gasped in pain, without any kind of sedative, praying for the end. The "good death" was one that did not last too long but delivered the living and turned them into cadavers with dignity, but quickly, in such haste that the overstuffed hospitals additionally accelerated.

Death has its rules; it is as organized as a concert. It is collective, public, active. The "good dying person" doesn't suffer, gesticulate, or complain too much. He thinks of his immortal soul and his loved ones. He informs them of his last wishes, leaning on his two crutches, testament and prayer, and turns his face to God, who awaits him. He is the agent of his own death, which he has felt approaching and whose tales he hopes will be told at least for a little while. The "good dying person" is a man more than a woman. Gender differences mark the deathbed, the stage where death is enacted. Women's deaths are carried out with discretion. Of course in the aristocracy there are some beautiful female deaths, which Bossuet praised and Saint-Simon recounted. They are ordinarily less heroic and more gentle than those of men, who often adopt the posture of dying on the field of battle. Feminine deaths must be sanctified to be famous—those of nuns, like Thérèse de Lisieux, or young devotees who hoped to die at the age of fifteen.[10] Death breaks the solitude of the cloister; the whole convent, or even the whole village, streams into the bedroom of the dying nun to contemplate her ecstatic smile and hear her last words, as if her death were the most important moment of her life.

The bedroom of the dying is invaded, to the point that in the eighteenth century doctors (like Vicq d'Azyr) complained that there were too many people present, and the large presence was corrupting the air.[11] This invasion was sometimes the dying person's desire. Madame de Montespan was afraid of dying alone. She "slept with her curtains open, with candles around her bedroom, and her women watching over her," Saint-Simon tells us. On 27 May 1707, feeling that she was about to die, "she did what she had to do."

This publicness also comes from a desire to accompany a parent or a neighbor (through solidarity or simple curiosity) in the final act of their existence—their ending, their "final judgment," which determines their passage to the great beyond. How would they take the final step? How would they "pass away"? In a dying person's bedroom, guests could enter even if they didn't know the person. People who passed the priest as he went jingling down the street could follow him to join in the prayers. A solitary death was a bad death. The good death was a chorus, where each person sang his part, sharing the duties, rites, and emotions.

The dying person was the soloist. He was expected to pronounce his final words and wishes in an audible voice and, at least in the more well-to-do households, to leave a will. Michel Vovelle has studied the ways in which this practice became widespread and the way wills changed in content. Civil matters having to do with the distribution of one's belongings slowly took precedence over religious preoccupations (masses, prayers, gifts), which nearly disappeared in the eighteenth century. This was a sign of secularization, to which the bedroom attests. The testament is usually written by someone who is alive and in more or less good health. But in case a will has not been arranged or the situation has changed, one can make a "deathbed will," according to the official terminology, with the notary or his representative bearing witness to the dying person's lucidity.

Custom regulates the organized ballet of entrances in a dying person's room: family, friends, neighbors, the priest who performs extreme unction, the doctor called in case there's hope. The well-established Christian scenario would last for centuries. The principal changes concern a mixture of the various elements and their order of precedence. Three major transformations affected the scene of death and the theater of the room: privatization, medicalization, and individualization. The family sent away the neighbors; the doctor replaced the priest; the dying person became one who was loath to leave (or hoped very much to) and whom we sometimes had trouble releasing.

The bedroom of the dying person has been medicalized. At one time the priest reigned unchallenged. He was the great master of a liturgy that consisted of sacraments and prayers. The doctor's presence and power were limited if not nonexistent. Their prominence grew in the seventeenth century for the well-off, especially at court; as Louis XIV lay on his deathbed, the doctors jostled for power, and the confessor looked a sorry sight. Doctors looked after Sand's sickroom, retiring from it when there was no more hope. Doctors don't like to attend their patients' deaths; this is to recognize their powerlessness. So they tiptoe out, making room for the priest as a last resort. For a long time there was a tacit complicity, organic and organized, between the doctor and the priest. We know the latter will have the last word; he is the only one who can help the dying person embark on the final voyage. To admit the priest is to give up. But in the eighteenth century, the priest was called on less and less often; the doctor, who put a human face on science, was called for instead. He became a familiar sight in the sickroom, at least for those with money. "We others, the poor, we die ourselves [j'nous mourrons nous-mêmes]," said a peasant who was asked why he didn't send for a doctor when his wife was dying.[12] The priest was enough for him and his ancestors, and that dictated his behavior. Preparing the dead, watching over them, laying them out, paying for a decent funeral—this was enough. The body had to be taken ever more quickly out of the communal room so as not to bother the other people living there; this haste made people fear the premature burial of the "dead" who were actually still alive, so custom imposed a delay of about thirty to thirty-six hours. In short, the room had to be emptied and purified: the windows had to be opened and the air changed, just as Louis XIV had required at Versailles, after his death, for his great-grandson. But this was not an unfamiliar action. "As soon as [the Comtesse de Fiesque] was dead . . . I went to Ratilly. . . . I spent five or six days in this desert to allow for the body to be opened and carried off and to air out the bedroom; for I loathe the smell of death in a house, and I cannot sleep when it is there," wrote Mademoiselle de Montpensier, who had a very keen sense of smell.[13]

Religious history and rural ethnography present a peaceful image of death at this time, one that doubtless bears little relation to the reality. The state of medicine and the lack of means to reduce suffering would have made it very painful. The deathbed was a bed of pain. In the nineteenth century, morphine began to be used, and it soothed George Sand. Later, opium would help Joë Bousquet, who is discussed below, to live. The lack of regulation made it easier, in a way, to use these drugs.

What we know for sure is the performance of death; the experience of it escapes us. The performance of it has changed. It became more dramatic in the eighteenth and nineteenth centuries and became an emotional moment. Julie's death scene in *La Nouvelle Héloïse* and the painting by

Jean-Baptiste Greuze are near contemporaries.[14] The death of the loved one—the *mort de toi* as Philippe Ariès puts it—was carried out amid an orchestration of cries, gestures, sighs, and tears. Women shed "torrents of tears." Men contained themselves, even if they were still allowed to cry until the nineteenth century closed off their tear ducts.[15]

The family strengthened its grip, a mix of heritage and sentiment. La Fontaine described it well: "A rich laborer, feeling death approach, / Drew his children near / And spoke to them without witnesses." It was to his children alone, "without witnesses," that he meant to speak. He wanted to pass on to them the work ethic that he believed to be essential to grow the assets he left them. The laborer is a cold, crafty entrepreneur, and his deathbed, a board meeting.

The deathbed became more private, a place for effusiveness, forgiveness, contrition, final revelations: "I'll tell you on my deathbed," a father would say, the keeper of secrets that he will perhaps never disclose; it is a place for reconciliation but also irreparable rifts. These are almost always the deaths of patriarchs—of the elder, the father, the uncle; these are the only family members whose deaths enter into legend. Women die in silence and in the dark.

There are tragic deathbeds—those where a suicide is found. Jules Renard found his father's body in his locked bedroom: "I forced it with my shoulder, and the door opened. There was smoke and the smell of powder. . . . He was there, lying on his back, legs out, torso raised, head to the side, his eyes and mouth open. Between his legs was his gun, his trusty walking-stick." The hunter had turned his arm against himself. "That man suffered too much," said a neighbor.[16]

We tend to keep children out of these rooms. According to Rousseau, they don't understand what's happened. "Whatever one tells children of death, they understand nothing; they don't fear it for themselves or for others; they're afraid of suffering, not of dying."[17] Marie d'Agoult remembered her exclusion like a wound. In 1819, her father had a stroke and died in three days. "I was not allowed under any circumstances to enter my father's bedroom. . . . While my mother gave a few orders, I slipped unseen into his room. The doctors had left it, and the nurse had gone into the next room. I

went up to the bed. Lord! What a spectacle. My father had begun the death
throes." He died soon after.[18] Pierre Loti similarly describes being banished
from his grandmother's deathbed. "They sent me downstairs and used different excuses to keep me away all day. I didn't understand why." When he
was readmitted, his grandmother was dead. "I was struck by the perfect
order that had been restored and the profound peace that had fallen over
the room." The bed curtains were open; her head was in the middle of the
pillow; she looked as if she were asleep, with "an infinitely sweet, tranquil
smile" on her lips.[19] Children were kept away from the tragedy of death in
order to preserve their innocence, but they saw everything. For many of
them, the death of a grandparent—especially a grandmother—is their first
decisive contact with death. It functions as a caesura, the end of an era.
There is a before and an after. For little Mona Sohier, the deathbed where,
at four years old, she kissed her father goodbye, is the "primal scene" of her
book and perhaps of her life.[20]

Women reigned over the death chamber and looked after the day-to-
day. The doctors left them the body to clean and dress with growing care.
At one time, it was enough to put the body in a nightshirt and a clean cap.
But in time, it became the custom to dress it in the deceased's most beautiful clothing, like a wedding outfit, which had been kept in a trunk. Dead
women, in the nineteenth century, were clothed again in their white wedding dresses; Flaubert was overwhelmed by the diaphanous sight of his sister Caroline: "They put her in her wedding dress, with a bouquet of roses,
everlastings, and violets. I watched over her all night. She was laid out on
her bed, in the room where you saw her play music. She seemed larger and
much more beautiful than when alive, with that long white veil down to her
feet."[21] Until the very end, women were held captive by the obligation to be
beautiful and often left instructions to ensure they would look seductive
even in death. George Sand's dying mother murmured to her, "Arrange my
hair." " 'I want to be pretty even in my coffin,' " said Balzac's Louise de
Chaulieu to her friend Renée de Maucombe, "languishing in bed for fifteen
days. In her room there was no trace of illness; medicines, resins, the entire
medical apparatus was hidden."[22] "If I could foresee my death in time," said
Martine Carol, suffering from cancer, "I would say: 'Put me in the dress that

I love. Do my hair. Make me up. I want the public and all the people I've known to remember that Martine."[23] Martine Carol was a star who hoped to live on through her image. But even nuns are prepared to meet their divine husbands.

Women looked after the death chamber—cleaning it, airing it out, tidying up—but left death at its threshold; its laying out was left to carpenters and its funeral to the men. For a long time, women were not allowed to attend funerals at the church or the cemetery, and this custom continued among the aristocracy throughout the nineteenth century, when they were not even mentioned in the death announcement. Then, veiled in black, little by little they were allowed to step into the funeral scene, eventually becoming its principal actors.

The death chamber progressively ceased to be a public space, open to anyone who cared to enter. But in fact, this desire to endure the death agonies in private is very old. In 1219, writes Georges Duby, the nobleman *Guillaume le Maréchal* wanted to die at home and had himself driven to one of his manors. When his state deteriorated, he called his closest friends and family together to let them know his wishes. Then, they waited. Finally, he said farewell to his wife and knights, leaving them to God: "I can no longer defend myself from death." This rare description of the death of a lord shows how the rites of separation and the distinction between public and private were refined, with the bedchamber as witness.[24]

In time, this distinction became more common. In the seventeenth century, Jansenism contributed to it. "We die alone," wrote Pascal. Madame de Sévigné extolled the death of "poor Saint-Aubin." "A room without noise, without disruption, without odors. . . . His mind free, a heavy silence, good and true speeches, no trifling; its like has never been seen." She reproached his wife's inappropriate exclamations: "This little woman cried out and was muffled by Father Morel, so there was nothing but Christianity in this sacred house."[25] A century and a half later, Stendhal was critical of the archaic way people had of dying in the provinces. "They don't do anything well in the provinces, not even die," he wrote. "In Paris, the dying person closes the door to rest in solitude and silence."[26] Less to please God than himself.

It was also because of advances in science that death was delayed, creating the death throes, the "long illness," the "sickbed," but also convalescence, and they gave the sickroom a much more pronounced material and literary existence—surreptitiously in the hospices of long ago, then at home, at least in more well-off social classes. There was more difficulty at the hospital, which had to deal with the demands of the collective, and only gradually gave the dying person some space. In the nineteenth century, the sickroom became less often a death chamber. That is when we began to see the mirrors veiled, the shutters closed, the fires put out, the vials removed, and the candles and the incense lit.

Hospital Beds

Illness, along with piety and birth, was one of the early causes for the individualization of beds. Epidemics forced the body into quarantine and divided people from each other. Hospices not only classified people (at Tournus they were divided into men, women, and the military), but also attempted to give a bed to each slowly dying person. The Hospices of Beaune offer an idyllic medieval example that is no doubt at several removes from reality but nevertheless gives us an idea of the ideal the others strove to attain.

In general, hospices and hospitals suffered from overpopulation. Beds were crammed into immense, difficult-to-heat rooms, often spilling into the corridor and containing up to three or four patients. In the civil hospices in Lyon under the Restoration, they were a terrifying sight. Inside, visitors and patients wandered through the same unpartitioned space, with the latter eating and urinating at will. The worst was the room where the mad were held. There was no water and no heat, apart from a wood-burning stove. The beds were only twenty inches apart, and it was common to find two people sharing a bed. An 1832 ruling made this illegal, "a crime against hygiene, health, and decency."[27]

Over time, hospitals became places to receive care, and they stopped being "general," beginning to practice a separation of patients. Terminal patients were sent to the hospice, the mad to the asylum, and hospitals kept on only those who could be cured, each in his own bed—especially in surgery. An operation was a hopeful (or hopeless) act that deserved its own space. Moreover, a practice of "paid beds" was implemented around 1835 and comprised 10 percent of the admittance rate; this was an illustration of the liberal principle according to which "society doesn't reward nothing with nothing," and it allowed hospitals to balance their budgets and keep up a more well-to-do clientele. A Parisian report from 1842 even recommended creating rooms in two hospitals, as had been done, for example, in Lyon and Brussels, indicating a very present demand: "On more than one occasion we have received offers of payment, on the condition of [the prospective patient's] not being assigned to a communal room." The report suggested partitions be used: "The paying sick should be gathered in a special area, with each receiving a room and sharing a gallery."[28] At the same time, in the hospices, older patients would hang sheets or laundry to isolate themselves—a sign of a general demand for individual space in Western society.[29]

But individualization was slow to be carried out, and when it was done, it was done timidly. Isolation and separation did not necessarily mean individualization. In 1852, a general congress on public hygiene held in Brussels had much to say on the matter of arranging rooms but little on the question of individual rooms. In 1864, the new Hôtel-Dieu hospital in Paris, which was designed as a series of smaller rooms, allocated fifteen to twenty beds per room and had a few isolated rooms for certain categories of patients. Iron beds were standard and curtains were eliminated.[30] In his *Traitié d'hygiène* (1869), Dr. Michel Lévy, an authority on the subject of hospital layouts, recommended smaller rooms with no more than twenty-five or thirty beds; the twelve beds prescribed by Dr. Trousseau seemed utopian to him. "One bed per person; only two rows of beds lined up against the walls, and not against the windows, where a draft might harm the patients. No rows in the middle of the room." This was the optimal arrangement to allow for a reasonable amount of ventilation. Light curtains would ensure women's modesty; they were pointless for men, who had nothing to hide, for "though they hid the sight of pain or agony, [the curtains] could do nothing to hide the sounds of it."[31] Dr. Lévy found it regrettable that people feared "apparent death" and therefore delayed removing the corpse; he advocated for its speedier removal. Except for women in childbirth, Dr. Lévy did not call for individual rooms; in his *Traité,* the word "room" doesn't even appear in the index.

The same is true of a 1930 *Encyclopédie de l'architecture* on the subject of hospitals and health facilities. The thirty-nine illustrations show rooms with at least four beds each, and sometimes seven, including the "isolation rooms" planned for the tuberculosis ward at the new Beaujon hospital! Tuberculosis and mental illness were often reasons for isolation and fragmentation in the hospital. The "moral treatment" of hysteria meant substituting smaller rooms in place of the communal room. Dr. Déjerine recommended an intensive milk diet (three to six liters a day), silence, and absolute rest in bed. "Each bed will be enclosed by white curtains marking off a smaller room"; this was the practice in the Salpêtrière by 1895.[32]

In short, isolation was related to treatment, to therapy, to a certain way of hoping for a cure; it was related to life rather than death. The hospital was a place of death deferred. Above all, the development of anesthesia and operating techniques allowed for more and more effective surgeries and meant longer hospital stays, though arrangements were not correspondingly modified.

Sickrooms

The sickroom belonged above all to the *grabataire* (bedridden person). In ancient Rome, the *grabat* (pallet) on which the bedridden lay referred to a soldier's camp bed or a bed for the poor, for slaves, or for Stoic philosophers; it was a second-rate cot with straps, low to the ground, without curtains, the sort of bed for the sick or impoverished, for whom nothing better could be found. In the seventeenth and eighteenth centuries, *être sur le grabat* meant to be sick: "I was alone the other day, in my little room/stretched out on my *grabat,* every limb in pain," writes Scarron in his *Épître chagrine.* And Voltaire apologized to the Duc de Richelieu: "Forgive me for not writing to you in my own hand; my detestable health has me on the *grabat,*" a frequent occurrence.[33] The *grabataire* is the invalid who cannot leave his

bed, whether he be rich or poor; the doctors of the Enlightenment paid
closer attention to them, and charity services counted them; *grabataires*
became a statistical category.

It was less certain that the road would end in death for the *grabataire;*
it was further off, the outcome of a lasting affection for life, which one sought
to prolong. The phrase "to die after a long illness" connotes a struggle
against it, having been carried off after an inexorable battle. "Nature scarcely
seems capable of giving us any but quite short illnesses. But medicine has
developed the art of prolonging them. . . . Natural illnesses are cured, but
never those that medicine creates, for it does not know the secret of their
cure," Proust writes on the subject of Bergotte's "long illness"; the writer
hardly ever left his house but was not a *grabataire;* he died suddenly while
looking at a Vermeer.[34] The narrator relates this aesthetically exemplary
death in *The Captive,* as if the enclosure of the sick were somehow a close
neighbor to love.

"Long illness" is a euphemism that refers to the desire not to name the
enemy—invisible, crouching in the shadows—that exists through these
words. Tuberculosis at one time, cancer or AIDS today, are seen as almost
shameful, illnesses to be hidden, as if they were a kind of moral error. "Aggressive therapies" are now a characteristic of society itself and are successful enough to explain the growth and longevity of the bedridden. The term
is now definitively medicalized and refers to an invalid who remains in bed
in a hospital or in his own home. There are two categories: the "horizontal"
invalid, who must continually lie down (the more dangerous case), or the
"vertical" invalid, who can move from his bed to a chair. The position of
the body makes all the difference to the risk and the care recommended to
home aides.

From this perspective, the sickroom is a consistent space. It is a refuge, a retreat, a place in which to live and struggle for life—and we must
avoid medicalizing it, at home above all. We might follow the model of
Proust's Aunt Léonie, which requires the space and relative comfort of a
provincial house, or at least its domesticity. After the death of her husband,
Octave, Aunt Léonie can barely rise from bed. She lives in her bedroom
(more specifically, in her bed), close to the window so that she can look out

the window, keeping watch over the comings and goings and receiving a few
close friends, like Eulalie, a peddler of news. To them, she exaggerates her
illness: "I must remember that I have not slept." "These were the sorts of
provincial rooms that . . . enchant us with [a] thousand smells" and a thousand tastes, like the madeleine dipped in tea, the key that unlocks the narrator's memories. Half-sick, half-reclusive, Aunt Léonie passes away (and
disappears from the narrative, which only mentions her briefly), going out
like the flame of a slowly consumed candle, in her room, no doubt in the
conjugal bed in which we can imagine her keeping to her side, like the widows of Noirmoutier, mourning their sailor husbands who've been lost at
sea. The old women of long ago died at home, elderly women turned *grabataires,* who mainly kept to their beds or moved sometimes to their chairs.
In the communal bedrooms in the countryside (more than in cramped urban lodgings), where a multi-generational cohabitation persisted, there
were disputes over their beds, which they often had to share with their
granddaughters, who likely did not much appreciate this lack of privacy.
As long as they could be of use, they were tolerated; when they became
impotent and confined to bed, their families lost patience with them. In
Gévaudan, they were kept outside in little huts. Death came to spare their
families the extra mouths to feed. In the nineteenth century, they died in
the communal rooms of hospices, where individual rooms are a very recent
invention, the sign of a late awareness of old age as a period of legitimate
retirement.[35]

In the nineteenth century, tuberculosis supplied rooms with patients
before they were sent to sanatoriums. "Consumption," as it was usually,
and pertinently, called, stretched out the body and closed the curtains. Initially, the people around the patient had a difficult time defending themselves from a disease that they did not understand; the husband or friends
of the patient continued to share the same bed. This was even a sign of
affection: Rousseau's Julie, as she lies dying, invites her dear cousin Claire
to sleep in her bed.[36] But whether they believed disease was spread by
contagion or a lack of air circulation, doctors alerted families to the risks
and separated their bodies. Confined to their rooms, the ill coughed themselves to death. Romantic ideas of melancholy led to the exchange of elegiac

letters, introspection, the keeping of a journal, the expression of one's feelings, like the family of La Ferronaye, or the Brontës, who interwove different
kinds of writings.[37] Tuberculosis was a great muse for writers, and, in a way,
it could be said to have produced the nineteenth-century novel. "Death and
illness are often beautiful, like . . . the hectic glow of consumption," wrote
Susan Sontag.[38]

    Nevertheless, the sickroom was not completely isolated. As early
as the seventeenth century, doctors were making house visits. They were,
then, the first observers of a rural way of life that left them troubled by
its lack of hygiene, as Lépecq de La Clôture wrote in his medical topogra-
phies.[39] His urban colleagues isolated their patients and made prescriptions, and the sickrooms were filled with preparations, with utensils, vials,
and flasks crowding the nightstands and mantelpieces. Women were in
charge of carrying out medical advice, taking the invalid's temperature,
airing out the room. That is to say, what they had done traditionally was
becoming more and more official within the medicalizing sickroom.

Nurses

Most women who helped in the sickroom were volunteers, but professional
nurses began to appear in the eighteenth century. In 1860, Florence Nightingale published a training guide called *Notes on Nursing,* which is a good
indicator of the preoccupations of the time. Nurses were still haunted by the
idea that the air might not be circulated enough; it was imperative to air the
room out, even if it was freezing. "People don't catch cold in bed." Blankets
and a hot water bottle were sufficient. Sometimes an invalid found himself
having to get up and close the windows. To keep the air fresh, Nightingale
recommended keeping the flues open on the chimney, using fans, "never
closing the curtains around the bed, or closing the shutters or curtains on
the window," and opening transom windows at night. An aerometer was
also a good investment. "Making the room cold is not airing it out; airing it
out is not making the room cold." Drafts should also be avoided, as well as
drying laundry; the bed should be opened and vases covered, preferably
earthenware so as to be more easily washed; no buckets or pails should be

allowed in the sickroom in case they should give off an unhealthy smell; the room should be cleaned every twenty-four hours, without the use of a feather duster, which would merely move the dust around, etc. This detail-oriented approach guaranteed good hygiene and prevented the sickroom from "becoming a sewer."[40]

Nurses were also meant to keep out inopportune visitors who might create noise and disruption; an entire chapter is devoted to this. Whispering, private conversations, the rustling of dresses—all these might fatigue the invalid. "The fidget of silk and crinoline, the crackling of starched petticoats, the rattling of keys, the creaking of stays and of shoes, will do a patient more harm than all the medicines in the world will do him good." Visitors should always sit in front of the invalid, never on the bed. Nightingale had a lively sensitivity to sensitivities. "Almost every step that crosses his room is painful to him; almost every thought that crosses his brain is painful to him." Another chapter concerns the bed: it should be made of iron, low to the ground, away from the wall on both sides, not far from the window so the invalid can see through it. Another has to do with lighting; the best exposition is at noon, facing east. The sun should be allowed into the room: "A light white curtain at the head of the bed is, in general, all that is necessary, and a green blind to the window, to be drawn only when necessary," for "where there is sun, there is thought."

Nurses were in charge not only of their patients, but also of their rooms, a necessary condition of their comfort. They must make the bed themselves, placing the pillows as required. "The suffering of dying patients is immensely increased by neglect of these points." The painter Edvard Munch called his childhood home, where so many in his family suffered from tuberculosis, "the house of pillows," as they were forever being rearranged. The pillow, with its creases, its shadowed folds, appears in many of his crepuscular paintings.

For Florence Nightingale, the invalid is a person who must be studied and treated like an adult, even if the truth about his state must be administered in small doses. In Lépecq de La Clôture's *Observations,* written under Louis XV, the level of personalization given to each patient is striking; the patients and their cases are minutely described. Nurses had to recognize the signs of approaching death and guide the dying person through it. This was never a question of religion but of professionalism; not of humanism, but of knowledge and psychology. In the art of dying, medicine and its treatments replaced faith. Today more than ever, nurses are there to help provide a "peaceful death."[41] Take the nurse whom Alice James addresses in her diary, a surprising mix of authority and indifference; her "little Nurse" speaks frankly and has clear ideas about how the room should be arranged; on this point, she is intransigent.[42]

But death was not the only outcome; Nightingale dedicates a chapter to "convalescence," about which Dr. Michel Lévy also writes at length. Both prescribe a change of diet and location, even if just from one floor to another. "The mere move to what *he* considers the 'convalescent ward' will give him a fillip." The convalescent spends a few hours in a chair near the fireplace, not far from the window. "The view of the horizon, the gardens, of greenery, will renew his thoughts and keep him from sad preoccupations." His first tentative walks should be taken at hours when the air is "at maximum purity."[43] The calm and quiet of the country will greatly aid in his recovery, for total recovery is now within the realm of possibility.

The sickroom can be escaped. At least for a while.

Private Hospital Rooms

Florence Nightingale addresses nurses working in private as well as public service, a sector she found more reliable. "I am bound to say, that I think more patients are lost by want of care and ingenuity in these momentous minutiae in private nursing than in public hospitals." In the 1860s, a health care professional like Nightingale trusted the hospital as a site of pioneering treatments, or at least a place where death was kinder.

This is more or less our fate today, when four out of five people in France die in a hospital. It is likely that that is where we will "end up." But in reality, it is a place where we only episodically spend time. "Long-term" establishments are in place to serve the bedridden. And then there are the retirement homes, which are more or less medicalized, where the comfort of the room, and its level of privacy, are markers of social and financial difference.

At the hospital, a private room remains just out of reach, reserved for those who have had operations or the most seriously afflicted, with attention constantly paid to the briefness of the stay and the circulation of admittance. Recall Dino Buzzati's short story "Seven Floors," which describes the gradual descent of a patient through the various floors of a hospital, ending in the basement mortuary and destined for a speedy evacuation, reflecting a social anxiety about overloaded hospitals that are shamed by death, the negation of their role as healing machines.

We no longer double up patients in beds, but we do place two to a room, at the risk of creating occasionally amusing conflicts—like the one Gérald Aubert describes in his 1990 play *Chambre 108,* which has three characters: seventy-five year-old René, forty-year-old Charles, and Janine, the nurse. René is a chatterbox whom Charles cannot tolerate; Charles asks for a private room. "You know, a private room can sometimes be even worse. The silence can be very noisy," Janine objects. The two men wait for test results, which, after a period of suspense, turn out to be favorable. This is a bonding experience: "We shared a room, we brushed our teeth in the same sink, we got better hand in hand. That creates a bond; it's logical," says René.[44] But they are unlikely to see each other again. The hospital is a temporary place where people encounter each other, then leave; it separates more than it brings together.

The hospital room also has hopeful associations, as in the case of an operation that is meant to cure a patient. This is the case for Isabelle, the first facial skin-graft patient, whose story has been reconstructed by Noëlle Châtelet. Isabelle has been mauled by her dog. In her room, she waits for the operation that will restore her face—but someone else's face. The room is the site of convergence for doctors, surgeons, and psychologists; her body is the object of care, of the gaze, of anguish, of all kinds of questions and hopes. This is why it is so difficult to leave the room for Lyon, where the final operation will take place, in a room without a number. But then Isabelle doesn't want to return to it: "Any room but number nine," she says.[45] Patients necessarily have a difficult time personalizing their hospital rooms in any way other than through the room number, like in a hotel, and through the events that have transpired there—major events that transform an anonymous place into an indelible memory. This is why hospital rooms play such a major role in contemporary narrative, in autobiography and fiction, and it explains the variations of experiences that take place there, often recounted by their survivors.

In this respect, Simone de Beauvoir was a pioneer. In *A Very Easy Death,* she describes her mother's death in 1963, after six weeks of hospitalization in a Parisian clinic. In this clinically and psychologically precise narrative, de Beauvoir is attentive to fluctuations in the space, without describing it too explicitly. This is striking. After fracturing her femur in a fall, Madame de Beauvoir is taken to the emergency room at the Hôpital Boucicault, which she detests, and from there to a clinic, whose merits she extols; it is calm, she can see a garden through the window, and the care she receives inspires a kind of joy at feeling like she matters. She asks for a variety of objects to be brought to her room (number 114)—vials, pills. She receives guests and gifts. "The room was full of flowers—cyclamens, azaleas, roses, anemones; on the nightstand accumulated boxes of *pâtes de fruits,* chocolates, hard candies"—sweets with which we deluge the sick. She "discovered the pleasure of being served, cared for, fussed over." She receives massages; her food is brought to her on a tray. The idea of returning to her apartment horrifies her: "I don't want to leave," she says.[46]

Then the situation changes; the tests indicate that Madame de Beauvoir has cancer. They decide to insert a tube into her nose "to clean out her stomach." The bed, which had been next to the window, "is returned to its usual position in the middle of the room, its head against the wall. On the left, connected to Mother's arm, there was an IV. There was a tube emerging from her nose, a transparent plastic that passed through some complicated machines then ended in a bowl." The doctors decide to operate. They hang a sign on the door: "No visitors."

"The decorations changed. The bed was returned to the place it had occupied the night before, leaving it open on both sides. The sweets were put away in the cupboard, and the books as well. On the big table in the corner there were no more flowers, but bottles, glass cylinders, test tubes." The patient wears no clothing; the body is bared at the same time as the room. Simone describes her mother's room with precision, as if to engrave the image: "Behind the door I find a short passage: on the left is the bathroom with the sink, the bedpan, cotton wool, jars; on the right there is a cupboard in which Maman's things have been put away. On a coat hanger there is her red dressing gown, covered in dust. . . . Before, I went through these places without really seeing them. Now, I know they will be a part of my life forever." The room changes at the same time as de Beauvoir's mother, who shrinks in on herself, has her hair cut, no longer eats, asks for the blue curtain in front of the window to be opened, demands "fresh air."

De Beauvoir takes over for her exhausted sister and sleeps beside her mother's bed for four nights. "As evening fell, the room grew gloomy, when it was lit only by the lamp on the bedside table." She describes the day care versus the night care, which she carries out herself, taking care to do so quietly. "The transition from my mother to a living corpse had been defini-tively accomplished. The world had been reduced to the size of her room," which had become a mortuary. Madame de Beauvoir dies one night, after having suffered for six weeks: "six weeks of intimacy ruined by betrayal," de Beauvoir writes, feeling as if she were playing the role of the mourner.

In the afternoon, the writer and her sister return to room 114. "As in hotels, the room had to be vacated before noon [of the next day]. We climbed the stairs, pushed open the doors: the bed was empty. The walls, the window, the lamps, the furniture, everything was in its place; and on the whiteness of the sheet there was nothing." The "no visitors" sign is taken down, in preparation for the next patient. They do not go to see the body at the morgue; what would be the use?

"She had a very easy death," Simone writes, "a privileged death." The dryness of these statements is shocking, but it underlines the limitations of the time. The "privilege" was precisely the private room, which even today so many sick people desire and which is very much the exception, in spite of a public relations campaign promising a "hospitality" that often bears a distant resemblance to the reality.[47] Some hospitals do have "short-term units" where the terminally ill are admitted just before death. Jacqueline L.'s mother was transferred to one from the emergency room, thanks to the help of a young doctor. "There," writes Jacqueline, "she was placed in a small, quiet room, where she died, peacefully I think, two days later. This room remains in my memory as a sort of gentle cocoon where my mother, her good mood restored, . . . could say goodbye to the people she loved. That was followed by the anonymity of the morgue."[48]

In her autobiography, Yoko Ogawa describes the last time she saw her younger brother, who suffered from cancer of the spinal cord, and her memories of their conversations on the fifteenth floor of the west wing of a large Japanese hospital.[49] This was the wing where they put the most extreme cases, and every room was private. What was surprising about this room was the centrality of the bed, "stocky, nestled there like a large animal," whose whiteness stood out against the cream-colored wallpaper. "All kinds of things were placed around this very white bed. Unlike in a normal room, or a hotel room, everything seemed to me to be much more significant. I felt like the entire sickroom unfolded around this bed." Ogawa describes the layout of the room: "Everything was clean and sober but not cold." What really strikes her is this cleanliness, this sobriety, how functional everything was, and the lack of anything organic; it calmed her, especially given the horrific memories she has of her mother, who was out of her mind, strewing trash and detritus around their house, creating a "dirty, disordered life." Here, purity reigned. "The impeccable cleanliness of his room was enough to make me happy."[50]

Nancy Huston visited her friend Annie Leclerc in the Hôpital Curie when she was dying. "I sat on the chair at the foot of the bed. Everything felt completely unreal." She, too, emphasizes the austerity of the room: "Bluish light. The room bare. . . . Minimal furnishing. No fuss; straight lines, almost nothing."[51] The bareness and asceticism of the hospital room prefigure the final absence. Sitting in the chair at the foot of the bed, we are finally face to face. It is time.

At the Sanatorium

The sanatorium was a place to experiment in long-term hospital rooms.[52] The tubercular poor were placed in dormitories, made unbearable by the nonstop coughing and nightmarish death throes. It wasn't until the 1920s that (at the Hôpital Laennec, for example) partitions were erected to set up areas of forty-five square feet each. Léon Bernard, director of the Hôpital Laennec, praised this innovation, which spared patients louse infestations and the spectacle of death, thanks to the American Red Cross.

Those who were well off could go away to palatial hotels in the mountains, which flourished in the early twentieth century in Switzerland and Germany. These rooms had their own verandas and were kept according to a strict hygienic code: simple furnishings that were easy to clean because the furniture was all rounded; walls covered in painted Liberty-style canvas, which was also easy to wash; oak parquet flooring polished with paraffin, which filled up the cracks; and no dust-attracting knickknacks, hangings, curtains, or portieres. The bareness of the decor, as well as the cold of the altitude—a major part of the therapy—contributed to the sensation of glacial purity worked up into a treatment. White is the color of the sanatorium and the hospital, a sad affirmation of a triumphant hygiene—as opposed to the black of death.

This describes the way the Berghof sanatorium functions in Thomas Mann's *The Magic Mountain* (1924); it is magisterially described through the experience of its hero. Hans Castorp has come to Davos simply to visit his cousin Joachim but discovers he is sick and stays for seven years, going through all the stages, treatments, sites, and events of the illness. He spends a lot of time on his balcony, stretched out on an "excellent chaise longue," wrapped in blankets that must be artfully arranged to withstand the key part of the treatment: the cold. The purity of the peaks, with the immaculate snow, endlessly renewed, is meant to ward off evil. Castorp has a fever, so the doctors put him to bed; its whiteness matches the landscape and performs a kind of exorcism. The way he uses objects and even his own body changes. His temperature is taken several times a day, becoming an obsessive leitmotif; meals are served on a special table, "a miracle of balance on one foot." His days are indistinguishable from one another, punctuated by visits from the doctor (with his enigmatic comments), the masseur, and his cousin, who brings him news from the dining room, the center of social life at the Berghof. The monotony of the daily rituals transforms the days into an undifferentiated stream of hours.

> It is incorrect to speak of repetition; a continuous present, an identity, an everlastingness—such words as these would better convey the idea. They bring you your midday broth, as they brought it yesterday and will bring it to-morrow; and it comes over you—but whence or how you do not know, it makes you quite giddy to see the broth coming in—that you are losing a sense of the demarcation of time, that its units are running together, disappearing; and what is being revealed to you as the true content of time is merely a dimensionless present in which they eternally bring you the broth.[53]

This is the way time moves in the sickroom and perhaps in life.

The Creative Illness: Joë Bousquet's Room

Many sickrooms are creative places. Georg Groddeck saw them as a home for art, or at least for the nocturnal, solitary exercise of writing.[54] Proust—the eternal invalid—wrote in his bed at night. The *Recherche* unraveled in his bedroom, to the point of being consubstantial with it.

Joë Bousquet transformed his own into a site of creativity, but also of an intense sociability, to such an extent that we have to ask: is this really a sickroom? Bousquet was paralyzed for life by a war wound in the spinal cord and became a paraplegic. On 27 May 1918, at Bois-le-Prêtre, he was standing behind the lines, exposed to German bullets—perhaps those of Max Ernst, who was in the opposite trenches. He stretched his arm out, a cigarette between his lips, as if—consciously or not—he wanted to give off an air of heroism or bravado. What really happened that day? It's an enigma. What did he see, what did he want, what did he choose? These are the question that François Berquin asks, as did a number of doctors who examined his mutilated body on the battlefield and in the thirty-two years that followed, until his death, in his bedroom, on 28 September 1950.[55] Neurologists, psychologists, and psychoanalysts hung around his house at 53, rue Verdun, in Carcassonne, where Bousquet had set up his den, to try to understand him—if not to cure him. Some posited trauma as the cause of his actions, while others hypothesized hysteria, the masculine version of which was established by World War I.[56] "You are content to reproduce, without realizing what you are doing, the state of childhood," said one eminent doctor. "You're cared for; there are women beside your bed; you're fed. You needed a serious wound so your body could fall under the control of your child's heart. Replace your nurse with a *valet de chambre,* and you will instinctively react against your inertia." Bousquet had, in a way, chosen his wound; he had consented to it and made it his medium: "Thanks to my wound, I have learned that all men are wounded like me." He "is" his wound. "I do not pity you," André Gide told him.[57]

But it was not as simple as that. Bousquet suffered—in the legs, in the bladder. He had erectile dysfunction, which complicated his relationship with women, whom he so desired that he sometimes felt they were aging him with their caresses. Bousquet sought treatment. He consulted his cousin, Adrien Gelly, an eye doctor, a disciple of the vitalist Barthez, who was passionate about psychoanalysis. A modest, attentive man, Gelly avoided jargon, while communicating the vocabulary and key scientific notions. "He spoke of my affection for being sick, and I held forth for hours, like a doctor." Adrien had his misgivings about the doctors' diagnoses, without rejecting them outright. He thought that healing was not a question of the wounds disappearing but "accessing a way of life that is not defined by our physical restrictions." He treated the body as if the illness were located in the soul. He calmed pain with morphine and opium (up to thirty pipes a day), which doctors distributed in spite of its being officially outlawed.[58] The smoke consumed the air in the dark room, which had become the heart of an artistic work and the center of a world.

The inner sanctum was accessed via a narrow hallway. A heavy wall hanging, in which you could catch your feet, had to be moved aside; in the dark it was difficult to make out the forms of objects and the outline of the master. It was an almost aquatic initiation, as Pierre Guerre described it: "To reach him, you had to go down dark corridors, onto dark landings, pass through dark doorways. . . . Through the doorway you entered into a kind of large wooden submarine cabin, in a subterranean chapel where the shadow and the silence make the angles disappear, and muffled voices," which modulated to a murmur.[59]

The room was small, with a modest bed; the constant lamplight was dimmed by 1930s lampshades. The shutters were almost always closed. No street noise reached the room. The walls were hung with paintings acquired by Bousquet or gifted by his painter friends: Max Ernst, Fautrier, Dubuffet, Miró, Bellmer, Dalí, Tanguy, Masson, Klee, Magritte. There were many objects, especially porcelain: a dog, a chicken, a little glass horse, fragile pieces that seemed as if they could break at any moment (and that did happen). Here, you had to "walk on soles of ashes." The room was dotted with bouquets of flowers, cut, faded, and renewed, like the young women who brought them, whom Bousquet tried to impress and whom he initiated into the arts of love, even as an impotent seducer. The heart and the crushed body embrace in one of the nightmares of the bedroom.

After his mother died, it was his old nurse, Cendrine, who looked after Bousquet. Always dressed in black, illiterate, a bit of a witch, she fed him, washed him, gave him his treatments, soothed his anguish. Bousquet noted and admired her little comments, typical of her origins in the Languedoc. Back then, there was still an image of the servant with the big heart. She allowed in his visitors—Gaston Gallimard, André Gide, Jean Paulhan, Henri Michaux, the Clanciers, Simone Weil, and many others. His close friends took the service stairway; the others, the central one. Bousquet was rarely alone. He would receive guests in bed, his torso emerging from the covers, elegantly dressed, smiling, like "a fish in the water of his room." He loved to have discussions and held lively debates about poetry and philosophy. He "reigned by speech as well as the written word." And he corresponded with those who were not present; for example, with Éluard when he was at a sanatorium. Tuberculosis formed the "magic mountain" for this generation.

Bousquet's room served as a gallery, a library, a reading room for never-ending reading, a writer's study, an opium den, a gaming table, a salon, a circle; it was "a dizzying place where anything was possible and nothing happened, a lofty place where a new notion of humanity evolved, a new idea of love."[60] Space and time ceased to exist. "No one enters my room without a ray of my interior life preceding him," he said, bragging of having "liberated [his] conscience from the tyranny of the sundial." "Night was given to him; he did not have to conquer it," wrote Maurice Blanchot, for Bousquet believed in eternal language, "the faculty through which one of our actions may outlast us," and left behind *L'Oeuvre de la nuit*.

Joë Bousquet spent much time reading, writing, playing never-ending games of solitaire. "Who is this bastard who shuffles the cards in my place?" he would say. He wanted to take control of the game, and he succeeded. In an inversion of the usual passivity we ascribe to illness, his was the motor behind his life. In his room, a metamorphosis took place, the opposite of the one described by Kafka; it was a place of invention, of exchange, of creation, of resistance in all senses of the word, especially during the Occupation, when it served as a hideout.

"The world didn't want anything to do with me. I want the world to belong to me," Bousquet wrote in a 1936 letter to Carlos Suarès; it was a magnificent subversion, that both hinged on and was cradled by the room.

Chronicle of a Death Foretold: The Diary of Alice James

Alice James (1848–1892) lived her life in her brothers' shadows: the psycho-analyst William and the writer Henry were equally famous. Alice suffered from depression and chronic neuralgia; she was prey to "women's ill-nesses," nervous afflictions and hysteria, all the characteristics of these conditions evident in the nineteenth century. She tried to quell her anxiety by writing; she was a diligent correspondent and kept a regular diary. Her brothers, whose fame condemned her to obscurity, were affectionate and attentive but condescending, convinced of the limitations inherent to her feminine condition of eternal malady. That is, they believed her to be incapable of genuine creation or of being a real writer. When she was diagnosed with incurable cancer, she decided to keep a journal, and during the last three years of her life (1889–1892), she recorded her life in her room and her daily experience of her illness, fed by medical consultations and by her reading books and newspapers. She noted events, gossip, and conversations with her various visitors—her brother Harry (Henry), her adored Katharine Loring, and the woman she calls her "little nurse," who is attentive and efficient.[61]

Having a reason to be cloistered in this way suited Alice: "The 'home' feeling which you can with good will . . . fabricate between four walls, is to my great delight possessing me more and more here in these two rooms."[62] This was true to such an extent that she is delighted by the bad weather, which relieves her from the obligation of being taken for a walk and allows her to close the window after the required period of airing out the room. "If I can get on to my sofa and occupy myself for four hours, at intervals, thro' the day, scribbling my notes and able to read the books that belong to me": this was the epitome of happiness for Alice James.[63] "The days I go out are twice as long as the shutup ones."[64] There is no obsession with pain or self-pity; on the contrary, the diary is distant and caustic toward British society, which she castigates for its "self-righteousness," and she demonstrates just the opposite in the detachment and humor that make her diary a masterpiece. Nevertheless, when Katharine Loring wanted to publish it after Alice's death, she met with fierce opposition from William and Henry, who were shocked by the publicity this "gossip" would bring. Henry even destroyed his own copy. Of course he admired his sister's pluck: "It is heroic in its individuality, its independence—its face-to-face with the universe by-and-for herself." But he thought the diary was futile and indiscreet: "she simplified too much, shut up in her sick room, exercised her wondrous vigour of judgment on too small a scrap of what really surrounded her."[65] The diary was published in its entirety only in 1982. It was decidedly no easier to be Henry James's sister than to be Shakespeare's.

A dying person has never seen death approach with such lucidity as did Alice James. It was lucidity toward herself, "dead for so long," since the terrible summer of 1878, when she "went down to the deep sea." It was lucidity on the disappearance of desire, which, more than the sharpness of her pain, indicated the end was near: "This long slow dying is no doubt instructive, but it is disappointingly free from excitements: 'naturalness' being carried to its supreme expression. One sloughs off the activities one by one, and never knows that they're gone, until one suddenly finds that the months have slipped away and the sofa will never more be laid upon, the morning paper never read, or the loss of the new book regretted; one resolves with equal content within the narrowing circle until the vanishing point is reached, I suppose." However, she experienced great satisfaction at "feeling as much myself as ever."[66] A month later, on 4 March: "I am being ground slowly on the grim sandstone of physical pain, and on two nights I had almost asked for K.'s lethal dose" of morphine, which her doctor brother had recommended her to use to diminish the pain. She wanted to die with dignity, without suffering; she did not want to be too agitated. She kept her journal until 4 March and died soon after.

The Mourning Room

A slow death by a long illness brings visitors to the sickroom; a protracted death allows enough time to see the loved ones before they go. This instills a desire to preserve a trace of them: we will not see them again. Their bodies will be taken from us, hidden, dissolved in earth or in flame. Soon we will forget the sound of their voices; we will find it difficult to remember their features. We want to keep something, some final relic, a lock of hair perhaps; we want to freeze the moving image while it's still possible.

We tend to exalt their final moments, when—beautiful or painful—life still beats within their veins. The religious tradition of the death story has over time transformed into an existential or even clinical narrative, related by those left behind in their journals or in their letters. They relate the manner in which the persons passed away, insisting less on their ardor and more on their suffering. In the United States, women tell these stories in "consolation books," recording the final words and moments of the departed.

The imprint of the death mask bears a more physical relationship to the dead. It is an ancient practice that was perpetuated for royalty, whose faces, or sometimes hands, were preserved by artists. These masks were touched up, idealized, taken out of context, much like recumbent statues, and were preserved for posterity. Into the twentieth century, this practice continued fairly systematically for politicians and more occasionally for writers (for example Proust, Gide, or Charles-Louis Philippe). It was also in use among families. Flaubert had molds cast of his sister Caroline's face and hand: "I saw these boors handling her with their paws, covering her with plaster. I will have her hand and her face. I asked Pradier to do her bust for me, and I will put it in my bedroom."[67] Edmond de Goncourt did the same for his brother Jules. Some refused; Delacroix forbid anyone to make an impression of his face or any sketch; he was all too familiar with the ritual of the "last portrait," the genealogy of which was recently explored in an exhibition at the Musée d'Orsay.[68]

One example of the "last portrait" was produced in Flanders as early as 1621, probably ordered by a family. An anonymous portrait shows a young woman lying in bed, her mouth open and her eyes unfocused, hands inert on a blue bedspread. She is composed, peaceful, still soft. In the nineteenth century, painters would spontaneously do the portraits of their deceased loved ones, but this was not always easy. Monet regretted showing the stained cheeks on his wife Camille's face. Marie Bashkirtseff was shocked at the state of her grandfather's bedroom and wanted to "arrange" him herself. "I draped a shawl around the bed, of white muslin; it had the same honest soul as he did and the purity of the heart that beats no longer." But how could she convey these impressions in paint? "The white pillows, the white nightshirt, the white hair, the eyes half-closed—it was very difficult to paint."[69] Is white really a color?

Private individuals could order these portraits. When Michelet's wife Pauline died on 24 July 1839, he called on a local painter to paint her death portrait, dressing her in a red scarf and a white bonnet not long before her death. "She left us beautifully . . . [head] on the white pillow." He blew out the candles, and the effect was striking. She had never been so beautiful. For fourteen hours, he directed the young painter, who we can imagine was worn out. "His final sketch is truly tragic. It captures the dismal quality of that night in that sepulchral room."[70] The death portrait is a double rite of passage, for the dead and for the living.

There is nothing spontaneous in these images, which are obsessed with the rules of theatrical presentation—a desire for order, peace, serenity, clarity. "The final portrait is only permitted once everything is in order"; the room must be tidied, the sheets changed, the bed made; the deceased must be cleaned, properly dressed, and laid out on the pillow, the face arranged in a calm expression, showing the hint of a fleeting smile that precedes rigor mortis. We erase the torment of the death throes, the final rictus, the marks of the accident or even the suicide. Dr. Gachet had Vincent Van Gogh transported on a suitable bed. Death must be beautiful. "In the most banal rooms of the Western bourgeoisie, death has finally coincided with beauty"—a beauty that disguised the reality.[71] And beauty was associated with whiteness: "All that white looking so sad, those tints fading away as if typical of the supreme end!"[72] Death was white.

Edvard Munch and Ferdinand Hodler introduced a tragic expressionism. Painting for them was a quest for truth and a work of mourning. Munch was obsessed by tuberculosis, which decimated his family. His notebook is full of sketches of bedridden adults and children; he tried to capture the degradation that ravaged them. In Paris, he spent his time sitting alone by the fire, meditating on the cemetery city. He was especially fascinated by the illness and death of his older sister, Sophie, who haunts his paintings between 1885 and 1896.[73] Ferdinand Hodler had a friend, Valentine, who died in a clinic in Vevey on 25 January 1915, after a seven-month-long illness. In those final days, he did not leave her side, and his sketches—more than two hundred drawings, gouaches, and oils—make up not only a diary of her death, but also a visual testimony to the ravages of cancer with Lake Léman in the background, captured in its luminous indifference.[74] They prefigure *The Magic Mountain,* in a Switzerland surrounded by a Europe at war.

Then came photography. Toward the middle of the nineteenth century, Nadar, Disdéri, and a constellation of ordinary photographers offered "after-death portraits" at home or in the studio, in an artificial decor or with a few objects representing the life of the deceased.[75] They were very successful, especially with deceased children shown in their cradles or on their mothers' knees. However, many people had their reservations about this "living portrait of a dead person" (as Roland Barthes put it). Man Ray detested the photograph he took of Proust. André Gide's daughter Catherine specifically asked that photographs of her father (which she had asked to be taken) not be published in the newspapers. Photography involved a form of manipulation, a distance, and especially a form of quasi-obscene publicity that some found unsettling.

A scandal was unleashed by a photograph of François Mitterrand. On 16 January 1996, *Paris Match* published an image of the president on his deathbed. The photograph is very posed, created according to a *mise-en-scène* described by *Le Monde*, which republished it ten years later (18 January 2006): "He lies in an anthracite-colored suit, a red-and-black striped tie over his white shirt. His right hand covers the left. Only his wedding ring shines. In a corner of the bare room are the walking sticks that attest to the president's habit of going for walks, even in his final days. On each of the nightstands there is a hardbound book. Above the bed, a painting of Venice." Next to the very low bed is a banal hospital-style chair. "In the bare room, on display for history," read the headline, reporting the controversy around the photograph and reminding the reader that Mitterrand had spent time in front of the anonymous photograph of Léon Blum on his deathbed at an exhibition at the Musée d'Orsay. "The meaning of socialism is the conquest of that kind of face," he commented. Could François Mitterrand be seen as on display for the history of socialism? Mitterrand's daughter, Mazarine Pingeot, confirms that her mother "found the photograph beautiful, worthy of a nineteenth-century tradition that inscribed Papa as a direct descendant of Victor Hugo," in a pictorial tradition that was at the same time formal and memorial.

The bedroom serves as a backdrop to the death portrait. We ask that it be "bare," "stripped" of its signs of life, as well as any traces of illness. The real bedroom is a different story. For some time it retains the presence of the deceased. Returning home from her grandmother's funeral, Aurore Dupin (the future George Sand) returned to her bedroom. "I thought I saw her there still, on the abandoned bed. In that deserted room, where no one had dared to enter since the funeral, and where everything was in the same place as it had been when she still breathed, I could finally unleash my tears." She opened the bed curtains, contemplated the mattress, which still preserved the shape of her grandmother's body, observed the vials, "the half-consumed potions. There it seemed to me as if nothing had changed," she wrote to Aurélien de Sèze on 24 October 1825.[76] Forty years later, at Palaiseau, after the funeral of her lover Alexandre Manceau, Sand partially returned to the bedroom where he had died and where she had watched over him. "I had been alone for two nights, watching over the poor sleeper who would never awaken. What a silence in that little bedroom, where I entered on tiptoe at all hours of the day and night!"[77] It was like one final contact with the loved one.

The return to the deceased's bedroom after the funeral becomes an act of tribute, a ritual, whose fleeting emotionality Flaubert captures. Charles Bovary has just buried his mother. "When everything was over at the cemetery, Charles went back to his house. He found no one downstairs; he went up to the second floor, into the bedroom, saw her dress still hanging at the foot of the alcove; then, leaning on the writing desk, he remained there till evening, lost in a sorrowful reverie. She had loved him, after all."[78]

Once the bedroom has been tidied up, we hesitate to make any changes to it. We close the door on it, to the point that it becomes mysterious, the lair of English phantoms and spirits that desert the cemetery in favor of corners of the bedroom and that sometimes appear in photographs as diaphanous silhouettes.[79] (We shall return to this.) "I constantly live in a room full of memories," says Alexandrine de la Ferronays, cultivating those of her husband, Albert. She is inspired in part by her grandmother, one of Balzac's heroines, old Madame de Portenduère (in *Ursule Mirouët*), who preserved her husband's memory in the room where he died. "The bedroom of the late M. de Portenduère remained exactly as he had left it the day of his death: all that was missing was the deceased." The marquise laid out the naval captain's uniform. She braided his white hair into a single lock curled above the font in the alcove. All his things have been preserved. "Nothing was missing. . . . The widow had stopped the hands of the clock at the hour of his death, to which they always pointed." She dresses in black to enter this room, at once bedroom, altar, and museum. "Entering there, he was once again visible in the many objects that indicated his daily habits."[80]

Edmond de Goncourt kept his brother Jules's room intact, on the third floor of his house. "It's the student's garret where my brother liked to work, the room he chose to die in; it remained as it was the day of his death, with the reclining armchair where he liked to smoke" or reread a page of *Mémoires d'outre-tombe*.[81] On sad days, Edmond would climb up here and sit in the chair next to the empty bed. He describes his brother's death throes (which lasted five days), his gestures, his murmurs, his cries, and the transformation of his face into the mask that resembled something by Da

Vinci. "Meditating in the half-dark, among those things that remind me of the beloved deceased, in the room where he died, I give myself over to the painful joy of remembering"[82]—in a Proustian experience of time, an infinite remembering. There is something carnal in the contact with an object that the deceased have touched, an armchair they sat in, or a painting they looked at. To keep the bedroom "as it was" is to maintain the illusion of their presence.

Queen Victoria wanted her beloved husband Albert's study and dressing room to remain in the state in which he left them. However, she made her own bedroom less of a temple of intimacy and more a "sacred room" saturated with memories of Albert, hung with paintings, decorated with busts.[83] It was an altar to his memory, like the kind we build in certain rooms by grouping together objects and photographs in some corner or in a cabinet, less to honor the dead than to encourage younger generations to remember a face, the fragments of a vanished life—that the dead were young once too. There are many ways to transform the room into a "place of memory." Inconsolable after his mother's death, Roland Barthes wanted to mark out the place where she lived: "In the room where she was sick, where she died, and where I now live, above the headboard of the bed I have placed an icon—not out of faith—and I always put flowers on a table. It's getting so that I no longer want to travel, so I can stay there, so the flowers never fade."[84]

Others, on the contrary, dread this morbid temptation to erect a museum to the departed with its derisory fetish for relics, and they speedily rearrange the room, clearing out the deceased's belongings. Dominique Aury kept Jean Paulhan's messy room "as it was," overflowing with papers, in their house in Boissise-la-Bertrand; she invited Régine Desforges to stay, who refused to sleep in a tomb and began to throw away papers and objects. Dominique watched her, stupefied, but began to understand, and accept, the purging.[85] In the seventeenth-century court, the deceased's clothes were distributed among the servants, and the furniture was changed. It was not a period with much taste for antiques or much time for memory, haunted as it was by the urgencies of the present.

The hospital made a radical practice of forgetting, through indifference and the need to make room for the survivors. Death in a hospital was a question of rapidly effacing all traces of the deceased. In that anonymous, transitory space, the individual is only a number who leaves no vestige behind. The embalming room desacralizes the body; its interventions are an updating of ancient funerary rites. They both practice a desire for total abolition. Why do we bury the dead? Cremation is the more logical solution; it has a terrible modernity to it.

Our era tries to replace the body's disappearance with a more and more ephemeral memory. We would like to extend the death notice, hold more colloquiums and conferences, write more books of memory. We do not know how to pay tribute to those who have left us, how to keep something of them. To close the door on their rooms, or to make the room disappear, is to draw out the ceremony of farewells.

No Exit

TO BE ABLE to close one's door and open it whenever we like; to come
and go; to possess a key and four walls in which to take refuge: these are the
desires woven into the bedroom. "We must stay in our rooms and cultivate
our gardens," writes Jean d'Ormesson, late in a life composed mainly of
writing. "That is where the flowers of the imagination grow." "You do not
need to leave your house. Stay at your table and listen," said Kafka.[1] These
men both chose to remain at home, even knowing the risks and experiencing anguish as a result. Others resigned themselves to it. Still others were
fleeing the constraints of a hostile world.

The dusky borderlands among choice, consent, and constraint are of
interest. Enter three figures who voluntarily sequestered themselves: the poet
Emily Dickinson, the artist Jean-Pierre Raynaud, and the schizophrenic artist
Jeannot. Emily Dickinson (1830–1886) spent most of her life in Amherst,
Massachusetts, in her family home, the Homestead. "Home is the definition
of God," she said. Her home was no doubt a warm one, although puritanical;
a cloud was cast over it by the death of her father and the paralysis and near-
mutism of her mother. "I cannot tell you how Eternity seems. It sweeps
around me like a sea." After her mother's death, Emily took refuge on the
third floor, in the bedroom that she would hardly ever leave again. Her physical horizon extended no further than the hedge that she could see from her
window. What good would it do to venture beyond it? "To shut your eyes is
to travel."[2] Like Proust, she would daydream about the names of countries.
Having her brother Austin and his wife Susan—"my crowd"—nearby was
enough—until she fought with them and stopped seeing them. She never
went to the village, where they called her "the Myth." When her father died,
she started to dress only in white; her sister Vinnie tried on the clothes she
had made for herself. It was all she could do to go downstairs to receive her

infrequent visitors. A childhood friend came to visit, and she spoke to her from the top of the stairs. Only the platonic (yet intense) love she felt for her editor, Bowles, and later for Judge Lord, could manage to dislodge her from her perch and then rarely. To the always disappointing human contact, she preferred words, letters read in secret with the door closed. She slept very little and worked at night: "I write to-day from my pillow," she said to one correspondent. In her poems, she praises the solitary bed: "Ample make this bed. / Make this bed with awe; / In it wait till judgment break / Excellent and fair. // Be its mattress straight, / Be its pillow round."[3] She was obsessed by the mystery of absence, by the tear, the hiatus, the blank; she was haunted like Mallarmé by snow, the white page. Yet she wrote nearly seven thousand poems. She kept them in groups of twenty, in notebooks that she sewed together herself and kept in a locked drawer. She asked to be taken to the cemetery not through the street but through the garden. She was obsessed with enclosure. But she was not a recluse, according to her biographer, Claire Malroux; rather, she was "entrenched" in her "room with a view of eternity."[4]

The contemporary artist Jean-Pierre Raynaud (born in 1939) made a different choice. His work is an architectural, symbolic gesture that subverts objects and forms, creating "psycho-objects" out of flower pots, no-entry traffic signs, and flags. He built a bunker for his home and studio, a minimalist space that is also a manifesto and that protects against intrusive, offensive light and against the outside, a source of aggression and death. There are no entrances except for a slit in one wall. In the center of the blockhouse, he placed a square room of an absolute purity, like the hospital room of a badly burned person, with a very sophisticated bed. "The degree zero of solitude and of the daily encounter with death takes place in a bedroom, which becomes a simple tiled tank, garnished with a mattress."[5] Was it inhabitable? Raynaud soon evolved, rediscovered light—maybe in the Abbaye de Noirlac in the Cher, whose stained glass windows he designed. In 1993, he decided to destroy his house, which he had finished in 1969. He showed a thousand containers made from its debris at the Centre d'art contemporain in Bordeaux. What was the meaning of this structure? How can we understand it in the context of his work and in the genealogy of the room? What will be its legacy?

The third example, which is much more dramatic, takes us to the edge of madness. In 1972, Jeannot died on a farm in the Béarn region. The son of a peasant who became a parachutist in Algeria after a love affair went wrong, he was deeply affected by his father's suicide in 1959. After a breakdown, he shut himself up more and more in his house with his mother and sister. When his mother died in 1971, he refused to be parted from her body and eventually arranged to have it buried under the stairway. He no longer left his bedroom and started to carve writings on a floorboard by his bed. Then he let himself starve to death in 1972. Twenty years later, after his sister's death, an antiquarian came across the floorboard. A psychiatrist, Dr. Guy Roux, discovered it, bought it, and had it exhibited as a major example of Art Brut. The text Jeannot carved is an almost delirious manifesto against religion, which "invented machines to control the minds of people and animals," and against the Church, which "made Hitler kill the Jews" and invented "electronic mind-control machines."[6] Jeannot's floorboard is currently owned by a pharmaceutical lab and is currently displayed at 7, rue Cabanis in Paris, across from the Hôpital Sainte-Anne, which specializes in psychiatry and mental illness.

What unites these three hermits if not the desire to make their retreat a way of life, of protest, and an expression of their freedom? The variation among these actions prompts questions: At what point do we become shut in? What is a wall? "Man is shut inside; he is ceaselessly linked to the walls that surround him and does not know he is imprisoned. These walls make one prison, and this prison is one single life, one single act," wrote Sartre. Michel Foucault was similarly preoccupied by the boundary between "inside" and "outside." But the "new cartographer" did not provide a metaphysical or abstract answer to this question; he preferred to think about historical, concrete "plans" for the sites of discipline—schools, hospitals, factories—and imprisonment (the psychiatric asylum, the prison), as well as their genealogy and their articulation.[7]

These "extreme rooms" at the limits of dominance and consent have fascinated contemporary artists, especially in the 1950s and 1960s. When writing *Les Bonnes* (1947), in order to show the ambiguity of the sisters' crime and the master/slave relationship, Jean Genet chose to concentrate the action—first the role-play, then the murder—in Madame's bedroom. "It was dark, and my sister had closed the shutters on the street," said Christine Papin when she was interrogated.[8] Harold Pinter's first play, *The Room* (1957), stages an impossible dialogue between a couple in a nearly bare stage set. "A room in a large house. A door down right. A gas-fire down left. A gas-stove and sink, up left. A window up centre. A table and chairs, centre. A rocking-chair, left centre. The foot of a double-bed protrudes from alcove, up right."[9] Francis Bacon's contorted bodies lie on beds around which he has drawn circles, creating the feeling of closed-off rooms that are striking for their embedded solitude (see *Study for Portrait of a Folding Bed,* 1963).[10] *A Man Asleep* (1967), by Georges Perec, fulfills Kafka's instructions (above), which Perec uses as an epigraph. After a disappointment, the *tu* who is addressed by the narrator shuts himself up in his tiny, bare room on the sixth floor of a Parisian building, "your den, your lair, your burrow." "You stay in your room, without eating, without reading, almost without moving. . . . You follow, on the ceiling, the sinuous lines of a thin crack, the futile meandering of a fly, the progress—which it is almost possible to plot— of shadows. This is your life. This is yours."[11] We can only possess the void.

Lovers

"Love is space and time made sensible to the heart."
—Marcel Proust, *La Prisonnière*[12]

Lovers seek privacy: face to face, body to body. Though they prefer to retire from the world together, they are fundamentally indifferent to the room itself. A bed is enough. There are, however, some forms of love that lead to separation from the world: the voluntary retreat of those who are so besotted with one another that they flee the world, an inconvenient distraction from each other, an obstacle to their passion. Marguerite Duras and Yann Andreas closed the windows and the curtains on their final encounter, like the disarmed, impotent hero of *The Malady of Death,* in his room overlooking the sea: "white sheets in the middle of the stage, and the sound of the sea surging in through the black door," Duras writes in her stage directions.[13]

There is the imprisonment of desire that can only be fulfilled by the possession, domination, or submission of the other: "the joy of slavery," as Jean Paulhan wrote in his preface to *Histoire d'O*.[14]

The *savoir-vivre* of the libertine may be read in the delicious folds of dissimulation, in the laying of traps, the game of hide-and-seek that exacerbates pleasure. Eighteenth-century libertines made subtle use of space.[15] Far from their mansions, they took refuge in the peripheries. All around Paris there are *petites maisons, folies,* where it was possible to escape the view of the public and the police. The layouts of these "little houses"—more modestly sized than urban dwellings—have been particularly studied by architects (Blondel, for example) who have been interested in creating a sense of comfort and intimacy. Instead of rooms succeeding one another (a layout that makes privacy difficult), they made use of hallways, corridors, angles, niches, hidden stairways where doors are camouflaged by hangings or secret mechanisms; these plans are directions for seduction, like that taken by Vivant Denon in *No Tomorrow:* "The vogue for *préciosité* represented love as a *carte du tendre,* or map of the stages of love. The libertinage of the following century replaced it with a map of desire, whose pathways bend and curve and reverse."[16] From the house to the garden and from the garden to the "derrières," which Louis XV's Versailles refined to a science, there were numerous paths available to the surprises of love. "It is less a case of seduction and more of surprising and seizing *[surpris et pris]*." The depths of the house were penetrated at the same time as those of the body. The unfolding of rooms in space formed a labyrinth, a spiral of conquest—antechamber, salon, cabinet, and boudoir—like a body undone, relinquished, not without a certain amount of resistance to whet the appetite, abandoned, finally, in the depths of a sofa or a divan that had to be low enough to accommodate "fainting, swooning, and falling." Some rooms featured mirrors judiciously arranged around the bed, permitting it to be contemplated from many different angles; in the *petite maison* of the Baron de La Haye, the strategically placed canopy bed allows for a panopticon of amorous frolicking.

The bedroom has been too strictly identified with conjugal activity. In fact, it played a secondary role in these provocations and charming deviations in which advances, subterfuge, evasion, approach, flight, and conquest count more than consummation. Lovers would move from the house to the garden, where the terrace could serve as a salon and the grove as a boudoir, becoming the preferred haunt of gallantry and secret affairs, though the nineteenth century would transform the terrace into a banal sitting room for ladies.[17] In the late eighteenth century, Sade and Nerciant "pushed this confusion of interior and exterior, house and garden, to their limits, also scrambling the real and the imaginary."[18] The conjugal bedroom—stable, established, regular—was intimidating. Lovers fled it, preferring *l'amour en carrosse,* love in a carriage, furtive and mysterious, like Emma Bovary, or, curtains drawn, Swann and Odette. The discretion and mobility of these forms of transportation, their impersonality, their anonymity, and their movement created the circumstances for a love without witnesses, without commitment, perhaps without a future.

O is undressed for the first time by her lover in a taxi.[19] She is brought to a "castle," where she enters "a round, vaulted room, very small and low," with the odor of a former prison and a hot, artificial light. She notices the colors and forms: the black and red of enclosed spaces; a "red boudoir" where she is prepared; a "small room" where she is given her meal through a hole in a wall; a "large, book-lined room . . . dimly lit," where she learns what awaits her, in the total dispossession of herself to which she secretly aspires. In these images there is a mix of the Gothic novel and Hitchcock's films: "the red tiles of the hallway, where doors succeeded doors, discreet and clean, with tiny locks, like the doors of the rooms in big hotels." She notices the bright red wall and the black carpet in the "cell" she occupies, which is furnished with just one piece of furniture: a large, low, square bed, covered in fur. The bed, the altar of the bed, is bare; O compares it to the more sophisticated poster bed that she usually shares with her lover. Decoration doesn't matter much; only objects matter, especially clothes, and even more the gestures, postures, words, treatment, blows, and humiliations inflicted, which O accepts unceasingly, consenting, demanding, ecstatic. "She received her lover like a god," and her abjection reinforces her pleasure, in a quasi-mystical annihilation that leaves no room for the picturesque or the comfortable.[20] There is only enclosure, in the text and around it. Pauline Réage/Dominique Aury wrote *Histoire d'O* in secret, in her room in her parents' house, at night, in the bed where she had a habit of working, due to her recurrent migraines. From her work in the Resistance she developed a taste for the clandestine that protected her double life, her love for Jean Paulhan, and her scandalous novel; it was rare for women to write erotic novels. Under the cloak of anonymity—retired much later— she hid her subversion. It was a subterranean life, darkly flamboyant, like her work.

The Captive

Jealousy is an essential mechanism in Proust's novels; it often results in closed doors.[21] "I once knew a woman who was loved by a man who in the end literally imprisoned her; she was never allowed to see anybody, she could only go out with trusted servants," writes Proust, summarizing the plot of *La Prisonnière* at the beginning of *Le Temps retrouvé*.[22] By imprisoning Albertine, the narrator hopes to control the people she sees, to know more about her friendships and her Sapphic affairs, to keep an eye on her movements but especially to seize her, to gain access to her interior life, dissolve her frustrating opaqueness, and take hold of her past, which haunts him. With this in mind, the narrator leads Albertine to believe that they will soon be married and invites her to share his Parisian apartment, in spite of his mother's reservations. For several months of an uncertain winter, he keeps her in a bedroom, next door to his absent mother's (a kind of profanation), at the end of a corridor. The washroom is next to his own room. "The partition which divided our two dressing-rooms was so thin that we could talk to each other as we washed in double privacy," in a proximity of bodies that is usually only possible in a hotel.[23] According to Proust's biographers, Albertine was based on Agostinelli, his driver and lover, who died tragically in a car accident (as would Albertine). This ambiguity between characters and sexes adds to the intensity of the drama. She or he? It doesn't matter; what matters is the object of love, the subject of passion.

The narrator enters Albertine's room only to watch her sleep, to look at her form under the sheets, and to be sure she has returned home safely. He watches her window from the street, as Swann once did for Odette, on the lookout for shadows and noises. It is she who enters his room, according to a ritual ordered by her host's fragility and manias: she may enter only when he rings for her; she must avoid closing the doors too loudly, as well as drafts. Françoise is defiant toward Albertine, whom she considers an intruder, and makes sure these rules are obeyed, "which Albertine had expressed in all innocence, [but] the latter realised with astonishment that she was now living in an alien world, where strange customs prevailed, governed by rules of conduct which one must never dream of infringing."

When the narrator wakes up, he does not send for her right away because he finds her more beautiful from afar. He considers her to be "a domestic animal which comes into a room, goes out"; a young woman who, cat-like, throws herself onto his bed for erotic play: intimate caresses, deep kisses. "Late every night, before leaving me, she used to slide her tongue between my lips like a portion of daily bread." The play does not, however, go as far as penetration: "You are not my lover," she says to him one day, and he admits it.

She sleeps often, and this is the height of pleasure. The narrator says, "I have spent charming evenings talking, playing games with Albertine, but never any so pleasant as when I was watching her sleep." Stripped of all artifice, she becomes vegetal, plant-like, her long hair placed beside her, like a fashionable woman's accessory in *Modern Style*. No conversation is necessary; "I knew that she was no longer looking at me, I had no longer any need to live upon my own outer surface." And love becomes possible once again. Marcel can caress, possess, dominate.[24] "In keeping her [body] before my eyes, in my hands, I had that impression of possessing her altogether, which I never had when she was awake. Her life was submitted to me." He touches her, kisses her, puts his leg against hers, rubs himself against her. "The sound of her breathing as it grew louder might give the illusion of the breathless ecstasy of pleasure and, when mine was at its climax, I could kiss her without having interrupted her sleep." He also likes to see her wake up. "In that first delicious moment of uncertainty, it seemed to me that once again I took a more complete possession of her since, whereas after an outing it was to her own room that she returned, it was now my room that, as soon as Albertine should have recognised it, was about to enclose, to contain her."

The room would "enclose her, contain her," keep her captive. Prevent her from loving anyone else. Watch over her, make those whom the narrator believes to be allies watch over her: Andrée or the driver. They would find out more about her and her lesbian affairs. Disrupt her social engagements, preventing her from attending a dangerous party at the Verdurins, where she might run into one or another of his female friends—Esther, Mademoiselle Vinteuil—who would trap her with insidious questions, make her contradict herself, catch out her lies, in a genuine strategy of suspicion and espionage that confines her more and more to her room.

Albertine likes baubles. He spoils her with gifts: jewelry, dresses, especially day dresses, asking for advice from his neighbor, the Duchesse de Guermantes. He promises her ever more sumptuous presents: a Rolls Royce, or even a yacht, luxuries of the era and ironic symbols of movement to someone trapped within four walls.

The narrator's jealousy and suspicions tighten the walls around Albertine. The act of remembering conversations and scenes that he doesn't know how to interpret plays a key role, filling the room with echoes and images that torture him. There is a logic of jealousy; it is that of the open boxes and sealed vessels," wrote Gilles Deleuze.[25] Jealousy leads to sequestration. "To imprison is, precisely, to put oneself in a position to see without being seen, that is, without the risk of being carried away by the beloved's viewpoint that excluded us from the world as much as it included us within it." To lock up Albertine is to try not to understand her, but to explain her, and to dominate her.

It is also to attempt to lock up Balbec and the *jeunes filles en fleurs*. "In the charm that Albertine had in Paris, by my fireside, there still survived the desire that had been aroused in me by that insolent and blossoming parade along the beach. . . . In this Albertine cloistered in my house . . . there persisted the emotion, the social confusion, the uneasy vanity, the roving desires of life by the seaside. She was so effectively caged that on certain evenings I did not even ask her to leave her room for mine." It is enough to know that she is there, secure, within reach. To *encage* Albertine is to dominate space, time, memory. Or at least to attempt to.

The bedroom is the center of the web that the narrator weaves around Albertine, in which he himself becomes progressively ensnared. In order to control her better, he gives up other women, travel, Venice, the theater, parties. Like Swann in the time of his love for Odette, he is no longer "seen"; he becomes invisible to a world whose insinuations he fears. Concerned about people getting curious—Bloch, for example, who tends to pry—he locks people out to lock Albertine in, to such an extent that he winds up imprisoning himself. "It was, moreover, principally from my bedroom that I took in the life of the outer world during this period." From there, through his curtains, he looks out at Paris, sniffs at the weather as soon as morning comes, takes in the sounds and cries of the city, which Proust renders superbly. "These habits of a life shared in common, this broad outline which defined my existence and within which nobody might penetrate but Albertine" describe a "lonely hermitage." "Day after day had gone by, these habits had become mechanical." When he speaks of "this life of seclusion which I carried so far as not to go any more to the theatre," it is Albertine who has taken center stage.[26] He covers her in expensive fabrics: "She walked about my room with the majesty of a Doge's wife and the grace of a mannequin. Only my captivity in Paris was made more burdensome by the sight of these garments which suggested Venice. . . . But gradually, by dint of living with Albertine, I was no longer able to fling off the chains which I myself had forged."[27] "The jailer is another kind of captive," wrote Nerval.[28]

At first, Albertine seems to submit to her seclusion to please her *chéri,* her "*petit* Marcel." She appears to easily accept the limits he imposes on her, as if she were indifferent to them; she gives in to his demands and receives his gifts with gratitude. But the confinement fades her beauty: "Albertine had lost all her colours." This "splendid girl," a captive bird of paradise, becomes "the grey captive, reduced to her dreary self." "Because the sea breeze no longer buffeted her skirts, because, above all, I had clipped her wings, she had ceased to be a Victory, was a burdensome slave of whom I would fain have been rid."[29] He no longer desires her but cannot let her go. Her captivity both drives and hampers the pleasure he derives from domination.

In reality, Albertine has escaped him. She dissembles, feints, lies, entraps him in the tangle of contradictions that he spends his time unraveling.

Her caresses become more distracted, her kisses less profound; she escapes his embrace. She withdraws, sad and tired, into silence.

Finally, she leaves him. "Mademoiselle Albertine asked me for her trunks . . ., off she went," Françoise announces, deploring (hypocritically) that her master has awoken later than usual.[30] She has left him just as he imagined leaving her, thinking to regain the upper hand by taking this initiative. To leave, to break captivity, is always possible. The slave may flee his master. Lost, Albertine regains her mystery, her attraction, the gleam of the *jeune fille en fleurs*.[31] "How slow the day is in dying on these interminable summer evenings!" says the narrator, who knows that he will never again hear Albertine ring for him, never see her lit window from the street, "the light which was extinguished for ever."[32]

The bedroom is the setting for drama, the center of the plot: amorous encounters and endless remembering. There, the narrator interminably evokes words, gestures, lies, the images of Albertine among the cyclists at the beach. The bedroom is also a way of understanding things, of fixing them, a box for keepsakes, as much as a structure for the narrative.[33] By cloistering Albertine, the narrator seeks to encapsulate the Balbec days, and the *jeunes filles en fleurs*. In the bedroom, he can keep the time he's lost.

Sequestrations

Where is love in this story? Is it the story of a mad love? A desperate desire to possess? The lover is greedy, jealous, obsessed. A father wants to rule his wife and govern his daughter. A brother dreams of destroying his sister. Roderick Usher locks himself in the melancholy bedroom of his shadowy house, "from whence, for many years, he had never ventured forth." He wants to bury his dead sister (having been the one to kill her) in one of the caves located deep below the house. Edgar Allan Poe's short story takes shape like a series of nesting boxes, forms of confinement governed by fear.[34]

Sequestration—amorous, exotic, sexual, familial—covers a desire for domination. The master wants to reserve the favors of the beloved, rupture any other relationships that might extend outside of him that provoke his jealousy, shut the beloved away from the world to keep for himself. He wants to shut the beloved up in an enclosed space—a bedroom, a cave—an invisible, inaccessible spot, to which he alone holds the key. There is a spatial logic to sequestration; the desire to hide implies recourse to a restricted, often minuscule space, as narrow as possible, so that one is hidden from the outside. Children know that when playing hide-and-seek that the best hiding places are in the least likely crevices; they make their small size work in their favor, like Hop O'My Thumb facing down the Ogre. Ferreting out these crevices is the detectives' principle aim, accustomed as they are to tracking down clues and prints in closed spaces that may appear otherwise unremarkable. The "Murders in the Rue Morgue" or *The Mystery of the Yellow Room* are classic examples.[35]

Imprisonment is a trope in the literature of sadism: forced sequestration, inflicted on one's prey, whose availability, debasing, bondage, and submission to the master's whims drive his pleasure. The underground caves in Sade's château extend for miles, a dark labyrinth where it is easy to get lost, where the imagination can run wild. Sometimes—as is the case for O—the submissive will voluntarily be imprisoned as part of the act of love, which requires her annihilation. It can also be the expression of bodily control that calls for unlimited access and obliteration. Sadism is not necessarily criminal. It desires an imaginary freedom from codes and norms. But it retreats far from the limits of the licit and is often exerted on the weak: children and women, especially virgins. Hence the discomfort it arouses.

Recent events have shown to what extremes certain perversions may run, almost always associated with sequestration or even burial. There are, for example, the horrors of the Dutroux Affair in Belgium, whose unfathomable black horror parents attempted to fight with their White March. There is the ongoing trial of Josef Fritzl, who for twenty-four years raped and imprisoned his daughter in Amstetten, in Austria.[36] Even stranger, because of the victim's personality, is the story of Natascha Kampusch, who was kidnapped at age ten and locked in a room halfway underground. The young Austrian never gave in to her imprisonment and managed to expand its limits; after six months, she persuaded her jailer to let her stay one floor up from where she was held. It took another two years to convince him to let her read newspapers and watch television. Her only access to the world came through the media, which is why these sources were so important to her after her escape. She imagined running away during the "outings" her kidnapper, Wolfgang Priklopil, took her on, but she was afraid he would kill her. When she was eighteen, she made an unthinkable choice and ran. Priklopil killed himself soon after, throwing himself under a train—and it seemed as if she experienced remorse.

The walls of the room were the horizon of Natascha's world. "I felt like a battery hen on a chicken farm," she said. "It was horrible. I was claustrophobic in that tiny room. I struck the walls with bottles of water or with my fists. If he hadn't let me up to the house to move around more, I think I would have gone crazy." But she didn't want anyone to see her bedroom, which had become a kind of second skin. "What bothers me the most? . . . All these photos of my cellar. It's no one's business. I don't go looking in other people's bedrooms. Why must all these people find themselves in my bedroom, the minute they open the paper?" This brutal exposure, after being hidden for so long, was difficult to endure. She grew dizzy from the too bright light shone on her by a hungry media. And yet she wanted to address her "dear public opinion," aware that by remaining silent she ran the risk of being further imprisoned in someone else's version of her story. But she experienced the attention paid to her bedroom as a violation of privacy, of a space where she had come of age during so many solitary years, in a room that both imprisoned and protected her. The bedroom—prison and refuge—was the armor and heart of her life.[37]

Isolation Cures

Children, women, and especially young women are the principal victims of these sexual crimes, where sequestration is a way in which their bodies are appropriated; it is a hallucinatory form of domination—usually male—that secretly dreams of breaking down all resistance through an imprisonment raised to the more dignified level of a cure. This is the story that Charlotte Perkins Gilman (1860–1935) tells in her autobiographical narrative "The Yellow Wallpaper," which was given the quite literal title of "La Séquestrée" in French and translated by Diane de Margerie, who saw it as the expression of the female condition in the Victorian era; women were kept under house arrest, a fate they fought against and that made them ill. Their malaise took the form of the famous "women's illnesses" of nineteenth-century psychiatry, the hysteria studied by Charcot and Freud and illustrated by Gilman's story.[38] Depressed by the pressures of daily life—marital, maternal, domestic—Charlotte submits to the isolation cure that her doctor husband prescribes for her. He loves her on the condition that she submit to his will. He is a man of science; he knows what's best for her. She must momentarily give up her children and her writing. The baby is handed off to a nurse, and they take away her ink and her pen; she hides a pencil. Then she is alone in a "magnificent" house, which she believes is haunted, with a "marvelous" garden that remains out of reach and that she can see only from the windows of the second-floor bedroom she occupies against her will (she wanted a room on the ground floor). It is a former nursery, judging from the bars on the windows and the yellow wallpaper with "sprawling flamboyant patterns"; she loathes the color, calling it "repellant . . . a smouldering unclean yellow . . . a dull yet lurid orange in some places, a sickly sulphur tint in others," and it gives off "a yellow smell."[39] Entire swaths of the paper have been torn away: "They must have had perseverance as well as hatred." She is bored, cries when she is alone, sprawls on the bed (which is nailed to the ground), and tries to decipher the paper. "I lie here on this great immovable bed—it is nailed down, I believe—and follow that pattern about by the hour." She makes out that "a broken neck and two bulbous eyes stare at you upside down. . . . Up and down and sideways they crawl, and those absurd, unblinking eyes are everywhere." Then she finds things she didn't realize were there: "Behind that outside pattern the dim shapes get clearer every day. . . . And it is like a woman stooping down and creeping about behind that pattern." One night, she thinks the woman is moving, creeping around behind the paper, trying to get out; it becomes imperative to tear it away, to see what's behind it, to help her escape. In solidarity with the woman in the wallpaper, she too creeps around the room, tearing off the paper in long sheets. She finishes the job in one night of insomniac revolt. In the morning, she tells her stupefied husband, " 'I've pulled off most of the paper, so you can't put me back!' "[40]

Charlotte loathed her fate. She married a man she didn't love out of weakness; he cheated on her; she resented the demands of motherhood, developed passions for women, and, above all, wanted to write. She regretted not having been born a man so that she could marry the woman she loved; doubtless she was a repressed lesbian; certainly she was a frustrated writer.[41] The rest cure she was given in 1887: "No pen, brush, or pencil," her doctor said; he, like his colleagues, was resolutely hostile to women's intellectual work, which was supposed to be the key to their emotionality and their hysteria. The same therapy was prescribed by most neurologists, especially the Americans (Silas Weir Mitchell in Philadelphia, Charles Fayette Taylor in Boston, William James (brother of Henry): distance from one's family, isolation, bed rest, stretching, massages, and a milk diet, the nutrient of femininity. It was applied to Edith Wharton and Alice James, as well as to Charlotte Perkins Gilman; they became sisters in depression.[42] Leonard Woolf contemplated it for his wife Virginia, whose passion for writing—her genius for it—resembled madness to him.[43] All seem to have experienced their "cure" as a kind of imprisonment.

Recluses

The typical form of religious retreat is the cell; it was perfectly suited to communal life, which counterbalanced its solitude. But was this enough? Especially in early and medieval Christianity, there is an ideal of reclusion that responds to several needs: the desire for asceticism, for penitence, for austerity, for prostrating the body and conquering carnal appetites to find God. Did Christ not dwell for nine months in the Virgin Mary's womb? Did he—the infinitely great, the incommensurable—not mean to give an example of rest in this sanctuary, *claustro materno*, triply enclosed—before, during, and after childbirth—the completely closed cavity that only the breath of God penetrated?

Men fled the desert, as Jean-Jacques Rousseau would: "I went with tranquil steps to find some wild spot in the forest."[44] But this wooded, eremitic lifestyle would not suit women, fragile and threatened by nature and by equally ferocious human beings. Female recluses lived in the city, where they found safety and familiarity. Jacques Dalarun has shown a surprising peak in their numbers in thirteenth- and fourteenth-century Italy, in a general expansion of feminine devotion; it was very popular among beguines and *pinzochere* and those who belonged to the Third Order.[45] There were 260 in Rome around 1320, 20 in Perugia, and dozens of others scattered around the country. Every town had its recluse or recluses. They came from varied social backgrounds, aristocratic or peasant; most of the time they were virgins or widows. Their goal was to find a recluse's cell near the church, if possible with a door to follow the service. This was the case for Humilité de Faenza: "They built a little cell into the side of the church, with a little window into the church, through which she could hear and receive the sacraments of the sacrosanct mother, the Church, as well as another on the outside, from which she could receive alms and satisfy at will those who came to see her." Iconography of the time shows her going from one window to the other. Humilité lived there for twelve years before leaving to found an order in Faenza and then in Florence, where she died. Saint Justine of Arezzo (who died in 1319) entered a monastery at age thirteen, where she joined another recluse, Lucia, in a cell so "low and narrow" that she could not stand up and had to pray on her knees. Not long after, she went to live in a precarious cell on the flank of the church of Sant'Antonio, with other nuns; when they were assaulted by highwaymen, they built a "little place" somewhere safer. When she went blind, she had heavenly visions.[46]

Clare of Rimini (who died between 1324 and 1329) is one of the most famous recluses. Noble and beautiful, she married twice after leading a frivolous youth. When she was widowed, she converted and decided to devote her life to Christ. She gave herself harsh penance and did everything to excess: went barefoot, dressed crudely, ate bread and water, "slept on bare boards." During Lent and Advent, she walked up and down the ancient Roman walls of the city, loudly announcing her sins. She left Rimini for Urbino, and during a tour of the bishop's palace, she stayed in a hovel whose door faced onto the church so that she was able to follow the nighttime services, so ardent was her thirst for the sacred, as was true of all these women. But her nocturnal cries exasperated the canons and the neighbors; they complained, and she was sorry not to have her own place to live. When she returned to Rimini, she set up camp near the Roman wall, outside, without a roof, among the marginal people who occupied that no-man's-land. "Lord, here I may have you," she said, happy for her salutary deprivation. The Christ of the Passion was her model. She had visions inspired by frescoes of the Apocalypse. She even felt a baby moving in her heart.[47] She founded a community of women who wanted to keep her among them, but whenever she returned from her travels (she moved around quite a bit), she preferred to return to her wall.

Whether individual or collective, at home or connected to a public building, reclusion was a fairly widespread form of devotion and was specifically feminine. There were recluses everywhere, including in southwestern France, in Auvergne; Saint-Flour had its own.[48] Religious orders were relatively closed off and could not accept all the women who sought to join them, a fact that explains the blossoming of recluses, capturing a desire for both asceticism and protection. Public opinion oscillated between respect and suspicion; the religious hierarchy mistrusted them. Clare of Rimini was accused of being a heretic. However, the Church tended to fear beguines, women who were active, lively, and sociable and who preached. They looked to Martha rather than Mary, claimed to support themselves by working or begging, organized their own spaces, wore nuns' habits, and spoke in public. The term *beguine* comes from *begge,* "to speak."[49] Women who spoke out were more dangerous than recluses, who were less visible and kept to themselves.

Teresa of Avila or the Castle of the Soul

Is solitude inherent to the feminine condition—the search for a secret garden, a "walled garden of the soul?"[50] With Teresa of Avila, the popular image of nuns became exceptionally mystic; she provided an example of this mysticism and gave an account of it in the founding of Carmel and in her celebrated *Las moradas o el castillo interior* (1577). Teresa advocated retreat, contemplation, and asceticism, and she built her monastery around these values. The cells were austere and cramped, with whitewashed walls; they were decent, clean, and impoverished, dedicated to solitude and piety.

Winters are harsh in Castile; snow falls on the handbooks; in the burning hot summers, the windows had to be constantly closed; no visitors were allowed. Teresa herself did not remain at the monastery but traveled a great deal on behalf of her communities. Accused of being "a vagabond and a rebel" by the papal nuncio Sega in 1577, she was condemned to confinement, like her disciple Saint John of the Cross, who was imprisoned by his order for several years, during which he composed his most beautiful writings: *The Dark Night* and *The Spiritual Canticle.* Their excess and religious individualism made them a kind of challenge to the Church. They described direct contact with God in the "castle of the soul," the "interior" where they believed they could find him, in the silence of their cell; even during sleep, they could encounter the beloved, as if in an embrace. Isolation was good for prayer, which did not necessarily need to be expressed in words but through entry into the "interior castle," which referred not only to the body, but also to the soul, which must be cloistered in order to access this interiority. Teresa described this in her book as a journey through the *manadas* (noisy crowds of people). Some have insisted on describing a literal topography of the castle of the soul; this is unnecessary. Julia Kristeva insisted on the fluidity of Teresa's thought, where water is the element of choice—springs, fountains, streams of tears—the link between the lover and the loved one. Water rushes through the borders between inside and outside, like writing, Teresa's passion. "One may not put in chains a soul that prays." Remaining in one room is not necessary, except for the room of self-knowledge.[51]

Any path—even the path to perfection—necessarily travels through spatial metaphors. How to describe it otherwise? In an introspective journey, Teresa asks us to "consider our soul like a castle, as if it were made of a single diamond or a very clear crystal, in which there are many rooms, just as in heaven there are many dwelling places." Our bodies are the outer walls of the castle, and we must leave them to enter it: "The castle has many dwellings, some above, some below, some on the sides, and in the center, in the middle of them all, is the main room, where the most secret things happen between God and the soul. . . . There is the main room, the palace where the King resides." In order to reach it, in order to cross the threshold, many obstacles must be overcome. There are rats and snakes. In the first through seventh dwellings, we must pass through several degrees of initiation. "Although I am speaking of only seven dwellings, the dwelling places contain rooms, upstairs, downstairs, on the sides, with beautiful gardens, fountains, and such delicious things that you will want to dissolve yourself in praise of God." God occupies the center. He can be reached through the "ears of the soul," by hearing in silence: "We feel without being able to see, neither with the eyes of the body, nor with those of the soul." Ecstasy is like being abducted; the person who prays is abducted from herself, from her body, from her thoughts; she is submerged in the water of life, invaded by God. What matters is to love and to desire. "We do not know perhaps what it is to love . . . for it is not a question of experiencing the greatest pleasure, but of having the greatest determination to desire forever," said Teresa. Love is not possession but desire. It is not a state but a perpetual movement—an interior movement. "The king hath brought me into his chamber," says the Song of Songs.

The Center of the Soul

Teresa's mystical experience and such experiences burgeoning in the seventeenth century, are examples of sensual knowledge that operates by intuition. The mystic feels the immediate presence of a transcendental being. His soul dilates, grows larger at the center. "All unions of love are knotted either at the center of the soul, or in the area closest to the center. . . . The union must consume the center of the soul; this seems so clear to the contemplative that in the description he makes of his experiences, he doesn't even think to situate his ecstatic love. We only ever form unions at the center of the soul, or at least very close by to it . . ., or at the peak of the spirit," wrote Abbé Bremond, the great seventeenth-century reader and historian of religious sentiment. Night is a trial as well as a possible revelation. To triumph over it, we must abandon ourselves, but without passivity; deliver ourselves to God to rediscover "this happy center of the soul, where, once the trial is over, the mystic union is consummated, and pure love is achieved."[52] A number of mystics have made reference to this nocturnal moment; Pascal described the fire that appeared as a sign of his "ravishing." "It is the heart that perceives God, and not the reason. That is what faith is: God perceived by the heart, and not by the reason."[53] Mother Agnes speaks of the "depths" where God lives and where he hides in the shadows, which are, rather, "unapproachable lights." "That is why we must adore God, who is hidden in the depths of our spirit, and give ourselves to him to carry this hiding place."[54] To find this god crouching within us, first we must retire within ourselves, like the hedgehog or the tortoise in his shell; empty out any words or images we have within ourselves; and banish the noise of the outside world to offer to ourselves and to God, who dwells inside us, a "vast, empty place."

Following Abbé Bremond and Michel de Certeau, Mino Bergamo has analyzed the mystical writings of the seventeenth century, specifically the *longue durée* of the "anatomy of the soul." At least since Saint Augustine and Meister Eckhart, Christian mystics have always sought to describe "a place or space in which to locate the highest graces and the supreme divine union."[55] Bergamo sketches out the diverse forms this has taken over the centuries. The ancient notion of *interiority* belongs to Augustinian thought, revisited and revalued in the seventeenth century by Surin, Camus, Olier, Bernières, Pascal, François de Sales, Fénelon, and the quietism of Jeanne Guyon. "All lines in their center are only a point," wrote Jean-Jacques Olier, "and the souls within God are all lost and become one soul in God. And just as these lines are naturally only this one point, it seems clear that these souls in God are singular. Hence the unity of will and light go together, so that they no longer need address each other, but see the same things in God."[56] Surin cites a letter from Marie Baron; that sainted woman, when she awoke, believed herself to be profoundly alone in a foreign land, but as if she herself were inhabited. "This single word, *interior,* completely ravished her. She told spiritual people to incessantly enlarge and dilate their interiors and to tolerate nothing that could shrink or limit it." For God, that infinite being, lives on the interior. That's why we must abandon the outside and "withdraw, sink into ourselves."[57] "Rest, joy, and solid contentment can only be found in the interior world, in the kingdom of God that we all have inside ourselves. . . . Peace can be found only in the interior life," said Father Lallemant.[58]

Seventeenth-century spirituality was a culture of interiority. It represented the soul as inherently interior, where oppositions between high and
low, superior and inferior, took shape; it was often seen in binary terms but
evolved toward the tertiary, making room in a median "center," as if a more
complex stratification were necessary. The most frequently recurring terms
are "the depths of the soul," "the center," "the pinnacle of the spirit," the
place where one can sometimes feel God, according to François de Sales
(*Traité de l'amour de Dieu,* 1616). De Sales inverted the representation
(which had been traditional since the time of Meister Eckhart) of the
"depths of the soul"; for him, the depths were not necessarily pure but
could be, on the contrary, quite muddy, requiring a topological inversion
that continually filtered and purified them. But it wasn't only a question of
topological inversion that prioritized verticality; François de Sales and later
Fénelon substituted psychological perception for an ontological analysis of
the soul. Union with God was consummated by "quiet prayer," "the pleasant rest of the soul." This could be practiced anywhere, not necessarily on
one's knees in a church or even in the silence of the bedroom, though this
was useful; ravishing could happen in the street. "Spiritual discernment"
was within the reach of all who were faithful, said Jeanne Guyon; she recommended a "short term" that would allow everyone to reach it "in their
center." The clergy found this kind of spiritual autonomy suspect and
locked her up for seven years because of it. They were fruitful years of meditation and writing; in her *Récits de captivité* she recounts her solitude and
anguish; in *Les Torrents,* she describes her mystical experience.[59]

According to Mino Bergamo, after a long inception, the seventeenth
century was the apogee of interiority. It was the culmination of a spatial
concentration that would greatly impact later representations of the soul,
which would become spirit, mind, consciousness, and unconsciousness in
a secular movement that has yet to receive a similar level of research.

Psychology takes the place of metaphysics; the self displaces God at
the center of the soul, and introspection replaces meditation. How is the
unconscious structured? Its development leaves little room for space.[60]
Psychoanalysis, which asks patients to lie down on a couch, is rich in bedroom stories; the parents' bedroom plays a major role in theories of the

libido and depth psychology—for example, in the case of Little Hans.[61] However, in spite of a certain vertical quality that superimposes the id, the ego, and the superego, it seems to me that this structure does not make specific reference to the bedroom itself or employ spatial metaphors.[62]

Of course, there are many other influences—especially scientific ones—on representations of interiority, which is above all related to our ability to be judicious.[63] The nineteenth century refers to "chambers of the mind," and it moved between topographical representations (as indicated by the recognition of the cerebral locations known as Broca's area) and the belief in fluids circulating in the body, which could be harnessed and tamed by hypnotists and mediums and concentrated in one cell.

The *camera obscura* had an even more direct influence on this conception of interiority. According to Émile Littré in the *Dictionnaire de la langue française,* "the *camera obscura* is a device where light may only enter through a small hole of an inch in diameter to which a lens is applied, which permits rays of light reflecting off of objects to appear on the opposite wall or on a draped sheet, allowing what is happening outside to be perceived on the inside." The discovery inspired Descartes, and perhaps Rousseau, who, at the beginning of his *Confessions,* announces his intention to work, "so to speak, in the dark room"; nineteenth-century thinkers like Marx, Nietzsche, or Freud were especially influenced by early photography, as Sarah Kofman has shown.[64] For Nietzsche, the *camera obscura* is the metaphor for forgetting, one that must be preserved or even cultivated. "The room of consciousness has a key, and it is dangerous to look through the keyhole: dangerous and impudent. Woe betide the curious! We must throw away the key." In the *Genealogy of Morals,* Nietzsche recommends "a shutting of the doors and windows of consciousness . . . a little silence, a little tabula rasa of consciousness, making room for the new."[65] Forgetting is a form of therapy, a necessary instrument, required in order to innovate. The selective *camera obscura* is the opposite of a room cluttered with souvenirs.

The mind is comparable to a room that must be cleared out lest it be suffocated with memories, a place that can easily become a prison. "I have a soul like a dungeon," said Jean Richepin. For Maeterlinck, what weakens

the life of the soul "is to remain, night and day, in the room of our little un-
generous thoughts."[66] For others, on the contrary, this precious sanctuary
must be preserved. "Each of us has a heart like a royal chamber. I've walled
it up, but couldn't destroy it," Flaubert wrote to Amélie Bosquet.[67] It is the
bottomless pit of memory; Proust and Perec made themselves its indefatigable explorers. "I remember," wrote Perec, a way of clearing out the murky
waters of memory, of dissipating the thick smoke of the crematory ovens
where his family were destroyed.[68]

But it is impossible to forget. "I cannot liberate myself from the image
of my mother in a gas chamber. I cannot rise above it," wrote Norbert Elias,
who, in an attempt to escape memory, participates more than ever in the
civilizing process.[69]

Go to Your Room! Children and Punishment

In all contexts, public and private, familial and legal, detention has been,
and continues to be, the preeminent form of discipline and punishment. It
is not necessarily in prisons, which are a very late development in penal history; this history has been written by Michel Foucault and other historians.[70] I do not intend to review this long and complex genealogy, which is
so bound up with a history of power, but to explore the place of the four
walls of the room or the cell in the configuration of this punitive obsession
with security, so widespread today.

"Go to your room!" mothers say to their children when they misbe-
have. For families who reject corporal punishment, sending a child to its
room and depriving it of dessert are the domestic equivalents of the more
lenient punishments that are more directed at the soul than the body. Victor
Hugo, like a good grandfather, thought it was excessive to punish Jeanne
with "dry bread in a small dark room" and brought her jam. The Comtesse
de Ségur, however, had no compunction about it. Her character, Madame
de Fleurville (in *Les Petites filles modèles*), locks Sophie in a "penitence
room" with bare furnishings, where the child breaks everything; she has
to copy "Our Father" over ten times and is given only soup, bread, and
water to eat—a real prisoner's "pittance" that made a great impression on

young readers. Sophie calms down and repents. Foloche, the cruel step-mother in Hervé Bazin's *Vipère au poing,* sentences her son to "three days in his room."[71]

Isolation in a dark room—not necessarily their own—was a common practice for punishing children in the nineteenth century. Plunging them into darkness—as if they had been thrown into a dungeon—was meant to inspire them to reflect on their wrongdoings and return to good behavior. The shadows are identified with hell, with punishment and suffering. And children are afraid of the dark. Writers rebeled against such treatment. Jane Eyre believes there was a ghost in the room in which she was locked up as a little girl; she was given such a nervous shock that she still feels its repercus-sions as an adult. This was an intolerable attack on the rights of children, an idea that was still vague at the time. Such punishment persisted in Quebec, however, until the middle of the twentieth century. An engraving in the jour-nal *L'Enseignement Primaire* from November 1919 shows a mother who very calmly and resolutely locks her little boy up while his sister looks on sadly and his grandmother wears a resigned, sorry expression.[72] As late as 1941, pedagogues who were eager to "fight fear" were advising never "to punish the child in a dark room."[73] At so late a date it was still necessary to warn against the harm caused by this method.

Some children are badly loved. When she was a servant in Paris, Jeanne Bouvier told the story of a little girl whose parents made her stay all day in her room, where she was brought her meals. "She had to live in her tiny little room," as though her parents dreamed of locking her up.[74] Nu-merous accounts mention "closet children," who were more or less seques-tered in a closet for several years. Very recently, it was discovered that a seven-year-old child has spent all of his life in a cubbyhole, where he was abused even further. What kind of will to negation and nihilism makes peo-ple do such things? Loving children clearly doesn't come naturally.

When they could no longer put up with their unruly children or teen-agers, families under the Ancien Régime appealed to the state, who could order them to be locked up by *lettre de cachet.*[75] The Revolution abolished this practice but replaced it with a paternalistic correction system.[76] Parents sought to place their children in reform schools that were meant to correct and discipline them. In the nineteenth century, such institutions functioned on both a social and sexual level. Unlike bourgeois families, who were concerned about autonomy, working-class families often voluntarily sent their daughters to such institutions, concerned about their moral "lightness"; sons were given more freedom. Bon Pasteur and other penal colonies would take on both sexes, including children who were sentenced to be there, many of whom were later sent to prison.[77] In all of these institutions, the children slept in dormitories, but the more hard-headed were frequently sent to solitary confinement. Chance reigned over these punishments; there were abuses, suicides, and deaths, especially at Mettray. The famous agricultural colony in Touraine was founded in 1840 by philanthropists to rejuvenate the corrupt urban family and its youth by having them working the land, and it degenerated into a tense, depressing place where there were constant revolts.[78]

The authorities were haunted by the fear that the children would corrupt one another. They had to be separated, isolated, taken away from the fomenting masses. Experiments with individual cells—to be occupied twenty-four hours a day—were carried out on children at La Petite Roquette, a prison opened in 1836 in Paris and built by an architect named Lebas according to plans derived from Bentham's panopticon.[79] It housed minors convicted of theft and vagrancy and children who were sent by their families to be reformed. It was oriented around the idea of radical isolation during both day and night. The young detainees were not to come in contact with one another but only with the guard, the teacher, or the priest. Mass was a fearful time of day, and the penal authorities would have willingly canceled it! To reach the chapel at the center of the building, the children had to hide their faces under "black veils," invented by the chaplain, who bragged about them to De Tocqueville; they were later replaced by hoods. Covered in this way, they took their places in separate compartments, like standing coffins. A narrow walkway came out of their cells, and they walked several steps forward onto it. When they weren't studying, they worked all day in their cells at creating detachable pieces of wood, like bars for chairs. Of course, their passion for communication was overstimulated by fear. They showed an unparalleled ingenuity in the system of noises, signs, and exchanges of *biftons* (little notes), declarations of love, for which they were starved. Confinement in the freezing cold, with a rudimentary level of hygiene and mediocre nutrition, gave rise to many cases of galloping consumption. Already in bad health, the children were susceptible to rickets and became scrofulous and tubercular; there was a high rate of mortality. Medical, philanthropic, and political opinion was very moved. Although De Tocqueville was a committed defender of a cellular penal system, he and Victor Hugo spoke out against La Petite Roquette. The children rose up several times, including once during a visit from the Empress Eugénie. The system was abolished and the children dispersed to various agricultural colonies.

For lack of funds and conviction, the cellular system was eventually abandoned in favor of dormitories, which were overcrowded and dirty. When they were adopted again in the 1950s, at Fresnes or Fleury-Mérogis, they were modeled on student *chambrettes;* times had changed.[80]

We don't know very much about the children's suffering. There are a few letters that indicate repentance and profound feelings of abandonment. Thirteen-year-old Philippe described his life in a letter to his father: "It is not very happy [here], but I am content to no longer be led by the whip, as I've been told. I am closed up in a cell all day where the furniture includes a bed with mattress, made of straw, two blankets, and two sheets; a table with a drawer; a stool; a pot for water and an earthenware pot, a chamber pot, a wooden broom, and a spittoon. When I need something, I have a wooden peg I put in the slot in the door to attract the guards' attention." Philippe's work was mind-numbingly monotonous, but he didn't complain. "Although we're not so badly off at La Roquette, I do regret having got myself put in here."[81] It is easy to stifle the tears of a child. Through her work in very rare archives, Martine Ruchat has reconstituted the history of Solon, "a child who was placed [in the facility], thief by trade," who could not be put right, in spite of the best efforts, principles, and recourse to solitary confinement of the philanthropists at the reform school in the Garance.[82]

The Dauphin Louis XVII—both an exceptional and exemplary victim—incarnates the figure of the unhappy child, the absolute victim. Françoise Chadernagor wrote an admirable novel about him, *La Chambre.*

The dauphin is locked in a room, an island detached from the continent; Chadernagor describes its layout, decoration, and progressive enclosure. The doors, windows, and even the chimney are sealed off, and locks appear everywhere in an attempt to bar the child from running away or being kidnapped. He was truly sequestered and ever more alone, rejected even by those close to him, if we believe the accusatory letter that was probably dictated by his sister, Marie-Thérèse, the future Duchess of Angoulême. Forgotten by all, he faded from view. But he did not complain or cry. He shut himself in by refusing to speak; he took refuge in silence, night, death. "What was there at the source of the crime?" What about those responsible for destroying the child—were they aware of it? Blind to it? The relationship between the center and the periphery comprises the political horizon and the sinister dynamic of this story. I wanted, Chadernagor writes in her epilogue, to write about evil and "about rooms: our walls, our hatreds, our solitude, our tombs."[83]

Prison Cells

Imprisonment is an ancient practice, even a habitual one. It was originally a political punishment. The sovereign "throws" his adversaries, his "captives," into the dungeon, the oubliettes of medieval castles. He banishes, isolates, and locks up his enemies, and the annals of royal history are brimming with narratives of imprisonment, often related to metal—Louis XI's iron cages, Louis XIV's iron mask; detainees were thrown to the very bottom of the fortress, locked up by official decree. In spite of regulations that were put in place over time, the Bastille was the very symbol of arbitrary royal power, and its "storming" marked the triumphant beginning of the French Revolution. But the revolution that aimed to destroy the prison walls would go on to employ them in its service.

The implementation of penal codes put an end to arbitrary imprisonment and placed the prison at the heart of the penal system. "Punish less to punish better": that was the idea behind the modern hostility to torture and corporal punishment (in spite of the fact that the death penalty was not abolished until 1982). Modern forms of punishment were concerned with

uniformity and consistency and worked toward dissuasion and rehabilitation, at least in principle. That is when the question of the "good prison"
became a central one, and with it, the idea of the cell. But this did not come
into play right away, not in practice (still subject to improvisation) or in
principle (which wavered). In his *Panopticon,* Jeremy Bentham argues for
the virtues of surveillance and circulation over that of separation; the cell
doesn't interest him. The scale of punishment imagined by Lepelletier de
Saint-Fargeau (1792) established a gradation that blended darkness and isolation. It distinguished the *cachot* ("solitary confinement in the dark") from
the *gêne* ("solitary confinement with a light"), from the prison, which involved isolation but also communal work. Darkness and the deprivation of
light were synonymous with punishment.

Many forces converge in the cell. Catholicism, which draws on the
monastic tradition, was attentive to the maintenance of communal links; it
fought against the practice of solitary confinement, a dangerous Protestant
invention that limited a prisoner's participation in and ability to attend
Mass.[84] There was a more rigorous influence of Puritanism, oriented toward
individual moral rehabilitation—for example, in the Quaker experiment at
Cherry Hill. Medicine, which is concerned with fighting contagion, fears
the kind of contact that creates a cholera epidemic like that of 1832. "The
best prison is the kind that doesn't corrupt," said De Tocqueville. Mesmer-
ism believed magnetic fluids to be an effective remedy, especially if they were
concentrated in a detainee's "cell," the "cradle of the criminal's healing."
The confluence of ideas in the nineteenth century around penitentiary discourse and psychiatric theories concerning isolation cures is also striking.[85]

The cell was the key to all therapies: moral, religious, hygienic, penal.
It provided three functions: punishment, social defense, rehabilitation. In
America, that laboratory of incarceration techniques, two models conflicted: Auburn, which practiced nightly isolation and daily communal
work, but in silence; and Philadelphia, founded on constant isolation, both
day and night; Bible reading; and self-reflection. At Cherry Hill, the Quak-
ers created an immense prison on a radiant plan entirely made of cells; it is
no longer in use but is open to visitors; this building, designed by John
Haviland, is the most impressive example of penitentiary architecture that

can be seen. On his 1832 trip to the United States, De Tocqueville wanted to carry out an inquiry into the penitentiary system; he was won over by Cherry Hill.[86] He disagreed with Charles Lucas, a well-reputed criminal lawyer who emphasized the physical and emotional drawbacks of isolation and was supported by a small number of doctors who worried about the risk of madness. In the 1840s, the debate raged.

The cell won out, both in France and abroad; in 1846, Parliament made it official policy. An architect named Blouet reconciled the panopticon with the cell in projects that marked the height of "cellular utopianism."[87] But the revolution of 1848 interrupted construction, and the Second Empire preferred to deport convicts to the far-flung colonies. The Third Republic returned to the ideal of the cell, and in 1875, it passed a law calling for cells to be installed in jails (where inmates carried out short sentences). But plans were stalled by financial reluctance on the part of the general councils—no matter how much money was spent on prisons, it was always too much. The Republic did not have very forward-looking policies when it came to penitentiaries; it preferred to "rid itself" of its "lost causes, . . . unfit for any kind of worksite," as the law regulating multiple offenders read (Waldeck-Rousseau, 1885), and sent them to Guyana or New Caledonia.[88] It nevertheless had the merits of adopting a deflationary attitude in its preference for shorter sentences and its use of suspended sentences and parole. The number of prisoners decreased and reached its low water mark in the 1930s: fewer than twenty thousand detainees, a dream of a figure.[89]

Building prisons was not a priority. After the Revolution, nationalized abbeys like Fontevraud, Clairvaux, or Melun were used; they were summarily furnished, cold, foul-smelling, sinister places of death. In the late nineteenth century, reports were less than mediocre. Radicals preferred the cell, especially in big cities. In Lyon between 1894 and 1896, 219 cells were inserted into the seven wings of the Saint-Paul prison. In its cells, painted "administrative yellow," summarily furnished with a small table and a cot, the inmate was given a few perfunctory belongings: a cup, a dish, a foot bath, and a broom. Cleaning the cell was part of his duties. In Paris, to clear out the capital in time for the world's fairs, the general council (on which sat several Communards, such as Louis Lucipia), decided to abolish Mazas, whose "implacable brutality" was critiqued even by the writer Maxime Du Camp, and to create a model prison at Fresnes that could house up to six thousand inmates. It was designed by Poussin, who practiced a new pavilion-style architecture, and it opened in 1898.[90] Located far from the city center, twelve miles away in the countryside, it was light and airy, laid out on a rectangular floor plan called the "telephone pole," and boasted the most modern conveniences (running water, electricity, heat); it was rigorously divided into cells. The inmate was completely alone, could walk a few steps along an adjoining narrow, fenced-in promontory, and the door to his cell was opened only on Sundays so that he could attend mass. "Prison is a tomb," wrote Louise, bored to death as an inmate in a woman's prison in 1906.

Each cell was about a hundred square feet, painted light colors, with an asphalt floor, and featured a large barred window and furniture bolted to the ground: an iron bed, a folding table, a chair, wooden shelves, and hooks; posted on the walls were rules and regulations and other administrative texts; there was electric lighting and a water closet that was also a sink. It was stingy (even repulsive) but unusual in a time when most of the population didn't have sewers or running water. Some criticized the excessive "luxury" of "Fresnes Palace": "Has the philanthropy driving those who built Fresnes not gone too far?" asked *Le Temps* on 21 July 1898. Popular opinion believed in the "iron law" that decreed that inmates should have a quality of life that was inferior to that of the poorest workers, lest prison should come to seem attractive. The level of suspicion aimed at the inmate called for the bare minimum required for survival. In this sense, the cell indicates national standards of consumption. The French worker was one of the worst-housed in Europe; the prisoner should be one of the worst-incarcerated. He was and is still.

The layout of cells was the object of much discussion among international penitentiary commissions, which debated the desirable or acceptable degree of comfort. Northern Europe had different ideas than southern Europe, especially when it came to toilets. France lagged behind in terms of hygiene. At the 1885 congress on penitentiaries in Rome, its delegates had refused to completely get rid of bathrooms but bragged (using illustrations) about implementing "a zinc vase with a hydraulic closure that rolls on small rails along the floor [and] that can be extracted in the corridor without entering the cell." The French "chamber pot" amused the Danes and the Belgians, more so as the lack of comfort was compensated by an abundance of posted signs: "an inventory of objects in the cell, a list of patrons and members of the disciplinary commission, names of factories found in the region, annual hours of the establishment, the law against repression, internal regulations, a list of lawyers, the price of supplementary food sold in the prison," etc.—all things that cost infinitely less than proper sanitation.[91] Thirteen years later, in spite of inarguable advances, Fresnes remained timid when it came to hygiene, although the penitentiary authorities made it a principle of rehabilitation: "Encourage self-respect through personal hygiene and proper clothing," said the president of the general council in his inauguration speech.

As was often the case in penitentiary matters, the reality was disappointing compared to the ideals laid out in speeches. In 1913, out of 370 prisons in France, only 62 had cells (42 built new and 20 rehabilitated). They were integrated into jails and reserved for defendants (a right) and shorter sentences (a precaution). In prisons under the Auburn system, they were limited to nocturnal isolation through a system of partitions and fencing, limiting the number of "sleeping cubbies," true "chicken cages," into which inmates were padlocked at night.

However, the cell became standard practice in Europe and conformed to relatively uniform norms. Witness the 1941 testimony of Victor Klemperer. In Dresden, where he fought Nazi persecution of the Jews, from which he was protected for a little while by his marriage to an "Aryan woman," he was condemned to eight days in prison for infractions against civil defense: he had inadvertently let electric light show from his window. In his journal, he gives a precise description of cell 89 at the police prefecture, where he was held from 23 June to 1 July 1941: "To the left, toward the window, was the bed. When it was folded up, it was hung up two feet on the wall, its feet held in by crampons that looked like bats. The comforter, the wool blanket, and the sheet were spread out along the side, and above the bolster, at an angle, were stenciled the letters PPD, Polizeipräsident-Dresden. . . . On the right, in front of the bed, a tiny folding table in crude wood, also attached to the wall, with a small bench. In front of the table, near the window, a small bookcase," whose contents he described: water jug, coffee maker, basin, a small jar in dark terracotta, a tin-plate box with salt in it; there was also a shelf with three hooks, the third of which had a PPD regulation bath towel. Behind the little bench, next to the door, at most six feet away from the table where inmates were supposed to eat, were the latrines. "They were the only thing that disturbed the superficial way I thought the cell would be. Instead of these modern, hygienic toilets, there should have been a simple pail. But even the bathroom made me feel my captivity—the toilet could only be flushed from the outside, . . . once in the morning and once at night." The air was still breathable, only "moldy and rank." Above the table they had posted the rules and regulations, which he had trouble reading because they had taken his glasses, under the pretext that he didn't need them in prison. The surroundings were fairly tolerable all in all, but it was the incarceration system that was hard to take; the food was almost better than in the outside world, in that period of intense rationing, but not being able to move was trying. He was not permitted to stretch out on his bed and had to spend his days sitting up or creeping about his cell. "I walked back and forth along the bed; it was, for me, a hyphen between today and tomorrow," surveillance and the passing of time, "the pure feeling of the cage and the abyss."[92] He was also deprived of writing materials until a guard relented and gave him a pencil. Klemperer tried to compose a dictionary of the "language of the third Reich," his masterpiece, by reciting it to himself.[93] He wrote his prison essay immediately after his release, with a level of detail that he took to be his duty.

Life in the Cell

We have learned much about the daily routine of life in the cell through the chatty, nitpicking reports made by penitentiary administrators and by investigations (from those of John Howard and Louise-René Villermé to those of contemporary sociologists) that saw their societies reflected in the prison. We have also learned much from prison narratives, which vary according to the culture of incarceration practiced by each nation. A subsection of

Russian literature as large as a gulag consists of stories from the camps and prisons, a recent example being *In Captivity Among the Dead,* by Eduard Limonov.[94] The prison narratives are a rich literature but full of gaps, and they are mainly recounted by men, due to the sexual dissymmetry found in prisons (in France, women make up only 4 percent of inmates); they are mainly written by political prisoners—Silvio Pellico, Nerval, Blanqui—more than regular inmates, and this is certainly one of their limitations. Earlier accounts written by intellectuals boast about their being locked up, as if it were a proof of honor; they are more able to adapt to solitude, to which they are more accustomed, especially for writing. Later, less articulate prisoners, who are more troubled by solitude, try to lose themselves in writing, except some well-known criminals, who, in the tradition of Lacenaire, glorify themselves and their exploits. Readers—perhaps less today, now that the politics of security has strengthened its grip—love big-hearted thieves, high-flying swindlers, daring burglars, those who defy the established order, like Mesrine; they have no tolerance for sexual offenders. Neither does the rest of the prison population, which stigmatizes "rapos." Dr. Alexandre Lacassagne and his competitor Lombroso promoted a criminal anthropology; Lacassagne systematically sought and gathered confessions from a dozen inmates in the Saint-Paul prison in Lyon. His and Lombroso's accounts were recently collected and published by Philippe Artières and bear astonishing witness to the "vile quality of life" and the everyday experiences of incarceration.[95] The past few decades have seen a flourishing of these narratives and have uncovered talented writers, like Albertine Sarrazin and Claude Lucas.[96]

Everyday life in the cell was the same generally for all inmates but varied in certain ways, depending on gender, temperament (some were more or less tolerant of isolation), diet, and the specific institutions where they were held. Madame Lafarge, who was condemned to life in prison for poisoning her husband, never stopped attempting to transform her cell into a bedroom. "Will I have books, pens, a table, or enough with which to rebuild the shadow of a home?" She was delighted with the furniture she was promised: "I will have my own iron bed and a fireplace, an armchair, two chairs, a walnut shelf for my books, and below it a little writing table. Another little table, which I can fold up, will do for my meals. Then I'll have a dresser in which a basin will be hidden, as well as a mirror and a few small bottles"; all that was necessary for an elegant woman.[97] It was a relief. But no sooner had this furniture been given to her than it was taken away (although the other prisoners refused to carry it out, out of solidarity), and she was left with only an iron bed and a wooden stool. Madame Lafarge was wrong about her era: she had no right to special privileges, and the pistol hadn't been invented yet.

Political prisoners were initially treated more severely; because they posed a threat to those who were in power, they were given arbitrary, indefinite sentences. Then democracies accorded them certain rights—for example, the right to private incarceration, which distinguished them for a long time from regular inmates.[98] Young leftists imprisoned during the 1970s wanted to eliminate this distinction and obtain the same rights for all prisoners; this unleashed a series of revolts in the following years.

Silvio Pellico, a member of the Carbonari, was imprisoned for ten years, eight of which were in *carcero duro,* or harsh incarceration, for a while in the ill-reputed Spielberg prison in Moravia. He was very sensitive to the "rooms" he occupied; to the views they had (in Venice, he could see the rooftops of the Piombi, where he was held); and to his neighbors (male and female, for the sexes were still imprisoned together). He deciphered the graffiti on the walls that made the cell a palimpsest. "Some only gave a name and the village of some unfortunate, along with the ominous date of his arrest. Others added slurs against their judge; still others inscribed moralizing maxims." He mentions the physical hardship: filth, vermin, cold, lack of exercise. At the Spielberg, he was given only a solitary walk, wearing his irons. A fellow inmate, Mazoncelli, came down with scurvy and had to have a leg amputated. Another, Oroboni, died. But in his cell, Silvio read the Bible and found God at the same time as he found himself. His narrative recounts his conversion and his resistance, as well as his detention. His book, *My Prisons,* was a bestseller, a guide to a personal irredentism that was profoundly romantic and Stendhalian in nature, according to which we are never so free as when we are in prison.[99]

Another prison hero: Auguste Blanqui (1805–1881). *L'Enfermé,* or "the prisoner," spent the better part of his life in prison: forty-three years and eight months.[100] His story illustrates the trials and tribulations of political life. In Mont-Saint-Michel (1840–1844), in the "lodges," conditions were archaic, worthy of the Spielberg; there were no mattresses, not even a straw pallet, only vermin-infested canvas mats; to eat there was only bread and water; for shoes, iron boots. "The general state of my body is deplorable. I no longer sleep or eat." Blanqui became mute and withdrew into his own thoughts. Near death, he was evacuated and liberated, only to return in full force to Paris in the midst of the revolution of 1848, which reinvigorated him. At the fortress on Belle-Île, where he was imprisoned in 1850, conditions were more liberal; his cell, number 14, became a meeting place and workplace. After trying to escape, he was put in solitary confinement, transferred to Corsica, then to Algeria, and eventually given amnesty in 1859. In 1863, he was incarcerated again, but the three years he spent in Sainte-Pélagie, the "prince's prison," he called "the happiest of my life." His "bedroom," which served as a study as well as a meeting room, was a hotbed of socialism. The Republic would go harder on this unrepentant rebel when, in 1872, it held him responsible for the flames of the Commune and condemned him to life imprisonment, which he served at Clairvaux, first in solitary confinement, in a five-by-eight foot cell. "On very cold days, he stayed in bed, wearing a hat; he wrote, his back turned to the light of the window," notes his biographer Gustave Geffroy. Then later, in a large room with eight windows, "he lived in a corner of the room, furnished with an iron bed, chairs, and armchair. He used the wood he chopped himself." He lived like a hermit on a mountain, an anchorite in the desert. Like a scholar, as well, shut up like Descartes in his heated room. On his table there were books; dictionaries; and treatises on mathematics, algebra, science, history, and geography, which his sisters obtained for him. He spent his days calculating and ruminating on astronomy, his great passion apart from politics. He was given amnesty again in 1879 and went to live with his friend Granger on the avenue d'Italie in Paris, but "they each had their room," and in his he reconstituted his "eternal cell" with his table and papers. He was "the most extraordinary beast in a cage there ever was," wrote Geffroy. "The prison followed the man, rebuilt itself around him, wherever he was, according to his own will." It had become a way of life, second nature. "He always carried inside him his cell and his tomb. He lived there strong and joyful," reads his epitaph.

Louis Perego and Claude Lucas left remarkable testimony on the regular inmate's experience of prison, where these two "professional" burglars and repeat offenders spent long years.[101] They experimented with all kinds of isolations—shared or individual cells, ordinary and disciplinary cells—and they were sensitive to the nuanced differences among these micro-spaces of daily life. They experienced the hardships of being *détenus particulièrement surveillés* (*DPS;* prisoners kept under close watch) and solitary confinement, a prison within a prison, a way of punishing those who rebelled. Solitary confinement meant four blank walls, at one time a straw pallet, today a low bed, with minimal food and utter solitude throughout the freezing night. It was often responsible for psychiatric and physical troubles and numerous suicides, and although it has been denounced any number of times, it persists as the expression of a penitentiary administration anxious to maintain its authority. In principle, solitary confinement is not meant to last more than forty-five days. But one inmate was recently shown to have spent thirteen years in isolation in approximately sixty prisons, and according to psychiatrists, he demonstrates "socio-sensory deprivation syndrome."[102] What an understatement.

Louis Perego was particularly interested in the details of everyday life, full of indefinitely repeated rituals meant to keep the population occupied. Claude Lucas describes the void of an interminable day in prison, where time is literally "killed," borne but not forgotten. It is "a parenthetical day: it doesn't belong to social time, and as such, it is abstract or fictional, a pure temporal vacuum." It introduces a radical break with reality and is productive of social exclusion. "It is the mold of this exclusion. It is sufficiently empty to be experienced as a punishment but 'furnished' enough to appear normal. It does not allow for a return to the self or to a confrontation with reality: it is a simulacrum of social time and creates the illusion of life. The epitome of this feeling of being shipwrecked comes in the evening, when the television is switched on." Lucas sees the television as a form of alienation and refuses to watch it. Perego and Lucas escape, in a manner of speaking, by studying and taking up writing. They do not take much issue with the cell; both appreciate its virtues of relative privacy and the retreat it offers. "It was a relief to finally be alone in the cell," Lucas writes after his roommate leaves; he was nice, but chatty and insomniac, two attributes that can quickly become irritating in a cell of one hundred square feet.[103] Once he was free, Lucas, like Blanqui, needed a small room in which to write. From this perspective, the ability to isolate oneself to read, write, and study is very helpful for the inmate. But Lucas and Perego denounce the way prison tends to alienate inmates, not only through its degraded material conditions, but also by its very essence, its openness, the way it feels like the void. Until very recently, it stood for a refusal to acknowledge certain basic individual rights.

The cell is only one part of a complex machine and the stage on which the drama of incarceration plays out. For it must be admitted that the cell is not a bedroom and should not become one. Anne-Marie Marchetti, the author of several detailed studies on contemporary prisons, has shown that inmates serving long-term sentences attempt to make themselves at home through photographs, knickknacks, personal objects, and pillows on the bed, the "most important piece of furniture"; her work has focused on women incarcerated in Rennes.[104] But prison authorities do not see this as a sign of settling in; they fear prisoners becoming too comfortable and appropriating the space of incarceration. The prisoners will often be suddenly moved from one cell to another, the peephole may be opened at any moment, and they are subject to surprise searches, which feel like invasions, especially when carried out by special squads hired for that purpose.[105] Everything is done to remind the inmates that they are not at home but under state control; that they have no privacy; that privacy is the luxury of free (and honest) men. Their mail is inspected; there are no private meeting rooms; they are subject to surprise body searches; all this contributes to a feeling of depersonalization that undermines the supposed goal of rehabilitating prisoners and reintegrating them into the outside world.

A cell is a punishment. For a long time it was associated with solitary confinement, which it resembles in some ways; it originally provoked the working classes to revolt and disrupted their ways of communicating and socializing. It also earned the ire of political prisoners, who wanted to be imprisoned together. Being brutally thrown into an individual cell could tip an inmate into depression. Suicides were frequent, especially in the early days of a devastating detention. In 2008, there were 115 deaths: one suicide every three days, most often carried out during a lonely night. Prisoners would hang themselves with sheets.[106] Having a roommate was hardly better. The young and the vulnerable, homosexuals, anyone who "deviated" from the norm ran the risk of serving as a punching bag for older and stronger inmates in these no-exit situations where the guards carefully turned a blind eye. In a remand center in Nancy, Johnny Agasucci, twenty-six, who was only a defendant, was murdered by his roommates in cell 118, who made him their "slave."[107]

For a minority of inmates, reading and writing was an escape, something to be discovered, a solution and an accomplishment. There are many strong links between prison and writing, from Dostoyevsky to Mahmoud Darwish, the great Palestinian poet who composed *State of Siege* while imprisoned in Ramallah.[108] Pellico decided to write his autobiography: "I would tell the story of everything that had happened inside of me, the good and the bad, since childhood."[109] Paper was rationed, so he wrote on the wood of the table, which he scraped off as he went, like a blackboard. Victor Klemperer was reborn when a guard returned his glasses to him and gave him a pencil: "At that moment everything became clear, yes, luminous even."[110] The inmates at the Saint-Paul prison whose testimonials Dr. Lacassagne collected, under the pretense that it would win them lenience (a lie: most of them would be executed), sometimes developed a real taste for it, like young Émile Nouguier, who blackened twenty-eight notebooks of eight hundred and fifty pages: "What is that impish spirit that put a pen in my hand? Tonight I can't stop; I've gone to bed three times, and three times I've gotten out of bed to write." This twenty-year-old gangster, a "Belle Epoque greaser," discovered the pleasure of writing while in prison. "To write is to resist and to refuse being negated," said Claude Lucas.[111] "This is my life," wrote a convict in the Saint-Paul prison on the front of his notebook. To write was to attempt to reclaim control over one's existence and to gain immortality.

To resist was also to remember. Camus's "stranger," Meursault, chose to remember his room by taking an inventory of it:

> At first it didn't take long. But every time I started over, it took a
> little longer. I would remember every piece of furniture; and on
> every piece of furniture, every object; and of every object, all the
> details; and of the details themselves—a flake, a crack, or a
> chipped edge—the color and the texture. . . . I could spend
> hours just enumerating the things that were in my room. And
> the more I thought about it, the more I dug out of my memory
> things I had overlooked or forgotten. I realized then that a man
> who had lived only one day could easily live for a hundred years
> in prison.[112]

Through poetry, through writing, and through memory freedom could be
reconquered.

For one brief, salvational, no doubt illusory moment, the cell became
a room of one's own. This minimal space, the necessity of which seems
more than usually clear, is constantly threatened by prison overcrowding,
which has peaked in France in recent years (more than sixty-seven thousand inmates in 2008) and made prisons—especially remand centers—
places of intolerable suffering and latent revolt.[113] The prison comptroller
general, Jean-Marie Delarue, has visited the "model" prison of Villefranche-
sur-Saône, where he has lodged numerous critiques. He especially has
complained of the *caillebotis,* the thick wire mesh attached to the windows
instead of bars to avoid all contact with the outside world, especially the
practice of *yoyotage,* in which, through the windows, prisoners send messages attached to bits of string that can be lowered and raised like a yo-yo.
The effect the *caillebotis* give is to "plunge the cells into near-darkness during the day," which reinforces "the impression of isolation and shadow" and
"aggravates feelings of depression or anger."[114]

Incarceration is very much in style. No more homeless people in the
street. They are cold, of course, but their misery disturbs the order of things.
We would prefer not to see them, so we place them in shelters, sometimes
against their will. We put twelve-year-old children in prison. We call them
"minors" until they grow up. A child of twelve is an "adolescent" who deserves
to be treated like an adult. In the slammer! Such a project was abandoned.

But that it even existed shows the obsession with fear. We also lock up the mad in a return to the asylum system with its strict isolation rooms. Rapists and pedophiles threaten us, the real or potential victims that we are. It would be more prudent to keep them in prison, even after they've served their time. It's safer. Incarceration, nevertheless, is an archaic solution, and modern technology ought to spare us the expense. The will to security has become a philosophy and a mode of governing and has given rise to a generalized control and system of registration (see the proliferation of all manner of dossiers) that poses with great perspicacity the question of limits.

Hiding Places

Sometimes we just want to hide. The famous painter Frida Kahlo, in the Casa Azul, her house in Mexico, collected papers, correspondence, love letters, and objects in the bathroom adjoining her bedroom, and she transformed it into a safe. These souvenirs attest to the betrayals and dramas that her life as a disabled recluse had imposed on her. She suffered from polio and was the victim of a terrible accident that resulted in the amputation of one leg; she hid her handicap under a corset and long Indian skirts. "Appearances can be misleading," she wrote in the margin of a drawing, a full-length image of Kahlo herself, superbly and sumptuously dressed. Behind the door, sealed up and hidden behind wall hangings, she had piled an impressive, dusty mess: dozens of cardboard boxes; piles of newspapers and thousands of books; armoires spilling with dresses and corsets; trunks; a little writing desk with sealed drawers, possessing secrets within secrets; and more than twenty-two documents, six thousand photos, and hundreds of drawings. In this safe room, which was unsealed on 8 December 2004, half a century after her death (in 1954) and that of Diego Rivera (1957), her unfaithful companion, the archives of this tormented, creative life were revealed.[115] All of this is now on display in the house, which was turned into a museum; the bedroom has a melancholy serenity that it is doubtful Kahlo knew herself.

War and oppression (be it religious or political) force populations to flee their persecutors. They take to the woods, the ancestral refuge of outlaws, or hide in all the nooks and crannies of a house: a trunk, a closet, an attic, under a stairway; they tunnel into basements or burrow into holes dug in the walls or gardens. The Camisards showed great ingenuity, as the Musée du Désert in Anduze reminds us. During the Occupation, many persecuted people (Jews, freemasons, resistance fighters) hid in bedrooms of apartments, with the windows closed and the curtains drawn. They couldn't leave any trace or make any noise that might give them away; in this they relied on neighbors and concierges not to denounce them—although they were denounced quite frequently. Michel Bernstein, who would later become a famous bookseller, was a member of the Défense de la France network and lived throughout the war in Paris without leaving his room, where he made false papers.

In this way, a number of Jews throughout Europe tried to escape the Nazi terror. Hiding was the only way any of them survived. In Amsterdam, Anne Frank and her family made it to 1944, when they were denounced, rounded up, and exterminated in the concentration camps. The same fate awaited "the lost" whom Daniel Mendelsohn tracked down in a Ukrainian village where, before the war, his great-uncle had been a prosperous butcher. He, his wife, and three beautiful daughters were all murdered. Mendelsohn describes his search, which lasted over several years in Europe and the United States, where most of his family had emigrated in the early twentieth century. When he began, he had only a few letters and the fragmented stories his grandfather had told him about his lost brother. After a long hunt through the forest, the brother had taken refuge in a *kessel,* which Mendelsohn, not speaking Yiddish, took to refer to a castle, but he could find no castles in the Ukraine. It was a false lead; a *kessel* is actually a hiding place. After years of interviewing elderly and sometimes reluctant witnesses, Mendelsohn finally found the *kessel* house, at the back of a garden. His uncle and his eldest daughter had survived the massacre of the Jewish community, in which his wife and two other daughters perished. They hid in a cave, which was more of a hole, disguised by a nearly invisible trap door. A drawing teacher had housed and fed them, with the help of a young non-Jewish Ukrainian who was in love with the daughter. But they were eventually denounced and were killed in the spring of 1944. Half a century later, at the end of his determined investigation, Daniel Mendelsohn found their final shelter. That was when he understood the meaning of his grandfather's *kessel:* a hiding place that was so narrow it resembled a thin box. A cassette.[116] It was one final room whose inaccessibility could not protect it from the ultimate betrayal.

Fugitive Bedrooms

WHAT REMAINS OF the bedrooms of the past? Do bedrooms have a future? Like the houses that contain them, they seem doubly uncertain. "Houses . . . are as fugitive, alas, as the years," said Proust.

Disappearing Traces

Of long-ago bedrooms, there remain few traces. The word sometimes refers to an archaic definition. "A room that continues to be called the child's bedroom": this comment opens the first act of Chekhov's *The Cherry Orchard.* "Your rooms, the white one and the violet one, have stayed just as they were, mama," says Varya to Lyubov Andreevna, who exclaims, "I slept here when I was little. . . . And it's as if I'm little now." Her identification with the room is so strong. But not for long: when the house is sold, she must leave. She takes one more look at the house: "It's as if I never saw before what kind of walls this house has, what sort of ceilings. . . . Our late mother liked to walk about in this room." She goes out. "The stage is empty. There is the sound of keys turning in both doors, then of the carriage driving off. Then all is quiet."[1] It is a parable of houses demolished, rooms fled, lives devoured.

The peasant's desire to exorcise the dead erases all evidence of them. In the countryside, after a death, the sheets are changed, as is the bedding, even the bed. Violette Leduc was devastated to see her grandmother's mattress and bedding destroyed under the pretext of disinfecting the house. "It burned in the garden after the funeral. The implacable smell of burnt pompoms. For me, that will always be the smell of death. . . . My grandmother was taken away a second time. . . . She disappeared in the smoke."[2]

In the city, demographics exert their pressure on interior space. The home, personal space itself—the way it's arranged, its small details, its objects, its uses—comes apart suddenly with the death of its occupant. What can be done with what is left behind? After Virginia Woolf's Jacob is killed in World War I, his mother and his friend enter his room and are surprised by the disorder he left: "Nothing arranged. . . . What did he [the friend] expect? Did he think he would come back?" Jacob's mother asks him, " 'What am I to do with these, Mr. Bonamy?' She held out a pair of Jacob's old shoes."[3] It is easier to throw away these superfluous relics, this troublesome inheritance, and tidy up the deserted room. This is not without its emotional baggage. "How can we clean out our parents' houses without liquidating our shared past?" asks Lydia Flem.[4] How to walk into such a room without knocking and find it intact, the two sides of the bed preserved, with the most personal objects in the drawers?

When the previous occupant has left, others will take his or her place, moving around the furniture; getting rid of a fireplace, the one with the mantelpiece that supported the pendulum, the shells, the knickknacks; or changing the purpose of the room by adding a partition. They will repaint or change the wallpaper, amused by the layers of different tastes they uncover—"What ridiculous taste!"—vaguely moved by this palimpsest of lost time. We hear about the disappointment of those who return to their childhood homes. They barely recognize the houses where they lived and even less the rooms in which they slept. After all, they were only boxes—emptied boxes, boxes that are empty without them. That others fill up in turn with the murmurs and rustling they think will last forever. "All the bedrooms of life are, in the end / Overturned drawers," wrote Aragon. "We will never return to the bedrooms, the houses / Will be demolished, as we now know / Demolished so that nothing remains, not even the imprint / of a foot."[5]

Bedrooms are "places of memory" only in rare cases; they are too private for that. The mourners' piety—erecting altars of relics, photos, objects, locks of hair—lasts only as long as the mourners survive. The cult of the bedroom exists only for "great men" (less frequently great women), politicians, philosophers, or writers, staged for the edification of a public that is more and more interested in the private lives of celebrities. In *La Chambre noire de Longwood*, Jean-Paul Kauffmann muses over the room where Napoleon was held in captivity; he wonders about the authenticity of the things found here, about his death, and reflects on his own ability to resist the captivity he himself experienced in Lebanon.[6] Apparently, Napoleon accorded great importance to the *coucher* ritual. As first consul, he had a stateroom built in which he installed a bed on a platform covered in red velvet and an English copper-trimmed dresser: a strange mix of styles, of the sacred and the domestic.[7] Next, he adopted a metal camp bed—simple, light, and easy to move, the elegant, austere mark of a general—that would emblematize his legacy: that of a man alone with his dreams, in love only with power, the kind you claim standing up.

On the second floor of the White House is the Lincoln Bedroom. It is an object of veneration, the sanctuary of the Republic, although it was never actually Lincoln's bedroom; rather, it was his office and a cabinet room where he signed the Emancipation Proclamation in 1863. Harry Truman turned it into a bedroom. Laura Bush restored it to its supposed original state, in the Victorian style. A large rosewood bed, with a large headboard, serves as the focal point. The bed is authentic; it was purchased by Mary Todd Lincoln when—as a good mistress of the house—she took care of the decoration. Although Lincoln probably never slept there, the ghost of the assassinated president haunts the room. Eleanor Roosevelt, Winston Churchill, Amy Carter, and Maureen Reagan all claim to have seen it! Ronald Reagan's dog barked at the door but refused to go in, and the maids would enter only reluctantly. The president in office receives distinguished guests there.[8] The White House is a family home that retains the memory of its most famous occupants. Chancellor Helmut Kohl did not see Lincoln's ghost, but he felt very moved to sleep in the legendary and somehow prophetic room.[9]

Does the French Republic have as long a memory? It is certainly less focused on the domestic side of things; it celebrates its heroes in the temple of the Pantheon. The honors of the republic remain strictly public. The occupants of the Elysée Palace are more interested in erasing all traces of their predecessors. The memorial to François Mitterrand is at Château-Chinon, in the Hôtel du Vieux Morvan, where, from 1959 to 1986, as deputy representing the Nièvre and later as president, he spent all his election nights. Starting in 1946 the young deputy began to occupy room 15, with a view on the Morvan, not far from Mont Beuvray, where he thought at one point that he and his wife Danielle would be buried. It was there that he learned he had been elected president, on 10 May 1981, and where he wrote his acceptance speech. With its old-fashioned enormous key, one hundred square feet of space (including the shower), and no frills—a stopover for traveling salesmen—room 15 was a proof of republican austerity when, during Mitterrand's second term, questions began to be asked regarding the president's costly expenditures. "Four monastic walls, between which a political destiny took shape, in a far-away century when the *banlieues* didn't exist yet," wrote Ariane Chemin.[10] The room has lost its feather duvet and its wallpaper with yellow flowers, but it retains its old-fashioned charm, and it's always booked out; the hotel is an obligatory stop on the François Mitterrand tour (theme tours: the cog rattle of memory) before it moves on to climb the Rock of Solutré.

Before becoming fashionable tourist attractions, writers' houses were often left in disrepair, their interiors neglected or dismantled; their inheritors did not necessarily understand their appeal.[11] Voltaire's niece conscientiously emptied the Château de Ferney of his belongings and sold them off; there remains almost nothing of the long years the philosopher spent there. Emily Dickinson's younger sister Lavinia—her last survivor—did not leave much behind in her bedroom in Amherst.[12] Restorations often destroy the feeling of proximity. There is nothing so valuable as writers' houses that have remained in situ, that haven't been too much tampered with. We have the illusion of discovering Victor Hugo more at Hauteville House than in the Place des Vosges, George Sand at Nohant, Mallarmé at Vulaines. At Malagar, the home of François Mauriac is less "fugitive" than the others because he wanted his *querencia,* his refuge, to be open to the public.[13] A number of bedrooms are on display: servants' quarters, guest rooms, and a surprising conjugal bedroom with two beds on rails, in case they needed to be brought together. At La Vallée-aux-Loups, a zealous conservator has swapped out a broke Chateaubriand's shabby furniture for fashionable decorations worthy of the author of *Mémoires d'outre-tombe* who would certainly not recognize his own home. Doubtless this *voyageur du siècle* was more interested in his tomb than his houses. At Combourg, we hear his father's footsteps.[14]

In these house-memorials, the bedroom is not necessarily the best preserved, unless (as often happens) it was a room in which the author wrote—a
creative room. The table, the inkwell, some manuscript whose jottings and
crossings-out attest to the fact that genius is the reassuring product of effort;
all this is greatly admired. At Wartburg Castle, in Thuringia, where from 1521
to 1522 an excommunicated Luther was welcomed by Frederick III of Sax-
ony, one can still see on the wall of the bedroom where he translated the New
Testament into German the traces of the inkwell that he threw at the head of
the devils who tempted him and prevented him from working. Much later,
Zola's writing tables would become objects of veneration; in Paris, in the rue
de Bruxelles, his immense desk has often been photographed. In Médan, the
table in his little garret was preserved; it had accompanied him since the beginning of his career, as had the large one, on which he worked in the middle
of the "sacred space" of his study.[15] The bed is embarrassing, or at least it
embarrassed someone; Zola talked about it too much or too little. In the room
he shared with his wife, the large copper bed is gone, replaced by a sort of
sainted rendering of François (the son of Jeanne Rozerot) and his wife Émilie
with their son: the real-life family restored to this place where it was illegitimate.[16] At Vézelay, the Zervos collection was installed in Romain Rolland's
house, the property of the Institut de France; the writer made just one request: that the bedroom should be conserved "as it was"; however, the bed
was replaced with the piano.[17] Museums are essentializing; they want to emphasize the principal strokes of a writer's life. The obsessive desire for an
evocative fidelity necessarily makes a space feel rigid. And so it is rare that
we have the opportunity to exclaim, like Georges Poisson at La Brède, "You
can visit Montesquieu's completely unchanged bedroom!"[18] Transpositions
bother us most of all because they weaken the link between an author and
the place he or she lived. It makes us uneasy to see Colette's bedroom transferred from the Palais-Royal to Saint-Sauveur-en-Puisaye—not in her mother
Sidonie's house but in the next-door château where the museum is housed.
Or, even worse, the scrupulously, impeccably rendered rooms of Proust,
Léautaud, and Anna de Noailles at the Musée Carnavalet.

Whether in fiction or autobiography, we discover writers' rooms
in their work, for which they are the cradle, the witness, a motif. Proust's

room is essential to his writing, which he carried out at all hours of the day and night, while the shadows moved across the walls and light filtered through the curtains, while doors slammed and people climbed the stairs or shouted in the streets; it evoked all of his sensations, anguish, insomnia, anxious awakenings, isolation. It was an existential, quasi-metaphysical place for Georges Perec, who as an amateur archaeologist attempted to make a precise inventory of the almost two hundred bedrooms in which he had slept: "The resurrected space of the bedroom is enough to bring back to life, to recall, to revive memories, the most fleeting and anodyne along with the most essential."[19] And yet he knows, "My spaces are fragile: time is going to wear them away, to destroy them. Nothing will any longer resemble what was, my memories will betray me, oblivion will infiltrate my memory."[20] Space itself is a doubt. Does it really exist?

A similar suspicion nags at François Mauriac. His mother—an indefatigable "modernizer"—has upset everything in the family home, where the photos on the walls remind him of so little:

> For stones do not keep the imprint of hands, the reflections of faces, the shape or shadow of those who are gone; only that which they leave behind: fabric, curtains, tapestries, whitewashed woodwork, objects, and colors that indicate their tastes, their preferences. These are the things that saw them move from one room to another, sit, lie down, smoke, eat, dream, die. When the decoration of everyday life is destroyed, the carcass that remains can no longer tell us anything.

These devastated places have been swallowed up by oblivion, like Proust, whom Mauriac cites: "The memory of a certain image is but the regret of a certain instant."[21] For something to remain, it must be deposited in writing, the only guardian of a history, be it domestic or tragic.

We can locate our bedrooms within ourselves. They are the cradle of our experiences; they live in our memories. It is up to us all to remember, to write our own bedroom stories, day and night.

Neglected Rooms

On architects' plans—witnesses and creation myths—lines multiply, carving out domestic and collective space in so many "rooms" that accord each resident her own bed, her own room. The puzzle of "how to live" has become more complicated and more rich. Rooms have proliferated, like cells in a beehive. They have changed places, been protected, but also been sent up to the second story of a house or to the back of an apartment, with a window on the courtyard, without a "view," relegated to private functions, to the unproductive night, dark and worrying, feared and desired. Some have gained in size to meet the required air cubage; some have shrunk substantially. They have been stripped of their many functions and have become specialized as places to sleep; from *rooms* they have become *bedrooms,* simple cubbies for sleeping. So they have become neglected. We are always trimming them down. In short, they bother us.

But are we simply postponing the day when we no longer need them?[22] What is the future of the bedroom? Architects say they don't really know what to do with them, except in secondary residences, where they take on renewed importance. They sometimes suggest personalizing them even more, especially for children, or opening them up to the point that they seem to lose their distinct purpose, by turning them into annexes to common areas or part of the bathroom, which receives so much architectural care, to the point where they will have no division between the two at all, creating a *chambre de bains* (bed-and-bathroom). Or, when transforming a shoe factory into a loft, they will create a mezzanine for them, as airy as a "California cabana."[23] The bedroom is losing its associations with confinement between four protective walls and becoming, for some, a glass room, visible to anyone who cares to look. For adults, the room no longer matters; they often sleep elsewhere. The guest room, once a symbol of intimacy and hospitality, has long since disappeared. People travel during the daytime; guests are put up at hotels or in a corner in the living room; they leave as quickly as they arrived, on trains or, more frequently now, on planes. It seems that only children still require their own bedrooms, especially in France, where, thanks to a rising birthrate, the market is expanding; parents and children can choose from an ever-more specific and personal range of furnishings. "The Smart Home, 2012" is expected to take into account technological advances, like a "well-being cocoon," a kind of bubble where children, under constant supervision by the adults, are safely curled up in bed, surrounded with toys and television screens. "With a constant supply of oxygen [the cocoon] guarantees a healthy environment for problem-free nights."[24] The grandfather's room features an alarm system in case he should fall. In the bedroom of the future, precaution is king—with the assistance of efficient robotics.

The bedroom has gotten lighter; much of its furniture and knickknacks have been cleared out.[25] The armoire has vanished, making room for closets, which open up to piles of colored towels, stacks of shirts, or clothing on hangers. Whatever furniture is there can be folded and put away; the drawers are hidden. There is barely anything that can be called a bed—no more fixed curtains or cumbersome headboards but four feet on the ground, covered with a duvet and layered with pillows or even a light futon thrown onto the ground. The lighting is subtle and soft. The overall impression of the furniture is that it is lightweight, conceived of for people who are always ready to decamp. When interviewed, the inhabitants of these bedrooms do not often say they're happy with them but don't know what exactly they want.[26] What they do want is a generalized space, malleable and modular, like a loft—something that matches their lives. "Before, we shopped for furniture; now we shop for partitions."[27] Japanese houses, with their sliding doors, fluid, free of furniture or curtains, furnished only with carpets or mats for an organic existence, where adaptive, supple people live, vaguely clad in kimonos, are the ideal for the postmodern bedroom, so far from the massive, stolid "bedroom" of department store catalogues, with its indispensable mirrored armoire, the trophy furnishing for young couples of yore. These interiors suggest another vision of the body, of the individual, and of love. The revenge of East on West?

How can we explain this "disappearing act"?[28] Above all, by economic factors related to urbanization, the housing crisis, and the high cost of living. It is a question of "enlarging your space, without moving a wall," through rearranging the space and the way it is divided up. Bedrooms often pay the price and through this partitioning end up reduced down to the most basic dimensions required. They seem to be undergoing a process of redefinition.

But there are more profound reasons at work. To understand them, we must work backward, retracing the many paths that coincide in the bedroom. Its familial, social, spiritual, and material foundations have eroded or collapsed. It has lost its anthropological importance. We are no longer born at home but in the maternity ward. We no longer "keep" to our rooms. We no longer die at home. Illness and death send us to the hospital, where three-quarters of French people currently die; hence the constant demand for a private room to occupy for a few days, or even a few hours, in order to die with dignity. We no longer even necessarily age at home. In the anonymous spaces of retirement homes, just a few personal objects keep up the link with a previous life. The conjugal couple and their matrimonial bed, which once invited a comment from François Mitterrand regarding the importance of his mother's presence and the continuity of his childhood home in Jarnac, are no longer the linchpin of the home. Blended families no longer valorize the permanent room and necessitate spare rooms in which to house the couple's various children, when the the couple has custody. Practices of lovemaking have become indifferent to the room and the bed. It is more common to seek transient spaces for a discreet coupling, the spontaneity, haste, and ardor of which take refuge in the hotel, the back room, the car, the tent, the beach, or the forest. An erotic affair no longer necessarily takes place in the routinized bedroom; in fact it fears it, like the eventual boredom that comes with a conjugal lifestyle.

The intellectual and even spiritual ideals underpinning the bedroom have similarly weakened. "Wherever we find the sacred, we find a wall. And wherever the enclosure fades . . . the sacred disappears," writes Régis Debray on the subject of public spaces.[29] In a society where transparency and the abolition of borders and boundaries are supreme values, the curtains tear. "It's not saying much if a voyeuristic society, which aspires to all that is transparent and forthright, no longer feels elective affinities with shells, screens, seals, and sacramental niches."[30] The same could be said of the bedroom. The essence of the couple and of the self is more exposed. They even want to expose themselves. Heads of state on the right as well as the left open the doors on their private lives.

The decline in reading in bed next to a bedside lamp—once a great pleasure—has shaken the alliance between the bedroom and the book, once a refuge for readers, especially female ones.[31] The television is its competitor; a more collective medium, it is enthroned in the living room, in front of the sofa with its coffee table. The same is true of the computer, which is still unequally individualized in interior spaces. Educators recommend not putting one in a child's bedroom in order to maintain parental control over potential predators—not even in a teenager's room, whose nights are spent on YouTube, Facebook, or Twitter.[32]

The prie-dieu has disappeared; solitary prayer is hushed. Contemplation is no longer the dominant mode of religious life. The projects and their ills command attention; humanitarianism has replaced mystic ecstasy. Abbé Pierre, Mother Teresa, Sister Emmanuelle, and Father Joseph Wresinski are our heroes today. Like Coluche or Doctors Without Borders, they take whatever roads they must to address the misery of the world. The odysseys of traveling people, the spectacle of Indian crowds, the urban conglomerations of Africa, the expansion of shantytowns and the ever-growing number of people without homes make the bedroom seem unimportant— but also desirable.

"Going Outside . . ."

FOR CENTURIES, WESTERN culture has sought and fought rest in the bedroom. The Greek *kamara,* the Roman *cubiculum,* the cloistral cell, the royal dungeon, the peasant's box-bed, the *précieuse*'s reception room, the alcove, the niche, the pensioner's sleeping car, or the first-class carriage—these are all sketches at modes of retreat, fluctuating like the steps of the ballet. I have followed the meandering paths that lead toward this bodily enclosure, without, however, exhausting its potential. I have not visited shepherds' cabins, or various kinds of student bedrooms, or the concierge's lodgings, or—to my great regret—the bedrooms of detective fiction (so often the scenes of the crime), which Edgar Allan Poe, Gaston Leroux, Raymond Chandler, and Paul Auster, among others, have explored with a detective's meticulous eye, expert in deciphering clues. These are a model for investigation that demands a knowledge of police culture that I do not possess. Beyond these sources, a historian is dependent on the gazes that have been cast on her subject. There are many other doors to open, other bedrooms to inventory, each of which could have been the subject of a book. This one is an invitation to travel.

The bedroom has been the cradle of civilization, at once productive of social norms, a place of creation, and a site for experience. In a long genealogy, which ranges from the king's bedroom to that of the palace, from the monk's cell to that of the prison, from the common room to the private bedroom, it corresponds to the ways in which we represent the body and its needs. It is a subject of observation for investigators, a way of surveying, regulating, and disciplining for those who have an idea of how it should function; priests, moralists, doctors, hygienists, and psychologists have each set out their theories regarding its layout and its hours, its air cubage, the kind of people who should live there, and different ways of sleeping.

Architects and decorators have constructed it, colored its walls, carpeted it, decorated it in various styles. The bed—a lair for sleeping, the altar of love, the sanctuary of reproduction—has invited a specific kind of attention to its materiality and its practices and especially to the time we spend there. The room is crammed with the anxieties and even the obsessions of a given society. The order of the room suggests the order of the world of which it is an elementary particle.

It plays, then, a double role. In the theater, its continuity and possibilities for entrances and exits have provided a setting for innumerable plays, especially in the contemporary era, which no longer hesitates to show a bed (at one time, this would have caused a scandal). In life, it is a site for encounter and exchange, of power and attraction, of tenderness and violence. Parents and children, young and old, rich and poor, men and women meet there, love each other, and sometimes confront each other. The individual both retires there and is abandoned there.

The bedroom has been a site of experiences that resemble and differ from each other, universal and singular experiences. It is timeless in the needs it fulfills and is also profoundly historical in its forms and uses. It is marked by the time that infiltrates each of its nooks and crannies; the time leaves its imprint on its objects and shapes our memory but also is inscribed in the immobility of the "time that does not pass," where daily life gives it an air of eternity for people of all ages and all conditions. Childhood and old age—which require more sleep—and the ages of illness and death nestle there more than others. Teenagers, women, and writers maintain profound links with the bedroom. And young people today, along with exiles and immigrants, are those who desire it the most. For them, the bedroom is not "neglected"; they feel neglected not to have one.

The bedroom represents a first step in inclusion, the minimum democratic requirement, as well as access to protective retreat, a foundational aspect of autonomy. "A door must be open or kept shut" says Alfred de Musset's Marquise; she is referring to her salon, which she would like to protect from people as well as drafts.[1] The door has the power of admission and choice and therefore allows the bedroom to feel protective. One ought not to enter without knocking; sneaking in would be an intolerable violation of privacy. And from the outside it is protected by shutters and curtains, even if for Baudelaire a lit-up window offers us a better view than an open one: "What we can see by the light of the sun is always less interesting than what happens behind a pane of glass."[2]

In a society that is ever more locked down and controlled, the bedroom retains its absolute right to secrecy. It represents the possibility of escaping the world, even more so as communication technologies improve to the point of putting the world on the computer screen. Connected in this way, the bedroom of the future will have infinite means of exploring the world. The door opens to desire, to other people, to the world; it invites us to discover them, to go outside.

These proliferating, enigmatic spaces—I have loved them for the scars on their walls, the murmurs they muffle, the emotions they contain, their intrigues, their existential density, and the dark paths of their imaginations. Dependent on the confidences I have received and surprised by how powerfully suggestive they have been, I have sometimes felt I have been indiscreet. But I have also felt as if I have hurled myself at a subject that is inherently ephemeral and unknowable. The inhabitants of bedrooms envelop themselves in protective secrecy and in silence; this wards off the historian's intrusion. The bedroom is a limit-experience, in Foucault's terms, whose opacity repels the researcher's (or the state's) prying gaze.

This is, no doubt, one of the reasons it seduces us.

Notes

Chamber Music

1. Michel Foucault, *Dits et écrits* (Paris: Gallimard, 1994), vol. 3, no. 195, p. 192 (taken from "L'œil du pouvoir," interview with Jean-Pierre Barou and Michelle Perrot, in Jeremy Bentham, *Le Panoptique ou l'œil du pouvoir* [Paris: Belfond, 1977]).

2. Blaise Pascal, *Pensées*, 8: "Divertissement," 126, in Blaise Pascal, *Œuvres complètes*, ed. Michel Le Guern (Paris: Gallimard, 2000), vol. 2, p. 583.

3. Philippe Hamon, *Imageries: Littérature et image au XIXᵉ siècle* (2001) (Paris: José Corti, 2007).

4. Xavier de Maistre, *Voyage autour de ma chambre* (1794), 2nd ed. (Paris: Dufort, 1797; repr. Paris: José Corti, 1984).

5. Cf. Edmond de Goncourt, *La Maison de l'artiste* (1881) (Dijon: L'Échelle de Jacob, 2003).

6. Walter Benjamin, *The Arcades Project*, trans. Howard Eiland and Kevin McLaughlin (Cambridge, Mass.: Belknap Press, 2002), p. 9.

7. "La nuit" (deals more with urban space), *Sociétés et Représentations* 4 (May 1997); Simone Delattre, *Les Douze heures noires: La nuit à Paris au XIXᵉ siècle*, intro. Alain Corbin (Paris: Albin Michel, 2000); Alain Cabantous, *Histoire de la nuit, XVIIᵉ–XVIIIᵉ siècle* (Paris: Fayard, 2009).

8. Léon Heuzey, in *Dictionnaire des antiquités grecques et romaines*, ed. Charles Daremberg and Edmond Saglio (1887), vol. 1, part 2, on "*camara*, or more usually *camera*."

9. Florence Dupont, "Des chambres avant la chambre," in *Rêves d'alcôves: La chambre au cours des siècles*, illustrated museum catalogue, Musée des Arts décoratifs (Paris: Réunion des musées nationaux, 1995), pp. 13–25.

10. Heuzey, in Daremberg and Saglio, eds., *Dictionnaire des antiquités grecques et romaines*.

11. Gustave Flaubert, *L'Éducation sentimentale: Histoire d'un jeune homme* (1869), in Gustave Flaubert, *Œuvres* (Paris: Gallimard, coll. Bibliothèque de la Pléiade, 1948), vol. 2, part 1, V, p. 100, SE, 78.

12. The same is true of nineteenth-century institutional dictionaries, in which administrative and legal definitions are numerous. Louis Charles Dezobry and

Théodore Bachelet's *Dictionnaire général de biographie et d'histoire* mainly deals with assemblies, while the *Grande Encyclopédie: Inventaire raisonné des sciences, des lettres et des arts,* ed. Henri Lamirault et al. (31 vols., 1886–1902, vol. 10, pp. 320–394) is more comprehensive.

13. The "Anjou room," so called because it was fitted with enormous armoires bearing the names of the provinces whose registers were filed there: Anjou, Normandy, etc.; *chambre de communauté:* "a room in which the guilds from each profession would gather to receive the master artisans who make their masterpieces"; whence the term *chambre syndicale.*

14. Cf. Henry Havard, *Dictionnaire de l'ameublement et de la décoration, depuis le XIIIᵉ siècle jusqu'à nos jours* (Paris: Maison Quantin, undated), vol. 1, pp. 666–714. Rich and subtle.

15. Jean-Philippe Heurtin notes this in *L'Espace public parlementaire: Essai sur les raisons du législateur* (Paris: PUF, 1999); he mainly deals with the hemicycle of the National Assembly in the absence of other work on its surroundings. Cf. as well Jean Starobinski, "La Chaire, la tribune, le barreau," in *Les Lieux de mémoire,* ed. Pierre Nora, vol. 2: *La Nation,* 3: "Les mots" (Paris: Gallimard, 1986), pp. 425–487. Neither devotes much space to the problem that concerns us here: the bedroom.

16. Meeting of the Chambre des Députés, 22 January 1839, cited in Heurtin, *L'Espace public parlementaire,* p. 129.

17. Timon, 1842, cited in ibid., p. 125.

18. Cf. Marc Fumaroli, *L'Âge de l'éloquence* (Geneva: Droz, 1980); "La conversation," in Pierre Nora, ed., *Les Lieux de mémoire,* vol. 3: *Les France,* 2: "Traditions" (Paris: Gallimard, 1992), pp. 679–743.

19. Works by Lucienne Roubin and Maurice Agulhon are discussed later in this book in the chapter titled "Workers' Rooms."

20. To cite only a few examples: Prosper Mérimée, *La Chambre bleue* (1872); Georges Simenon, *La Chambre bleue* (1964); August Strindberg, *La Chambre rouge* (1879); Gaston Leroux, *Le Mystère de la chambre jaune* (1907); Nicolas Bouvier, *La Chambre rouge* (Geneva, 1998); Christine Jordis, *La Chambre blanche* (Paris: Seuil, 2002).

21. Pascal Dibie, *Ethnologie de la chambre à coucher* (Paris: Métailié, 2000); Philippe Ariès and Georges Duby, *Histoire de la vie privée: De l'antiquité à nos jours,* 5 vols. (Paris: Seuil, 1985–1987).

22. "The English word *room* means at the same time a chamber and the space we physically occupy, and, mentally, the place we take up in someone else's thought. In other words, the English word has a double meaning that is untranslatable in French" (Pierre Nordon, preface to Virginia Woolf, *La*

Chambre de Jacob [Jacob's Room], in *Romans et nouvelles* [Paris: LGF, coll. La Pochothèque, 1993], p. 22). [The term "room" is given in English in the original.—Trans.]

23. Traces are found especially in the works of Monique Eleb and Anne Debarre, to whom I make frequent reference; cf. *Rêves d'alcôves.*

24. In French, the etymology of *huissier* traces back to the door.—Trans. Foundation of research by Daniel Roche and Annick Pardailhé-Galabrun, *La Naissance de l'intime: 3 000 foyers parisiens, XVIIᵉ–XVIIIᵉ siècles* (Paris: PUF, 1988).

25. A reference to the police novel *Le Mystère de la chambre jaune,* by Gaston Leroux (1907). Virginie Berger in *Sociétés et Représentations,* no. 18 (October 2004); the author looks at a series of studies of criminal cases in the Deux-Sèvres in the nineteenth century; sketches show the arrangement of the furniture and note how frequently two beds are found in the same room.

26. "Examination of blood samples found in the child's bedroom could affect investigation"; once they were gone over with ultraviolet detectors, the walls of the bedroom of little Maddie McCann (an English toddler kidnapped in Portugal) showed traces of hemoglobin (*Le Monde,* 13 August 2007).

27. Michelle Perrot, "Espaces privés," in *Il Romanzo,* ed. Franco Moretti (Milan: Einaudi, 2003), vol. 4.

28. In the nineteenth century, the outdated term "physiognomy" referred to the science of the face. Cf. Jean-Jacques Courtine and Claudine Haroche, *Histoire du visage: Exprimer et taire ses émotions du XVIᵉ siècle au début du XIXᵉ siècle* (Paris: Payot-Rivages, 1988). "Most observers could reconstruct nations or people in the truth of their habits, from the remains of their public monuments or by an examination of their domestic relics. Archaeology is to social nature what comparative anatomy is to organized nature" (Honoré de Balzac, *La Recherche de l'absolu* [1834], in Honoré de Balzac, *La comédie humaine* [Paris: Gallimard, coll. Bibliothèque de la Pléiade, 1979], vol. 10, p. 658).

29. Honoré de Balzac, *César Birotteau* (1833), in Balzac, *Œuvres complètes,* vol. 6, p. 120. Pillerault is a generous, idealistic republican who supports the perfumer through all of his trials and tribulations.

30. Honoré de Balzac, *Ursule Mirouët* (1841), in Balzac, *Œuvres complètes,* vol. 3, p. 836. The novel is built on a symbolic notion of place that has been analyzed by Madeleine Ambrière (in Balzac, *Œuvres complètes,* vol. 3, pp. 766ff.).

31. Pierre-Marc de Biasi, ed., *Les Carnets de travail de Gustave Flaubert* (Paris: Balland, 1988), p. 238 (written during the period in which Flaubert was preparing to write *Bouvard et Pécuchet*).

32. Mario Praz, *Histoire de la décoration d'intérieur: La philosophie de l'ameublement* (Paris: Tisné, 1990).

33. Mario Praz, *La Maison de la vie* (1979), preface by Pietro Citati (Paris: Gallimard-L'Arpenteur, 1993), p. 379: "These watercolors manage to retain the flavor of their era so well that it is as if the doors and windows they depict have not been opened since then and that we may inhale the spirits preserved within them."

34. Roland Barthes, *La Chambre claire* (Paris: Gallimard-Seuil, 1980). For an attempt at understanding this, see Arlette Farge, *La Chambre à deux lits et le Cordonnier de Tel-Aviv* (Paris: Seuil, 2000); images by Sophie Ristelhueber.

35. Eugène Atget, *Intérieurs parisiens,* museum catalogue, Musée Carnavalet, intro. Bernard de Montgolfier (Paris: Gallimard, 1982); *Atget: Une rétrospective,* museum catalogue, BNF Richelieu (Paris: BNF-Hazan, 2007).

36. Claude Dauphiné, "Les chambres du narrateur dans la *Recherche*," *Bulletin des Amis de Marcel Proust,* no. 31 (1981): 339–356.

37. Franz Kafka, "La métamorphose" (1915) and "Le terrier" (1931), in Franz Kafka, *Œuvres complètes,* vol. 2: *Récits et fragments narratifs,* ed. Claude David (Paris: Gallimard, coll. Bibliothèque de la Pléiade, 1980).

38. Georges Perec, *Espèces d'espaces* [Species of Spaces] (1974) (Paris: Galilée, 2000).

The King's Bedroom

1. Joël Cornette, ed., *Versailles: Le pouvoir de la pierre* (Paris: Tallandier, 2006), p. 14.

2. André Félibien, *Description sommaire du chasteau de Versailles* (Paris: Desprez, 1674). See also Louis Marin, *Le Portrait du roi* (Paris: Minuit, 1981), esp. pp. 221–235, "Le palais du prince."

3. Julien Green, *Journal,* 12 December 1935, in Julien Green, *Œuvres complètes* (Paris: Gallimard, coll. Bibliothèque de la Pléiade, 1977), vol. 5, p. 394. Green reports the observations of a friend, Rolland de Renneville, who believed this to be the case.

4. Hélène Himelfarb, "Versailles, fonctions et légendes," in Pierre Nora, ed., *Les Lieux de mémoire,* vol. 2: *La Nation,* 2, pp. 235–292.

5. William R. Newton: *L'Espace du roi: La cour de France au château de Versailles, 1682–1789* (Paris: Fayard, 2000), and *La Petite Cour: Services et serviteurs à la cour de Versailles au XVIIIᵉ siècle* (Paris: Fayard, 2006); Emmanuel Le Roy Ladurie, *Saint-Simon ou le système de la cour* (Paris: Fayard, 1997).

6. Édouard Pommier, "Versailles, l'image du souverain," in Pierre Nora, ed., *Les Lieux de mémoire,* vol. 2: *La Nation,* 2, pp. 193–234.

7. Cf. Lucien Bély, *La Société des princes, XVIᵉ–XVIIIᵉ siècle* (Paris: Fayard, 2000); Monique Chatenet, *La Cour de France au XVIᵉ siècle: Vie sociale et architecture*

(Paris: Picard, 2002), esp. pp. 147–150, "La chambre du roi," and its public and private uses in the sixteenth century.

8. Cf. Newton, *L'Espace du roi*, p. 124.

9. Régis Debray, *Le Moment fraternité* (Paris: Gallimard, 2009), p. 42.

10. Joël Cornette, "La réception des ambassadeurs," in Cornette, ed., *Versailles*, p. 199.

11. Saint-Simon, cited in Daniel Dessert, *Saint-Simon: Louis XIV et sa cour* (1994) (Paris: Complexe, 2005), p. 69 (anthology of excerpts from Saint-Simon's *Mémoires*).

12. The Marquis is mocking the bailiff's mistake: "Monsieur, vous profanisez la chambre du roi," earning this retort: "Monsieur, je préconerai votre exactitude." [*Profanisez* is not the *vous* form of *profaner*, but *profanez.*—Trans.]

13. Pommier, "Versailles, l'image du souverain," p. 225.

14. Saint-Simon, in Dessert, *Saint-Simon*, p. 337. For an example of the use of "details," see the use of chairs in Emmanuel Le Roy Ladurie, "Saint-Simon: Mémoires d'un Petit Duc," in Cornette, ed., *Versailles*, p. 185.

15. Béatrix Saule, *La Journée de Louis XIV: 16 November 1700* (Arles: Actes Sud, 2003).

16. Saint-Simon, in Dessert, *Saint-Simon*, p. 69. Unless otherwise indicated, all following citations concerning the king's bedroom are from Saint-Simon.

17. Newton, "La chambre du roi," in *La Petite Cour*, pp. 33ff.

18. Norbert Elias, *La Civilisation des mœurs* (1939) (Paris: Calmann-Lévy, 1976).

19. Saint-Simon, in Dessert, *Saint-Simon*. Mathieu Da Vinha, *Les Valets de chambre de Louis XIV* (Paris: Perrin, 2004).

20. Cited in Cornette, ed., *Versailles*, p. 22.

21. Saint-Simon, in Dessert, *Saint-Simon*, p. 346.

22. Saint-Simon, cited in Da Vinha, *Les Valets de chambre de Louis XIV*, p. 233.

23. Saint-Simon, Versailles, 29 March 1699, letter cited in Dessert, *Saint-Simon*, p. 33.

24. Saint-Simon, in Dessert, *Saint-Simon*, p. 262.

25. Ibid., p. 300.

26. Ibid., pp. 201–205.

27. The *remueuse:* "A woman who had the special task of caring for the child of a prince, or a great lord, that is, to wash him and change his swaddling clothes."—Trans.

28. Guy Chaussinand-Nogaret, "Les familles du roi," in Cornette, ed., *Versailles*, pp. 107–115. The author refers to the "Versailles harem that prevailed, at least until the king's marriage to Mme de Maintenon."

29. Saint-Simon, in Dessert, *Saint-Simon*, pp. 366–367ff.

30. Ibid., p. 377.

31. Hélène Himelfarb, "Les logements versaillais de Mme de Maintenon: Essai d'interprétation," in Himelfarb, *Saint-Simon, Versailles, les arts de la cour* (Paris: Perrin, 2006), p. 208.

32. The word *privance* conveys intimacy, familiarity. This medieval term disappeared after the seventeenth century, according to Alain Rey. Saint-Simon uses it often with regard to the king.

33. Élisabeth-Charlotte d'Orléans, *Lettres de la princesse Palatine* (Paris: Mercure de France, 1999), pp. 111 and 52. Cf. Arlette Lebigre, "La Palatine, une Allemande à Versailles," in Cornette, ed., *Versailles,* pp. 223–232.

34. Saint-Simon, in Dessert, *Saint-Simon,* p. 399.

35. Ibid., p. 122.

36. Ibid., p. 359.

37. On this subject, see Pierre Birnbaum, *Un Récit de meurtre rituel au Grand Siècle: L'affaire Raphaël Lévy, 1669* (Paris: Fayard, 2008). Birnbaum emphasizes the protective role played by royal power in this respect.

38. Antoine Vallot, Antoine Daquin, and Guy-Crescent Fagon, in *Journal de santé de Louis XIV,* ed. Stanis Perez (Grenoble: Jérôme Millon, 2004); Stanis Perez, *La Santé de Louis XIV: Une biohistoire du Roi-Soleil* (Seyssel: Champ Vallon, 2007).

39. Perez, *La Santé de Louis XIV,* p. 239, ch. 7, "Les nouvelles de la santé du roi en tant qu'informations stratégiques."

40. Ibid., p. 308.

41. Quotes in this paragraph and in the remainder of this chapter are from Saint-Simon, in Dessert, *Saint-Simon,* pp. 245–270 and following citations.

42. A jeering term that means "bottom of the bottle, mixture of old wines, treacle." [The Palatine princess was the mother of the Duc d'Orléans.—Trans.]

Rooms for Sleeping

1. Dibie, *Ethnologie de la chambre à coucher; Rêves d'alcôves.* [*Chambre à coucher:* literally, room for sleeping.—Trans.]

2. Aurélien Sauvageot, *Découverte de la Hongrie* (Paris: Alcan, 1937).

3. Louis Lépecq de La Clôture, *Collection d'observations sur les maladies et constitutions épidémiques: Années 1763 à 1770 et 1771 à 1773* (Rouen: Imprimerie privilégiée, 1778).

4. Prosper Mérimée, *La Chambre bleue,* a short story written for the Empress Eugénie, 1872.

5. Article from *La Science Illustrée,* 18 October 1875, cited in Jacques Léonard, *Archives du corps: La santé au XIXe siècle* (Rennes: Ouest-France, 1986); this volume gives other examples.

6. Ibid.

7. Jules Renard, *Journal,* 1905, cited in Jacques Léonard, *Médecins, malades et société dans la France du XIXe siècle* (Paris: Sciences en situation, 1992).

8. Émile Guillaumin, *La Vie d'un simple: Mémoires d'un métayer* (Paris: Stock, 1979), p. 98.

9. Françoise Zonabend, *La Mémoire longue: Temps et histoire au village* (Paris: PUF, 1980), pp. 27ff., "Manières d'habiter." Quotes in the following paragraph are also from this work.

10. Daniel Roche, *Histoire des choses banales: Naissance de la consommation dans les sociétés traditionnelles, XVIIe–XIXe siècle* (Paris: Fayard, 1997), pp. 183–208, "Meubles et objets."

11. Jean Guéhenno, *Journal d'un homme de quarante ans* (Paris: Grasset, 1934), pp. 57–58.

12. Katerina Azarova, *L'Appartement communautaire: L'histoire cachée du logement soviétique* (Paris: Sextant, 2007). This book (which grew out of a doctoral dissertation) calls on a variety of sources, including a field report made between 1996 and 2003 interviewing more than twenty families across several generations. It includes many photographs and floor plans.

13. Ibid., p. 272. Part 4, "Communal Life," is full of stories similar to Nina's.

14. Viktor Borisovitch in ibid., p. 270.

15. Françoise Huguier, *Kommunalki* (Arles: Actes Sud, 2008); cf. *Le Monde 2,* 19 April 2008.

16. The bibliography is extensive; for example, André Burguière, Christiane Klapisch-Zuber, Martine Segalen, and Françoise Zonabend, *Histoire de la famille,* 2 vols. (Paris: Armand Colin, 1986). A recent contribution: Agnès Walch, *Histoire du couple en France de la Renaissance à nos jours* (Rennes: Ouest-France, 2003).

17. Cf. Odile Nouvel-Kammerer, "La création de la chambre conjugale," in *Rêves d'alcôves,* pp. 104–127.

18. Louis-Georges Tin, *L'Invention de la culture hétérosexuelle* (Paris: Autrement, 2008).

19. Émile Littré, *Dictionnaire de la langue française,* vol. 3: *"Privé"* (Paris: Hachette, 1863–1872). The expression *mur de la vie privée* (wall around private life) came into use during the 1820s.

20. Florence Dupont, "Des chambres avant la chambre," in *Rêves d'alcôves,* pp. 13–25.

21. Sylviane Agacinski, *Métaphysique des sexes: Masculin/féminin aux sources du christianisme* (Paris: Seuil, 2005).

22. Cited in Françoise Collin, Évelyne Pisier, and Eleni Varikas, eds., *Les Femmes de Platon à Derrida* (Paris: Plon, 2000), p. 96; emphasis added.

23. Father Féline, *Catéchisme des gens mariés* (Caen: Gille Le Roy, 1782), p. 31.

24. Anne-Claire Rebreyend, *Intimités amoureuses: France, 1920–1975* (Toulouse: Presses universitaires du Mirail, 2008).

25. Louis Aragon, *Les Chambres: Poème du temps qui ne passe pas* (Paris: Éditeurs français réunis, 1969), p. 105.

26. Honoré de Balzac, "Code conjugal," note in *Physiologie du mariage* (around 1830), in Balzac, *Œuvres complètes,* vol. 11, p. 1892, note 1.

27. Anne Debarre-Blanchard and Monique Eleb-Vidal: *Architectures de la vie privée: Maisons et mentalités, XVIIᵉ–XIXᵉ siècles* (Brussels: Archives de l'architecture moderne, 1989); *Invention de l'habitation moderne: Paris, 1880–1914* (Paris: Hazan, 1995); and "Architecture domestique et mentalités: Les traités et les pratiques, XVIᵉ–XIXᵉ siècles," *In extenso,* no. 5 (April 1985) (analysis of architectural plans).

28. Nicolas Le Camus de Mézières, *Le Génie de l'architecture ou l'analogie de cet art avec nos sensations* (Paris, self-published, 1780).

29. As Debarre-Blanchard and Eleb-Vidal point out in *Invention de l'habitation moderne,* pp. 139–160, ch. 6, "La chambre."

30. Julien Guadet, *Éléments de composition dans l'habitation* (1902), cited in Debarre-Blanchard and Eleb-Vidal, *Architectures de la vie privée,* p. 145.

31. Dr. P. de Bourgogne, *Le Mariage: Conseils médicaux d'hygiène pratique,* 5th ed. (Paris: Vigot, 1923), pp. 88–110, ch. 7, "La chambre à coucher et le cabinet de toilette." Thanks to Philippe Artières for bringing this text to my attention.

32. Marion Segaud, Sandrine Bonvalet, and Jacques Brun, eds., *Logement et Habitat: L'état des savoirs* (Paris: La Découverte, 1998), esp. pp. 68–74, the chapter by Monique Eleb, "L'habitation entre vie privée et vie publique"; Monique Eleb and Anne-Marie Châtelet, *Urbanité, sociabilité et intimité: Des logements d'aujourd'hui* (Paris: L'Épure, 1997), pp. 175–191, "Les chambres en souffrance."

33. The Victoria and Albert Museum in Kensington, London, is a museum of decorative arts abounding in furniture and *objets d'art.*

34. Dr. Michel Lévy, *Traité d'hygiène publique et privée,* 3rd ed. (Paris: Hachette, 1862), vol. 1, pp. 549–628, article VI, "Des habitations privées et de l'air confiné." Cf. as well Jacques Léonard, *Archives du corps,* ch. 2, "L'air vicié."

35. Cf. Jean-Pierre Goubert, *La Conquête de l'eau: L'avènement de la santé à l'âge industriel,* with introduction by Emmanuel Le Roy Ladurie (Paris: Laffont, 1986).

36. Bourgogne, *Le Mariage.*

37. Michela de Giorgio, "La bonne catholique," in *Histoire des femmes en Occident,* 5 vols., ed. Georges Duby and Michelle Perrot (Paris: Plon, 1990–1991), vol. 4, p. 187.

38. Havard, *Dictionnaire de l'ameublement et de la décoration,* vol. 1.

39. Rivka Bercovici, "La privatisation de l'espace familial: Chambre à coucher conjugale au XIXe siècle," in *La Maison: Espaces et intimités,* ed. Anne Debarre-Blanchard and Monique Eleb-Vidal, *In extenso,* no. 9 (1986): 345–368; Bercovici scrutinizes a thousand inventories in twenty-four different Parisian studies between 1840 and 1880.

40. Jean-Pierre Chaline, *Les Bourgeois de Rouen: Une élite urbaine du XIXe siècle* (Paris: Fondation nationale des sciences politiques, 1982).

41. Marcel Proust, "Journées de lecture" (1905), *Pastiches et Mélanges,* in Marcel Proust, *Contre Sainte-Beuve* (Paris: Gallimard, coll. Bibliothèque de la Pléiade, 1971), p. 164.

42. Cited in Claude Mossé, *La Femme dans la Grèce antique* (Paris: Albin Michel, 1983), p. 28.

43. Françoise Frontisi-Ducroux, *Ouvrages de dames: Ariane, Hélène, Pénélope* (Paris: Seuil, 2009), p. 103 (with regard to Penelope and the "strange sequence of the bed test").

44. Michel Rouche, in Ariès and Duby, *Histoire de la vie privée,* vol. 1, p. 465.

45. Évelyne Patlagean, in Ariès and Duby, *Histoire de la vie privée,* vol. 2, p. 555.

46. Georges Duby: *Le Chevalier, la femme et le prêtre* (Paris: Hachette, 1981), and "L'amour en France au XIIe siècle" (1983), in *Féodalité* (Paris: Gallimard, 1996), p. 1405.

47. Cited in Philippe Ariès, *L'Homme devant la mort* (Paris: Seuil, 1977), vol. 1, p. 224.

48. Cited in Havard, *Dictionnaire de l'ameublement et de la décoration,* vol. 3, p. 374.

49. Cf. Roche, *Histoire des choses banales.*

50. Anne Fillon, *Fruits d'écritoire: Société et mentalités aux XVIIe et XVIIIe siècles* (Le Mans: Laboratoire d'histoire anthropologique du Mans, 2000), "Comme on fait son lit on se couche: Trois cents ans d'histoire du lit villageois, population et cultures," pp. 109–127; Agnès Fine, "À propos du trousseau: Une culture féminine?" in *Une histoire des femmes est-elle possible?* ed. Michelle Perrot (Marseille: Rivages, 1984), pp. 155–189.

51. Joëlle Guillais, *La Chair de l'autre: Le crime passionnel au XIXe siècle* (Paris: Olivier Orban, 1986).

52. Honoré de Balzac, *Physiologie du mariage,* Méditation XVII, "Théorie du lit," and Méditation XIV, "Des appartements," in Balzac, *Œuvres complètes,* vol. 11, pp. 1060ff. and 1038ff.

53. The article "Lit" in Havard, *Dictionnaire de l'ameublement et de la décoration,* vol. 3, is detailed and encyclopedic. Cf. Nicole de Reyniès, *Le Mobilier domestique: Vocabulaire typologique,* 2 vols. (Paris: Imprimerie nationale, 1987); Alecia Beldegreen, *Le Lit* (Paris: Flammarion, 1992).

54. Diane de Furstenberg, *Lits de rêve* (Boulogne-Billancourt: Éd. du May, 1991).

55. Claude Langlois, *Le Crime d'Onan: Le discours catholique sur la limitation des naissances, 1816–1930* (Paris: Les Belles Lettres, 2005); Agnès Walch, *La Spiritualité conjugale dans le catholicisme français, XVIe–XXe siècle* (Paris: Le Cerf, 2002).

56. "Ils vivent ensemble avec tant de politique, de réserve et de cérémonie, qu'ils ne se donnent pas seulement de la liberté dans les choses naturelles, et ne se peuvent souffrir en mesme lit, en mesme chambre, ny en mesme appartement. Ils s'éloignent autant qu'ils peuvent par une aversion naturelle de nature et de tout ce qui en dépend" (Catherine Levesque [on the seventeenth century] in ibid., p. 279).

57. Alain Corbin, *L'Harmonie des plaisirs: Les manières de jouir du siècle des lumières à l'avènement de la sexologie* (Paris: Perrin, 2008), pp. 255–290, ch. 8, "Le lit conjugal; ses interdits et ses plaisirs."

58. Cf. Martine Sèvegrand: *Les Enfants du Bon Dieu: Les catholiques français et la procréation (1919–1969)* (Paris: Albin Michel, 1995), and *L'Amour en toutes lettres: Questions à l'abbé Viollet sur la sexualité (1924–1943)* (Paris: Albin Michel, 1996).

59. Ibid., p. 256.

60. Ibid., "Débat autour du lit conjugal," pp. 201–205 (correspondence published in the newsletter of the Association pour le mariage chrétien, 1926).

61. Dr. Charles Montalban, *La Petite Bible des jeunes époux* (1855), ed. Alain Corbin (Grenoble: Jérôme Millon, 2008).

62. Évelyne Bloch-Dano, *Madame Zola* (Paris: Grasset, 1997), p. 272; this was in March 1899, when *Fécondité* had recently been published.

63. Évelyne Bloch-Dano, *Chez les Zola: Le roman d'une maison* (Paris: Payot, 2006), p. 113. Cf. Émile Zola, *Lettres à Jeanne Rozerot, 1892–1902,* ed. Brigitte Émile-Zola and Alain Pagès (Paris: Gallimard, 2004).

64. Cited in Anne Martin-Fugier, *Une nymphomane vertueuse: L'assassinat de la duchesse de Choiseul-Praslin* (Paris: Fayard, 2009).

65. Alexis de Tocqueville, *Œuvres complètes* (Paris: Gallimard), vol. 8: *Correspondance avec Gustave de Beaumont* (1967), p. 277, letter of 18 January 1838.

66. Letter to Mary Motley, 28 October 1837, archives, Beinecke Library, Yale University.

67. Rebreyend, *Intimités amoureuses*, pp. 122–135. The APA was founded by Philippe Lejeune to receive personal writings and today includes more than two thousand documents. It is held in the Bibliothèque d'Ambérieu-en-Bugey (Ain).

68. Agnès Varda, *Quelques veuves de Noirmoutier;* it aired 17 October 2006 on Arte.

69. Cf. Jean-Pierre Bois, *Les Vieux* (Paris: Fayard, 1989).

70. Élisabeth Claverie and Pierre Lamaison, *L'Impossible mariage: Violence et parenté en Gévaudan (XVIIᵉ–XIXᵉ siècles)* (Paris: Hachette, 1982), shows through trial cases the extreme tension of the communal lifestyle in the *oustal;* it was no match for the power of a litigious individual.

71. Sylvie Lapallus, *La Mort du vieux: Une histoire du parricide au XIXᵉ siècle* (Paris: Tallandier, 2004).

72. Vincent Gourdon, *Histoire des grands-parents* (Paris: Perrin, 2001), p. 60.

73. Irène Théry, *Le Démariage: Justice et vie privée* (Paris: Odile Jacob, 1996).

74. Cf. *Le Monde,* 7 February 2004, on an investigation with commentary by Pascal Dibie.

A Room of One's Own

1. Jules Vallès, *L'Insurgé* (1871), in Jules Vallès, *Œuvres,* vol. 2: *1871–1885,* ed. Roger Bellet (Paris: Gallimard, coll. Bibliothèque de la Pléiade, 1990), p. 879.

2. Cited in Marie-Claire Hoock-Demarle, *La République des lettres: Réseaux épistolaires et construction de l'espace européen* (Paris: Albin Michel, 2008), p. 78 (letter of 4 August 1789).

3. Cited in ibid., p. 83 (9 November 1793).

4. Joris-Karl Huysmans, *En ménage,* cited in Victor Brombert, *La Prison romantique: Essai sur l'imaginaire* (Paris: José Corti, 1975), p. 160.

5. Michel Foucault, *Surveiller et Punir: Naissance de la prison* (Paris: Gallimard, 1975).

6. Michel de Certeau, *La Prise de parole* (Paris: Seuil, 1994), p. 247.

7. Victor Dézamy in *Rêves d'alcôves,* p. 115.

8. Philip Roth, *The Human Stain* (New York: Random House, 2010), p. 236.

9. Cited in Havard, *Dictionnaire de l'ameublement et de la décoration,* vol. 1, p. 678.

10. Cited by Dibie in *Rêves d'alcôves,* p. 31.

11. Perec, *Espèces d'espaces,* p. 25.

12. Danièle Régnier-Bohler, in Ariès et Duby, *Histoire de la vie privée*, vol. 2, pp. 325–328.

13. Maria Bakhmeteva, *Journal*, 1805, in Elena Gretchanaia and Catherine Viollet, *"Si tu lis jamais ce journal": Diaristes russes francophones, 1780–1854* (Paris: CNRS, 2008), p. 170.

14. According to Roche, "Even everyday people had real beds, a comfort attained by the end of the seventeenth century," at least in Paris (*Histoire des choses banales*, p. 199). The dominant model was a bed on pillars with curtains.

15. Cited in Guillais, *La Chair de l'autre*, p. 124.

16. Perec, *Espèces d'espaces*, pp. 33–39, "Le lit."

17. George Sand, *Histoire de ma vie* (1847) (Paris: Gallimard, 2004), p. 770.

18. Franz Kafka, "Un célibataire entre deux âges," in Kafka, *Œuvres complètes*, vol. 2, p. 355, with relevant note on p. 993, letter to Felice Bauer, 11 February 1915.

19. Marcel Mauss, *Manuel d'ethnographie* (Paris: Payot, 1967).

20. Lévy, *Traité d'hygiène publique et privée*, vol. 2, pp. 409–415, "Hygiène du sommeil."

21. Cf. Stéphane Audouin-Rouzeau, *Combattre: Une anthropologie historique de la guerre moderne (XIXᵉ–XXIᵉ siècle)* (Paris: Seuil, 2008), p. 89.

22. Violette Leduc, *Je hais les dormeurs* (1948) (Rigny: Éd. du Chemin de fer, 2006).

23. Paul Fluchaire, *La Révolution du lit: Pour un sommeil de rêve* (Paris: Artylen, 1991).

24. Michel Pastoureau, *Noir: Histoire d'une couleur* (Paris: Seuil, 2008), p. 160.

25. Mona Ozouf, *Composition française: Retour sur une enfance bretonne* (Paris: Gallimard, 2009), p. 46.

26. Henri Michaux: "Dormir," *La nuit remue* (1967), in Henri Michaux, *Œuvres complètes* (Paris, Gallimard, coll. Bibliothèque de la Pléiade, 1998), vol. 1, p. 472, and *Un certain Plume*, in Michaux, *Œuvres complètes*.

27. *La nuit remue*, or *The Night Is Stirring*, is the title of the book by Henri Michaux cited above.—Trans.

28. Cf. William C. Dement and Christopher Vaughan, *Avoir un bon sommeil* (Paris: Odile Jacob, 2000); Paul Fluchaire, *Guide du sommeil* (Paris: Ramsay, 1987).

29. Michel Covin, *Une esthétique du sommeil* (Paris: Beauchesne, 1990). On this matter literature is a bit more explicit than art.

30. *Faire la grasse matinée* is to spend the morning in bed.—Trans.

31. Jeremy Bentham, *Esquisse d'un ouvrage en faveur des pauvres* (1797), in Adrien Duquesnoy, *Recueil sur les établissements d'humanité* (Paris, 1802), p. 112. The *Panopticon* is a famous circular prison plan that aimed at reducing the costs of

surveillance. Cf. Michelle Perrot, "L'inspecteur Bentham," in Michelle Perrot, *Les Ombres de l'histoire* (Paris: Flammarion, 2001), pp. 65–108.

32. Cited in Gretchanaia and Viollet, *"Si tu lis jamais ce journal,"* p. 163.

33. Cf. Yannick Ripa, *Histoire du rêve: Regards sur l'imaginaire des Français au XIXᵉ siècle* (Paris: Hachette, 1988).

34. Cf. Fanny Déchanet-Platz, *L'Écrivain, le sommeil et les rêves, 1800–1945* (Paris: Gallimard, 2008).

35. Baudelaire cited in Max Milner, *L'Imaginaire des drogues: De Thomas de Quincey à Henri Michaux* (Paris: Gallimard, 2000), cited in ibid., p. 148.

36. Cited in Déchanet-Platz, *L'Écrivain, le sommeil et les rêves,* p. 170.

37. *Un lit défait* (around 1827), Musée Eugène Delacroix, Place de Furstenberg, Paris.

38. On this subject, see Pauline Réage's remarkable confessions in *Histoire d'O* (Paris: Ed. Jean-Jacques Pauvert, 1954), and the results of studies on sexuality.

39. Marie Chaix, *L'Âge du tendre* (Paris: Seuil, 1979), p. 89, "La chambre de jeune fille."

40. Tin, *L'Invention de la culture hétérosexuelle.*

41. Jules Renard, *Journal* (Paris: Gallimard, 1960), p. 27 (25 July 1889).

42. James Baldwin, *Giovanni's Room* (New York: Dial Press, 1956); a classic of gay literature.

43. Lytton Strachey, "Lancaster Gate" (1922), in Lytton Strachey, *The Shorter Strachey,* ed. Michael Holroyd (Oxford: Oxford University Press, 1980), pp. 1–13. Lytton Strachey (1880–1932), critic, writer, and friend of Virginia Woolf, is one of the most striking figures in Bloomsbury, famous for his biographies *Eminent Victorians* and *Queen Victoria.* "Lancaster Gate" is a beautiful description of a family home. He was later the lover of Duncan Grant, a central member of the group.

44. *L'Astrée,* cited in Danièle Haase-Dubosc, in *Séduction et Sociétés,* ed. Cécile Dauphin and Arlette Farge (Paris: Seuil, 2001), p. 61.

45. Charles Baudelaire, "La mort des amants," in Charles Baudelaire, *Les Fleurs du mal* (Paris: Auguste Poulet-Malassis, 1857).

46. Sainte-Beuve, *Port-Royal* (Paris: Robert Laffont, 2004), vol. 1, p. 443.

47. Mary Carruthers, *Machina memorialis: Méditation, rhétorique et fabrication des images au Moyen Âge* (1998) (Paris: Gallimard, 2002).

48. Elegy by Motin, cited in Henri Bremond, *Histoire du sentiment religieux en France depuis la fin des guerres de religion jusqu'à nos jours (1916–1933)* (Grenoble: Jérôme Millon, 2006), vol. 1, p. 392.

49. Antoine de Nervèze, *Le Jardin sacré de l'âme solitaire* (late sixteenth century), cited in ibid., p. 295.

50. Jacques-Joseph Duguet, 1731, cited in ibid., vol. 4, p. 487.

51. Cited in Julia Kristeva, *Thérèse mon amour* (Paris: Fayard, 2008), p. 375.

52. Ibid., p. 384; emphasis added.

53. Bremond, *Histoire du sentiment religieux en France,* vol. 1, p. 718.

54. Ibid., vol. 6, p. 830. Dom Claude was the son of Marie Martin-Guyard, who became Marie de l'Incarnation, founder of the order of that name and a Quebecois evangelist.

55. Kristeva, *Thérèse mon amour,* p. 377.

56. Bremond, *Histoire du sentiment religieux en France,* vol. 1, p. 513.

57. Ibid., vol. 6, p. 735.

58. Ibid., vol. 8, p. 459. "Recollections" *(recueillis)* are spiritual retreats, and *récollets* are those who practice them.

59. Alberto Manguel, *Une histoire de la lecture* (Arles: Actes Sud, 1998; 2nd paperback ed., Paris: J'ai lu, 2001).

60. Ibid., p. 81.

61. Ibid., p. 211.

62. Jean-Paul Sartre, *L'Idiot de la famille: Gustave Flaubert de 1821 à 1857* (Paris: Gallimard, 1971), vol. 2, p. 1363.

63. Laure Adler and Stefan Bollmann, *Les femmes qui lisent sont dangereuses* (Paris: Flammarion, 2006). Richly illustrated.

64. *Delacroix et ses amis de jeunesse* (Paris: Musée Eugène Delacroix, January 2008).

65. Marcel Proust, *À l'ombre des jeunes filles en fleurs,* in Marcel Proust, *À la recherche du temps perdu,* vol. 1 (Paris: Gallimard, coll. Bibliothèque de la Pléiade, 1973), p. 607.

66. Jean-Marie Goulemot, *Ces livres qu'on ne lit que d'une main: Lecture et lecteurs de livres pornographiques au XVIIIe siècle* (Paris: Minerve, 1994).

67. Marcel Proust, "Journées de lecture," *Pastiches et Mélanges,* pp. 161–194.

68. "Les déchiffreurs: Voyages en mathématiques," *Le Monde 2,* 24 January 2009, p. 29.

69. Cited in Gretchanaia and Viollet, *"Si tu lis jamais ce journal,"* p. 204 (17 September 1821).

70. Cited in Hoock-Demarle, *La République des lettres,* p. 420 (30 December 1879).

71. Ibid., p. 271.

72. Cited in ibid., p. 14.

73. Marcel Proust, *La Fugitive,* in Proust, *À la recherche du temps perdu,* vol. 3 (Paris: Gallimard, coll. Bibliothèque de la Pléiade, 1977), p. 571.

74. Letter to Felice Bauer, 14–15 January 1913, in Franz Kafka, *Œuvres complètes,* vol. 4 (Paris: Gallimard, coll. Bibliothèque de la Pléiade, 1989), p. 232.

75. Letter to Felice Bauer, 11 February 1915, in ibid.

76. Ernst Jünger, *Journaux de guerre* (Paris, Gallimard, coll. Bibliothèque de la Pléiade, 2008), vol. 2, p. 34 (4 May 1939).

77. Simone de Beauvoir, *La Force des choses* (1963) (Paris: Gallimard, 1977), vol. 1, p. 123 (16 May 1945).

78. Cited in Francis David, *Intérieurs d'écrivains* (Paris: Le Terrain vague, 1982).

79. Cited in ibid.

80. "This is how he surrounded himself," said Karl Grün, who visited Proudhon in December 1844; cited in Michel Winock, *Les Voix de la liberté* (Paris: Seuil, 2001), p. 270.

81. Edmond et Jules de Goncourt, *Journal*, ed. Ricatte (Monaco: Imprimerie nationale de Monaco, 1956), vol. 8, p. 44 (4 August 1867). The text accuses not only women, but also Troubat, the secretary whom the Goncourts took for a babbling idiot.

82. Louis Chauvin, *Manuel de l'instituteur* (1889), cited in Francine Muel-Dreyfus, *Le Métier d'éducateur: Les instituteurs de 1900, les éducateurs spécialisés de 1968* (Paris: Minuit, 1983).

83. Honoré de Balzac, *Les Proscrits,* in Honoré de Balzac, *La Comédie humaine,* vol. 1 (Paris: Gallimard, coll. Bibliothèque de la Pléiade, 1976), lxxii (regarding Dante).

84. Letter to Ernest Delahaye, in Arthur Rimbaud, *Œuvres complètes* (Paris: Gallimard, coll. Bibliothèque de la Pléiade, 1946), "Parmerde, Juinphe 72," pp. 269–271. A commemorative plaque was hung by the "Friends of Arthur Rimbaud" at 8 rue Victor-Cousin, with this inscription: " 'Just now, I have a pretty room.' Arthur Rimbaud, Hôtel de Cluny, June 1872." This plaque was pointed out to me by Maurice Olender.

85. Marcel Proust, *La Prisonnière,* in Proust, *À la recherche du temps perdu,* vol. 3, p. 18. This is one of the rare passages in the *Recherche* in which the narrator uses real first names: Céleste for Françoise, Marcel for himself. See also Marcel Proust, *Cities of the Plain,* trans. C. K. Scott Moncrieff (New York: Random House, 1934), p. 389.

86. Proust, *À l'ombre des jeunes filles en fleurs,* p. 872.

87. Orhan Pamuk, "La valise de mon père," acceptance speech, Royal Swedish Academy, 2006, cited in *Le Monde,* 15 December 2006, trans. Maureen Freely. https://www.nobelprize.org/nobel_prizes/literature/laureates/2006/pamuk-lecture_en.html.

88. Olivier Nora, "La visite au grand écrivain," in Pierre Nora, ed., *Les Lieux de mémoire,* vol. 2: *La Nation, 3*, pp. 563–587, "Les mots."

89. The Château de Ferney-Voltaire is empty.

90. Jean-Claude Bonnet, *Naissance du Panthéon: Essai sur le culte des grands hommes* (Paris: Fayard, 1998), pp. 243–251.

91. Madame de Flesselles, *Les Jeunes voyageurs en France* (1822), cited in Patrick Cabanel, *Le Tour de la nation par des enfants* (Paris: Belin, 2008), p. 123.

92. Victor Brombert, "Baudelaire: claustration et infini," in Brombert, *La Prison romantique,* pp. 139–152; on "Huysmans et la thébaïde raffinée," see pp. 153–174.

93. Séverine Jouve, *Obsessions et perversions dans la littérature et les demeures à la fin du XIXᵉ siècle* (Paris: Hermann, 1996).

94. Edmond de Goncourt, *La Maison de l'artiste* (1881) (Dijon: L'Échelle de Jacob, 2003).

95. Robert de Montesquiou, *Les Pas effacés: Mémoires et souvenirs* (Paris: Émile-Paul Frères, 1923), vol. 3, p. 246.

96. On the reasons for choosing orange, see Huysmans, *En ménage,* in Brombert, *La Prison romantique,* pp. 92–93. On colors more generally, see the work of Michel Pastoureau.

97. Patricia Falguières, *Les Chambres des merveilles* (Paris: Bayard, 2003). Falguières historicizes these *Wunderkammern.* They are only distantly related to museums and therefore have a subtle relationship to the "mysteries of the State."

98. Montesquiou, *Les Pas effacés,* p. 126.

99. Mario Praz, *L'Ameublement: Psychologie et évolution de la décoration intérieure* (Paris: Tisné, 1964); renamed in the second edition: *Histoire de la décoration d'intérieur.* Luxuriously illustrated.

100. Praz, *La Maison de la vie,* p. 483.

101. Ibid., p. 157.

102. The apartment included a foyer, dining room, hallway, living room, and two bedrooms. The author worked in the living room, a fact that surprised some of his friends; how could he work in such a richly furnished room "when Goethe himself could only work in a bare room?" (ibid., p. 410). This is the monkish writerly ideal.

103. There was a special auction (February 2009) for an exceptional collection, the result of two extraordinary lives.

104. Daniel Roche, *Humeurs vagabondes* (Paris: Fayard, 2003), ch. 3, "Le voyageur en chambre," pp. 95–136, on Xavier de Maistre and his numerous imitators.

105. *Lettre sur les voyages,* cited in ibid.

106. De Maistre, *Voyage autour de ma chambre,* and Xavier de Maistre, *Expédition nocturne autour de ma chambre* (1825), ed. Michel Covin (Paris: Le Castor astral, 1990).

107. On the indispensable dressing gown, cf. Daniel Roche, *Le Culte des appar-ences: Une histoire du vêtement, XVIIᵉ–XVIIIᵉ siècles* (Paris: Fayard, 1989), p. 486. Napoleon had a dozen, according to one inventory; cf. Frédéric Masson, *Napoléon chez lui: La journée de l'empereur aux Tuileries* (Paris: Ollendorf, 1906).

108. Marcel Proust, *Du côté de chez Swann,* in Proust, *À la recherche du temps perdu,* vol. 1, "Combray," p. 9.

109. Marcel Proust, "À mon ami Willie Heath," July 1894, *Les Plaisirs et les Jours* (Paris: Gallimard, coll. Bibliothèque de la Pléiade, 1971), p. 6.

110. *Libération,* 9 September 2001.

111. Refusing a "bedroom revolution" was one of the main goals of members of the "establishment," the students and intellectuals who, around 1968, chose to work in factories, fleeing the enclosure of the bourgeois interior. They thought that only direct contact and immersion in manual labor could allow them to understand and improve it.

112. Ivan Goncharov, *Oblomov* (1859), trans. Luba Jurgenson, preface by Jacques Catteau (Lausanne: L'Âge d'homme, 1988).

113. Ibid., p. 199.

114. Ibid., p. 14.

115. Ibid., p. 166.

116. Ibid., p. 167.

117. Ibid., pp. 456–457.

118. Paul Lafargue, *Le Droit à la paresse* (Paris: Henri Oriol, 1883).

119. André Gide, *Les Nourritures terrestres,* cited in Covin, *Une esthétique du sommeil,* p. 108.

The Children's Room

1. Laurence Egill, *Chambre d'enfant: Histoire, anecdotes, décoration, mobilier, conseils pratiques* (Paris: Le Cherche-Midi, 2002). In the citations in this para-graph from this book, the emphasis is added.

2. Daniel Féau, *Le Magazine,* 2008, "Dream bedrooms," pp. 68–69. These per-sonalized models require prior agreement from both parents and children.

3. Corinne Bullat, *Une chambre d'enfant saine et écologique* (Paris: Ulmer, 2009); "Maison bio. La chambre d'enfant: La pièce prototype," *Le Nouvel Observa-teur,* March 2009.

4. Daniel Roche, *Histoire des choses banales,* ch. "Meubles et objets." Mention of the child's bed is late and not generalizable; the same thing is nearly true for the cradle, "a piece of furniture that was basically unknown to the notaries of

the French Vexin." However, in Alsace, which was richer and more evolved, the baby's bed is mentioned in every other document.

5. Jean-Jacques Rousseau, *Émile,* in Jean-Jacques Rousseau, *Œuvres complètes* (Paris: Gallimard, coll. Bibliothèque de la Pléiade, 1964), vol. 4, book 1, p. 278. Rousseau recommends "placing the baby in a large, well-padded cradle where he can move around as he likes without dangers" but adds, "I use the word 'cradle,' although it is outdated, for lack of a better one."

6. "Berceau," *Nouveau Larousse illustré:* "It is not advised to let young children become used to going to sleep only if they are rocked; better to see the cradle as a bed and not as something to be rocked."

7. *Barcelonnette:* A small cradle that, in order to facilitate rocking, is suspended on two crescent-shaped feet.—Trans.

8. Cf. Michel Foucault, *La Volonté de savoir* (Paris: Gallimard, 1976).

9. Cited in François Furet and Jacques Ozouf, *Lire et Écrire* (Paris: Minuit, 1977), vol. 1, p. 87.

10. According to Marc Soriano's reading in *Les Contes de Perrault: Culture savante et traditions populaires* (1968) (Paris: Gallimard, 1989), prefaced by an interview with *Annales.*

11. George Sand, *Histoire de ma vie,* ed. Georges Lubin (Paris: Gallimard, coll. Bibliothèque de la Pléiade, 1971), vol. 1, p. 743.

12. Cited in Nancy Huston, *Passions d'Annie Leclerc* (Arles: Actes Sud, 2007), p. 285. Annie Leclerc was planning to write a book about the middle of the bed.

13. The song is "Aux marches du palais" (On the Steps of the Palace). The verse in question goes as follows:

Dans le mitan du lit. / In the middle of the bed
Dans le mitan du lit. / In the middle of the bed
La rivière est profonde, Lonla. / The river is deep, Lonla
La rivière est profonde. / The river is deep. [Trans.]

14. Cf. Françoise Barret-Ducrocq, *L'Amour sous Victoria: Sexualité et classes populaires à Londres au XIXe siècle* (Paris: Plon, 1989); Jean-Marie de Gérando (1772–1842), *Le Visiteur du pauvre* (Paris: Colas, 1820). Cf. Michelle Perrot, "L'œil du baron ou le visiteur du pauvre," in *Du visible à l'invisible: Pour Max Milner,* ed. Stéphane Michaud (Paris: José Corti, 1988), vol. 1, pp. 63–70.

15. Newton, *L'Espace du roi,* p. 246.

16. Letter of 12 June 1778, in ibid., p. 220.

17. Cf. Debarre-Blanchard and Eleb-Vidal, "Architecture domestique et mentalités."

18. Le Camus de Mézières, *Le Génie de l'architecture,*

19. Ibid., p. 220.

20. Cars Larsson, in *Das Haus in der Sonne* (Königstein im Taunus and Leipzig: Karl Robert Langewiesche Nachfolger, 1909), gives a joyful, even erotic, image of the little girls' room.

21. Rousseau, *Émile,* book 1, p. 252.

22. Ibid., p. 301.

23. Rousseau added: "No mirrors, no porcelain, no luxurious objects" (ibid., p. 323). Only things Émile would make himself, the products of his own labor.

24. Cited in Debarre-Blanchard and Eleb-Vidal, *Invention de l'habitation moderne,* pp. 161–187, ch. 7, "La place des enfants."

25. Roger Perrinjaquet, "La genèse de la chambre d'enfant dans la pensée architecturale," *L'Architecture d'aujourd'hui,* nos. 204–206 (1979): 89–93 (summary of his PhD dissertation, supervised by Marie-José Chombart de Lauwe). Perrinjaquet refers to Jaoul's autobiography, "La maison Jaoul."

26. Quotes are from "La maison Jaoul," in ibid.

27. Comtesse de Ségur, *La Santé des enfants* (Paris: Hachette, 1857); repr. in Colette Misrahi, *La Comtesse de Ségur ou la mère médecin* (Paris: Denoël, 1991).

28. Émile Cardon, *L'Art au foyer domestique* (Paris, 1884).

29. Francis Marcoin, *La Comtesse de Ségur ou le bonheur immobile* (Arras: Presses universitaires de l'Artois, 1999).

30. Quotes in this paragraph are from Berthe Bernage, *Brigitte maman* (Paris: Gautier-Languereau, 1931); republished many times until 1951.

31. On the subject of CF, see Martine Sèvegrand: *Les Enfants du Bon Dieu; L'Amour en toutes lettres;* and *L'Affaire Humanae Vitae: L'Église catholique et la contraception* (Paris: Karthala, 2008).

32. Sand, *Histoire de ma vie,* vol. 1, p. 530. Sand remembers the buzzing of the flies, the flicker of the candles, the way the things in the room would double, "pale amusements of my captivity in the cradle and of this life within the cradle, which seemed incredibly long and plunged into a soft ennui."

33. Ibid., pp. 618–619.

34. Letter of 7 October 1847, in George Sand, *Correspondance,* ed. Georges Lubin, vol. 8: *Juillet 1847–décembre 1848* (Paris: Garnier, 1985), p. 98.

35. Anatole France, *Le Livre de mon ami* (Paris: Calmann-Lévy, 1885); repr. in Anatole France, *Œuvres* (Paris: Gallimard, coll. Bibliothèque de la Pléiade, 1984), vol. 1, pp. 437–438. *Paul et Virginie* (1788) was a well-known novel by Jacques-Henri Bernardin de Saint-Pierre.

36. Praz, *La Maison de la vie,* p. 378.

37. Annie Renonciat, current director of the Musée de l'Éducation in Rouen, has renewed interest in the subject and is writing a book on the decoration of children's bedrooms. I thank her for sharing her work with me.

38. Cardon, *L'Art au foyer domestique.* Cf. Annie Renonciat, "Quatre murs à la page: Le livre et la chambre d'enfant," in *Livres d'enfants, livres d'images, 1848–1914* (Paris: Dossiers du Musée d'Orsay, no. 35, 1989).

39. Let us not forget that Jean-Jacques Rousseau dedicated an entire book of *Émile* to adolescence. He sees it as a space, not a period of education.

40. However, on this subject, see Rebecca Rogers, *Les Bourgeoises au pensionnat: L'éducation féminine au XIXe siècle* (Rennes: PUR, 2007).

41. Cf. Agnès Thiercé, *Histoire de l'adolescence (1850–1914)* (Paris: Belin, 1999).

42. Cited in Daniel Roche, *Le Peuple de Paris* (Paris: Aubier, 1981), p. 120.

43. *Journal de Clotilde: Pages sérieuses commandées à son retour de pension par Mlle S. W.*, 7th ed. (Lille and Paris, 1864); cited in Thiercé, *Histoire de l'adolescence.*

44. Balzac, *César Birotteau,* in Balzac, *Œuvres complètes,* vol. 6, p. 169.

45. Balzac, *Ursule Mirouët,* in Balzac, *Œuvres complètes,* vol. 3, p. 836.

46. Johann Wolfgang von Goethe, *Faust,* trans. Gérard de Nerval, in Johann Wolfgang von Goethe, *Théâtre complet* (Paris: Gallimard, coll. Bibliothèque de la Pléiade, 1951), p. 1020.

47. Hélène Cixous, "The Laugh of the Medusa," trans. Keith Cohen and Paula Cohen, *Signs* 1, no. 4 (Summer 1976): 878.

48. Chaix, *L'Âge du tendre,* pp. 83–91, "La chambre de jeune fille." One of the most beautiful texts on this "ungrateful landscape."

49. *Journal* (1912), cited in Loukia Efthimiou, "Les Femmes professeurs dans l'enseignement secondaire public en France," thesis, Paris-VII, 2002.

50. Praz, *La Maison de la vie,* "La chambre de Lucia," pp. 231–342.

51. Ibid., p. 236. The bed prompts long descriptions of the various kinds of Empire beds taken from La Mésengère's book, *Meubles et objets de goût,* and collected especially at the Museum of Applied Arts in Vienna.

52. Praz complains of the absence of a museum devoted to toys in Italy and cites a number of major Anglo-American works on doll houses and the hidden meanings of miniatures.

53. Mario Praz describes his wife Vivien embroidering: "During this idyllic time, Vivien was a woman of the north who had utterly abandoned herself to the charms of the south; submission seemed light to her, and her dedication to her embroidery was a symbol of this." But he lost all his virility when he began to embroider as well: "It was as if I had discovered within myself some unspeakable proclivity" (*La Maison de la vie,* p. 363).

54. Ibid., p. 295.

55. Anatole France, *Le Petit Pierre* (Paris: Calmann-Lévy, 1919); repr. in France, *Œuvres,* vol. 4, pp. 1000ff., "Ma chambre." The scene takes place around 1855 to 1860.

56. François Mauriac, *Commencement d'une vie* (Paris: Grasset, 1932); repr. in François Mauriac, *Œuvres autobiographiques* (Paris: Gallimard, coll. Bibliothèque de la Pléiade, 1990), pp. 78 and 91.

57. François Mauriac, *La Robe prétexte,* in François Mauriac, *Œuvres romanesques et théâtrales complètes,* vol. 1 (Paris: Gallimard, coll. Bibliothèque de la Pléiade, 1978), p. 99.

58. Cf. Anne-Marie Sohn, *Âge tendre et tête de bois: Histoire des jeunes des années 1960* (Paris: Hachette, 2001). The Trente Glorieuses were the thirty years following the end of World War II in France (1945–1975), when the economy grew rapidly and the standard of living improved dramatically.

59. Catherine Rollet, "Le journal d'un père pendant la Première Guerre mondiale," in *Histoire des familles, de la démographie et des comportements: En hommage à Jean-Pierre Bardet,* ed. Jean-Pierre Poussou and Isabelle Robin-Romero (Paris: PUPS, 2007), p. 687.

60. Cf. Emmanuelle Maunaye, "Quitter ses parents," *Terrain,* no. 36 (March 2001); cited in *Libération,* 2 February 2007: "When it is time to leave, [the child's room] is given a different purpose or reserved like a relic of the past."

61. Cf. Lydia Flem, *Comment je me suis séparée de ma fille et de mon quasi-fils* (Paris: Seuil, 2009).

62. Pietro Citati, *Le Monde,* 11 May 2007.

63. *Francs Camarades,* no. 36 (15 November 1945), provides precise guidelines on how to manufacture quilts, pillows, rugs, curtains, lamp shades, vases, and wall designs. Information provided by Jacqueline Lalouette.

64. Proust, "Journées de lecture," *Pastiches et Mélanges,* p. 172. On the pleasures of reading, cf. François Mauriac, *La Robe prétexte.* Mauriac locks himself in his room to abandon himself to "the inexpressible pleasure of reading." In that way, "the world was annihilated."

65. Marcel Proust, *Jean Santeuil* (Paris: Gallimard, coll. Bibliothèque de la Pléiade, 1971), "Le baiser du soir," p. 205. This draft of the *Recherche* is even more explicit.

66. François Mauriac, *Les Maisons fugitives* (Paris: Grasset, 1939); repr. in Mauriac, *Œuvres romanesques et théâtrales complètes,* vol. 3 (Paris: Gallimard, coll. Bibliothèque de la Pléiade, 1981), p. 909.

67. Jean-Jacques Rousseau, *La Nouvelle Héloïse,* in Rousseau, *Œuvres complètes,* vol. 2, "Inscription de la 11ᵉ planche," p. 770. Although Rousseau does not say for sure, it is probably something Julie said to Claire d'Orbe, her cousin.

68. Cited in Sigmund Freud, *Trois Essais sur la théorie sexuelle* (Paris: Gallimard, 1987), p. 168, note 1. Thanks to Lydia Flem, who brought this text to my attention.

69. Pierrette Fleutiaux, *Nous sommes tous éternels* (Paris: Gallimard, 1990), composed, using her own sounds, the themes for a similar opera around Estelle and Dan, her brother. Jean Cocteau, *The Holy Terrors,* trans. Rosamond Lehmann (New York: New Directions, 1957), p. 40.

70. Robert Musil, *L'Homme sans qualités* (Paris: Gallimard, 2007), vol. 1, p. 90.

71. Virginia Woolf, *To the Lighthouse.*

72. Louis-René des Forêts, *La Chambre des enfants* (1960) (Paris: Gallimard, 1983). Jean-Bertrand Pontalis offers an enlightening comment in the *Nouvelle Revue de psychanalyse,* no. 19 (Spring 1979), "L'Enfant": "By keeping watch over what happens in the children's room—by staying close to the door or inventing reasons to intrude—we run a strong risk of hearing only the noise of our own interior monologues."

The Women's Room

1. Virginia Woolf, *Une chambre à soi,* trans. Clara Malraux (Paris, Denoël, 1977; repr. Paris: UGE, coll. 10/18, 1992), p. 131.

2. Cf. Pierre Bonte, *Le Monde,* July 2007.

3. Bernard Edelman, *La Maison de Kant* (Paris: Payot, 1984), ch. 2, "La femme apprivoisée."

4. Sigmund Freud, *The Interpretation of Dreams* (1899), trans. James Strachey (1953) (New York: Basic, 2010), p. 365, note 3: "In dreams of speakers of French and other Romance languages a room is used to symbolize a woman, though these languages have nothing akin to the German expression *'Frauenzimmer.'*"

5. Emmanuel Levinas, *Totalité et Infini: Essai sur l'intériorité* (1971) (Paris: LGF, 1990), p. 319; "La demeure," pp. 162–203.

6. Danièle Régnier-Bohler, in Ariès and Duby, *Histoire de la vie privée,* vol. 2, p. 357.

7. Monseigneur Dupanloup, *Femmes savantes et femmes studieuses,* 5th ed. (Paris: Douniol, 1863), p. 76.

8. Cf. Véronique Leroux-Hugon, "Infirmières des hôpitaux parisiens: Ébauche d'une profession (1871–1914)," PhD dissertation in history, Université Paris-VII, 1981.

9. Gilman's writing is discussed below in the chapter titled "No Exit."

10. Françoise Flammant, *À tire d'elles: Itinéraires de féministes radicales des années 1970* (Rennes: PUR, 2007).

11. Paul Veyne, ed., *Les Mystères du gynécée* (Paris: Gallimard, 1998), p. 10.

12. François Lissarague, "Images du gynécée," in ibid., pp. 157ff.; cf. Françoise Frontisi-Ducroux, *Ouvrages de dames.*

13. Rétif de La Bretonne, *Les Gynographes, ou idées de deux honnêtes femmes sur un projet de règlement proposé à toute l'Europe pour mettre les femmes à leur place, et opérer le bonheur des deux sexes* (The Hague, 1777).

14. Cf. Altan Gokalp, *Harems: Mythe et réalité* (Rennes: Editions Ouest France, 2008). Superbly illustrated, this synthesis by one of the foremost specialists in this field appeared after this chapter was written.

15. Alain Grosrichard, *Structure du sérail: La fiction du despotisme asiatique dans l'Occident classique* (Paris: Seuil, 1979); esp. part 3, "L'ombre du sérail," from which I have taken the bulk of my information. Cf. Malek Chebel, *L'Esprit du sérail*, 2nd ed. (Paris: Payot, 1995).

16. Grosrichard, *Structure du sérail*, p. 178.

17. Jocelyne Daklia, "Harem: Ce que les femmes font entre elles," in "Clôtures," *Clio*, no. 26: (2007): 61–87.

18. Fatima Mernissi, *Le Harem et l'Occident* (Paris: Albin Michel, 2001).

19. Fatima Mernissi, *Rêves de femmes: Une enfance au harem* (Paris: Albin Michel, 1996), p. 71.

20. Cf. Tin, *L'Invention de la culture hétérosexuelle.*

21. Jeanne Bourin, *La Chambre des dames* (Paris: La Table ronde, 1979), p. 316.

22. Ariès and Duby, *Histoire de la vie privée*, vol. 2, pp. 88ff. On the intensity of the historiographic and ideological controversy provoked by Jeanne Bourin's books, especially with Robert Fossier, professor at the Sorbonne, see Delphine Naudier, "Jeanne Bourin: Une romancière historique aux prises avec les universitaires en 1985," in *Histoires d'historiennes*, ed. Nicole Pellegrin (Saint-Étienne: Publications de l'université de Saint-Étienne, 2006).

23. Cf. Corbin, *L'Harmonie des plaisirs*, pp. 352ff.; Goulemot, *Ces livres qu'on ne lit que d'une main.*

24. Cf. Marcel Bernos, *Femmes et gens d'Église dans la France classique (XVIIe–XVIIIe siècles)* (Paris: Le Cerf, 2003).

25. Cf. Nicole Pellegrin, "La clôture en voyage (fin XVIe–début XVIIIe siècle)," in "Voyageuses," *Clio*, no. 28 (2008): 76–98.

26. Cf. Geneviève Reynes, *Couvent de femmes: La vie des religieuses cloîtrées dans la France des XVIIe et XVIIIe siècles* (Paris: Fayard, 1987); Nicole Pellegrin, "De la clôture et de ses porosités: Les couvents de femmes sous l'Ancien Régime," in *Le Genre des territoires*, ed. Christine Bard (Rennes: PUR, 2004); Odile Arnold, *Le Corps et l'âme: La vie des religieuses au XIXe siècle* (Paris: Seuil, 1984).

27. Colette, *La Maison de Claudine* (1922), in Colette, *Œuvres*, ed. Claude Pichois (Paris: Gallimard, coll. Bibliothèque de la Pléiade, 1986), vol. 2, p. 1012.

28. Cf. Rebreyend, *Intimités amoureuses;* Rebreyend drew on autobiographical material deposited at the APA in Ambérieu-en-Bugey (Ain).

29. From our vantage point in the spring of 2008, we can only be shocked by the preoccupation with virginity that still nags at our society: the Affaire Fourniret, the "monster" hungry for virgins his wife procured for him; the case of the marriage in Lille in which the groom sued his bride for not being a virgin and for therefore, in his view, having broken their marriage contract. The judges dropped the case, preserving the intimacy of marriage, a private sphere in which the court refused, justly, to interfere.

30. Cf. the work of Jacques Gélis, Mireille Laget, Marie-France Morel, Scarlett Beauvalet-Boutouyrie, Françoise Thébaud, and especially Yvonne Knibiehler, *Accoucher: Femmes, sages-femmes et médecins depuis le milieu du XXᵉ siècle* (Rennes: ENSP, 2007); Knibiehler traces the decline of the profession of midwife and its contemporary manifestations; cf. ch. 1, "L'accouchement: Affaire privée, affaire de femmes."

31. Cf. Nicole Aronson, *Madame de Rambouillet ou la magicienne de la chambre bleue* (Paris: Fayard, 1988); Myriam Dufour-Maître, *Les Précieuses: Naissance des femmes de lettres en France au XVIIᵉ siècle* (Paris: Honoré Champion, 1999). According to Marc Fumaroli, the gilded legend of the blue bedroom gained traction starting in the nineteenth century; cf. *La Diplomatie de l'esprit* (Paris: Hermann, 1994).

32. Comtesse de Bassanville, *L'Art de bien tenir une maison* (Paris: Broussois, 1878).

33. Paul Reboux, *Le Nouveau savoir-vivre* (Paris: Flammarion, 1948), p. 191.

34. Annick Tillier, *Des criminelles au village: Femmes infanticides en Bretagne (1825–1865),* preface by Alain Corbin (Rennes: PUR, 2001), pp. 175ff.

35. Gustave Flaubert, *Un cœur simple* (1877), *Trois Contes,* in Flaubert, *Œuvres,* vol. 2, p. 573. Translated in *A Simple Heart,* trans. Charlotte Mandell (New York: Melville House, 2011.)

36. In Flaubert's novella, the house is not sold. Félicité makes an altar of Loulou. She dies in her room, incarnating the continuity of a vanished family.

37. Anne Martin-Fugier, *La Place des bonnes: La domesticité féminine en 1900* (Paris: Grasset, 1979; repr. Paris: Le Livre de Poche, 1985). See especially vol. 1, ch. 4, "Le logement." On interpersonal relationships, see Geneviève Fraisse, *Femmes toutes mains: Essai sur le service domestique* (Paris: Seuil, 1979).

38. Azarova, *L'Appartement communautaire.* These maid's rooms often served as storage for neighboring apartments.

39. Bécassine, a French maid character from a comic strip, was created by *La Semaine de Suzette,* a newspaper for little girls printed by Gautier-Languereau in the early twentieth century.

40. Singer was the most widespread American brand, next to several German brands, which enjoyed lively publicity, the traces of which we can still see on the walls of cities.

41. Ministère du travail, Office du travail: *Enquête sur le travail à domicile dans l'industrie de la lingerie*, 5 vols. (Paris: Imprimerie nationale, 1911), and *Enquête sur le travail à domicile dans l'industrie de la fleur artificielle* (Paris: Imprimerie nationale, 1913). On the Office du travail, see Isabelle Moret-Lespinet, *L'Office du travail, 1891–1914: La République et la réforme sociale* (Rennes: PUR, 2007).

42. Cf. Anne Lhuissier, *Alimentation populaire et réforme sociale au XIXe siècle* (Paris: Maison des sciences de l'homme, 2007); Michelle Perrot, *Les Ouvriers en grève*, 2 vols. (Paris: Mouton, 1974), vol. 1, "L'ouvrier consommateur," p. 216, on the question of rents.

43. Ministère du travail, Office du travail, *Enquête sur le travail à domicile dans l'industrie de la fleur artificielle*, XLIII, p. 204; Madame A. devoted her mornings to cleaning the house; she ate no meat and drank no wine; she wore only the clothes that were given to her.

44. Ministère du travail, Office du travail, *Enquête sur le travail à domicile dans l'industrie de la lingerie*, vol. 1, XLV, p. 329.

45. Ibid., XVII, p. 661.

46. Ministère du travail, Office du travail, *Enquête sur le travail à domicile dans l'industrie de la fleur artificielle*, XXIV, p. 175.

47. Ibid., XXX and XXXI, pp. 187–189.

48. *Les Ouvriers des Deux Mondes*, 3rd series, vol. 1, no. 98, observations gathered by L. de Maillard in 1903.

49. Alexandre Parent-Duchatelet, *De la prostitution dans la ville de Paris* (Paris: Jean-Baptiste Baillière, 1836), vol. 1, pp. 285–287. Quotes in the following are from this work.

50. Cf. Danièle Poublan, "Clôture et maison close: Les mots des écrivains," *Clio*, no. 26 (2007): 133–144. Poublan shows that the expression *maison close* appeared in the beginning of the twentieth century and became widespread during the 1930s, often as an outdated concept; "women who belonged to what were once called *maisons closes*," writes Proust in *La Prisonnière*.

51. Cf. Christelle Taraud, *La Prostitution coloniale: Algérie, Tunisie, Maroc, 1830–1962* (Paris: Payot, 2003).

52. Germaine Aziz, *Les Chambres closes: Histoire d'une prostituée juive d'Algérie*, preface by Christelle Taraud (Paris: Stock, 1980; repr. Paris: Payot, 2007). Germaine Aziz (1926–2003) managed to escape the prostitution ring and became a journalist at *Libération*.

53. Ibid., p. 77.

54. Alain Corbin, *Les Filles de noce: Misère sexuelle et prostitution au XIXe siècle* (Paris: Aubier, 1978).

55. Émile Zola, *Nana* (1880), in Émile Zola, *Les Rougon-Macquart* (Paris: Gallimard, coll. Bibliothèque de la Pléiade, 1977), vol. 2, p. 1347. The *hôtel particulier* belonged to Valtesse de La Bigne, a well-known courtesan who lived in the boulevard Malesherbes and whom Zola visited with the painter Guillemet; fragments of the house may be seen at the Musée des Arts décoratifs, rue de Rivoli.

56. Ibid., p. 1287.

57. A *grisette* was a young working-class Frenchwoman who worked in fashion and lived on her own and whose independence sometimes led to her being associated with an easy morality.

58. Map reprinted in Zola, *Les Rougon-Macquart,* p. 1730.

59. Marcel Proust, *À l'ombre des jeunes filles en fleurs,* pp. 615–616. Compare with the description of Odette's rooms during her Far East phase, p. 220.

60. Anne Martin-Fugier, *Comédienne: De Mlle Mars à Sarah Bernhardt* (Paris: Seuil, 2001). On the bedrooms of actresses, see Séverine Jouve, *Obsessions et perversions dans la littérature et les demeures à la fin du XIXe siècle,* pp. 181ff.

61. Émile Zola, *La Curée* (1872), in Zola, *Les Rougon-Macquart,* vol. 1, p. 477. Translated as *The Kill,* trans. Brian Nelson (Oxford: Oxford University Press, 2004), pp. 150–151.

62. Testimony of the historian Jacqueline Lalouette: "The fights with my sister had become so much more frequent and so bitter that during our last year of high school . . . my parents rented a room in the neighborhood where we lived, with a divorced woman, who lived alone. So I left the family home every evening after dinner," until the family moved and the two sisters could each have their own rooms (letter of 21 February 2009).

63. Simone de Beauvoir, *La Force de l'âge* (1960) (Paris: Gallimard, 1986), p. 17. It will be noted that the narrative begins with this move.

64. Jeanne Bouvier, *Mémoires* (Paris: Maspero, 1983).

65. Marguerite Audoux: *Marie-Claire* (1910) (Paris: Grasset, 1987) the novel that won the Prix Femina. See also Marguerite Audoux, *L'Atelier de Marie-Claire* (1920) (Paris: Grasset, 1987).

66. Perla Serfaty-Garzon, *Enfin chez soi? Récits féminins de vie et de migration* (Paris: Bayard, 2006). These migrants passed through France en route to Canada, where they settled.

67. The novels of Virginia Woolf—like *Mrs. Dalloway* or *To the Lighthouse*—are novels of the home and the bedroom, although the latter is more often evoked than described.

68. Virginia Woolf, *The Diary of Virginia Woolf,* vol. 1: *1915–1919,* ed. Anne Olivier Bell (New York: Harcourt, 1977), p. 196 (18 September 1918). Sydney and Beatrice Webb founded the Fabian Society, a well-known Socialist group, and the Woolfs saw them often.

69. Christine de Pisan, *La Cité des dames* (1404–1405), trans. and ed. Thérèse Moreau and Éric Hicks (Paris: Stock, 1986), p. 19.

70. Cf. Sylvain Maréchal, *Projet de loi portant défense d'apprendre à lire aux femmes* (Paris, 1801; repr. Paris: Fayard, 2007).

71. Cf. Anne-Marie Thiesse, *Le Roman du quotidien: Lecteurs et lectures populaires à la Belle Époque* (Paris: Chemin vert, 1984).

72. Séverine Auffret has edited and published a few of these texts: *Traité de la morale et de la politique* (1693) (Paris: Éd. des femmes, 1988); *Petit Traité de la faiblesse, de la légèreté et de l'inconstance qu'on attribue aux femmes mal à propos* (1693) (Paris: Arléa, 2002).

73. Cf. Christine Planté, *La Petite Sœur de Balzac: Essai sur la femme auteur* (Paris: Seuil, 1989).

74. Manguel, *Histoire de la lecture,* p. 219.

75. De Beauvoir, *La Force de l'âge,* p. 105 (in Marseille in 1931).

76. Ibid. (autumn 1932). "I had the impression that I lived in Paris, in some faraway suburb" (p. 140).

77. Ibid., p. 576.

78. Ibid., p. 319.

79. Ibid., p. 219.

80. Ibid., p. 125.

81. Ibid., p. 231.

82. Ibid., p. 321.

83. Claude Lanzmann, *Le Lièvre de Patagonie* (Paris: Gallimard, 2009), p. 218.

84. Ibid., p. 250.

85. Francis David, *Intérieurs d'écrivains;* Manguel, *Histoire de la lecture,* p. 219.

86. Cited in Francis David, *Intérieurs d'écrivains,* pp. 176–177.

87. Simone de Beauvoir, *Le Deuxième Sexe* (1949) (Paris: Gallimard, 1998), vol. 1, p. 139.

88. This was in an era when women walked by themselves very infrequently. Sand is cited in Catherine Nesci, *Le Flâneur et les flâneuses: Les femmes et la ville à l'époque romantique* (Grenoble: Ellug, 2007).

89. Cf. Rosi Braidotti, *Nomadic Subjects: Embodiment and Sexual Difference in Contemporary Feminist Theory* (New York: Columbia University Press, 1994).

90. Translated in *Madame Bovary,* trans. Lydia Davis (New York: Viking, 2010), p. 111.

91. Gustave Flaubert, letter of 6 June 1857, *Correspondance,* vol. 2: *1851–1858* (Paris: Gallimard, coll. Bibliothèque de la Pléiade, 1980), p. 732.

Hotel Rooms

1. Whence the effort in some hotels (usually luxury ones) to create personalized rooms that borrow elements from history or regional culture.
2. Roche, *Humeurs vagabondes,* esp. ch. 3, "Le voyageur en chambre"; Catherine Bertho-Lavenir, *La Roue et le stylo: Comment nous sommes devenus touristes* (Paris: Odile Jacob, 1999).
3. Francisque-René Michel and Édouard Fournier, *Le Livre d'or des métiers: Histoire des hôtelleries, cabarets et courtilles et des anciennes communautés et confréries d'hôteliers, de taverniers et de marchands de vin,* 2 vols. in quarto (Paris: Adolphe Delahaye, 1859).
4. Arthur Young, *Voyages en France* (Paris: UGE, 1989), vol. 1 (1787), pp. 112–113, "Observations générales." Original English text: http://oll.libertyfund.org/titles/young-arthur-youngs-travels-in-france-during-the-years-1787-1788-1789.
5. Ibid., vol. 2 (1790), pp. 485ff. On the uses of the bidet, cf. Roger-Henri Guerrand and Julia Csergo, *Le Confident des dames. Le bidet du XVIIIᵉ au XXᵉ siècle: Histoire d'une intimité* (1997) (Paris: La Découverte, 2009).
6. Young, *Voyages en France,* vol. 1, pp. 114–115.
7. Stendhal, *Mémoires d'un touriste* (1838), in Stendhal, *Voyages en France,* ed. V. Del Litto (Paris: Gallimard, 1992). Quotes in the following paragraphs are from this work.
8. Alain Corbin, *Le Territoire du vide: L'Occident et le désir du rivage, 1750–1840* (Paris: Aubier, 1988).
9. Stendhal, *Mémoires d'un touriste,* p. 337 (July 1837).
10. Ibid., p. 189 (20 June 1837).
11. Cf. Catherine Bertho-Lavenir, *La Roue et le stylo,* esp. pp. 217–239, "Réformer l'hôtellerie." Bertho-Lavenir describes these transformations in detail, on which these rooms clearly depended.
12. Cf. Roger-Henri Guerrand, *Les Lieux: Histoire des commodités* (Paris: La Découverte, 1985; 2nd ed., 2009).
13. Bertho-Lavenir, *La Roue et le stylo,* p. 228.
14. The *Chambres à coucher et cabinets de toilette,* competition organized by the Automobile Club of France (Paris: P. Schmid, no date), twenty-four images.
15. Émile Zola, *Lourdes* (1894), ed. Henri Mitterand (Paris: Stock, 1998).
16. Jean d'Ormesson, intro. to *Palaces et grands hôtels d'Europe* (Paris: Flammarion, 1984); lavishly illustrated.

17. Cf. *Du palais au palace,* exhibition catalogue, Musée Carnavalet, 1998. (This is the most thorough work on this question.)

18. There is quite a lot of writing on the Ritz. In addition to the catalogue cited above, see Stephen Watts, *The Ritz of Paris* (New York: Norton, 1964).

19. Proust, "Journées de lecture," *Pastiches et Mélanges,* p. 164.

20. Cf. Émile Litschgy, *La Vie des palaces: Hôtels de séjour d'autrefois* (Paris: Tac Motifs, 1997).

21. Henri Michaux, "La chambre," *Un certain Plume* (1930), in Michaux, *Œuvres complètes,* vol. 1, p. 675.

22. According to Aury's biographer, Angie David, *Dominique Aury* (Paris: Léo Scheer, 2006), p. 313: "They spent nights making love in hotel rooms, sometimes returning to the same one (often at the Auberge du Cheval blanc), or any other room, as chance would have it." Or more precisely, in the rooms let by the train station hotels in the Seine-et-Marne.

23. Aragon, *Les Chambres,* p. 13.

24. Alice James, *The Diary of Alice James* (Harmondsworth: Penguin, 1964), p. 150 (7 November 1890).

25. Furstenberg, *Lits de rêve,* p. 51, featuring a photograph of the room in question. In spring 2009, room 16 was restored by the interior decorator Jacques Garcia, who "identically reconstituted the poet's lifestyle. He also redid the other twenty rooms, as memorials" (*Le Monde,* supplement of 5 March 2009).

26. Cited in *Le Monde,* 17 August 2006.

27. Victor Klemperer, *Mes soldats de papier: Journal, 1933–1941* (Paris: Seuil, 2000), vol. 1, p. 696, note 35 (25 March 1934). Klemperer reminds us that the inventor of that mortal poison Veronal, Emil Fischer (1852–1919, winner of the Nobel Prize in 1902), put an end to debates about its name with this exasperated wisecrack: "My train is leaving in a half hour; I've already reserved a room in Verona."

28. Cited in Lorenzo Mondo, *Cesare Pavese: Une vie* (Paris: Arléa, 2009); cited in *Le Monde des livres,* 2 May 2009.

29. Valéry Larbaud, *A. O. Barnabooth: Journal* (1913), in Valéry Larbaud, *Œuvres* (Paris: Gallimard, 1957), p. 129: "What a blemish it is to own property! A string of houses, luxury, social importance: how ridiculous for a single young man!"

30. Ibid., p. 117.

31. Ibid. The only way to free himself would be to marry a poor girl, an actress perhaps. He courts one, but she refuses to give up her freedom: "I prefer to be poor and free rather than rich and bound," she tells him (p. 156). He understands her perfectly.

32. Ibid., p. 277.

33. Ibid., pp. 891–907.

34. Marcel Proust, *Swann's Way,* trans. C. K. Scott Moncrieff (New York: Henry Holt, 1922), p. 9

35. Marcel Proust, *Within a Budding Grove,* trans. C. K. Scott Moncrieff (New York: Henry Holt, 1922).

36. Marcel Proust, *The Guermantes Way,* trans. C. K. Scott Moncrieff (New York: Henry Holt, 1922).

37. Proust, *Jean Santeuil,* "Une chambre d'hôtel," p. 554. The original room that prompted this description is the one the author occupied in October 1896 at the Hôtel de France et d'Angleterre in Fontainebleau.

38. Proust, "Journées de lecture," *Pastiches et Mélanges,* p. 167.

39. "The Café Man" is what Roger Troisfontaines called Sartre in 1945; see text and interview in Roger Troisfontaines, *Œuvres romanesques* (Paris: Gallimard, 1980), p. 1745, note.

40. Sartre interview with John Gerassi, 1972; cited in ibid., p. lxiv: "In my view, having an apartment is a mistake. That's why I gave Mathieu one [in *L'Âge de raison*]: it represents the limits of his freedom."

41. The Hôtel Printania is the name of the hotel where Sartre stayed when he taught in a *lycée* in Le Havre.

42. Troisfontaines, *Œuvres romanesques,* p. 1736. The long footnote published on pages 1732–1740 and entitled "Dans la nuit de mercredi à jeudi," not included in the novel, is essential to understanding Roquentin's relationship to the bedroom and to bedrooms in general, as well as Sartre's own philosophy of rooms.

43. Ibid., p. 1738.

44. On this, see Michèle Le Dœuff, *L'Étude et le rouet* (Paris: Seuil, 2008). Sartre profoundly desired a room of his own, separate, empty. He had a phobia of mixing things; he feared the proximity of domestic life and the life of the mind (p. 203).

45. The Hôtel Mistral in the fourteenth arrondissement, the Welcome Hotel on the rue de Seine, the Grand Hôtel de Paris on the rue Bonaparte, the Hôtel Chaplain on the rue Jules-Chaplain during the war, the Hôtel Louisiane on the rue de Seine from 1944 to 1946.

46. In late June 2008, Cossery was found dead in his hotel room. Cf. *Libération,* 23 June 2008.

47. Edmund White, *Jean Genet* (New York: Knopf, 1993). See also Ivan Jablonka, *Les Vérités inavouables de Jean Genet* (Paris: Seuil, 2004); Albert Dichy and Pascal Fouché, *Jean Genet: Essai de chronologie, 1910–1944* (Paris: Bibliothèque de littérature française contemporaine, 1988).

48. Jean Genet, *Prisoner of Love* (1986), trans. Barbara Bray (New York: NYRB Classics, 2003), pp. 366, 367, 368; emphasis in original.

49. See Pellegrin, "Voyageuses"; Nicolas Bourguinat, ed., *Le Voyage au féminin: Perspectives historiques et littéraires* (Strasbourg: PUS, 2008); the author devotes a section to the 1835 travels of Liszt and Marie d'Agoult in Switzerland.

50. Zola, *Nana*, p. 1485. According to Gabrielle Houbre, *Le Livre des courtisanes: Archives secrètes de la police des mœurs* (Paris: Tallandier, 2007), loose women were frequent visitors to the Grand Hôtel.

51. Cf. Véronique Olmi, *Sa passion* (Paris: Grasset, 2006). A female author finds herself alone in a shabby hotel room in Sologne, where she weathers a breakup.

52. Colette, *L'Entrave* (1913), in Colette, *Œuvres complètes*, vol. 2, p. 355. The novel's resolution is, however, very conventional. Renée Néré, after indecisive thoughts of independence, gives in to her lover's desires, letting him take her place in the role of the vagabond. Colette would later disavow this ending.

53. Thanks to Élisabeth Roudinesco, who sent me the text of this talk and informed me of this controversy. Cf. Lydia Flem, *La Vie quotidienne de Freud et de ses patients* (Paris: Hachette, 1986).

54. Sigmund Freud, *"Notre cœur tend vers le Sud": Correspondance de voyage, 1895–1923,* ed. Christfried Tögel, intro. Élisabeth Roudinesco (Paris: Fayard, 2005).

55. Julien Gracq, *Un beau ténébreux* (Paris: Corti, 1945).

56. Olivier Rolin, *Suite à l'hôtel Crystal* (Paris: Seuil, 2004; 2nd ed., 2006). Rolin also published a collection entitled *Rooms in 2006,* which featured twenty-eight authors describing "their" hotel rooms.

57. Letter to Felice Bauer, 21 November 1912, in Kafka, *Œuvres complètes*, vol. 4, p. 76.

58. Letter to Felice Bauer, 26 June 1913, in ibid., p. 423.

59. Letter to Felice Bauer, 3 November 1912, in ibid., p. 34.

Workers' Rooms

1. As Jacques Rancière has shown in *La Nuit des prolétaires: Archives du rêve ouvrier* (Paris: Fayard, 1981).

2. Barrie M. Ratcliffe and Christine Piette, *Vivre la ville* (Paris: La Boutique de l'histoire, 2007), take issue with Louis Chevalier's overdramatic account; they underscore the power of the city to integrate and attempt to shine a light on migrants and their practices. They also critique the statistician from the INED for having sacrificed quantitative data in favor of literature overwhelmed by

representations. Louis Chevalier, *Classes laborieuses et classes dangereuses à Paris pendant la première moitié du XIXe siècle* (Paris: Plon, 1958).

3. Lépecq de La Clôture, *Collection d'observations sur les maladies et constitutions épidémiques,* pp. 228 and 252.

4. Ange Guépin and Eugène Bonamy, *Nantes au XIXe siècle: Statistique topographique, industrielle et morale* (Nantes: Sébire, 1835), p. 485.

5. Louis-René Villermé, *Tableau de l'état physique et moral des ouvriers employés dans les manufactures de coton, de laine et de soie* (Paris: Renouard, 1840), vol. 1, p. 270.

6. Ibid. See Pap Ndiaye on racist associations of the color black in *La Condition des Noirs: Essai sur une minorité française* (Paris: Calmann-Lévy, 2008).

7. Villermé, *Tableau de l'état physique et moral des ouvriers,* vol. 1, p. 83.

8. Ibid., p. 287.

9. Cited in Judith Lyon-Caen, "Une histoire de l'imaginaire social par le livre," *Revue de synthèse,* nos. 1–2 (2007): 172, letter from Ernestine Duval to Eugène Sue (13 July 1843). The author studied letters sent to novelists and authors of feuilletons like Balzac and Eugène Sue; these provide lively testimony of public opinion.

10. Cf. Pastoureau, *Noir.*

11. Émile Zola, *Pot-Bouille,* in Zola, *Œuvres complètes,* vol. 3, p. 65; Madame Vuillaume is speaking here.

12. The 1832 cholera epidemic prompted a pioneering investigation: *Rapport sur la marche et les effets du choléra-morbus dans Paris et le département de la Seine: Année 1832* (Paris: Imprimerie royale, 1834), in-quarto, fifty-one maps.

13. Alain Cottereau, "La tuberculose: Maladie urbaine ou maladie de l'usure au travail? Critique d'une épidémiologie officielle: Le cas de Paris," *Sociologie du Travail,* April–June 1978.

14. Dr. Octave du Mesnil, "Les garnis insalubres de la ville de Paris," *Annales d'hygiène publique et de médecine légale* (1878), brochure BHVP 928027.

15. Lion Murard and Patrick Zylberman trace a nuanced genealogy of the politics of hygiene in *L'Hygiène dans la République: La santé publique en France ou l'utopie contrariée, 1870–1918* (Paris: Gallimard, 1996).

16. Louis Rivière, "L'habitation, le mobilier et le jardin de l'ouvrier," *La Réforme sociale,* 1 October 1907. Abbé Lemire created the Association des jardins ouvriers.

17. Agricol Perdiguier (1805–1875), author of the *Livre du compagnonnage* (1839), served as a model for *Compagnon du tour de France* (1840), by George Sand, who had befriended him. He wrote *Mémoires d'un compagnon* (1855), a relatively rare example of a worker's autobiography.

18. Jean-Paul Flamand, ed., *La Question du logement et le mouvement ouvrier français* (Paris: La Villette, 1981). The Social Palace was an industrial and residential community, a society of workers.

19. Alain Faure and Claire Lévy-Vroelant, *Une chambre en ville: Hôtels meublés et garnis à Paris, 1860–1990,* intro. Andrée Michel (Paris: Créaphis, 2007); an impressive summary. Alain Faure is preparing a book on the history of working-class housing in nineteenth-century Paris; Claire Lévy-Vroelant looks at precarious housing today.

20. Michel de Certeau, *L'Invention du quotidien,* vol. 2: *Habiter, cuisiner,* with Luce Giard (Paris: UGE, 1980).

21. Maurizio Gribaudi has studied this process in Turin from 1880 to 1920.

22. Villermé, *Tableau de l'état physique et moral des ouvriers,* vol. 1, pp. 269–270.

23. Ibid., p. 346.

24. Lucienne Roubin, *Chambrettes des Provençaux: Une maison des hommes en Méditerranée septentrionale,* intro. Roger Bastide (Paris: Plon, 1970); Maurice Agulhon, *La République au village: Les populations du Var de la Révolution à la Seconde République* (Paris: Seuil, 1971), and "Les chambrées en Haute-Provence: Histoire et ethnologie," *Revue Historique,* April–June 1971; repr. in Agulhon, *Histoire vagabonde* (Paris: Gallimard, 1988), vol. 1, pp. 17–59. Cf. as well Pierre Chabert, *Les Cercles: Une sociabilité en Provence* (Aix-en-Provence: Publications de l'université de Provence, 2007).

25. Text from 1957, cited in Paul Imbs, ed., *Trésor de la langue française: Dictionnaire de la langue du XIXe et du XXe siècle* (Paris: CNRS, 1977), vol. 5.

26. Pierre Vinçard, *Les Ouvriers de Paris* (around 1850), cited in Faure and Lévy-Vroelant, *Une chambre en ville,* p. 98.

27. Michel Cordillot, *Eugène Varlin* (Paris: Éd. ouvrières, 1991), p. 120. What was the extent of this woman's freedom?

28. Imported by a factory in Jujurieux (Bonnet), the French system was a pale imitation of the Lowell cotton mills, near Boston, which were much more ambitious.

29. Cf. Faure and Lévy-Vroelant, *Une chambre en ville,* pp. 94–101. Faure argues that a version of Paris as being full of workers' rooms is excessive. He traces the fluid boundary between bedsits and *chambrées.*

30. Ibid., p. 98 (text from 1852).

31. Ibid.; Faure reproduces about thirty of these photographs.

32. Ibid., pp. 66ff.

33. Cited in ibid., p. 68.

34. Ibid., pp. 71ff.

35. See plates in ibid., p. 89.

36. Jean-Claude Caron, *Générations romantiques: Les étudiants de Paris et le Quartier latin, 1814–1851* (Paris: Armand Colin, 1991), pp. 131–135, "Se loger."

37. Jules Vallès, *Le Bachelier* (1881), in Vallès, *Œuvres,* vol. 2, pp. 567–574, ch. 18, "Le garni."

38. Andrée Michel, *Famille, industrialisation, logement* (Paris: CNRS, 1959), esp. ch. 5, "Les conditions d'habitat des locataires de l'enquête."

39. Faure and Lévy-Vroelant, *Une chambre en ville,* part 3, "Des années 1920 aux années 1990: Grandeur et décadence des garnis parisiens." A sociologist, Lévy-Vroelant is also a member of the Observatoire des hôtels created by the Mairie de Paris. Cf. Claire Lévy-Vroelant, *Logement, accueil et mobilité: Contribution à l'étude des statuts d'occupation incertaine en France (1831–1999)* (Paris, 2002).

40. Cited in Faure and Lévy-Vroelant, *Une chambre en ville,* p. 156.

41. Grave and Bouvier cited in ibid., p. 157.

42. Georges Navel, *Travaux* (1945) (Paris: Gallimard, 1979), p. 104.

43. Édouard Ducpétiaux, *De la condition physique et morale des jeunes ouvriers et des moyens de l'améliorer* (Brussels: Meline, 1843), vol. 1, p. 337.

44. Cf. Michel Frey, "Du mariage et du concubinage dans les classes populaires à Paris (1846–1847)," *Annales ESC,* no. 4 (July–August 1978).

45. On Le Play, cf. Antoine Savoye, *Les Débuts de la sociologie empirique: Études socio-historiques (1830–1930)* (Paris: Méridiens-Klincksieck, 1994); Lhuissier, *Alimentation populaire et réforme sociale au XIXᵉ siècle.*

46. Cf. "La chambre des dames," in Moret-Lespinet, *L'Office du travail.*

47. Jean-Louis Deaucourt, *Premières Loges: Paris et ses concierges au XIXᵉ siècle* (Paris: Aubier, 1992); Jean-François Laé, *Les Nuits de la main courante: Écritures au travail* (Paris: Stock, 2008), chapter on the concierge who is at once inspector and witness to social suffering; Société d'économie sociale, *Les Ouvriers des Deux Mondes,* vol. 1, no. 1, pp. 27–68, "Le charpentier de Paris," observations gathered in 1857 by Le Play and Focillon. This early monograph has become a classic. Around a hundred monographs are concerned with workers' families.

48. Société d'économie sociale, *Les Ouvriers des Deux Mondes,* vol. 1, no. 7, pp. 299–372, observations gathered in 1857 by E.-F. Hébert and E. Delbet.

49. Ibid., vol. 2, no. 11, pp. 63–104, observations gathered in 1856 by E. Avalle and A. Focillon.

50. Ibid., vol. 2, no. 17, pp. 321–362, observations gathered in 1858 by E. Avalle.

51. Ibid., vol. 2, no. 13, pp. 145–192, observations gathered in 1856 by A. Focillon.

52. Linen seamstress: ibid., vol. 3, pp. 247–284, observations gathered in 1861 by L. Auvray. Toy maker: ibid., 2nd series, no. 73 (1893).

53. *Sublime* was a term given to alcoholic workers—for example, by Denis Poulot, *Question sociale: Le sublime ou le travailleur comme il est en 1870 et ce qu'il peut être* (1870), 2nd ed. (Paris: Lacroix, 1872).

54. Société d'économie sociale, *Les Ouvriers des Deux Mondes*, vol. 5, no. 42, pp. 201–259, observations gathered in 1878 by Jacques de Reviers.

55. Ibid., 2nd series, vol. 4, no. 74, pp. 53–100, observations gathered by Pierre du Maroussem, who devoted several studies to workers in the furniture industry.

56. Ibid., vol. 4, no. 73, pp. 1–53, observations gathered in 1884 and 1890 by Urbain Guérin.

57. Michel Lallement, *Le Travail de l'utopie: Godin et le familistère de Guise* (Paris: Les Belles Lettres, 2009), the most recent study in a richly studied field. The majority of lodgings in the *familistère* had two rooms and a smaller room.

58. Cf. Lhuissier, *Alimentation populaire et réforme sociale au XIXe siècle.*

59. I once had a tendency to do so, after reading Maurice Halbwachs, who saw the worker's disinterest in his lodgings in contrast to the employee's; see his foundational study *La Classe ouvrière et les niveaux de vie: Recherches sur la hiérarchie des besoins dans les sociétés industrielles contemporaines* (Paris: Alcan, 1912). Perrot: *Les Ouvriers en grève*, vol. 1, "Logement: Un poste modeste," pp. 216–224, and "Les ouvriers, l'habitat et la ville," in Flamand, ed., *La Question du logement et le mouvement ouvrier français*, pp. 19–39.

60. Lhuissier, *Alimentation populaire et réforme sociale au XIXe siècle*, "Cuisines et cuisinières: La préparation des repas au quotidien," pp. 65–68.

61. Cf. Guerrand, *Les Lieux.*

62. Charles Garnier and Auguste Amman, *L'Habitation humaine* (Paris: Hachette, 1892), cited in Debarre-Blanchard and Eleb-Vidal, *Invention de l'habitation moderne*, p. 69.

63. In this and the following paragraphs, references to Gervaise and quotes are from Émile Zola, *L'Assommoir*, in Zola, *Œuvres complètes*, vol. 2, pp. 472ff.

64. Charles Blanc, *La Grammaire des arts décoratifs* (1880), cited in Joëlle Deniot, *Ethnologie du décor en milieu ouvrier: Le bel ordinaire*, intro. Michel Verret (Paris: L'Harmattan, 1995), p. 90.

65. *Atget: Une rétrospective*, p. 212. Cf. Molly Nesbit and Françoise Reynaud, *Eugène Atget. Intérieurs parisiens: Un album du musée Carnavalet* (Paris: Carré, 1992).

66. A tinsmith in Aix-les-Bains created an engraving of "a surprise in the wheatfields" that was judged to be "bawdy" by the investigator. Société d'économie sociale, *Les Ouvriers des Deux Mondes*, vol. 2, no. 10 (1857), pp. 1–53.

67. Zola, *L'Assommoir*, p. 472.

68. Gauny to Ponty, 1856, cited in Rancière, *La Nuit des prolétaires*, p. 91.

69. Jérôme-Pierre Gilland, cited in Rancière, *La Nuit des prolétaires;* Société d'économie sociale, *Les Ouvriers des Deux Mondes,* 2nd series, vol. 3, no. 70, pp. 325–368, "Le charpentier indépendant de Paris," observations gathered in 1889 by Pierre du Maroussem, who underscores the politicization of the carpenter.

70. Pascale Marie, "La bibliothèque des Amis de l'instruction du IIIe arrondissement: Un temple, quartier du Temple," in Pierre Nora, ed., *Les Lieux de mémoire,* vol. 1: *La République* (Paris: Gallimard, 1984), pp. 323–351.

71. Exhibition at the Mairie du XIIIe arrondissement de Paris, Spring 1980, of the photos conserved at the Bibliothèque historique de la Ville de Paris.

72. Gilland, cited in Rancière, *La Nuit des prolétaires,* p. 42.

73. Virginia Woolf, *The Diary of Virginia Woolf,* vol. 1: *1915–1919,* ed. Anne Olivier Bell (London: Hogarth Press, 1977), p. 4 (2 January 1915).

74. Foundational work in this area has been undertaken by Roger-Henri Guerrand: *Les Origines du logement social en France* (Paris: Éd. ouvrières, 1966), and *Le Logement populaire en France: Sources documentaires et bibliographie* (Paris: École nationale supérieure des beaux-arts, 1979).

75. Cf. the work of the CERFI: Lion Murard and Patrick Zylberman, *Recherches,* no. 25 (November 1976).

76. Rolande Trempé, *Les Mineurs de Carmaux de 1848 à 1914* (Paris: Éd. ouvrières, 1971), vol. 1, pp. 259ff.; Trempé looks at the design and size of workers' lodgings in miners' settlements.

77. Émile Zola, *Germinal,* in Zola, *Les Rougon-Macquart,* vol. 3, pp. 1444–1145.

78. Cf. Émile Cacheux, *État des habitations ouvrières à la fin du XIXe siècle* (Paris: Baudry, 1891); it includes numerous plates and architectural plans of workers' houses.

79. Christian Devillers and Bernard Huet, *Le Creusot: Naissance et développement d'une ville industrielle, 1872–1914* (Seyssel: Champ Vallon, 1981); *Les Schneider, Le Creusot: Une famille, une entreprise, une ville (1856–1960),* exhibition catalogue, Musée d'Orsay (Paris: Fayard, 1995), esp. Yves Lequin, "De l'usine à la ville: Une politique de l'espace," pp. 342–352; the author stresses the overall success of the system.

80. Cf. Frédéric Moret, *Les Socialistes et la Ville: Grande-Bretagne, France, 1820–1850* (Fontenay-aux-Roses: ENS, 1999).

81. Michel Verret, *L'Ouvrier français: L'espace ouvrier* (Paris: Armand Colin, 1979).

82. Deniot, *Ethnologie du décor en milieu ouvrier;* the author visited seventy workers' homes in the Nantes region and took four thousand photographs. She is less interested in space as such and more in the objects that fill it.

83. Jean-François Laé and Numa Murard, "Mémoires des lieux: Une histoire des taudis," seminar 1986–1988, duplicate copy, Bibliothèque du CEDIAS, 46336 V4. "Henceforth the worker is no longer poor; a thousand indications allow us to show that the poor are no longer workers, a thousand writings proclaim this truth. Being a worker is no longer a destiny but a profession, with diplomas, status, and employment. While being poor is simply a fate."

84. The INED carried out the first census in the 1980s. The most recent investigation was carried out by INSEE: Marie-Thérèse Jouin-Lambert, "Une enquête d'exception. Sans-abri, sans-domicile: Des interrogations renouvelées," *Économie et Statistique,* nos. 391–392 (October 2006).

85. Lydia Perreal, *J'ai vingt ans et je couche dehors: Le combat quotidien d'une jeune SDF* (Paris: J'ai lu, 2002).

86. Robert Castel, *Les Métamorphoses de la question sociale: Une chronique du salariat* (Paris, Fayard, 1995).

87. Colette Pétonnet, *Espaces habités: Ethnologie des banlieues* (Paris: Galilée, 1982), p. 25.

88. Crépin-Massy, *L'Identité sociale* (Paris: École des hautes études en sciences sociales, 1980), p. 268.

89. *Ouest-France,* 12 January 2009.

90. Speech by Jean-Noël Guérini, senator for Bouches-du-Rhône, in the Senate, 10 October 2007.

91. Xavier Godinot, *Éradiquer la misère: Démocratie, mondialisation et droits de l'homme* (Paris: PUF, 2008). This fieldwork was gathered from the collection of life stories of the most indigent, restored to their control.

92. Ibid., pp. 141–191, ch. 3, "Résister pour exister: L'histoire de Farid, Céline et Karim, entre l'Algérie et la France."

93. "Cabanes des clandestins," *Le Monde 2,* 19 July 2008. This investigation won the World Press Photo Prize in 2008. Louis Mesplé critiqued Jacques Revillard for aestheticizing misery, but he was congratulated for capturing it. Philippe Lioret's film *Welcome* (2008) is another kind of memorializing of it.

94. Mike Davis, *De l'explosion des villes au bidonville global* (Paris: La Découverte, 2006). Cf. as well the interview with the author by Olivier Pascal-Mousselard, *Télérama,* January 2008.

Sickbeds and Deathbeds

1. George Sand, *Correspondance,* ed. Georges Lubin, vol. 24: *Avril 1874–mai 1876* (Paris: Garnier, 1990).

2. George Sand, *Agendas* (1852–1876), ed. Anne Chevereau (Paris: Touzot, 1990), 5 vols. + index of names mentioned.

3. Georges Lubin published Dr. Favre's account (previously unpublished), as well as that of Henry Harrisse (1904), in annexes 3 and 4 of vol. 24 of Sand, *Correspondance,* pp. 654–672. He believes the testimony given by Wladimir Karénine in his biography of Sand is debatable. There is also an unpublished account by Solange, who kept a journal of her mother's final moments. This document is conserved in the collection of the late Dina Vierny and was brought to my attention by Martine Reid.

4. Georges Lubin provides the exchange of letters between Maurice and Lina on this subject. Maurice appears as "Baron Dudevant" and Lina as merely "Mme Maurice Sand-Dudevant" (ibid., p. 650, n. 1).

5. Georges Lubin gives the main elements of this debate. On Sand and religion, see Bernard Hamon, *George Sand face aux églises* (Paris: L'Harmattan, 2005). On the question of free thought and secular burials during this period, see Jacqueline Lalouette, *La Libre pensée en France, 1848–1940* (Paris: Albin Michel, 1997).

6. Philippe Ariès: *Essais sur l'histoire de la mort en Occident du Moyen Âge à nos jours* (Paris: Seuil, 1975), and *L'Homme devant la mort;* Michel Vovelle, *La Mort et l'Occident de 1300 à nos jours* (Paris: Gallimard, 2000).

7. Joan Didion, *The Year of Magical Thinking* (New York: Knopf, 2005), p. 3.

8. According to the testimony of the volunteer group Morts de la rue, the life expectancy for a homeless person is forty years and twice that for those who live indoors.

9. Zola, *L'Assommoir,* p. 410.

10. Cf. Arnold, *Le Corps et l'Âme,* part 3, "Devant la souffrance et la mort."

11. Cf. Jean-Pierre Peter, *Annales* 22, no. 4 (1967): 712.

12. Cited in Jacques Léonard, *La Vie quotidienne des médecins de province au XIXᵉ siècle* (Paris: Hachette, 1977), p. 198.

13. Mademoiselle de Montpensier did not want to remain in the dying countess's room "because it smelled very bad, and this kept me from entering the next day." Bernard Quilliet, ed., *Mémoires de la Grande Mademoiselle* (Paris: Mercure de France, 2005), p. 371 (1st ed., 4 vols., Chéruel, 1858–1859).

14. Rousseau, *La Nouvelle Héloïse,* part 6, letter XI, from M. de Wolmar, pp. 703–740. This narrative of Julie's death includes numerous details on the sickroom, which she wanted to keep serene and full of flowers.

15. Ariès, *Essais sur l'histoire de la mort en Occident du Moyen Âge à nos jours;* Anne Vincent-Buffault, *Histoire des larmes, XVIIIᵉ–XIXᵉ siècle* (Marseille: Rivages, 1986; 2nd ed., Paris: Payot-Rivages, 2001).

16. Renard, *Journal,* pp. 418–419 (19 June 1897).

17. Rousseau, *La Nouvelle Héloïse*, p. 711. Wolmar makes the children leave Julie's room after she has left them to her cousin Claire.

18. Marie d'Agoult, *Mémoires, souvenirs et journaux* (Paris: Mercure de France, 1990); memoirs composed under the Second Empire; cited in *Le Dernier portrait*, exhibition catalogue, Musée d'Orsay, March–May 2002 (Paris: Réunion des musées nationaux, 2002), p. 198.

19. Pierre Loti, *Le Roman d'un enfant*, 1890; cited in *Le Dernier portrait*, exhibition catalogue, Musée d'Orsay, March–May 2002, p. 199. "On nous tenait à l'écart," said Paul Klee with regard to his grandmother.

20. Ozouf, *Composition française*, p. 17.

21. Gustave Flaubert to Maxime Du Camp, 25 March 1846, in Gustave Flaubert, *Correspondance,* vol. 1: *1830–1851,* ed. Jean Bruneau (Paris: Gallimard, 1973), p. 258. Flaubert's sister died in childbirth in March 1846.

22. Honoré de Balzac, *Mémoires de deux jeunes mariées* (1841–1842), in Balzac, *La Comédie humaine,* vol. 1, ed. Pierre-Georges Castex (Paris: Bibliothèque de la Pléiade, 1976).

23. Cited in Louis-Vincent Thomas, *Anthropologie de la mort,* 3rd ed. (Paris: Payot, 1980), p. 195.

24. Ariès and Duby, *Histoire de la vie privée,* vol. 2, p. 94. Georges Duby published the knight's tale: *Guillaume le Maréchal ou le meilleur chevalier du monde* (Paris: Fayard, 1984).

25. Cited in Vovelle, *La Mort et l'Occident de 1300 à nos jours,* p. 325.

26. Stendhal, *Mémoires d'un touriste.*

27. Olivier Faure, *Genèse de l'hôpital moderne: Les hospices civils de Lyon de 1802 à 1845* (Lyon: PUL, 1982), p. 175.

28. Report presented to the Conseil général des hôpitaux et hospices civils de Paris, signed Blondel, BHVP 132594.

29. Charles Coquelin and Gilbert Guillaumin, *Dictionnaire de l'économie politique,* 4th ed. (Paris: Guillaumin, 1873), article titled "Hospices."

30. Cf. *L'Architecture hospitalière au XIXᵉ siècle: L'exemple parisien,* exhibition at the Musée d'Orsay (Paris: Réunion des musées nationaux, 1988). See also Yannick Marec, ed., *Accueillir ou soigner? L'hôpital et ses alternatives du Moyen Âge à nos jours* (Rouen: Publications des universités de Rouen et du Havre, 2007). Marie-Christine Pouchelle, *L'Hôpital corps et âme: Essais d'anthropologie hospitalière* (Paris: Seli Arslan, 2003), focuses on interpersonal relationships but says very little about the space itself.

31. Lévy, *Traité d'hygiène publique et privée,* vol. 2, pp. 531–535.

32. Cf. Nicole Edelman, *Les Métamorphoses de l'hystérique: Du début du XIXᵉ siècle à la Grande Guerre* (Paris: La Découverte, 2003), p. 254. Listening,

separation from the family, and persuasion were some aspects of this authoritarian treatment.

33. Voltaire, letter of 17 August 1767, cited in Littré, *Dictionnaire de la langue française.* [The English term "bedridden" comes from the Old English *bedreda,* itself composed of *bed* (bed) and *rida* (rider); the term eventually moved from being a noun to an adjective, from describing the person to describing the state.—Trans.]

34. Proust, *La Prisonnière,* pp. 182–183. *The Captive,* in *In Search of Lost Time,* vol. 5: *The Captive and The Fugitive,* trans. C. K. Scott Moncrieff and Terence Kilmartin; revised D. J. Enright (London: Random House, 2010), p. 202.

35. Élise Feller shows how late individualization began. A 1926 ruling orders dormitories with around twenty beds, placed about 3–4 feet apart, made of iron without curtains; there was no space to put anything away; one sink for every five people, one toilet for every ten. Cf. *Histoire de la vieillesse en France, 1900–1960: Du vieillard au retraité* (Paris: S. Arslan, 2005).

36. Rousseau, *La Nouvelle Héloïse,* p. 735.

37. Cf. Ariès, *L'Homme devant la mort.*

38. Susan Sontag, *Illness as Metaphor;* cited in Jean Strouse, *Alice James: A Biography* (1980) (New York: New York Review Classics, 2011), p. 101.

39. Lépecq de La Clôture, *Collection d'observations sur les maladies et constitutions épidémiques,* for the year 1770.

40. Florence Nightingale, *Notes on Nursing* (1860). In England in 1851, there were 22,466 professional nurses and 39,139 home nurses, whose training was of great interest to Nightingale.

41. Élise and Michaëlle Gagnet, *La Mort apaisée* (Paris: La Martinière, 2007). Élise was a night nurse with a palliative care service, and she recounted this fact to her sister Michaëlle, who was a journalist.

42. James, *The Diary of Alice James.*

43. Lévy, *Traité d'hygiène publique et privée,* vol. 1, pp. 249–260.

44. Gérald Aubert, *Chambre 108* (Arles: Actes Sud, 2003).

45. Noëlle Châtelet, *Le Baiser d'Isabelle: L'aventure de la première greffe du visage* (Paris: Seuil, 2007).

46. Simone de Beauvoir, *Une mort très douce* (Paris: Gallimard, 1964).

47. For example, on the internet, competing clinical groups boast of the furnishings in their rooms.

48. "I had never had this kind of experience of a sickroom, and I can never thank the young emergency room doctor enough for allowing my mother to leave his care, where he was overwhelmed with patients, and letting her die in the haven

of the hospice," Jacqueline Lalouette wrote to me (31 January 2009); I thank her for allowing me to mention her experience and cite her letter.

49. Yoko Ogawa, *Une parfaite chambre de malade* (Arles: Actes Sud, 2003). [The Japanese title is *Kanpeki na byōshitsu;* it has not been translated into English.—Trans.]

50. Ibid.

51. Huston, *Passions d'Annie Leclerc,* February 2006.

52. Pierre Guillaume, *Du désespoir au salut: Les tuberculeux aux XIXe et XXe siècles* (Paris: Aubier, 1986).

53. Thomas Mann, *The Magic Mountain* (1924), trans. H. T. Lowe-Porter (New York: Knopf, 1927), pp. 452–453.

54. Georg Groddeck, *Conférences psychanalytiques à l'usage des malades prononcées au sanatorium de Baden-Baden, 1916–1919,* 3 vols. (Paris: UGE, 1993).

55. François Berquin, *Hypocrisies de Joë Bousquet* (Lille: Presses universitaires du Septentrion, 2000) (and see its important bibliography). Cf. Édith de La Héronnière, *Joë Bousquet: Une vie à corps perdu* (Paris: Albin Michel, 2006), esp. ch. 6, "Camera obscura"; Pierre Cabanne, *La Chambre de Joë Bousquet: Enquêtes et écrits sur une collection,* intro. Pierre Guerre and Louis Pons (Marseille: André Dimanche, 2005).

56. Cf. Nicole Edelman, *Les Métamorphoses de l'hystérique.*

57. Joë Bousquet, *Exploration de mon médecin,* intro. Pierre Nouilhan (Toulouse: Sables, 1988); article published in 1943.

58. Jean-Jacques Yvorel, *Les Poisons de l'esprit: Drogues et drogués au XIXe siècle* (Paris: Quai Voltaire, 1992).

59. Pierre Guerre in Cabanne, *La Chambre de Joë Bousquet.*

60. La Héronnière, *Joë Bousquet,* p. 96.

61. James, *The Diary of Alice James.* Cf. Jean Strouse, *Alice James: A Biography* (Boston: Houghton Mifflin, 1980).

62. James, *The Diary of Alice James,* p. 106 (30 March 1890).

63. Ibid., p. 113 (5 May 1890).

64. Ibid., p. 70 (16 December 1889).

65. Cited in Leon Edel's introduction in ibid.; Edel provides the complicated historical context of the diary's publication.

66. Ibid., p. 230 (2 February 1892).

67. Gustave Flaubert to Maxime Du Camp, 25 March 1846, in Flaubert, *Correspondance,* vol. 1, p. 258.

68. *Le Dernier Portrait,* exhibition catalogue, Musée d'Orsay, March–May 2002.

69. Diary entry, 24 August 1878.

70. Excerpts from Michelet's *Journal* (Paris: Gallimard, 1959); cited in ibid., p. 208.

71. Ariès, *L'Homme devant la mort,* vol. 2, p. 182.

72. Émile Zola, *L'Œuvre;* cited in *Le Dernier Portrait,* exhibition catalogue, Musée d'Orsay, March–May 2002, p. 207. The section focuses on Claude Lantier's final portrait of a dead child. *His Masterpiece (L'Œuvre),* trans. Ernest Alfred Vizetelly (London: Chatto and Windus, 1902), p. 277.

73. *Study for the Sick Child,* 1885–1886; *Death in the Sickroom,* 1893; *By the Death Bed (Fever),* 1896.

74. *Ferdinand Hodler, 1853–1918,* exhibition at the Musée d'Orsay, Paris, 2007.

75. Joëlle Bolloch, "Photographie après décès: Pratiques, usages et fonctions," in *Le Dernier Portrait,* exhibition catalogue, Musée d'Orsay, March–May 2002, pp. 112–145.

76. Sand, *Correspondance,* vol. 1, no. 89, p. 217.

77. Ibid., vol. 29, p. 371, letter of 22 August 1865.

78. The translation from *Madame Bovary* is by Lydia Davis (London: Penguin, 2010).—Trans.

79. Cf. Nicole Edelman, *Voyances* (Paris: Seuil, 2008).

80. Balzac, *La Comédie humaine,* vol. 3, p. 881.

81. Edmond de Goncourt, *La Maison de l'artiste,* vol. 2, p. 369.

82. Ibid.

83. Cf. Ginette Raimbaut, *Parlons de deuil* (Paris: Payot, 2004), p. 35.

84. Roland Barthes, *Journal de deuil,* ed. Nathalie Léger (Paris: Seuil, 2009), p. 204 (18 August 1978).

85. Cf. Angie David, *Dominique Aury,* p. 56.

No Exit

1. Jean d'Ormesson, *Qu'ai-je donc fait ?* (Paris: Laffont, 2008).

2. Emily Dickinson, *The Letters of Emily Dickinson,* vol. 3, ed. Thomas H. Johnson (Cambridge, Mass.: Belknap, 1958), p. 750.

3. Emily Dickinson, *Complete Poems,* ed. Thomas H. Johnson (New York: Back Bay, 1997), p. 402.

4. Claire Malroux, *Chambre avec vue sur l'éternité* (Paris: Gallimard, 2005). Malroux has edited a number of Dickinson's poems, mainly published by José Corti. Cf. Christian Bobin, *La Dame blanche* (Paris: Gallimard, 2007).

5. Cited in Monique Eleb, ed., "La Maison: Espaces et intimités" (conference in Paris, 1985), *In extenso,* no. 9 (1986): 104.

6. Emmanuel de Roux, "Gravé par un fou, un joyau de l'art brut," *Le Monde*, 21 July 2007. Emmanuel de Roux, who provides these excerpts, writes: "[This is] a delirious text that makes the reader ill at ease, from the mute suffering of his unaccented, unpunctuated sentences."

7. As Gilles Deleuze has put it; "Ecrivain non: Un nouveau cartographe," *Critique*, no. 343 (December 1975): 1207–1227.

8. Cited in Muriel Carduner-Loosfelt, "Une affaire ténébreuse," *Sociétés et Représentations*, no. 4 (May 1997): 240–249.

9. Harold Pinter, *The Room* (1957), in Harold Pinter, *Plays One* (London: Faber and Faber, 1996).

10. Painting shown at the Tate Modern, London, Autumn 2008.

11. Georges Perec, *A Man Asleep* (1967), in Georges Perec, *Things: A Story of the Sixties with A Man Asleep*, trans. David Bellos (London: Random House, 2011), pp. 141–142.

12. Proust, *La Prisonnière*, p. 385 (English ed., p. 519). In it we hear an echo of Pascal: faith is "God perceived by the heart."

13. Marguerite Duras, *The Malady of Death*, trans. Barbara Bray (New York: Grove/Atlantic, 2015).

14. Pauline Réage, *Histoire d'O*, rev. ed., preceded by Jean Paulhan, "Le bonheur dans l'esclavage" (Paris: Pauvert, 1974). We now know the author of the text is Dominique Aury.

15. Michel Delon, *Le Savoir-vivre libertin* (Paris: Hachette littératures, 2000), esp. ch. 6, "Lieux et décors," pp. 115–144.

16. Ibid.

17. Michel Delon, *L'Invention du boudoir* (Toulouse: Zulma, 1999).

18. Delon, *Le Savoir-vivre libertin*, p. 135.

19. On the composition of *Histoire d'O*, cf. Angie David, *Dominique Aury*.

20. Pauline Réage, *Story of O*, trans. Sabine d'Estree (New York: Grove, 1966). The author is of course Dominique Aury, and Richard Seaver translated, also using a pseudonym.—Trans.

21. Nicolas Grimaldi, *La Jalousie: Étude sur l'imaginaire proustien* (Arles: Actes Sud, 1993).

22. Marcel Proust, *In Search of Lost Time*, vol. 6: *Time Regained*, trans. C. K. Scott Moncrieff, Terence Kilmartin, and D. J. Enright (New York: Modern Library, 2003), p. 23.

23. This and all following quotes, unless otherwise noted, are from *In Search of Lost Time*, vol. 5: *The Captive and The Fugitive*, trans. C. K. Scott-Moncrieff, Terence Kilmartin, and D. J. Enright (New York: Modern Library, 2003).

24. Oddly, sometimes the names in the text are undisguised: Marcel, Céleste Albaret.

25. Gilles Deleuze, *Proust and Signs,* trans. Richard Howard (London: Continuum, 2008), p. 90.

26. Proust, *The Captive,* p. 99.

27. Ibid., p. 679.

28. Cited in Brombert, *La Prison romantique,* p. 136.

29. Proust, *La Prisonnière,* pp. 370–371.

30. Ibid., p. 649.

31. But she dies shortly thereafter in a banal accident (denied later), as if there were no other possible outcome for her or for the narrator. A long pursuit follows that provides the framework for *The Fugitive.*

32. Proust, *La Fugitive.*

33. Cf. Gilles Deleuze, *Proust et les signes* (Paris: Presses Universitaires de France, 1964), ch. 2, "Les boîtes et les vases," as structures within Proust's narrative.

34. Edgar Poe, "The Fall of the House of Usher," *The Works of the Late Edgar Allan Poe* (New York: J. S. Redfield, 1850), vol. 1, p. 297.

35. Edgar Poe, "The Murders in the Rue Morgue," *Collected Works of Edgar Allan Poe* (New York: Walter J. Black, 1927); Leroux, *Le Mystère de la chambre jaune.*

36. *Le Monde,* 17 March 2009, gives an unbelievable description of the bunker at 40, Ybbstrasse, in Amstetten in southern Vienna.

37. Cited in *Le Monde,* 2 September 2006.

38. Nicole Edelman, *Les Métamorphoses de l'hystérique.*

39. Charlotte Perkins Gilman, "The Yellow Wallpaper" (1890), *"The Yellow Wallpaper" by Charlotte Perkins Gilman: A Dual-Text Critical Edition,* ed. Shawn St. John (Athens: Ohio University Press, 2006), p. 44.

40. Ibid.

41. She was at least bisexual. Her second marriage was very happy.

42. On Charlotte Perkins Gilman, beyond "Écrire ou ramper," Diane de Margerie's postface to "La Séquestrée," cf. Mary A. Hill, *Charlotte Perkins Gilman: The Making of a Radical Feminist, 1860–1896* (Philadelphia: Temple University Press, 1980). On Alice James, cf. Strouse, *Alice James.* On Edith Wharton, cf. Diane de Margerie, *Edith Wharton: Lecture d'une vie* (Paris: Flammarion, 2000).

43. Cf. Viviane Forrester, *Virginia Woolf* (Paris: Albin Michel, 2009). As a preventive measure, Woolf was prescribed "milk, food, rest" and was not permitted to write (p. 308); this was the recommendation of the psychiatrist Octavia Wilberforce.

44. Cited in Jean Starobinski, *La Transparence et l'obstacle* (Paris: Gallimard, 1971), p. 59.

45. Jacques Dalarun, *Dieu changea de sexe "pour ainsi dire": La religion faite femme, XIᵉ–XVᵉ siècle* (Paris: Fayard, 2008), esp. pp. 211–240, ch. 7, "Hors des sentiers battus: Saintes femmes d'Italie aux XIIIᵉ–XIVᵉ siècles."

46. Ibid., p. 217.

47. Ibid., p. 285. We are exceptionally well informed about Clare of Rimini's life, thanks to the narratives of a brother at the convent who wanted to set her as an example to "all vain ladies."

48. Paulette L'Hermite-Leclercq, "Reclus et recluses dans le sud-ouest de la France," in *La Femme dans la vie religieuse du Languedoc (XIIIᵉ–XIVᵉ siècle)* (Toulouse: Privat, 1988). Several years ago, the town of Saint-Flour rebuilt a fictive hermitage on the old bridge.

49. Cf. Jean-Claude Schmitt, *Mort d'une hérésie* (Paris: Mouton-EHESS, 1978). The poorest recluses were the most mobile; beguine convents attracted the most well off and tended to keep families, especially daughters and mothers, together.

50. Paul Vandenbroeck, ed., *Le Jardin clos de l'âme: L'imaginaire des religieuses dans les Pays-Bas depuis le XIIᵉ siècle,* exhibition catalogue (Brussels: Martial-Snoeck, 1994).

51. Thérèse d'Ávila, *Le Château intérieur ou les demeures;* cited in Kristeva, *Thérèse mon amour.* Quotes in the following paragraph are also from this work.

52. Bremond, *Histoire du sentiment religieux en France,* vol. 1, pp. 811ff.

53. Cited in ibid., vol. 2, ch. 9; on Pascal, see pp. 241–296.

54. Ibid., p. 170.

55. Mino Bergamo, *L'Anatomie de l'âme: De François de Sales à Fénelon* (Grenoble: Jérôme Millon, 1994); cf. esp. the second half, pp. 137ff., "La topologie mystique."

56. Jean-Jacques Olier (1608–1657), *L'Âme cristal: Des attributs divins en nous,* ed. Mariel Mazzocco, intro. Jacques Le Brun (Paris: Seuil, 2008), p. 178. Maurice Olender brought this text to my attention; it was written by the founder of the Compagnie de Saint-Sulpice and was taken from a book he edited that is itself a treatise on interiority.

57. Bergamo, *L'Anatomie de l'âme,* p. 9.

58. Ibid., p. 16.

59. Jeanne Guyon: *Récits de captivité* (previously unpublished), ed. Marie-Louise Gondal (Grenoble: Jérôme Millon, 1992); *Les Torrents* (1683), ed. Claude Morali (Grenoble: Jérôme Millon, 1992); *Le Moyen court et autres écrits spirituels* (1685) (Grenoble: Jérôme Millon, 1995).

60. Henri-Frédéric Ellenberger, *Histoire de la découverte de l'inconscient* (Paris: Fayard, 1994).

61. In Sigmund Freud, *Cinq Psychanalyses* (Paris: PUF, 1979); summarized by Ellenberger, pp. 543ff.

62. The word "bedroom" does not appear in the numerous dictionaries of psychoanalysis I consulted or in Ellenberger's book, *Histoire de la découverte de l'inconscient.* But here I fully acknowledge my incompetence.

63. I use this term in a figurative sense, implying the judgment of conscience. Cf. Claudine Haroche, ed., *Le For intérieur* (Paris: PUF, 1995).

64. Sarah Kofman, *Camera obscura: De l'idéologie* (Paris: Galilée, 1973); in an appendix Kofman provides the text of Willem Jacob S'Gravesande, "Usage de la chambre obscure."

65. Friedrich Nietzsche, *On the Genealogy of Morals: A Polemic,* trans. Douglas Smith (Oxford: Oxford University Press, 2008), p. 39.

66. Maurice Maeterlinck, *La Sagesse et la destinée* (1898), cited in *Trésor de la langue française.*

67. Gustave Flaubert, *Correspondance,* vol. 3: *1859–1868* (Paris: Gallimard, 1991), p. 61, November 1859.

68. Georges Perec, *Je me souviens* (Paris: Hachette, 1978).

69. Cited in Audouin-Rouzeau, *Combattre,* p. 51. "I would have preferred to avoid all conflict," wrote the author of *La Civilisation des mœurs,* published as early as 1939.

70. Foucault, *Surveiller et Punir;* Jacques-Guy Petit, *Ces peines obscures: La prison pénale en France, 1780–1875* (Paris: Fayard, 1989); Jacques-Guy Petit, ed., *Histoire des galères, bagnes, prisons, XIIIᵉ–XXᵉ siècles* (Toulouse: Privat, 1991).

71. Comtesse de Ségur, *Les Petites filles modèles* (Paris: Bibliothèque des chemins de fer, 1858). Hervé Bazin, *Vipère au poing* (Paris, Grasset, 1948).

72. Cited in Marie-Aimée Cliche, *Maltraiter ou punir? La violence envers les enfants dans les familles québécoises, 1850–1969* (Québec: Boréal, 2007).

73. *Nos Enfants,* no. 8 (August 1941); cited in ibid., p. 169.

74. Jeanne Bouvier, *Mémoires,* p. 79.

75. Arlette Farge and Michel Foucault, *Le Désordre des familles: Lettres de cachet des archives de la Bastille* (Paris, Gallimard, 1982).

76. Bernard Schnapper, "La correction paternelle," *Revue Historique,* April–June 1980.

77. Élise Yvorel, *Les Enfants de l'ombre: La vie quotidienne des jeunes détenus au XXᵉ siècle en France métropolitaine* (Rennes: PUR, 2007).

78. Frédéric Chauvaud, *Justice et déviance à l'époque contemporaine* (Rennes: PUR, 2007), pp. 362ff.

79. Michelle Perrot, "Les enfants de la Petite Roquette," *L'Histoire,* no. 100 (May 1987); repr. in Perrot, *Les Ombres de l'histoire.*

80. The *chambrettes* in Fresnes measured thirteen by sixteen feet and were equipped with toilets and summary but decent furnishings; "Look after your room" was one of the rules and regulations. At Fleury-Mérogis, the norms imposed resembled those of student housing at the *cité universitaire:* 110 square feet, solid oak closets, and "no bars or walls."

81. Letter from an inmate at La Roquette, 17 May 1891. This model student was an inveterate runaway; this is why his father, a Parisian shopkeeper, sent him to reform school.

82. Martine Ruchat, *Le Roman de Solon: Enfant placé, voleur de métier (1840–1896)* (Lausanne: Antipodes, 2008).

83. Françoise Chandernagor, *La Chambre: Roman* (Paris: Gallimard, 2002).

84. Cf. Petit, *Ces peines obscures,* pp. 53ff. Mabillon (1632–1707) had critiqued the severity of isolation used by religious orders and insisted on the importance of communal work and gardening. Cf. *Réflexion sur les prisons des ordres religieux* (1690).

85. Cf. Marcel Gauchet and Gladys Swain, *La Pratique de l'esprit humain: L'institution asilaire et la révolution démocratique* (Paris: Gallimard, 1980).

86. De Tocqueville was not won over right away; at first he was an Auburnian, and then he converted to the individual cell. Cf. Alexis de Tocqueville, *Œuvres complètes,* vol. 4: *Écrits sur le système pénitentiaire en France et à l'étranger,* 2 vols., ed. Michelle Perrot (Paris: Gallimard, 1984).

87. Cf. Petit, *Ces peines obscures,* pp. 244–245.

88. Cf. Robert Badinter, *La Prison républicaine (1871–1914)* (Paris: Fayard, 1992).

89. However, we should not be fooled by these figures; because sentences were so short, many people spent time in prison; this was a penal objective.

90. Christian Carlier, *Histoire de Fresnes, prison "moderne": De la genèse aux premières années* (Paris: Syros, 1998).

91. *Congrès pénitentiaire de Rome,* 1885, vol. 3, p. 51, featuring four plates.

92. Klemperer, *Mes soldats de papier,* vol. 1, pp. 582–618, "Cellule 89, 23 June–1 July 1941." Klemperer's journal is an act of resistance, as well as one of the most affecting testaments to the everyday lives of German Jews persecuted by the Nazis during the war. Klemperer and his wife Eva were about to be deported when they were saved by the bombing of Dresden, which, by destroying any trace of their identity cards, allowed them to sink into the anonymity that saved them.

93. Victor Klemperer, *LTI: La Langue du IIIe Reich* (1947), trans. Élisabeth Guillot (Paris: Albin Michel, 1996; repr. Paris: Pocket, 1998).

94. Édouard Limonov, *Mes prisons* (1990), trans. A. Roubichou-Stretz, intro. Ludmila Oulitskaia (Arles: Actes Sud, 2008). [This book is unavailable in English.—Trans.]

95. Philippe Artières, *Le Livre des vies coupables: Autobiographies de criminels (1896–1909)* (Paris: Albin Michel, 2000).

96. Albertine Sarrazin, *L'Astragale* (Paris: Jean-Jacques Pauvert, 1965); Claude Lucas, *Suerte: L'exclusion volontaire* (Paris: Plon, 1995).

97. Marie Lafarge, *Heures de prison,* 2 vols. (Paris: Librairie nouvelle, 1854), vol. 1, p. 199.

98. Jean-Claude Vimont, *La Prison politique en France: Genèse d'un mode d'incarcération spécifique, XVIIIᵉ–XXᵉ siècles* (Paris: Anthropos-Economica, 1993). There has never been a "right to resist"; hence the massive deportations of insurgents in June 1848, after the Commune, and later of anarchists.

99. Silvio Pellico, *Mes prisons* (French translation, 1843); republished in many editions, notably Éditions de Septembre in 1990 by Alain Vuyet. [This book was published in English in 1836, 1900, and 1928 but is now out of print—Trans.] Cf. Brombert, *La Prison romantique.*

100. Gustave Geffroy, *L'Enfermé,* 2 vols. (Paris: Fasquelle, 1926), intro. Julien Cain; quotes in this section come from this work.

101. Louis Perego, *Retour à la case prison* (Paris: Éd. ouvrières, 1990), afterword by Christian Carlier; Lucas, *Suerte.*

102. *Le Monde,* 13 December 2008; ruling of the Commission nationale de déontologie de la sécurité (CNDS).

103. Lucas, *Suerte,* "La journée carcérale," pp. 452–458.

104. Anne-Marie Marchetti, *Perpétuités: Le temps infini des longues peines* (Paris: Plon, 2001), and *Pauvretés en prison* (Paris: Érès, 1997). Marchetti, a sociologist and recently deceased, carried out numerous field investigations.

105. Perego, *Retour à la case prison,* p. 33; Perego describes a cell search at the Saint-Paul prison in Lyon carried out by a special squad that has come specifically for that purpose from Paris; the search systematically destroyed all personal touches to the decoration.

106. *Le Monde,* 16 January 2009, p. 3.

107. *Le Monde,* 14 January 2008: "In Nancy prison, Johnny Agasucci was beaten for hours, until he was dead; the guards noticed nothing."

108. Mahmoud Darwish, *État de siège* (Arles: Actes Sud, 2008).

109. Pellico, *Mes prisons,* p. 58.

110. Klemperer, *Mes soldats de papier,* vol. 1, p. 612.

111. Nouguier cited in Artières, *Le Livre des vies coupables,* p. 377. The author, who mainly studies prison writing, shows how prison becomes a "creative writing workshop" (pp. 380–398).

112. Albert Camus, *The Stranger,* trans. Matthew Ward (New York: Vintage, 1989), pp. 78–79.

113. The rate of overpopulation is 141 percent in remand centers; cf. *Le Monde,* 19 December 2008. At Fleury-Mérogis, the cells always hold two inmates and are in lamentable condition. Broken tiles are replaced with paper; it is freezing. See Jean Bérard and Gilles Chantraine, *80,000 détenus en 2017? La dérive et l'impossible réforme de l'institution pénitentiaire* (Paris: Éd. Amsterdam, 2008).

114. Jean-Marie Delarue, "Recommandations sur Villefranche-sur-Saône," *Dedans, dehors,* revue de l'Observatoire international des prisons, section française, nos. 67–68 (April 2009): 11. This text precedes the report made public in April 2009. It looks at fifty-two establishments, including sixteen prisons and eleven detention centers for foreigners. It is very critical and sheds light on the arbitrary rules in these institutions, in particular the intolerable infringements on privacy. Cf. *Le Nouvel Observateur,* 25–28 April 2009. I have not been able to obtain a copy of the report.

115. Cf. Babette Stern, "La chambre secrète de Frida," *Libération,* 6 July 2007.

116. Daniel Mendelsohn, *The Lost: A Search for Six of Six Million* (New York: HarperCollins, 2006).

Fugitive Bedrooms

1. Anton Chekhov, *The Cherry Orchard,* trans. Richard Nelson, Richard Peaver, and Larisa Volokhonsky (New York: Theatre Communications Group, 2015), pp. 7, 94, 96.

2. Leduc, *Je hais les dormeurs,* p. 43.

3. Virginia Woolf, *Jacob's Room* (1922), ed. Kate Flint (Oxford: Oxford University Press, 2008), p. 246.

4. Lydia Flem, *Comment j'ai vidé la maison de mes parents* (Paris: Seuil, 2004), p. 67, "Au bord du lit."

5. Aragon, *Les Chambres,* pp. 99 and 101.

6. Jean-Paul Kauffmann, *La Chambre noire de Longwood: Le voyage à Sainte-Hélène* (Paris: La Table ronde, 1997).

7. Cf. Masson, *Napoléon chez lui.*

8. Information taken from the documented entry on Wikipedia (accessed 10 January 2009).

9. Television special on the White House, *Arte,* 17 May 2008.

10. Ariane Chemin, "Hôtel du Vieux Morvan. Chambre 15," *Le Monde,* 3 January 2006.

11. The regional and national bibliography on writers' houses is impressive. Cf. esp. Georges Poisson, *Guide des maisons d'hommes et de femmes célèbres en France: 600 lieux: Écrivains, artistes, savants, hommes d'État,* 7th ed. (Paris: Horay, 2003); Aliette Armel, *Marguerite Duras: Les trois lieux de l'écrit* (Saint-Cyr-sur-Loire: Pirot, 1998); Évelyne Bloch-Dano, *Mes maisons d'écrivains* (Paris: Tallandier, 2005).

12. To the chagrin of Dickinson's biographer, Claire Malroux, *Chambre avec vue sur l'éternité,* p. 131.

13. Mauriac, *Les Maisons fugitives,* p. 889.

14. François-René de Chateaubriand, *Mémoires d'outre-tombe* (Paris: Gallimard, 1946), vol. 1, p. 82: "For the rest of the evening, all that could be heard was the measured sound of footsteps, my mother's sighs, and the murmur of the wind."

15. Bloch-Dano, *Chez les Zola,* p. 78; Bloch-Dano also cites, on p. 54, the description of Edmond de Goncourt, who was very critical of Médan: "The cabinet is respectable enough, grand enough, but it is ruined by its atrocious accumulation of curios."

16. Ibid., pp. 113–114.

17. Cf. Dominique Pety, "Maisons d'écrivains du XIXe siècle: Habitations d'hier et musées d'aujourd'hui," *Dix-Neuvième Siècle,* no. 25 (June 1977).

18. Poisson, *Guide des maisons d'hommes et de femmes célèbres en France.*

19. Perec, *Species of Spaces and Other Pieces,* trans. John Sturrock (London: Penguin, 1997), p. 21.

20. Ibid., p. 91.

21. Mauriac, *Les Maisons fugitives,* p. 888.

22. Eleb et Châtelet, *Urbanité, sociabilité et intimité,* "Les chambres en souffrance," pp. 175–191. It is a very good summary, with plans and illustrations, of the evolution of the bedroom; Eleb, "L'habitation entre vie privée et vie publique," pp. 68–74.

23. *Journal du dimanche,* 3 May 2009.

24. "Visite de la maison intelligente telle qu'on l'attend pour 2012. Près de Bruxelles, une bâtisse témoin fonctionne avec les technologies de demain," *Le Monde,* 8 August 2008.

25. Marie-Pierre Dubois-Petroff, *La Chambre: Recettes d'architecte* (Paris: Massin, 2004). To personalize the space that has been sacrificed, "a space to be *exploité* [taken advantage of]," the author suggests employing curtained headboards, "which seem right out of a fairy tale."

26. SRERP, *Histoire de cellules: Étude d'anthropologie sociale sur le vécu de certains logements* (Paris, 1975); a precise study of six housing projects in the

region of Paris, this investigation, which is already out of date, testifies to the families' dissatisfaction with the size and layout of the bedrooms.

27. Philippe Demougeot, *SOS Maison: Libérons l'espace* (Paris: Hoëbeke, 2007); cited in "Agrandir l'espace sans pousser les murs," *Le Monde,* 30 May 2008. The author appeared on France 5 on the program *Question maison,* on 18 February 2009: "SOS maison: Adapter une chambre pour un enfant et un ado."

28. François Jollant-Kneebone, "La chambre contemporaine ou la disparition," in *Rêves d'alcôves,* pp. 154–174.

29. Debray, *Le Moment fraternité,* p. 41, "Enclore."

30. Ibid., p. 50.

31. A woman's bed jacket, in French, is even called a *liseuse,* or "woman who reads."—Trans.

32. "Les adolescents en manque chronique de sommeil: La faute aux écrans," *Le Monde,* 7 April 2009.

"Going Outside . . ."

1. Alfred de Musset, *Il faut qu'une porte soit ouverte ou fermée* (1845), in Alfred de Musset, *Théâtre complet* (Paris: Gallimard, 1947).

2. Charles Baudelaire, "Les fenêtres," *Le Spleen de Paris* (1869), XXXV, in Charles Baudelaire, *Œuvres complètes* (Paris: Gallimard, 1976), vol. 1, p. 470.

Acknowledgments

THE SOURCES FOR this book are too wide ranging to compose a proper bibliography. Beyond the volumes in *Histoire de la vie privée,* dictionaries, exhibition catalogues, various treatises, the work of ethnologists and sociologists, and a vast number of literary works, each chapter has its own sources, as referenced in the notes.

I benefited from the wise and generous concern of a number of friends. Thanks to Aliette Armel, Philippe Artières, Fabienne Bock, Marie Chaix, Jacques Espagnon, Lydia Flem, Pierrette Fleutiaux, Jacqueline Lalouette, Jean Leymarie, Anne Martin-Fugier, Stéphane Michaud, Mona Ozouf, Françoise Prunier-Dreyfus, Martine Reid, Elisabeth Roudinesco, Claude Schkolnyk, Leïla Sebbar, and Michel Vernes. I would like to express my particular gratitude to Maurice Olender.

Index

adolescence, 102, 107, 324 n.39

adultery, 54

Agasucci, Johnny, 286

Agnes, Mother, 268

Agulhon, Maurice, 185

Alain-Fournier, 77

À la recherche du temps perdu (Proust), 61,
63, 128, 237, 319 n.85; the bedroom as
leitmotif in, 13, 110, 259; *Du côté de chez
Swann,* 61; nocturnal anxiety in,
164–166; *La Prisonnière* (The
Captive), 227, 252, 255–259; *Le Temps
retrouvé,* 255; *Within a Budding Grove,*
157. *See also* Proust, Marcel

Albert, Maurice, 212

Albert, Prince, 44, 247

Amiel, Henri-Frédéric, 76

Amman, Auguste, 201

Andreas, Yann, 252

Anne of Austria, 29

Anselme, Saint, 69

Antelme, Robert, 65

Anthony, Saint, 113

Aragon, Louis, 42, 161, 292

Argerich, Martha, 161–162

Ariès, Philippe, 2, 217, 221

Aron, Marguerite, 104

art: the bedroom in, 12–13, 73, 113, 123; in
children's rooms, 100–101

Artières, Philippe, 281

Art Nouveau, 47

Atget, Eugène, 13, 200, 203, 204

Aubert, Gérald: *Chambre 108,* 232

Audoux, Marguerite, 77, 141–142

Audry, Colette, 105

Augustine, Saint, 19, 41, 122, 268

Aury, Dominique, 160, 247, 254–255, 333
n.22

Austen, Jane, 59, 104, 143

Auster, Paul, 173, 301

Automobile Club of France, 153–155

Avignonnais la Vertu. *See* Perdiguier,
Agricol

Azarova, Katerina, 38–39

Aziz, Germaine, 137

Bacon, Francis (artist), 252

Balbein, Nanon, 26

Baldwin, James, 67

Balzac, Honoré de, 103, 222; on the bed,
49; on the bedroom, 42; *La Comédie
humaine,* 11; *Eugénie Grandet,* 67;
The Rise and Fall of César Birotteau,
11; *Ursule Mirouët,* 11; on writing,
79

banlieues, 189–190

Baron, Marie, 268

Barthes, Roland, 13, 244, 247

Barthez, Paul Joseph, 238

Bashkirtseff, Marie, 104, 243

Bassanville, Comtesse de, 126

Bastille, 275

Baud, Lucie, 187

Baudelaire, Charles, 10, 65, 68, 81, 303

Bauer, Felice, 76, 176

Baum, Vicki: *Grand Hotel,* 174–175

Bazin, Hervé, 272

Béat de Murat, 85